Democracy and Executive Power

Democracy and Executive Power

Policymaking Accountability in the US, the UK, Germany, and France

Susan Rose-Ackerman

Yale
UNIVERSITY PRESS
NEW HAVEN AND LONDON

Published with assistance from the foundation established in memory of
Amasa Stone Mather of the Class of 1907, Yale College.

Yale University Press books may be purchased in quantity for educational, business, or promotional use. For information, please e-mail sales.press@yale.edu (U.S. office) or sales@yaleup.co.uk (U.K. office).

Set in Fournier MT type by IDS Infotech Ltd.
Printed in the United States of America.

Library of Congress Control Number: 2021930104
ISBN 978-0-300-25495-2 (hardcover : alk. paper)

A catalogue record for this book is available from the British Library.

This paper meets the requirements of ANSI/NISO Z39.48-1992 (Permanence of Paper).

10 9 8 7 6 5 4 3 2 1

For Bruce,

My face in thine eye, thine in mine appears,
And true plain hearts do in the faces rest; . . .
If our two loves be one, or thou and I
Love so alike, that none do slacken, none can die.

—John Donne, *The Good-Morrow*

Contents

Acknowledgments

Comparative law, almost by definition, requires help from others as one moves beyond comforting realities to learn something new. I am deeply grateful for the generous and ongoing help that I have received from coauthors, students, visiting scholars, practitioners, librarians, language teachers, and academic colleagues. A number of institutions hosted me in ways that made my research possible and provided wonderful environments for intellectual discussion and fun.

My first and deepest thanks go to my coauthors Thomas Perroud and Stefanie Egidy. Thomas coauthored several articles with me resulting from my visit to Sciences Po in 2011. We carried out interviews with policymakers and discussed our work with a number of academic interlocutors. Thomas, now a professor as the University of Paris-Assas, has been an unfailing source of insights on current developments in French public law. Stefanie was a graduate student at Yale when we started talking with another student, James Fowkes, about "due process of lawmaking." The three of us wrote a book of that title published in 2015, with chapters on Germany and the EU. I have drawn on our joint work here. I also coauthored a paper with Edgardo Jordão on judicial review of executive policymaking in the US, Canada, France, and Italy that deepened my knowledge of countries with contrasting common law and civil law traditions.

Second, I have been very fortunate in calling on the talents of an extraordinary group of research assistants and students. Paul Shortell, a Yale Law School student, helped immensely with the material on the US, especially keeping me up to date on current developments. He was a perceptive reader of my early drafts, helping me to fine-tune my arguments. Edgar Melgar, while earning joint degrees in law and history, commented insightfully on the entire manuscript and helped especially with the US, UK, and

French cases. Akis Psygkas, a former Yale doctoral student in law, now on the law faculty of Western University in London, Ontario, thoughtfully read the manuscript and shared his knowledge of the UK and French cases and their interactions with the EU. On Germany, Lena Riemer seemed always to anticipate what I was looking for both while a visiting scholar at Yale Law School and after her return to Berlin. Franziska Bantlin, an LLM candidate from Germany, was especially diligent in tracking down sources and carefully reading the entire manuscript as I prepared it for publication. Joachim-Nicolas Herrera, a visiting student from Paris, helped me better to understand the French political and regulatory system.

The third group to thank are the academics and practitioners who spent time with me discussing aspects of the project. I cannot list everyone here, but I want to mention several scholars and policymakers who helped me to understand their own country's public law. In Germany: Martin Eifert, Dieter Grimm, Bernd Holznagel, Matthias Ruffert, Sabine Schläcke, Eberhard Schmidt-Aßmann, and Annegret Groebel. In the UK: Paul Craig, Elizabeth Fisher, Ruth Fox, Carol Harlow, Aileen Kavanagh, and Margaret Russell. In France: Cécile Blatriz, Jacques Chevallier, Florence Denier-Pasquier, Charlotte Halpern, Pierre Lascoumes, Jacky Richard, and Olivier Schrameck. My debts to American scholars of public law are extensive and longstanding and too numerous to list. However, I want to express special gratitude to Peter Strauss at Columbia Law School and Jerry Mashaw at Yale Law School, who in the 1980s accepted me, an interloper from economics and public policy, as a colleague and friend into the field of administrative law.

Fourth, I have worked to increase communication between administrative law scholars worldwide through the resources of the Yale Law School. To help that effort, Peter Lindseth and I organized two conferences at Yale on comparative administrative law, the second with the addition of Blake Emerson. I thank Peter and Blake for their hard work, insights, and enthusiasm. As editors, we are grateful to the participants for contributing to two excellent edited volumes that are helping to define the developing field at the intersection of comparative law and political economy.

Fifth, I want to express my appreciation to several institutions that provided financial support as well as congenial environments for research. First and foremost, the Yale Law School has been an incredible home base, with supportive faculty colleagues and an atmosphere that encourages creative thinking. The Law School has the resources to make comparative research possible, and, more important, its librarians and staff smooth the way. I want especially to thank my assistant, Cathy Orcutt, for all her help and patience, and the librarians for their wonderful willingness to respond to my requests for sources and background information with amazing speed.

My case studies were made possible by several visits outside the US. My interest in comparative public law began with a year in Berlin in 1991–1992, under Fulbright and Guggenheim fellowships, that produced a book on environmental policymaking in the US and Germany. The broader frame of the current book took nascent form in 2008 during a one-month stay at the Rockefeller Foundation's Bellagio Center. The democratic legitimacy of executive rulemaking percolated in my mind for several years. In 2011, I learned about France as a visitor at Sciences Po's Centre for European Studies. Professor Jean Bernard Auby helped to arrange that visit and put me in touch with Thomas Perroud. In 2014–2015, I updated my work on Germany as a fellow at the Wissenschaftskolleg zu Berlin. I interviewed academics and public officials, and had outstanding help from the institute's librarians. In addition, I organized a fellows' workshop that helped me better to understand the relationship between the EU and its member states. I came late to the UK, helped by an important two-month stay at Queen Mary University of London in 2018 that allowed me to conduct interviews in London and Oxford. Before arriving in London, I spent a very productive two months at the Stellenbosch Institute for Advanced Study in South Africa, organizing and writing a draft of this manuscript, learning about administrative law in South Africa, and beginning to work on the UK.

Finally, I want to thank those at Yale University Press who supported my project and shepherded the book through to publication: Bill Frucht, Karen Olson, and Jeff Schier, as well as the copy editor, Harry Haskell, the indexer, Fred Kameny, and the proofreader, Robin Charney.

Obviously, none of these individuals and institutions is responsible for the errors of law and fact that likely remain. I have tried to be as accurate as possible, and I would have made many more mistakes without the help of the people and institutions mentioned here. Thank you!

As always, I am grateful to my husband, Bruce Ackerman, who has continuously supported my adventures in scholarship and in travel. He has been my cheerleader, my best critic, and my emotional anchor for over fifty years.

Democracy and Executive Power

Introduction

Bureaucrats are the source of pointed jokes and public frustration. Critics call them venal, arbitrary, or incompetent. Starry-eyed reformers dream of governments that operate through direct public participation based on give-and-take. Charismatic leaders sidestep established hierarchies to unite the populace in support of a cause and to rally behind their compelling personalities. The downsides of demagogy are obvious from history and current experience. In practice, charismatic leaders stay in power through well-oiled bureaucracies, hierarchical military capacities, and organized domestic surveillance.

Governments that hold power over time need bureaucratic organizations to work along with elected politicians. Even bureaucracy's critics must come to terms with its necessity. The challenge is to establish a public law that enhances the democratic accountability of bureaucrats and political appointees. Yet, too often, administrative law limits itself to the protection of individual rights and ignores the way that law can further democratic values in executive policymaking.

The stereotypical bureaucrat with a green eyeshade pores over books of figures, mechanically granting permissions and imposing costs. Of course, some do perform routine tasks that only require them to follow the rules, obey the commands of their superiors, and refuse bribes. In fact, public officials are much more important than that. They do not merely implement clearly articulated policies from parliaments or presidents. If that were all they did, a bureaucracy could operate as a pure hierarchy with officials reporting up the chain of command. A stereotypical military model could prevail, requiring absolute deference to higher authority. At the limit, governments could eliminate the human element through on-line portals programed to a set of rules.

Public policymaking in democracies necessarily requires discretion and judgment inside government ministries, independent agencies, and quasi-public bodies. Political appointees work with bureaucrats to make policy under statutes that delegate authority either explicitly or through vague language requiring interpretation.

Bureaucrats' technical expertise and programmatic experience are centrally important. However, giving discretion to technocrats, full stop, is insufficient in a democracy that depends upon popular support. A skeptical public may be difficult to convince if complex policies rely on officials' claims to esoteric knowledge. Even if the bureaucracy's analysis is easily understandable, the general public will not necessarily agree with its policy prescriptions. Some will bear the costs; others may want a distribution of benefits skewed toward the poor or other worthy groups; still others may disagree on how to weigh aesthetic or cultural values. Even if analysis removes some disputes over facts, technocratic methods cannot resolve disagreements over values. Fairly managing the distribution of gains and losses is necessary for broad public acceptance. Administrative law can help legitimate these choices in the eyes of citizens.

Disparate policy views are normal in a democracy. Unanimous consent is not a realistic goal for most policy choices. Sometimes, after an informed debate, almost everybody will agree that a particular policy is the best alternative to the status quo, but serious disagreements will typically persist. Consultation is necessary, but nothing would ever move forward if open-ended participatory processes must seek unanimous consent with no time limits.

Instead, citizens must agree on an institutional framework for making political choices, with the understanding that they will not always obtain their preferred policy outcomes. Majority rule in the legislature is one option that produces legally enforceable norms legitimized by the democratic process. Once a statute delegates authority to a government ministry or agency, however, new legitimacy issues arise.[1] Technocratic methods, such as cost-benefit analysis, balance gains and losses, but these evaluations differ from majority rule. A policy may pass a cost-benefit test but fail to obtain broad popular support. Democratic legitimacy requires that the contesting normative frameworks be transparent to the public, not hidden in esoteric language. Even for an agreed set of facts, there are alternative ways of aggregating costs and benefits to produce a policy recommendation. These options depend not on science, but on competing views of the public good and on the proper role of the state in society.

The tension between expertise and public acceptance is endemic to democratic government. Competent, technically trained bureaucrats are necessary but not sufficient. Individuals and organized groups should be able to present their relevant concerns and to articulate how the proposed alternatives will help or hurt them. They should not have the power to override statutory and political imperatives, but officials should be required to take account of outside input as they build on the statutory choices of the legislature to make their final policy decisions.

Bureaucratic discretion is necessary and inevitable, but two familiar conceptions of delegation to the executive fail to do justice to the realities of modern government. These are the closely related "transmission-belt" and "chain-of-legitimacy" models. Each of these models is anchored in an idealized vision of legislative activity and its ties to political party platforms.

The transmission-belt model supposes that the statutory text resolves all the key policy issues.[2] The bureaucracy then carries out its mandate in a legalistic, adjudicatory fashion; policymaking only occurs during statutory drafting. Advocates of this model worry that public input into executive actions will inject biased or partisan concerns into what should be an apolitical, professional policy decision. To them, public opinion at the time of executive rulemaking is irrelevant. Those who claim to speak for the "public interest" during rulemaking are likely to undermine the goals of the political-party coalition behind the original legislation. Worse yet, wealthy or well-organized interests may dominate the hearings and have too much influence on the outcome.[3]

The unrealistic model of the legislative process embodied in the transmission-belt view contrasts with an alternative approach that takes a more sympathetic view of bureaucratic discretion. Under the chain-of-legitimacy model (*Legitimationskette* in German), the democratic mandate flows from the voters to the political parties that they support to the legislature. It then extends beyond legislative enactments to policy implementation by the cabinet and the bureaucracy.[4] In contrast to the transmission-belt model, this conception acknowledges that statutes can leave policy gaps for the executive to fill with secondary norms or regulations. Administrative discretion is consistent with democracy because policymakers in the executive are ultimately accountable to the voters along the chain of legitimacy. This view opposes policymaking by agencies that are independent of cabinet departments because they break the chain of democratic legitimacy and, on that view, are not ultimately accountable to the voters.

Hence, under the transmission-belt model, bureaucratic policymaking is anti-democratic; under the chain-of-legitimacy model, official policy discretion is acceptable so long as it can be traced back to the will of the voters. Neither model sees a role for administrative law in enhancing the democratic pedigree of delegated power through public participation in bureaucratic policymaking.

Both models are unrealistic—but about different things. The transmission belt is blind to the reality of bureaucratic policymaking; the chain of legitimacy ignores the weaknesses of the link between voting behavior and the democratic justification for regulatory policies. In other words, I begin from the proposition that voting and political parties are not the only proper routes for public sentiment to influence political/policy choices.

A citizen's support for a party or candidate running on a broad, diverse platform bears only a weak relationship to his or her views of particular executive decisions made months or years after the election. The ongoing policy problems facing incumbent governments need a stronger connection to the public than a paragraph in a composite platform issued during an election that may be several years in the past. Incumbent parties remain relevant to voters by performing what is called "casework," that is, satisfying the individual demands of their supporters. Some public input into executive policymaking may take that form, but public input can also invite participants to consider the broader merits of policy options, not only their own individual interests. Such considered evaluations of alternatives are a central link between citizens and officials in the administration and contribute to the democratic legitimacy of delegation.

Thus, I defend administrative procedures that require bureaucracies to reach beyond official circles and consult broadly with the public. Consultation and public reason-giving contribute to the democratic legitimacy of discretionary regulatory actions. Government accountability to the electorate extends beyond case-by-case decisions directed at individuals and property-owners; it also ought to include larger policy initiatives with broad, diffuse impacts on society. Many legal commentators have failed to recognize this basic point. The public-law literature emphasizes the protection of individual rights—a valid goal, to be sure—but public consultation and reason-giving are no less important.

Democracies, worldwide, ought to further policymaking accountability of that kind inside executive ministries and agencies. To keep my project manageable, though, I concentrate on four established democracies—the United States, the United Kingdom, Germany, and France. In the final chapter of this book, I argue that the lessons learned from these comparisons can inform government-reform debates elsewhere, especially in emerging democracies and those in transition from an authoritarian past. I urge others to take up my invitation to engage in broader comparative work that takes seriously both democratic values and the distinctive features of each political, economic, and social system.

My four case studies represent different forms of representative democracy—two presidential systems (the US and France) and two parliamentary systems (the UK and Germany). France, with both a directly elected president and a prime minister, may appear to be a hybrid, but, in practice, it has a strong president. Two countries, the US and UK, have a common-law background, while France and Germany are rooted in civil law. Each system connects administrative law to bureaucratic policymaking, and I will be assessing their strengths and weaknesses. For introductory purposes, though, it is enough to identify four interrelated issues.

First, why is executive-branch policymaking necessary? Shouldn't democratic legislatures resolve all the policy issues in the text of statutes?

Second, even if delegation to bureaucracies is a practical reality, how can it operate consistently with democratic principles? How ought policymakers to balance expert knowledge with openness to public input? It is all very well to call for public participation, but who should participate, when should participation occur, and how should governments organize consultations? Can administrative law help to frame the answers to these questions, or are they purely political choices?

Third, there are many ways to organize executive-branch institutions and associated agencies and commissions. How can these organizational choices encourage public input and bureaucratic competence? Can private bodies fulfill some policymaking functions, and if so, should they conform to the participatory and transparency practices of public agencies?

Fourth, how can public law monitor and control policymaking without limiting exercises of political judgment? What role should courts play in enforcing the requirements of administrative law? How should judicial oversight interact with systems of political accountability inside the executive branch?

Four Democracies

The answers to these questions in the United States differ fundamentally from those given in the United Kingdom, Germany, and France, each with a different public-law tradition. Despite important differences, the three European cases resemble each other in generally avoiding American-style competition between the legislative majority and the executive. They rely heavily on bureaucratic expertise and place greater confidence in the public-service ethic of the professional staff. None of them has legal provisions, such as the notice-and-comment procedures of the US Administrative Procedure Act (APA), that mandate public consultation and reason-giving in the production of rules with the force of law. At the same time, national courts in my European cases play a significant oversight role, and European Union law imposes additional constraints on national executives in member states.

The German and French constitutions interact with an idealized view of the law, distinct from policy or politics—terms that cannot be distinguished in either language (*politique* in French and *Politik* in German). Their civil-law traditions affect the interpretation of their written constitutions and result in different but related approaches to executive rulemaking.

Conventional German administrative law focuses on the administrative act (*Verwaltungsakt*), a term that refers to a public measure taken by a state authority to regulate an individual case under public law.[5] Germany has a strong civil service that plausibly ensures the citizenry of its seriousness in pursuing the public interest. Here, the chain-of-legitimacy model has achieved maximum credibility—moving from the voters to political parties to elected representatives to the prime minister and cabinet to the bureaucracy. A separate hierarchy of administrative courts considers the legality of administrative acts and related material. Within this overarching structure, public participation in administrative rulemaking may seem unnecessary or downright pernicious. The courts seek to protect the fundamental rights of individuals, but they have seldom self-consciously furthered policymaking accountability to the citizenry in the making of general rules. Some German scholars do recognize the limits of this model,[6] and civil-society activism is pushing officials, as well as some scholars and jurists, to take public participation seriously. Especially in the environmental area, the EU has allied with those seeking more public input into national policy.

As in Germany, French public law also refers to the *acte administratif*, but defines it more broadly.[7] Law and politics are deeply intertwined, with the Conseil d'État acting as both a higher administrative court and an advisor to the government that reviews proposed statutes and rules. Its members are elite generalists who move in and out of government ministries and independent agencies. French law takes a significantly different view of bureaucratic discretion than German law. The French Constitution rejects strict parliamentary government and establishes a strong president. Voters directly elect the president to a five-year term, and he or she can dissolve the National Assembly and call a new parliamentary election without resigning.[8] The president nominates the prime minister, subject to approval by the National Assembly, but so long as the president has a parliamentary majority, an ally will hold that post.[9] Civil servants implement the statutory law, working under a thin layer of political appointees. France, like Germany, has no general statute governing rulemaking procedures, in spite of the passage of a first-ever administrative code in 2015.

The British Westminster government, with first-past-the-post voting rules, usually vests the prime minister with a stable majority in the House of Commons. Even if the parliamentary opposition and some backbenchers object to particular bureaucratic decisions, the prime minister can implement government policy choices by issuing statutory instruments (SIs) that have the force of law. Most SIs require parliamentary approval, but with the same party or coalition controlling both the House of Commons and the government, approval is generally pro forma.[10] The British constitutional tradition is skeptical both of judicial supervision of executive policymaking and of the democratic value of public participation in government policymaking. The exceptions on both counts involve the violation of rights and, in recent years, environmental policies with broad societal effects.

The polarizing debate over Britain's exit from the European Union (Brexit) tested the premises of the Westminster model. Yet, it did not challenge the reliance on SIs. To the contrary, bureaucratic discretion is filling many gaps in the law opened up by Britain's departure from the EU. Even the divided Parliament that governed before Boris Johnson's victory at the polls in December 2019 provided little review of hundreds of Brexit-related SIs.

In contrast, in the United States public law seeks to ensure the political accountability of executive rulemaking to the American public, as well as to those directly affected. Under its version of the separation of powers, the president's party may fail to control one or both houses of Congress. This results in partisan competition between the House, the Senate, and the president for effective control over bureaucratic decisions. Even when a single party controls all three institutions, the electoral system gives each member of Congress an individual constituency with priorities that need not match those of the president or the leaders of the House and Senate. Thus, legislation typically involves compromises that generate vague language and inconsistent provisions. As a consequence, implementing departments and agencies have broad discretion to interpret their responsibilities.

The APA creates a framework to check potential abuse. It requires administrators to provide public notice, open-ended hearings, and reason-giving before issuing legally binding rules. The first two factors allow citizens, economic interests, and civil-society advocacy groups to make their views known to both bureaucrats and political appointees. The department or agency must justify its decisions to the public, and courts have the authority to check compliance with the APA's demands. Hence, the United States does not rely on the chain of legitimacy but embraces a process that connects directly to those outside of formal government structures. At present, this process is under strain as presidents from both major parties attempt to enhance their power over agency actions. Nevertheless, there remains much to learn from America's successes and failures as democratic reformers in both established and emerging democracies seek better ways to connect bureaucratic policymaking to their citizens' concerns.

Consider a final dimension of the basic problem—the technocracy/democracy tension that arises in "independent agencies" that challenge the conventional separation of powers. Such agencies arose first in the US, but variants are now common, including in Germany, France, and the UK, often in connection with the privatization policies of the EU.

These bodies aim to deal with technically complex issues via insulation from day-to-day political pressures. Yet, their decisions often have important political consequences. Unless labeled as a court, a truly independent body does not satisfy the chain of legitimacy in a parliamentary regime. Hence, for both political and conceptual reasons, such agencies in Europe usually are nominally under a cabinet ministry, lack rulemaking authority, and concentrate on case-by-case adjudication. Nevertheless, some operate with almost as much independence as their US counterparts, especially those created by member states in response to EU directives. At the same time, the independence of US regulatory commissions is currently under attack. Cross-country comparisons help to highlight the tensions generated by different constitutional traditions and rationales for agency independence. The difficulties that have arisen in my case-study countries are repeated throughout the world and can provide insights that may be applicable elsewhere.

Private or quasi-public bodies that make rules face the same legitimacy questions as public agencies. If they take on regulatory responsibilities, should they be subject to consultation and transparency requirements, or do their private-sector credentials act as a substitute? In all four countries, such organizations set standards, and some professions have self-regulatory authority. If their decisions are enforced as law, should civil society demand a role in their deliberations? The mixture of public and private roles sometimes produces hybrids that fail both as publicly accountable bodies and as effective private associations.

Public participation in executive policymaking interacts with each state's constitutional structure in different ways. The incentives for making policymaking accountable to the public differ between alternative forms of parliamentary and presidential government. Formalistic theories of the separation of powers are insufficient; they place government activities too rigidly into predetermined boxes. In spite of cross-country differences, citizen agitation for more effective public input into major government decisions is commonplace. Especially in Europe, such activism may encourage systemic changes that go beyond episodic responses to particular high-visibility government actions. An analysis of the strengths and weaknesses of public input thus can provide bases for reform, not only in established democracies but elsewhere as well.

My analysis leads to a paradoxical conclusion. Although American politics is riven by inter-branch conflicts, the implications for the law of bureaucratic rulemaking have been generally salutary. I will argue that notice-and-comment rulemaking under the APA comes closest to the democratic ideal of public involvement in delegated policymaking. Although under pressure from presidential overreaching and subject to justified criticism for failing to live up to its promise, the APA, at least, does confront the political and technocratic values at stake in rulemaking.

Monitoring the Rulemaking Process

Judicial review can help to promote accountable executive-branch policymaking even though the courts are the least democratic of the branches. Their traditional mandate is often limited to the protection of individual rights. Nevertheless, their isolation from day-to-day politics can permit them to provide impartial review of executive policymaking, as well as of rights violations. Judicial review can focus on procedures that encourage public input, on officials' public reasons, and on the consistency of executive rules with underlying substantive statutes and constitutional provisions.

In providing oversight, the courts walk a tightrope. Judges should set the parameters for government policymaking and monitor its agents' performance, without meddling in politics. A good balance is not easy to achieve. Each country's legal structure determines which issues are appropriate for judicial review and which should be left to the discretion of politically responsible institutions. My four case studies reveal marked differences in the oversight role assigned to courts. The comparative analysis will provide a grounded sense of institutional possibilities, as well as assessing their strengths and weaknesses.

Generalist courts in the US and UK decide disputes involving executive rulemaking. The advantages are their broad perspective and their independence from the public administration. However, these virtues have potential downsides. Judges may fail to recognize the distinctive features of the administrative process—in particular, the political/policy aspects of rulemaking. In practice, both countries have introduced some specialization within their judiciaries. Thus, the US federal appellate court in the District of Columbia hears a large share of challenges to executive-branch rules. The UK recently established a specialized section of the High Court to hear appeals from tribunals covering particular policy areas.[11]

In contrast, in France and Germany specialized administrative courts are the main locus of judicial oversight. Judges are career public officials who are close to the civil service in training. This knowledge has both benefits and costs. These judges have the expertise to evaluate the actions of the administration, but they may not have a sufficiently critical perspective. In essence, the debate over the value of specialized administrative courts repeats the controversy over the merits and disadvantages of specialized expertise that arises in the rulemaking process itself.

Courts also have intrinsic limits as monitors. They cannot set their own agendas; they only intervene in response to litigation. They manage their caseload by refusing to accept certain kinds of cases—by refusing jurisdiction, by judging ripeness and timing, and by limiting standing. Some courts permit public-interest standing, while others insist that plaintiffs suffer individualized harm. As to timing, courts can pause agency proceedings to resolve judicial challenges, hear a case after the rule takes final form, or hear complaints only after the agency has applied the rule to a particular case. Each aspect of review has different implications for the effectiveness of judicial monitoring.

The judicial role is also shaped by each country's stance on the inherent prerogatives of the executive branch. How much information must the executive disclose? Is agenda-setting a purely executive function, or can plaintiffs use lawsuits to force the government's hand? Should the internal organization of the bureaucracy and government contracting practices be subject to judicial review? May the courts impose limits on executive orders if they are not based on statutory grants of authority? If legislation creates an institution not contemplated in the explicit constitutional text, is the innovation constitutionally acceptable?

In the United States, independent regulatory commissions have survived most constitutional challenges, but the Supreme Court has recently limited the options open to statutory drafters. The judiciaries in France, Germany, and the UK are currently struggling with analogous problems as they review unconventional institutions, such as regulatory commissions, that do not easily fit into their standard separation-of-powers categories. Whatever the criteria for access to the courts, judges will be ineffective monitors if society does not contain advocacy organizations capable of bringing appropriate lawsuits.

Responding to these potential weaknesses, most countries have developed additional institutions to enhance accountability. Audit offices, such as the US Government Accountability Office, evaluate program performance but spend much of their time uncovering fraud and the misuse of funds. Ombudsmen outside the US concentrate on resolving individual complaints, but can compensate for the weaknesses of judicial and legislative oversight by carrying out programmatic reviews of executive policies.

In all four countries, civil-society organizations are pushing the courts and other oversight institutions to take more aggressive stands to encourage public input into the actions of public bureaucracies. Much of this activity, especially outside the US, focuses on the violation of individual rights. However, a deeper look at these developments suggests an enhanced concern with the democratic status of executive rulemaking. Reformers elsewhere can learn from studying the interactions between courts, government monitors, and civil-society watchdogs in my cases. These reformers may face very different levels of institutional capacity and public involvement, but the imperfections of even established democracies should promote critical and creative thinking about institutional design.

Overview

This book aspires to establish some basic principles of public law that apply to democracies everywhere. However, it recognizes that there are no hard and fast recipes for managing the tensions at the boundaries between politics, professionalism, and public accountability. Some reformers respond to the democratic deficit in rulemaking by seeking to limit delegation and to increase legislative oversight. My argument is different. I accept executive policymaking as a realistic necessity in modern states, but I seek ways to make administrative procedures more open to public input without giving up the value of technical competence. The cases of the US, the UK, Germany, and France show how four democracies are struggling with this issue, even as some proposed reforms clash with traditional models of democratic accountability.

Chapter 1 introduces the basic framework for constructing a public law that promotes the democratic exercise of bureaucratic discretion. It distinguishes three types of accountability—performance, rights-based, and policy-oriented. The first two are familiar concepts in administrative law. The third has not been central to traditional public law, but it is at the core of my framework. I then outline four overlapping models of policymaking accountability that combine accountability to the citizenry with the use of expertise. They are: 1) political decision-making with expert consultation, 2) decisions by experts with public consultation, 3) public institutions structured to provide incentives for political appointees to make impartial decisions, and 4) statutory delegations to private or quasi-governmental bodies to regulate with the force of law. The chapter concludes by considering the diverse ways in which administrative law interacts with these models.

Chapter 2 develops the relationship between constitutional structures and executive policymaking. It assesses the incentives and disincentives for policymaking accountability that arise under alternative forms of representative democracy.

Chapter 3 reviews policymaking processes in the executive with a focus on democratic accountability and competence. Major public infrastructure projects and local development plans generally require public input, but, outside the US, these requirements do not routinely apply to rulemaking. Environmental policymaking is a partial exception. In my European cases, environmental law has been open to input from civil-society advocacy groups, and I ask why. The EU and a specialized treaty are part of the explanation, but the broad-ranging nature of many environmental harms is also relevant.

Chapter 4 turns to the added complexity of independent public authorities and quasi-public bodies. It also considers independent agencies that monitor the behavior of public officials themselves.

Chapter 5 moves from process to substance. It examines the policy-evaluation techniques used by professional civil servants and assesses their relationship to principles of democratic government. It considers the role of impact assessment and cost-benefit analysis, and discusses their underlying normative structures and the possibility that interest groups and politicians will manipulate them for narrow partisan ends. A key theme is the impossibility of entirely isolating expertise from politics. The state must find ways to manage that interaction, not assume it away.

Chapter 6 considers how public participation can help to bridge the legitimacy gap that arises when the executive exercises policymaking discretion. It discusses private-sector and civil-society input, the transparency of regulatory processes, and officials' justifications for policy choices. It focuses on alternative routes to public participation that are consistent with both political accountability to citizens and technical competence. There is no perfect way to achieve a balance, but I explore the options, drawing on experiences with alternative routes for public participation.

No matter which institutions make policy, oversight gives officials incentives to comply with procedural requirements for public input and public reason-giving. Thus, Chapter 7 deals with the courts. Judges must provide oversight without becoming policymakers themselves. Are courts so determined to avoid interfering in politics that they refrain from any oversight of policymaking discretion? What principles could help judges to provide oversight of process without turning them into de facto policymakers?

Chapter 8 concludes by arguing that my comparative and normative analysis, although focused on four countries, has relevance for representative democracies everywhere. The details depend upon country-specific facts and legal norms, but the basic concerns are very general. Although history and legal doctrines are deeply interrelated, that link is not necessarily deterministic. Historical legacies need not prevent reform. Rather, administrative law should place a greater focus on policymaking accountability as part of the ongoing struggle to build and consolidate democracy.

1. *Policymaking Accountability and Public Law*

"Enforcing the rule of law holds governments to account"—this familiar claim hides a multitude of difficulties. What does "accountability" mean? To whom is government accountable? How can one identify the "law" that should "rule"? Should public and private institutions operate under different understandings of the basic principle? If so, where is one to draw the line?

In short, the "rule of law" stands for a number of different ideas.[1] To some, the phrase implies nothing more than clear and market-friendly rules. Under that view, the courts should resolve legal challenges to government actions in ways that limit burden-shifting and interest-group capture while enhancing the efficacy of policymaking. To others, the talismanic phrase requires the protection of individual rights and legal redress for past wrongs. An alternative view simply asks if the law on the books, whatever its content, is enforced in practice.

My emphasis differs from these formulations. In stressing policymaking accountability, I focus on ways in which public law can promote democratic legitimacy and effective policy design, considering the private law only where it overlaps with this effort. My focus is on the way democracies make policies that reflect the preferences and values of voters, and on how bureaucracies implement the statutory and constitutional decisions made by popularly elected institutions.

Central to my argument is the practical understanding that statutory and constitutional texts cannot resolve all the important policy issues confronting the modern regulatory/welfare state. This reality raises a crucial issue of democratic legitimacy: Even if they are ultimately responsible to elected officials, unelected officials make policy that is of great importance to the voting population. Hence, executive branch agencies ought to engage in public consultation in their efforts to fill the constitutional and statutory gaps that are a precondition for effective policymaking. Public consultations do not provide definitive solutions to the problems of bureaucratic legitimacy raised by the modern regulatory state. However, if creatively combined with "the chain of legitimacy" linking agency expertise to democratically elected officials, such procedures can help connect the modern policymaking enterprise to a nation's citizens.

Of course, it is unrealistic to expect that everyone will applaud the ultimate decisions made by executive officials. Nevertheless, transparent procedures, if working well, invite bureaucratic decision-makers to be open to input from concerned constituencies and outside experts as the government weighs its policy choices. This democratic commitment to transparency and reason-giving motivates the book's inquiry into comparative public law. My aim is to clarify the extent to which the public law of four leading democracies—the US, the UK, Germany, and France—in fact, redeems the promise of public accountability embedded in their constitutional values.

From this perspective, the rule of law should constrain self-serving policy choices by politicians, bureaucrats, and private-interest groups. However, it must do so without stifling valid exercises of discretion. Complex and fast-changing policy areas require the flexible application of professional expertise—not just when a statute is passed, but as ministers and their bureaucracies confront new data and problems over time. Administrative law must frame these ongoing exercises of discretion in ways that are compatible with democratic values. Judicial review should strengthen democracy, not restrict it through rigid, formalistic requirements.

Sometimes statutes contain clear rules, but in many cases, legislatures grant broad discretion to the executive. Regulatory bodies issue many kinds of documents, from guidelines to interpretive rules to policy statements. If they want to issue rules with the force of law, their procedures should be transparent and open to outside participation. Judicial review should then ensure that the rulemaking process was sufficient and that the agency's rationale is consistent with the statute. In other words, courts should not just consider the substantive legality of rules. They should also require agencies to comply with procedures for public consultation and public justification. This is the procedural framework that ideally prevails in the United States, but US practice does not always live up to its ideals. Even if one accepts the democratic case for American-style accountability, the US suffers from one great practical disadvantage. It takes considerable time and trouble to invite broad participation and to respond to public comments with a reasoned defense of the final decision. The department or agency must deal with outside critics who are poorly informed about the issues on the table, and months can turn into years, especially if its decision is challenged in court.[2] However, these difficulties do not undermine the basic principle of accountability to the public for regulatory policy. The dangers of gridlock and delay can be surmounted if administrative law takes them seriously.

In subsequent chapters, I argue that the risks are outweighed by the democratic deficits that exist if administrative law fails to require public input and reason-giving when agencies and ministries make policy. A deeper problem in the US is the president's incentive to accumulate power and to limit outside input if it does not align with his or her political program. My other case-study countries, the United Kingdom, Germany, and France, do not require a notice-and-comment process for rulemaking, so the lack of democratic accountability may not be so obvious to outside observers. I will be critiquing both current US practice and the more hands-off approach of my other cases.

This chapter introduces three concepts of public accountability, highlighting what I call "policymaking accountability." It next outlines two views of public law—narrow and broad—that differ in their relationship to policymaking accountability. Building on the broad view, I present alternative approaches to policymaking accountability and conclude by suggesting how to combine the various approaches.

Three Types of Public Accountability

In English, German, and French, the term "accountability" is sometimes limited to fiscal rectitude, that is, compliance with the principles of the accounting profession.[3] My interest, instead, is in the broader questions of public input into policymaking and the oversight of government policy choices. Because I focus on regulatory policies that leave little trace in the public budget, I concentrate on the way the government explains and justifies its actions, not just through balance sheets and income statements but also through rules that influence private-sector behavior. To begin, I distinguish three ideal types: performance accountability, rights-based accountability, and policymaking accountability.

Under **performance accountability**, political actors set the goals, and expert professionals carry them out in a competent and cost-effective way—using their specialized knowledge. The key word, "competence," has two facets. It requires a corps of hard-working civil servants with integrity, who refuse to take bribes, to embezzle funds, or to engage in more subtle conflicts of interest.[4] It also demands that the heads of bureaus ensure that their subordinates comply with statutory requirements. To gain credibility, performance accountability demands both transparency—so that the public can check bureaucratic performance—and sanctions that discipline officials for illegal or incompetent actions.[5] It goes beyond the prevention of fraud and waste in government budgets to include the operation of public programs that influence private-sector behavior.

Performance accountability has always been a central concern of US public law, which regulates private industry to achieve objectives, such as the control of monopolies, protection of the environment, and the reduction of risk. This form of accountability has also become increasingly important in the UK, Germany, and France as they privatized state-owned enterprises and discovered a "new type of administration called regulation" that "consists of mostly sector-specific rules establishing markets and specific public obligations with regard to competition and certain social interests."[6]

For American public lawyers there is nothing new here. In Europe, with its established state-owned utilities, the switch to privatized firms led to the regulation of network industries—telecoms, energy, water, railroads—along with the regulation of public health, public transport, and financial services. Hence, "regulatory law does not simply restrict economic freedoms in order to avert dangers for public or private interests. Instead, regulation organizes markets proactively, constructs new options for economic activities and directly or indirectly demands certain economic or social outputs."[7] This statement expresses the aims of a system focused on performance accountability so long as one extends it to include environmental and social areas, as well as regulations affecting the performance of particular sectors.

Rights-based accountability focuses on the protection of individuals against the abuses of arbitrary power by public bodies. Even if an agency fulfills the requirements of performance accountability, it may violate fundamental rights. In the US, the Bill of Rights plays a central role; across the Atlantic judicial concepts of "natural justice," or *principes généraux du droit*, fulfill an analogous function.[8] In Europe, over and above national constitutions, the European Court of Human Rights hears cases under the Convention on Human Rights of the Council of Europe. The European Court of Justice of the EU has become increasingly aggressive in enforcing the EU's own Charter of Fundamental Rights.[9] Some rights, such as those to education and health, require signatories to spend public resources under legislative mandates. Others state prohibitions or outlaw types of discrimination that can only be effectively enforced through statutory guarantees.[10] Such rights must be embodied in statutes that demand performance accountability to help ensure member states' compliance.

These first two modes of accountability are crucial, but they are not sufficient. Modern statutory regimes delegate vast discretion to public and quasi-public agencies, and this can create a democratic deficit. Election campaigns seldom emphasize technical regulatory matters, and elections are too infrequent and too rough-grained to link voter sentiment to the implementation of specific policies. Referenda are a poor substitute because of voter ignorance. Hence, additional steps must assure citizens that officials of the modern regulatory/welfare state are using their power in a way that is consistent with democratic values.

Policymaking accountability goes beyond issues of competence, honesty, and the protection of rights. Statutes are frequently vague, unclear, and inconsistent, and they often leave difficult policy issues to the implementation stage. Delegation then requires the exercise of policy discretion by cabinet ministers, experts, and bureaucrats. Whatever the risks and the countervailing political pressures, legislatures worldwide believe that the benefits of delegation outweigh the costs. In addition, executives make policy on their own without any statutory framework, and these actions need democratic justification. Administrative law can help further that goal.

Policymaking accountability aims to inform citizens and interest groups that a policy choice is imminent and to give them an opportunity to express their opinions. Policymakers also need to consult the best experts and to mediate conflicts between them in a transparent way. The views of the public and experts may diverge, and regulatory authorities should consider the evidence and the nature of public concerns before promulgating a rule. The authority should publish the final rule along with a justification that acknowledges the disputed nature of the choice. A next step in the process is the possibility of independent review by courts that check the policy decision for conformity with the underlying substantive statute and with the procedural constraints designed to ensure public accountability. Once a policy is in place, retrospective review by watchdog groups and public oversight bodies can check to see if the policy has achieved its goals.

Using such procedures, the agency with delegated power makes the ultimate policy decision, but it must consult ex ante and justify its action ex post, subject to limited external review. The review process will check to see that the policymaker has taken public input into account and made a well-reasoned, publicly justified decision. This basic framework is normatively relevant for all modern democracies, but it is currently most evident in US administrative law. Even if representative political institutions provide some oversight of delegated authority, I will argue that they are generally insufficient taken alone.

The three types of accountability can seldom be neatly cabined into watertight compartments. I emphasize policymaking accountability but consider its overlap with performance and rights-based accountability.

Performance accountability and policymaking accountability intersect in familiar ways. Technocratic techniques, such as cost-benefit analysis and impact assessment, are not value-neutral and require policymaking accountability to satisfy the demands of democratic legitimacy. Rights-based accountability can help ensure that public participation incorporates the rights of citizens. Furthermore, policies that themselves protect rights—for example, those dealing with freedom of expression, freedom of assembly, or anti-discrimination—cannot be comprehensively addressed through individual lawsuits. Legislative enactments in these areas need implementation by the public administration in ways that satisfy both performance and policymaking accountability.

Particularly difficult issues arise when a government decision both resolves an individual case and expresses a general policy—for example, when an individual's treatment highlights the way an identifiable class of people (such as, the poor, the elderly, a minority group, or women) is treated by the law. Alternatively, an "individual" decision to build a rail line, a highway, or an airport may be a major undertaking that affects a sizable share of the population and has nationwide effects. In these situations public-law values may come into conflict, and policymaking accountability ought to be a requirement.

Procedures may differ depending upon the type of policy choice and the decision-making environment. Quasi-governmental or private organizations might follow procedures that differ from those imposed on government ministries. The nature and extent of external review might vary by issue and the locus of policy choice. In emergencies, the law may exempt public officials from certain requirements depending on whether they are natural, military, terrorist-related, financial disasters—or a disease that develops into a national or international epidemic. Resolutions of the trade-offs between expertise and public accountability or between speed and transparency may differ, but the core principles remain.

Principles of public accountability also ought to apply to the legislative process. The political self-interest of legislators will frequently lead them to consult widely, hold hearings, and explain their actions to the press and their constituents. The legislature's own rules may mandate public hearings, control amendments and debate, and produce a public record of testimony and committee reports. Laws and internal rules may constrain campaign finance, conflicts of interest, lobbying, and the acceptance of gifts. Even so, in practice, parliaments often add special-interest clauses to general bills, rush through massive legislative packages at the end of the session, and hold truncated hearings.[11] These are very serious failures, but I will not be considering them here because many others have addressed those problems with representative government. In contrast, the behavior of politically responsible executive agencies has not been studied as thoroughly by either democratic theorists or administrative lawyers, especially outside the United States.

Narrow and Broad Views of Public Law

Two stylized models of democratic accountability dominate the field of administrative law and have different implications for the role of the courts in reviewing executive actions. The narrow model focuses on administrative decisions in particular cases. The broad model incorporates this concern but adds a role for law in constraining and managing government performance and policymaking. I will be defending the broader view.

Under the **narrow model**, judicial review of administrative action concentrates on the protection of individual rights against state overreaching. These rights can be procedural, such as the right to be heard and to be judged by an impartial decision-maker, or they can be substantive and broad-ranging, such as the right to "the free development of personality" affirmed in the German Basic Law or *Grundgesetz*.[12] Here, the judiciary's task is to determine whether the bureaucracy's treatment of the individual is compatible with legally binding regulations, statutes, the constitution, and international human-rights norms. In discharging this function, continental jurists characteristically distinguish between disputes in public and private law—with different legal principles and different courts often operating in each sphere.[13]

In deciding cases under the narrow model, courts deny jurisdiction if the judge finds that individuals have been adversely affected by a "political" decision. They defer to such decisions, regardless of whether the political heads of the agency are checked and balanced by other institutions. Even in contexts, such as civil-service law, that include provisions for judicial review, courts only hear individual cases of maladministration and do not adjudicate the propriety of general regulations, which is left to politicians to resolve. There are a few exceptions to this general approach: constitutional provisions, the requirements of international treaties, and criminal offenses. Generally speaking, however, the narrow model assumes that the transmission belt is sufficient and that, in any case, the courts are not the appropriate institutions to fix broken linkages.

The **broad model**, in contrast, takes policymaking accountability seriously. It rejects the notion of a transmission belt that minimizes executive policymaking. I construct my argument for the broad approach from five basic building blocks: first, the inevitability of policymaking delegation; second, the need for technical expertise; third, the importance of political accountability, both to elected officials and to voters; fourth, an openness to outside opinions, not just to input from elected politicians; and fifth, recognition by the judiciary that administrative law can play a constructive oversight role in promoting accountability.

Parliaments have limited time, expertise, and staff resources to confront the complexity and fluidity of real-world problems. At best, generalist legislators outline the policy that should guide the elaboration of technical and legal rules and guidelines, as well as the resolution of individual disputes. Realistically, that framework will leave many policy choices for the administration to elaborate. Referenda are not a good alternative because they are especially likely to delegate detailed elaboration to the government.

In short, the narrow model contains a large gap that places much of the executive's work outside the realm of law. Of course, the legislature provides oversight of the bureaucracy through its power to determine budgets, review spending, hold hearings, establish commissions of inquiry, and the like. Members of opposition parties play an important role. However, just as the legislature does not have the time, expertise, or foresight to write detailed statutes in the first place, it lacks the ability to provide comprehensive oversight ex post. Current political imperatives determine legislative priorities, and so the legislature is likely to overlook a wide range of government activities.

Policymaking accountability should not depend on the shifting attentions of the legislature. Nor is the presence of an honest and technically trained bureaucracy sufficient. Writing rules with the force of law is a deeply political enterprise, but administrative law should nevertheless play a central role in their promulgation. Political leaders inside the executive may not have strong incentives to be accountable to the public, even if they do seek approval, at least pro forma, from the legislature. The broad view recognizes the legitimacy gap that this disconnect poses. It seeks ways to bring interest groups, stakeholders, environmental and social welfare advocates, labor unions, and business associations into the policy discussion, always understanding that no group can, on its own, claim to represent "the public interest." Political accountability operating through an electoral connection has a superior claim to democratic legitimacy, but that claim is not sufficient to fill the gap.

There is no magic formula for solving this problem. To move the discussion forward, I advance four ideal types that crystallize different options. In the chapters that follow, I give these models specific content by considering how four leading democracies have put them into practice.

Models of Policymaking Accountability

My four models differ in their organizational forms, appointment processes, and decision-making procedures. Call them the chain-of-legitimacy model, the expertise model, the partisan-balance model, and the privatization model. Matching the options to substantive problems and finding ways to draw on the strength of each are major aspects of good institutional design.

The **chain-of-legitimacy model** builds in accountability by relying on officials who can trace their authority back to the voters at the beginning of the chain. The justification for delegation is straightforward. The legislature, an elected political body, reviews its own limited staff resources and time, and it passes on the political responsibility of implementation to the president, the prime minister, or a member of the cabinet. The civil service may help frame the issues, and legislation may require consultation with experts or the public. However, decisions are in the hands of political actors. The route for redress is the ballot box or a focused campaign to amend the statute or to replace those charged with implementing it.

Taken to its extreme, the model empowers presidents or prime ministers to issue decrees with the force of law in the absence of explicit delegation by statute.[14] These decrees have external effect on society; they are not just internal orders to the bureaucracy.

A strong form of this model gives little oversight role to the judiciary because of its position outside the political structure. "Administrative law" is a suspect category authorizing political meddling by judges with no democratic legitimacy. The courts resolve individual cases of maladministration but stay clear of issues related to regulatory processes and the substance of policy. They intervene most confidently when governmental bodies are involved in archetypal private-law disputes dealing with contracts, torts, and property.

Under the **expertise** model, a statute delegates authority to neutral, expert decision-makers. They may or may not need to accommodate, or at least to consult with, the public or politicians before making their final decisions. In extreme cases, the regulatory body does not depend on legislative appropriations to sustain its day-to-day operation. Central banks, for example, sometimes achieve this extraordinary degree of independence.

Some issues are not politically contentious. The legislature may safely delegate them to specialists inside a government department. For example, a statute might appropriate funds for basic scientific research and leave it to an expert agency to apportion the funds.[15] Pure performance accountability is sufficient. However, many issues, although highly dependent on scientific competence, generate wide-ranging controversy. Such cases call for appropriate forms of public accountability, in which government experts reach beyond the scientific community to produce democratically acceptable policies. A common response is to set up a broad-based advisory committee representing relevant groups in society. Although bureaucratic experts must consult with these outsiders, government professionals have the final say on the agency's decision.

The model of expert dominance assumes a reasonably objective set of criteria for choice. To work well, the agency must attract high-quality professionals through a combination of prestige and material rewards. It must also access state-of-the-art research in the private sector and academia. By following these strategies, the agency can credibly claim to be pursuing the public interest in a scientifically informed fashion.

To frame the agency's discretion, statutory drafters may pinpoint policy dimensions that are not just matters of scientific expertise. For example, a statute might require both cost-benefit analysis to set priorities and broad consultation, both expert and lay, on contested issues with no "right" answers. A pervasive issue involves the selection of an appropriate discount rate for future costs and benefits. Similarly, the value of human life and ecological integrity raise issues that transcend the teachings of standard welfare economics.[16]

Finally, the policy choice could be subject to judicial review, even if judges defer to the agency's expertise. For example, statutes might seek to enhance economic efficiency by limiting monopoly power; overcoming negative externalities, such as air or water pollution; enhancing product information; or improving health and safety. In reviewing rulemaking under these statutes, courts could require agencies to carry out cost-benefit analyses, unless the substantive statute explicitly outlaws the technique. Judicial review would then evaluate policies in terms of this criterion and remand decisions that appear to be in conflict, recognizing that all such analyses involve value judgments. Agencies could defend themselves by claiming that the statute forbids the use of cost-benefit analysis or that their application of the technique produced results within the range of acceptable policy choice.[17]

This type of review could limit opportunities for the pathologies associated with regulatory capture that tilt so-called "expert" analyses in favor of the regulated industry.[18] More subtly, a biased consultation that is dominated by the regulated industry could affect the good-faith decisions of experts. External review by courts could check the agency's discretion in the name of more democratically justified choices. Although such review is a modest response to a major problem, officials, at least, would need to conduct an open and publicly justified process that permits oversight by individuals, non-governmental organizations, and business interests that were pushed to the periphery of the captured agency's concern.

Next, the **partisan-balance** model explicitly acknowledges the tension at the heart of modern regulatory policy: the conflict between political accountability and expertise. A multi-member board makes decisions through a collegial process, operating by a majority or a supermajority rule or by consensus. The political branches make appointments to the board under rules designed to ensure partisan balance. Paradoxically, explicit partisan balance aims to produce impartial decisions by forcing board members to compromise to fulfil their statutory mandates. There are three important variants based on institutional constraints, balanced membership, and decision-making by establishment figures. The first two are common in the United States, although a recent Supreme Court case contains dicta questioning their constitutionality.[19] The UK, Germany, and France also have multi-member regulatory commissions created in response to EU privatization policies. In other cases, the UK uses bodies composed of establishment figures to deliberate on contested policy issues.

Under the *institutional-constraints* variant, politics enters at the appointment stage, but the institutional design creates incentives for incumbents to operate as impartial professionals while in office. Sometimes the appointment process seeks candidates who are broadly acceptable across the political spectrum. In the US, a highly politicized process requires top agency appointees to be acceptable to both the president and the Senate majority. In a parliamentary system, if approval requires a supermajority, the government must often gain support from political opponents to win confirmation of its nominees.[20] Alternatively, different bodies each select a portion of the agency's membership. This happens in France, where the National Assembly, the Senate, and the president independently choose officials to serve on multi-member commissions.[21] Similarly, each house of the German parliament proposes sixteen members from each legislative house to serve on an Advisory Council for the Federal Network Agency (*Bundesnetzagentur*).[22]

Board members typically have diverse political priorities. Yet, they must transcend narrow partisanship to play a constructive role. Of course, the meliorating force of this technique diminishes during periods of one-party dominance.[23] Nevertheless, once partisans gain appointment, other institutional constraints play a role. In my case-study countries, a number of devices are at work. One involves the terms of employment—for example, long or life-time tenure with discharge only "for cause." Members may receive high salaries balanced by restrictions on subsequent employment in the regulated industry. Their terms of office may overlap and not match those of elected officials. These options encourage official independence from politics, limit self-dealing, and encourage appointees to develop professional expertise.

However, efforts at partisan balance generate distinctive pathologies. The downside risk is that the organization, operating independently, could settle on an idiosyncratic, minority view of good policy. For example, a central bank might limit economic growth with an overly tight monetary policy. Alternatively, it could fuel inflation by printing money or making credit too easily available, undermining government macroeconomic policy.

The *balanced-membership* approach responds to the risk of narrow partisanship by requiring that members span the political landscape. The need to obtain multi-party agreement dampens factional infighting. Its basic form is a multi-member agency that decides policy issues by majority or supermajority vote. To contrast this version with the institutional-constraints variant, imagine a multi-member agency without insulation from short-term partisan influence. Partisan appointees represent their factional supporters. Nevertheless, partisanship is constrained by limiting the number of members each political party can name to the agency. In a two-party regime, such as the US, a five-member commission might be limited to three members from one party.[24] Because appointments are meant to include a range of political opinion, members have an incentive to reach decisions that will seem reasonable to broad sectors of the public. The dangers, however, are partisans who fail to transcend their disagreements and condemn the agency to gridlock, or the appointment of political hacks lacking expertise.[25]

In contrast, the third version of the partisan-balance model envisions a multi-member commission set up to evaluate a technical but politically charged issue. The appointees are *establishment figures* with reputations for practical wisdom and dedication to the public good. The danger is that they have little knowledge of the particular controversies under their mandate. Policy recommendations might be public-spirited but uninformed. They might also merely undertake retrospective efforts to assign blame for past mistakes. To remedy these difficulties, the commission might have an expert staff and consult with representatives of the regulated industry and other stakeholders. This model bears a family resemblance to common-law adjudication except that their proposals may be only advisory. The notables on the commission hear arguments from experts, advocacy groups, and stakeholders with private interests in the outcome. As a practical matter, this process typically ends with a return to political accountability. The establishment figures make a recommendation to the responsible minister who makes the final decision, sometimes after obtaining parliamentary approval.[26]

Finally, the **privatization** option turns over the regulatory task to an institution that is largely independent of the legislature and the executive. Often, these entities claim inherent or historical authority to regulate themselves. There are three variants: professional self-regulation, industrial standard-setting, and corporatist self-government by a broader group of stakeholders.[27]

Doctors, engineers, and lawyers serve as paradigms for *professional self-regulation*. Their associations have a long history, predating the modern state, but they now hold public charters specifying their legal authority and institutional form. Today, many professions operate in similar fashion. Governing boards, consisting of members of the profession, typically control entry, specify the proper way of doing business, and can strip violators of their licenses to provide professional services.

Just as professions regulate themselves, firms also organize to set *industry-wide standards*. These may mandate industrial designs that permit various products to fit together, for example, plugs and sockets, batteries and appliances. They may set safety standards that give customers confidence in the quality of the goods that they buy. If these self-regulatory bodies work well, they draw on the industry's own expertise to set workable standards. Sometimes these consensus standards are subsequently enacted into law.

However, there is a downside to professional and industrial self-regulation. Both are vulnerable to self-seeking behavior that raises entry barriers and entrenches monopoly profits. For example, a profession's governing board might impose overly strict limits on entry and an industry could agree upon anti-competitive constraints on product characteristics.[28] Hence, public accountability may be necessary. As the process of consultation, reason-giving, and review proceeds over time, it may become clear to the larger public that the professional or industry association is abusing its prerogatives, and that its regulation should be shifted to the state bureaucracy. Even the prospect of such a shift could encourage more responsible decision-making within self-regulatory bodies.

Under the *corporatist* alternative, the state turns over regulatory decisions to a body of stakeholders—typically including labor unions, business firms, and perhaps representatives of consumers and concerned citizens. Government ministries sometimes also participate, but they cannot impose their preferred choices.[29] The Scandinavian countries provide archetypal examples. Because corporatist structures are strong and labor union membership is high, few workers and businesses lack representation. Germany also has peak associations at the industry level that negotiate over labor/management issues, manage insurance funds, and regulate some aspects of workplace health and safety.[30]

However, if important groups lack stakeholder status, corporatist institutions suffer from the same problem as professional and industrial self-regulation. In such cases, the decision-making bodies may systematically ignore the interests of excluded groups. For example, those who consume the industry's products or suffer from its impact on the environment typically lack a seat at the table.[31] Moreover, some stakeholder representatives may fail to speak responsibly for the larger group that they claim to represent. The closed nature of the regulatory body gives outsiders little recourse if problems arise.

Conclusion: Mixed Models

Each of my four models of policymaking accountability has distinctive strengths and weaknesses. I have been treating them separately for analytic purposes, but in the real world, the chain-of-legitimacy, expertise, partisan-balance, and privatization models overlap and interact. I have already suggested that the privatization model ought to include a role for governments to check on private bodies' accountability to the public. Consider some additional hybrids with analogues in my case-study countries.

First, those who make policy at the end of the chain of legitimacy often require expertise. In one variant, the political officials who hold the top positions must also have technocratic credentials. Alternatively, a staff of specialists can advise the political appointees. A common pattern, most fully developed in the US, is a politically appointed agency head who collaborates with division chiefs with recognized expertise. These professionals depend upon their deep knowledge of particular substantive areas, but they understand that their basic role is to further the policy agenda of the agency head.

Second, an agency run by expert technocrats could add a staff of savvy operatives to deal with hot-button political issues.[32] Even if the technocrats resist the urge to play politics, they may find that they cannot further their goals without political support. Oversight by the legislature inevitably introduces political calculations into agency decisions.

Third, an agency controlled by a commission with partisan membership will likely depend on an expert staff of career civil servants or academic experts. This will add a layer of technocratic knowledge or, at least, nonpartisan advice to the mix. Expertise provides an additional route to the impartial choices anticipated by partisan balance and may take certain extremely partisan options off the table. Multi-member commissions will not be competent unless they have technocratic support. Impartiality is not valuable unless the agency has the capacity to make competent choices.

Fourth, a state may hedge its bets by subjecting an agency with a single head or a multi-member commission to oversight from a cabinet minister. This represents a partisan check on what may appear to be an independent agency. In all my cases except the US, most agencies are ultimately responsible to a cabinet minister. Political accountability to the government overlaps with expertise and limits the authority of an agency's board. Such an institutional arrangement, however, is problematic because independent technocratic decision-making and the compromises anticipated by a balanced board are both in tension with cabinet responsibility.

Fifth, both partisan and expert decision-makers might benefit from outside input from individuals and organized groups. Thus, although the decision-maker has the ultimate authority to make policy, the law may require consultation and permit judicial challenges to enforce that requirement. On the one hand, consultation complements both the political and the expert models. It can be a source of additional technocratic input if the government lacks state-of-the-art expertise. The downside is that technocratic input may not be impartial but rather may tilt the outcome toward particular organized interests. On the other hand, consultation could focus on ordinary citizens without scientific expertise who are concerned about the policy's impact either on their own lives or on the broader society.

Sixth, specialized expertise is usually the justification for allowing a profession to regulate itself. However, critics point to the incentives for such bodies to favor insiders and restrict competition. The very expertise that can produce effective regulatory rules is bound up with the economic interests of these bodies.

No combination represents a perfect solution. The challenge for the public administration is to balance political accountability to voters and elected politicians with technical competence. Policy choices should reflect the political values of the sitting government, incorporate state-of-the-art knowledge, and facilitate public input between elections. Comparative administrative law can help in the construction of legitimate, responsive modern states. This requires cross-disciplinary dialogue and a search for common themes where the perspectives of political science, public administration, economics, history, and public law are in conversation. Protecting the rights of individuals and businesses against an overarching state is important, but it is not sufficient. Public law should also help constrain excessive assertions of executive power and monitor private or quasi-public entities that carry out public functions.

Some recognize the importance of this goal but argue that hearings and dialogue are imperfect methods. They urge the greater use of public opinion polls and focus groups. They see open-ended public hearings as biased and unreliable measures of public opinion, and they claim that modern social-science techniques would do a better job. Advocates for this position, however, too often understand "public opinion" in simplistic terms. In a representative democracy, bureaucratic policymakers should not merely seek a snapshot of public sentiment, especially because citizens' opinions often lack an informed confrontation with the problem at hand. Rather, the administration should create public fora to enable citizens to engage in meaningful discussion and debate. As I show in Chapter 6, constructing such real-world structures is not an easy task, but it is fundamentally different from simply trying to locate views that are "out there" in the populace.

Political accountability also can be approached from a different angle. Some contend that public hearings on proposed rules are an ineffective way to incorporate public sentiment into bureaucratic decisions. They argue that the public ought to be deeply involved in proposing options, debating the choices, and making the final decisions.[33] The problem is figuring out how to accomplish such an ambitious goal. Positive examples exist at the local level in dense urban neighborhoods, small villages, and affinity groups. However, such intense public involvement is infeasible for policy issues affecting tens of millions of citizens. Think of national environmental regulations or the construction of a new high-speed rail line. Furthermore, seeking widespread agreement on any change from the status quo is not a desirable goal if the distribution of power and wealth is unjust. Existing inequalities should not be baked into the menu of feasible options, especially when the poor and other marginalized communities lack the time, resources, and energy to reflect on their concrete interests in contested matters.

There is a final check on bureaucratic abuses of discretion: popular protest, with marches and rallies denouncing government initiatives.[34] Even here, well-established forms of policymaking accountability matter. If they exist, it is more likely that the state will engage in constructive efforts to incorporate popular grievances into ongoing consultative processes or other efforts at popular inclusion. Of course, these measures may reduce, but won't eliminate, the risk of violent confrontations that may shake the foundations of a democracy. In the final analysis, there is no substitute for responsible political leadership and thoughtful bureaucratic administration to sustain the credibility of modern activist government. Political accountability, as I have articulated it here, can play a valuable role in sustaining this project.

To conclude, the accompanying box summarizes the modes of political accountability, which may, in practice, interact and overlap. Subsequent chapters move beyond this abstract outline and explore the concrete ways in which my four case-study countries have developed these options and their interrelations in the real world. The analysis of the strengths and weaknesses of existing practice sets the stage for my effort to propose ways forward—and to leave the way open for my readers to do the same.

A TYPOLOGY OF PUBLIC ACCOUNTABILITY

- Performance Accountability
- Rights-Based Accountability
    - Narrow model of public law
    - Broad model of public law
- Policymaking Accountability—Broad Model of Public Law
    - Chain of legitimacy
    - Expertise
    - Partisan balance
        - Institutional constraints
        - Balance of power
        - Establishment figures
    - Privatization
        - Professional self-regulation
        - Industrial self-regulation
        - Corporatist self-government

2. *Constitutional Paradoxes*

Democratic systems provide key actors with very different incentives for promoting political accountability. Moreover, they do so in ways that challenge much conventional wisdom. Comparative law traditionally draws a sharp distinction between presidential and parliamentary systems. My exercise in political economy, however, leads to a boundary-crossing conclusion. The methods of holding government to account in different countries do not conform to a sharp presidential/parliamentary dichotomy. I will be demonstrating this point by exploring the practices of my four case-study countries.

To clarify the argument, I assign a label to each democracy. The United Kingdom is a common-law parliamentary regime; Germany has a written-constitution parliamentary system. Similarly, I distinguish between strong presidentialism in France and separation-of-powers presidentialism in the United States. I highlight the differences between Britain and Germany and then argue that executive-branch accountability in France is more similar to the practices prevailing in parliamentary Germany than to those in Britain. In contrast to all three European cases, the separation of powers in the United States creates political incentives that have produced statutes requiring policymaking accountability in the executive.

This chapter introduces the key elements in my political-economic analysis. The following chapters fill in the basic argument by outlining the current practices of each regulatory/welfare state. I concentrate on four dimensions of the problem. One is the impact of legislative/executive relationships on structures of accountability to citizens. The second is the role of the courts. The third is the place of technocratic expertise in policymaking. The fourth is the relationship between the legislative-executive-judicial institutions and the citizenry in general, with special emphasis on civil-society advocacy groups.

Parliamentarianism: The United Kingdom and Germany

Begin with a stripped-down model that highlights the common features of the parliamentary systems in Britain and Germany. In this simple model, voters choose between competing candidates selected by party leaders.[1] The party or party coalition that gains majority support has sweeping lawmaking authority. Once installed in office, the prime minister or chancellor has the right to call an election if a majority of the legislature threatens to overthrow the government with a "vote of no confidence." Generally speaking, this electoral threat will keep party members in line because the leadership will respond to their defection on the confidence vote by denying them the party's endorsement in the coming election. As a result, the government will govern for its full term in office—unless public opinion polls indicate that a "snap election" will reward the established leaders with an even larger parliamentary majority.

To be sure, victory at the polls is never guaranteed.[2] But, the governing coalition has no short-term reason to constrain its own discretion by empowering outside private interests or the courts to intervene in administrative rulemaking.

This basic point also shapes the government's relationship to the bureaucracy. Because it is politically secure until the end of its term, the governing coalition has much to gain from cultivating an apolitical civil service dominated by long-time professionals with the expertise required to implement the government's legislative program. Similarly, there is little long-term political gain from rigid restrictions on the promulgation and the repeal of executive rules.

These political and bureaucratic dynamics shape the nature of electoral competition. Each political party has an incentive to present a platform that emphasizes its fundamental policy commitments, and voters have good reason to expect that parliament will pass, and the bureaucracy will implement, the winner's program. Within this system, the chain of legitimacy supporting the exercise of bureaucratic discretion arises from the clear connections between voters, party platforms, and electoral victories.

Despite these linkages, the victorious government may find that real-world complexities require unexpected revisions in its initial policy pronouncements—leading to exercises of bureaucratic discretion that may generate controversy in society, especially if they appear to violate legislative mandates. This may lead the government to respond by asserting political control over the civil service, invoking principles rooted in rights-based and performance accountability. It might do this either through internal controls on recruitment and promotion or through procedures that permit individual citizens and firms to lodge complaints about their treatment. The government might also create specialized tribunals or administrative courts to check particular injustices.

Nevertheless, governing coalitions are unlikely to support laws that give citizens strong independent routes to demand policymaking accountability through appeals to the courts or other bodies. Instead, political parties are meant to reflect popular sentiment.

The cabinet may establish general oversight bodies, such as an audit office or an ombudsman, to promote performance accountability. Their task is to be sure that professional civil servants respect the law and do not exceed their delegated authority or waste resources. These bodies aim to check the abuse of legal authority but will not help to further the democratic accountability of the governing parliamentary coalition. The same is true of judicial review. At most, cabinet officers and top civil servants will support review of decisions made by low-level officials, especially when they involve the abuse of individual rights or indicate subpar bureaucratic performance. But they are unlikely to seek limits on their own policymaking discretion. Of course, politicians do not operate in a vacuum. They may gain an electoral victory only to find that existing statutes or the independent courts restrict their power.

An extreme example of the limits of executive power is the practice of allowing certain groups, such as doctors, engineers, lawyers, and other professional organizations, to regulate themselves with little oversight from public bureaucracies. To mask this anomaly, parliamentary regimes characteristically indulge in legal fictions. They may treat these regulatory grants to professional groups as if they were merely "private-law" arrangements similar to those regulated by consensual agreements.

As I shall show, these parliamentary themes are visible in both Britain and Germany. Nevertheless, they play out very differently in the two systems—generating more serious efforts at political accountability in written-constitution Germany than in its common-law analogue.

UK: Common-Law Parliamentarianism

The UK constitution is unwritten, leaving it open to shifting interpretations over time. As Paul Evans writes, "the UK constitution is rather like an ice sculpture—no sooner have you put the finishing touches to a description of it and placed it on display, it begins to melt."[3] Even so, the British system provides a relatively pure example of the basic parliamentary model. The government is ordinarily in firm control of a majority in the House of Commons, although the Fixed-Term Parliament Act of 2011 limits the prime minister's ability to call an early election. Parliamentary sovereignty means that its statutes are not subject to judicial review by the nation's courts.

Parliament's absolute sovereignty was tested by the UK's membership in the European Union and the Council of Europe. The "provisions" of the country's unwritten constitution have been a source of controversy, especially where individual rights are concerned. Over recent decades, there have been ongoing disputes over the impact of the Council of Europe's Convention on Human Rights and the EU's Charter of Fundamental Rights. With European courts challenging Westminster's sovereignty, Parliament passed the Human Rights Act in 1998. That act reconciled parliamentary sovereignty with European interdependence by granting the UK Supreme Court a role in reviewing statutes and secondary legislation for compatibility with European rules and principles. If, however, the Court found an incompatibility, the act did not grant it the power to declare Westminster's law invalid or unenforceable. Rather, it authorized the judges to interpret legal provisions in ways that minimized the tension and to propose amendments that, if adopted, would make British law consistent with European requirements.[4] Post-Brexit, of course, the EU Charter does not apply to the UK, but the UK remains a member of the Council of Europe.

The government also issues regulations with the force of law—usually called statutory instruments (SIs). Unlike statutes, most important SIs must be approved by both the House of Commons and the House of Lords, and they are subject to judicial review. However, parliamentary oversight is of relatively little significance; both houses of Parliament typically enact government regulations by rubber-stamping SIs without any serious debate on the floor or in committee. As we will see, the courts have sometimes intervened, but they have not been very active. At present, statutes impose procedural requirements on bureaucratic policymaking in specific areas, most notably the environment and major infrastructure investments. Compliance with these procedures has engaged the courts in disputes over the adequacy of the administration's procedures.

Putting together the protection of rights, scrutiny by the House of Lords, and statutory constraints on bureaucratic discretion, there has been a discernible shift toward greater policymaking accountability inside the government, despite political dynamics granting authority to an expert bureaucracy in the service of the prime minister. It remains to be seen whether this tendency survives the UK's exit from the European Union.

Germany: Written-Constitution Parliamentarianism

Germany departs more decisively from the simple model than the United Kingdom. Two institutional factors produce a stronger version of political accountability. The first is the role of courts; the second, the status of the upper house.

The written constitution reinforces the legitimacy of the German courts. The Basic Law, or Grundgesetz, gives the Constitutional Court the power to authoritatively interpret its content. Government actors must respect fundamental rights, rules about state organization, and democratic self-government.[5] In contrast, the common-law British tradition demands judicial deference to parliamentary sovereignty.

Just as in Britain, however, judicial scrutiny is constrained by the political dynamics of parliamentary government. The Basic Law authorizes parliament to delegate policymaking discretion to the bureaucracy so long as the statute states the "content, purpose, and scope" of executive-branch discretion.[6] However, the text does not regulate the process of issuing legally binding regulations that implement statutory objectives.[7]

No government has tried to fill this vacuum during the life of the modern German republic. A statute like the US Administrative Procedure Act, setting out enforceable procedural requirements for public participation in rulemaking, could interfere with the government's power to pursue its high-priority political initiatives. Instead, the government operates under a set of internal guidelines that are not judicially enforceable.[8]

The German rejection of US-style rulemaking procedures, however, is not only based on power politics. As Chapter 1 suggested, the chain of legitimacy that goes from voters through elected politicians to the dominant party coalition to the government and the professional bureaucracy is not merely a metaphor in Germany. Under this view, bureaucratic rulemaking should be subject to political, not legal, constraints. Indeed, many German jurists go so far as to argue that the chain of legitimacy implies that independent efforts by the judiciary to ensure bureaucratic accountability are unconstitutional, but the Constitutional Court has never passed a definitive judgment. However, the administrative-law statute only authorizes judges to adjudicate grievances generated by particular agency decisions; it does not contemplate supervision of the processes leading to the issuance of rules and guidelines.[9]

Over the past decade, these long-standing principles have been challenged by selective statutes requiring public consultations, mostly involving capital-intensive infrastructure projects affecting particular communities. Article 20a of the Basic Law protects the "natural foundations of life" (*die natürlichen Lebensgrundlagen*) and animals, and it gives the state the power to legislate and to take executive and judicial actions. These provisions have encouraged environmental activists to campaign for greater public consultation in bureaucratic decision-making, even where this is not required by statute. In response, elected politicians have granted limited forms of citizen participation.

At present, however, these concessions are only attempts to accommodate activist pressure, not a general recognition of the democratic value of policymaking accountability. Nevertheless, some academic commentators recognize a distinction between formal dogmatic public law and a regulatory approach better adapted to modern realities.[10] As later chapters explain, these developments could signal an increasing appreciation of the fundamental significance of democratic values in the legitimation of executive-branch policymaking. Perhaps the Constitutional Court will reinterpret the Basic Law's commitment to democratic self-government to affirm a more active judicial role in the process. A similar reorientation is far less likely in common-law Britain.

The second difference between the UK and Germany is that the upper house of parliament, the Bundesrat, expresses the Basic Law's deep commitment to federalism. In contrast to Britain's House of Lords, its members, even though indirectly elected, reflect the party composition of the provincial governments (*Länder*) weighted by population.[11] Under the Basic Law, the Länder administer most federal laws, and the upper house must approve central-government rules that apply to them.[12]

Overall, then, in spite of a parliamentary structure, the German written constitution generates a stronger version of political accountability than prevails in common-law Britain. Indeed, its emerging practice more closely resemble that which prevails in presidentialist France.

France: Strong Presidentialism

The French president is more powerful than a parliamentary chief executive. Although the British prime minister and the German chancellor can call snap elections, they will lose office if their opponents win. The French president does not need to take the same risk. He or she remains in office for the rest of the office's five-year term, whatever the outcome of the snap election.[13] Given this fact, it is unlikely that the president's allies in the National Assembly will provoke its dissolution. American presidents are also weaker vis-à-vis Congress because they lack the power to dissolve Congress and call for an election.

The French Constitution provides for a prime minister, appointed by the president and subject to approval by the National Assembly. If the president has a majority in that body, he or she will appoint a pliable ally.[14] Unified control is likely, at present, because elections for the National Assembly occur only six weeks after the presidential poll. That timing gives supporters of the winning candidate popular momentum in the legislative contest. Even if the opposition parties manage to gain a majority in the Assembly, the president remains a powerful force. He or she chairs weekly cabinet meetings, determines their agenda, and must sign all regulations approved by the Council of Ministers.[15]

The president and the prime minister can propose statutes that delegate policymaking authority to the executive. Some topics have to be governed by statute, but in many policy areas, the government can issue ordinances and decrees (*ordonnances* and *décrets*) even if no statute exists. Presidents would have no interest in statutes that impose procedural limits on executive rulemaking, and no wide-ranging constraints appear in the statute books.

In practice, the most effective potential checks on presidential power do not come from political opponents but from the bureaucracy itself. The authority of the elite corps in the Conseil d'État (CE) predates the 1958 Constitution of the Fifth Republic by at least a century.[16] Traditionally, the

CE has consisted of about 150 elite jurists, most of whom dedicate their professional lives to public service, sometimes moving for a time into top positions inside the cabinet. This remains true, but, recently, exits to the private sector have become more common.[17]

The CE has two roles. First, it sits at the apex of the administrative court system. Second, it reviews the government's statutory and bureaucratic proposals before they are considered by parliament and the voters. It can also review legislative proposals originating in the parliament, if requested by either house. The *avis* (reports) of the CE focus on the extent to which proposals are compatible with the values and principles of French public law, and they are generally not made public. A recent report of the CE, made public by President Macron, confirms the CE's focus on basic legal principles. In late 2020, President Macron proposed a constitutional amendment that would guarantee (*garantir*) protection of the environment. The CE's report objected to the use of that term, rather than "preserve," claiming that it risked giving environmental values priority over other rights.[18] Although only advisory, if the government resists the CE's judgments in any case, it risks subsequent enforcement difficulties if the law or decree returns to the CE in its judicial role. The constitutional structure, in short, combines strong presidential leadership with a significant check from an elite juristic institution.[19]

In contrast, France's constitutional tribunal, the Conseil Constitutionnel (CC), has played a less significant role than its German counterpart. Until 2011, only parliamentarians or the president could bring constitutional challenges. Moreover, they could do so only before bills were enacted into law. Once a statute was on the books, the regular courts refused to rule on analogous objections. A 2008 constitutional amendment authorized the CC to hear such challenges, based on referrals from France's two high courts, one of which is the CE. In contrast to Germany, this grant of authority challenges a centuries-old French tradition rejecting "government by judges." The CC has begun to exercise its new power in recent years, and it has become an important actor within the legal system. The French Constitution includes a Charter for the Environment, and the courts have enforced it to require certain forms of public input into policy choices.

Another recent reform suggests recognition of the value of public reason-giving. In 2015 France enacted its first Administrative Procedure Code, which focuses on the adjudication of individual cases and largely codified the case law of the CE.[20] Despite this legislative affirmation of the status quo, other institutions have been more responsive to demands for greater public participation in bureaucratic initiatives. Judicial decisions mandating participation have concentrated on environmental law, in part because of the constitutional mandate included in the Charter for the Environment appended to the Constitution.[21]

United States: Separation-of-Powers Presidentialism

The American Constitution provides that the president shall "take Care that the Laws be faithfully executed," but it says nothing about the executive branch institutions needed to fulfill this demand.[22] Given that lacuna, the separation of powers generates political incentives for the legislature to act. Its most comprehensive response was the Administrative Procedure Act (APA) enacted in 1946. Among my case-study countries, the APA represents the strongest commitment to public accountability for executive rulemaking.[23]

The American Constitution combines a separately elected president and legislature with the president's inability to dissolve Congress. Hence, the chief executive may face a Congress where a rival political party controls the House or the Senate or both. Even if the president's party has a majority in both branches, some members may oppose presidential initiatives that are unpopular in their home districts. Congressional leaders have a political interest in constraining executive-branch discretion.

One option is to draft detailed substantive statutes. The president may accept restrictive language to gain congressional consent to executive-branch initiatives. Such provisions will be more enduring than in Europe. In the US, when the presidency shifts to the opposing party, the new administration will find it hard promptly to repeal or amend statutes, given the system's multiple veto points.[24] Even when delegation occurs, Congress has a strong incentive to keep it in check through oversight hearings, budgetary control, and commissions of inquiry.

However, given the broad range of government regulatory activities, elected politicians have limited capacity to engage in intensive, ongoing oversight. Instead, the legislature has sought to constrain executive actions through procedural controls and judicial review, rather than micro-manage the executive's substantive decisions.[25] The result in 1946 was strong congressional support for the APA—an effort to achieve many of the same purposes as direct oversight.[26] It enlists the courts to enforce its requirements and to limit the electoral damage caused by policies hostile to the interests of legislators.[27] In other words, the legislature recognizes the pragmatic value of delegation but uses the courts to constrain its exercise. This implies that the courts are both competent and have limited jurisdiction. Judicial oversight can then focus on assuring democratic control, not enacting the judges' policy preferences—a delicate balancing act.

According to the APA, a rule is "an agency statement of general or particular applicability and future effect designed to implement, interpret, or prescribe law or policy or describing the organization, procedure, or practice requirements of an agency."[28] The key words here are "future effect": a rule looks forward even if it also resolves a particular issue. The "notice-and-comment" rulemaking procedures articulated in § 553 of the act require general notice in the Federal Register of proposed rules, hearings open to all "interested persons," and publication of final rules along with "a concise general statement of their basis and purpose."[29] The APA exempts certain rules and administrative actions—for example, "general statements of policy"—and some policy areas—for example, military or foreign affairs—but its reach is broad. Even some agencies not required to follow notice-and-comment processes voluntarily follow them.

The APA states that a reviewing court can set aside actions if an agency did not follow the procedures required by law, where these procedures include violations of the APA's notice-and-comment procedures.[30] Requirements for notice, hearings, and public reason-giving are broad and neutral. They do not favor particular political or economic interests. In practice, wealthy and well-organized interests are better represented at hearings and provide input both into proposed rules and in the post-comment period. In the end, however, the agency must docket all comments and provide a public, reasoned justification for its rules.[31]

How, then, do the APA's procedures square with the claim that narrow economic interests have captured Congress? Critics argue that single-purpose agencies risk capture by the very industries they must regulate, or even that the legislature intended to enshrine industry dominance when it passed the law.[32] Others make the same claim for groups supporting environmental and workplace regulation. If judicial review checks these tendencies, why would Congress build it into the structure of the law? One answer is that judicial review allows legislators to avoid making difficult policy choices. Because they face pressure from both special interests and ordinary voters, they write statutes that nominally favor interest groups but then set standards for judicial review that limit the damage. The legislators, in David Mayhew's phrase, "claim credit" for benefiting a powerful constituency while avoiding a severe impact on the general public.[33] To some, this tendency argues for revival of the disused non-delegation doctrine that would limit the ability of Congress to include vague terms such as "feasibility" in statutes.[34]

So far, my political-economy explanation for the APA has avoided an important question. The APA limits the freedom of the executive, but presidents seek to put their stamp on policy.[35] Why, then, did President Harry S. Truman sign the bill into law? One possibility is that he expected his party to lose the next election and believed that the procedural constraints in the APA would make it difficult for future administrations to undo the New Deal legacy of Franklin Roosevelt. Perhaps, he accepted the APA as part of a political compromise that led to a post-war reorganization to improve government performance.[36]

The APA's combination of public participation, reason-giving, and judicial review is a powerful tool, but it does not exhaust the congressional repertoire. For example, over the decades, Congress gained presidential support for the creation of Offices of Inspectors General (OIGs) in most cabinet departments to report on fraud, waste, abuse, and mismanagement. The president or the department head appoints the inspector general with the consent of the Senate; thus, these officials are not completely independent. Nevertheless, a study of the OIGs in the Departments of Justice and Homeland Security shows that they have gone beyond investigations of malfeasance to consider rights and performance accountability, respectively.[37] Although their role is only advisory, and they lack a mandate to assess policy, some OIGs act as policy advisors. Other bodies help Congress monitor the executive and the independent agencies. The most important is the Government Accountability Office. It reports to Congress and can assess both financial integrity and programmatic accomplishments and failures.

Finally, Congress has created independent regulatory agencies such as the Securities and Exchange Commission and the Federal Communications Commission, not under the direct control of the president. These institutions are generally multi-member bodies whose members have staggered terms. Although the president nominates candidates, they must be confirmed by the Senate. The incumbents do not report to the president or a cabinet member, but they are accountable to congressional committees and subject to judicial review. In some respects, independent agencies operate much like lower courts, but over time they have taken on rulemaking responsibilities in important areas of economic and social life. Presidents continue to try to bring them into the orbit of the core executive, but, so far, with limited success.[38]

Conclusions

Political economy helps to explain policymaking accountability under the APA in the United States and the absence of such a statute in my other cases. American separation-of-powers presidentialism produced political incentives for the APA. The legislature, facing practical reasons to delegate policymaking to the executive, found ways to hold the executive to account. Going forward, however, that pattern may not be a stable equilibrium. Critics of notice-and-comment rulemaking in the US see it as pure window-dressing. They argue that it covers a deeply biased process that favors major economic actors. Others worry that it takes too much time and money and involves the courts in political/policy battles. At the same time, presidents, going back at least to Ronald Reagan, have attempted to take control of the administrative state, concentrating power in the White House.[39] These centralizing moves limit the role of notice-and-comment rulemaking in cabinet departments and generate more executive control of independent agencies. Downplaying notice-and-comment rulemaking and increasing presidential power leave little space for diverse, outside voices. If critics of APA procedures succeed, they may find that the administration has become more closed and the president more powerful.[40]

At the same time, an opposing trend exists in Europe. The parliamentary systems of the UK and Germany and French-style presidentialism have no general statutory requirements for public input into executive rulemaking. Yet, the very lack of such laws is leading to organized pressure for more open and accountable policymaking.

In Europe the expertise of the bureaucracy and its insulation from day-to-day politics were traditionally meant to preserve the public interest from the short-term partisan pressures of political actors. Today, these states face demands for more openness and public participation, on the one hand, and for more systematic, publicly justified reason-giving, on the other. Some polities have begun to respond to pressures for more analysis and for expanded public participation, but public officials frequently resist them, and reforms have not coalesced around a uniform response. Future developments are by no means clear, but the elements are in place to build upon recent reforms. There is room for innovative, cross-country learning as democracies struggle to produce well-reasoned policies that are responsive to popular concerns, not just to the interests of professional politicians or technocratic elites.

3. *Policymaking inside the Executive*

Prime ministers and presidents are both chief executives and political leaders, and these roles are in tension.[1] Some theories of executive power try to shoehorn heads of government into a managerial box that downplays political aspects. Under that view, they are chief executive officers (CEOs) of a large, complex organization who also happen to be elected politicians. In the United States, a classic statement of that view is the 1937 Brownlow Report, produced by a committee of public-administration specialists advising President Franklin Roosevelt.[2] The report characterized the president as a top manager who implements the legislature's will, aided by staff assistants. Evaluation of a president's performance would then depend upon one's view of good public administration. For example, a traditional Weberian model envisages a state that is organized hierarchically with a CEO at the apex. That model competes both with the new public management (NPM) model that focuses on supplying services to citizen-consumers and with other management theories that deemphasize hierarchy.[3] Whatever the particulars of the various management models, however, they emphasize performance accountability, that is, the competent and efficient implementation of statutes.

One version of the CEO model incorporates a strong non-delegation doctrine that prevents the legislature from delegating policymaking authority. This constraint would imply both little legislative action in politically contested areas and highly detailed statutes in others where the legislative majority agrees on the policy details. The latter option can result in rigid frameworks that do not respond to evolving scientific developments or the facts on the ground.

In a representative democracy, the managerial model of executive power is drastically incomplete. Politics cannot and should not disappear when the executive makes choices. The head of government and the cabinet necessarily make policy, constrained by statutory and constitutional provisions.[4] In my four cases, policymaking accountability and political deal-making coexist with the protection of rights and with efforts to make the government run more effectively.

Two issues are important for comparative analysis. First, does the constitution permit the executive to make policy in areas not covered by statute? Second, how do policymakers in the executive balance political accountability with professional expertise?

I begin with the parliamentary systems of the UK and Germany, where the head of government is politically accountable to the governing coalition in the legislature and is also responsible for maintaining a competent public administration. I then move to France with its strong president and (usually) subordinate prime minister. One might imagine that the president could focus on government performance, with the prime minister leading the parliamentary majority. In practice, the French president is both the government's top manager and the nation's political leader.

I conclude with the American system, where the opposition may control one or both houses of Congress, and presidents must both exert political leadership and oversee the bureaucracy. However, as David E. Lewis has astutely argued, the US president and the legislature have little incentive to concentrate on the functioning of the administrative state.[5] The president's fixed term and mandate from the voters frame negotiations with Congress. Statutes are often vaguely worded to achieve passage in times of divided government. Laws are both difficult to pass and hard to repeal. In order to implement vague or broadly worded statutes, the executive must make policy choices before taking action.

Governments in all four cases deal with issues of democratic accountability as they make policy outside the formal legislative process. A popular mandate at the ballot box is essential, but it is not the only route to public accountability.

The United Kingdom

The UK state has a unitary structure where the political party (or coalition) with the dominant position (usually a majority) in the House of Commons forms the government. The party leader becomes prime minister and selects members of Parliament for his or her cabinet. Within this unitary framework, Parliament can delegate the implementation of statutes to the government. Administrative law stresses performance and rights-based accountability; Parliament itself is presumed to provide sufficient policymaking accountability.[6] Acts of Parliament are exempt from judicial review. However, under the 1998 Human Rights Act, the courts can issue declarations of incompatibility if a statute violates the human rights norms of the Council of Europe.[7] Moreover, when the UK was part of the EU (and during the transition period), courts could refuse to apply statutes that violate EU law.[8]

Parliament must approve most secondary legislation (rules with the force of law) issued by the government, and such rules can be subject to judicial review on limited grounds.[9] The executive is directly accountable to the Parliament, although "the Crown" retains some prerogative powers, especially in foreign affairs.[10] The extent of this power is contested and has narrowed over time, but it remains a remnant of the British monarchy, now exercised by government ministers on behalf of the Crown.

However, the partisan battle over Brexit led the Supreme Court in *Miller I* to take the bold step of establishing a strong presumption in favor of parliamentary involvement in major policy choices.[11] The long-run implications of *Miller I*, however, are unclear. Two days after the decision, the government submitted its bill to Parliament. The bill, became law less than two months after the court's decision. There was debate in both houses, and a few members proposed amendments; none passed, and the Commons enacted the government's text. Although the case was read as a victory for Parliament, the rapid disposition of the key issues hardly illustrates the democratic benefits of parliamentary involvement. The text had only one operative clause, which stated:

> 1. Power to notify withdrawal from the EU:
>
> The Prime Minister may notify, under Article 50(2) of the Treaty of the European Union, the United Kingdom's intention to withdraw from the EU.
>
> This section has effect despite any provisions made by or under the European Communities Act of 1972 or any other enactment.[12]

The constitutional crisis escalated when Prime Minister Boris Johnson tried to prorogue Parliament to force through Brexit without serious debate.[13] The

Supreme Court intervened in *Miller II* to declare that his action violated constitutional principles, highlighting ongoing difficulties in the relations between the legislature and the executive.[14] With the Tories' decisive victory in the December 2019 election, these tensions have eased, but they may resurface as Brexit proceeds and Britain seeks to define a new place for itself in the twenty-first century.[15]

The contemporary situation highlights three contrasting difficulties: weak parliamentary oversight in some key cases, Parliament's inability to provide an effective democratic check even when it is involved, and the risk of using referenda to decide complex policy issues. These weaknesses mean that, in practice, much policymaking occurs under statutory delegations to the government. Although the UK's statutory instruments (SIs) have the force of law, they are often described as filling in "technical" details or improving bureaucratic implementation. In practice, they often make policies with social costs and benefits, much like US rules with the force of law.[16]

Delegation in the UK sometimes takes the form of "Henry VIII clauses" that permit the government to "amend" statutes using SIs, thus avoiding the more time-consuming process of passing a statutory amendment through the Parliament. This power will sound illegitimate to American ears, especially given the association with that monarch. However, such clauses are not unilateral exercises of executive power. Rather, they are written into statutory texts that have passed the Commons.[17] Hence, in practice, they resemble the broad delegations of rulemaking authority in US statutes.

As a check on executive overreaching, SIs and Henry VIII amendments ordinarily require the approval of each house, with no power to amend the text.[18] Approval is usually pro forma, although a small number of SIs have been voted down and sent back to the government to be revised or dropped. With few exceptions, Parliament's veto power over SIs provides little democratic accountability over and above the imprimatur of the underlying statute.

However, there may be limits to parliamentary deference. A test of the executive's ability to obtain broad regulatory powers arose in the Internal Market Bill, designed to manage the UK market after it leaves the EU. The bill invoked sharp criticism, including by the House of Lords Constitution Committee. Among the many sources of disquiet were the bill's extensive Henry VIII powers that would permit the government to amend, repeal, or otherwise modify legislation to further the law's aims. The Committee called this "the most extreme form of Henry VIII clause, representing an indiscriminate rather than a targeted approach to delegating powers to ministers." The Lords cannot prevent the Commons' passage of the bill into law, but it did vote against some of the bill's provisions during its review of the legislation.[19]

SIs, including Henry VIII amendments, can be subject to judicial review, unlike statutes enacted under the sovereignty of Parliament. Nevertheless, no general administrative procedure act applies to their promulgation, so there is no overall statutory check on the procedures used.

Much of the reform discussion in the UK focuses on making parliamentary oversight stronger and more effective, not on codifying rulemaking procedures inside the government or requiring more public input. However, the House of Commons faces a conundrum as a check on government rulemaking. Although possessing the political legitimacy of popular election, it is unlikely to be an effective check on the government because the cabinet and the majority in the Commons are members of the same party or party coalition. MPs from the government's party who are not in the cabinet (backbenchers) and the opposition may raise objections, but they will generally be unable to vote down an SI if the prime minister insists on party discipline (that is, on a whipped vote). Most MPs in the majority would not find it in their interest to oppose an SI and risk retaliation from the government on future issues of concern to them. Dissident MPs from the governing party or coalition might try to trigger a change of leadership, but such a drastic step is unlikely to result from opposition to a single statutory instrument.

The House of Lords, an appointive and hereditary body, only has an advisory role with respect to statutes.[20] However, it can quash an SI even if the Commons approves.[21] Apparently recognizing its lack of democratic legitimacy, the Lords uses this power selectively. The Parliament's Joint Committee on Conventions states that the Lords should not regularly reject secondary legislation, but could do so "in exceptional circumstances."[22] Peers spent only 6 percent of the chamber's time on delegated legislation in 2016–2017.[23] The Lords first voted against an SI in 1968, when it vetoed one dealing with sanctions against Rhodesia;[24] it did not veto another SI until 2000.[25] Between 1999 and 2010 "there were 22 defeats on whipped business other than on government bills; 17 of these involved delegated legislation (statutory instruments); 53 votes upheld SIs."[26] In 2015 the Lords voted down an SI that would have cut tax credits for poor working families with children.[27] The Lords argued that the government should have proposed a statute, not an SI. It suggested that if the government expected deference from the Lords, it should have included the policy in its party manifesto.[28] They objected, not to the policy per se, but rather to the stealthy way that the government introduced it with little publicity or consultation, making the Lords the only institution willing to hold the government to account.[29] Along the same lines, some argued that using SIs to smooth the process for exiting the EU undermined constitutional principles because of the inadequacies of parliamentary oversight of delegated legislation.[30] Perhaps the Lords' objections to some aspects of the Internal Market Bill signals its willingness to provide intensive review of the corresponding SIs, especially those enacted under Henry VIII powers.

Policymaking processes inside the government frequently include consultations with stakeholders, including civil-society groups and members of the public.[31] However, no general administrative procedure act applies to SIs. Unless a substantive statute mandates consultation, it is not a legally enforceable right and is left to the discretion of government departments or agencies. Consultations are described as making sure that the policymaker has all the relevant information and acts fairly, not as enhancing democratic legitimacy. Nevertheless, both the executive and the courts have sometimes acknowledged the democratic value of participation. There is a nascent recognition of the democratic benefits of more open and participatory processes in the drafting of secondary legislation.[32]

Civil servants with relevant experience are central to policymaking. They must carry out their duties "(a) with integrity and honesty, and (b) with objectivity and impartiality."[33] Individual ministers and the prime minister have relatively small political staffs, often including one or two "special advisors." These officials are personally appointed by ministers to further their policy goals. They are formally part of the civil service but are not required to be objective and impartial. Instead, they help to further the goals of the minister and of the government as a whole.[34] The prime minister's office has expanded as a result of the need to coordinate across government departments.[35] Coordination involves both "managing for results" and checking on the political accountability of departments, that is, enhancing both performance and policymaking accountability at the apex of government. Many commissions and authorities also provide advise.[36]

Delegation of rulemaking gives considerable drafting influence to expert professionals in the civil service or in advisory bodies. Of course, ministers retain the right to interfere in highly politicized or contested cases, aided by their special advisors.[37] Their actions should reflect the prime minister's priorities. Overall checks on executive policymaking are concentrated inside Parliament, not in procedures for consultation with the public.

As we will see in discussing Germany and France, environmental policymaking in the executive is a partial exception. Input from organized civil-society groups is especially important because the benefits and costs of regulations are often spread broadly across the population, so that individuals have little incentive to participate absent an association that speaks for their concerns, both moral and economic. The Convention on Access to Information, Public Participation in Decision-Making and Access to Justice in Environmental Matters of the UN Economic Commission for Europe (the Aarhus Convention) has been crucial in encouraging public-law protections for civil-society participation in environmental decisions. It establishes three rights of the public, both individuals and associations: (1) access to environmental information held by government officials, (2) public participation in environmental decision-making, and (3) access to justice to remedy infringements on the two previous rights.[38] The convention has been ratified by forty-six states, including my three European cases, plus the EU. For EU members, the European Court of Justice (ECJ) gives legal force to what is otherwise a weak treaty.[39] After exiting the EU, the UK remains under the Aarhus Convention, but, after a transition period, the ECJ will have no jurisdiction, and EU law that is consistent with the goals of Aarhus will no longer apply.

The UK government has replaced much EU law with statutory instruments, as part of the Brexit process, with little or no public consultation. The European Union (Withdrawal) Act of 2018 granted the government time-limited powers to issue SIs to amend existing legislation to remove references to EU institutions, EU treaties, or other similar "deficiencies."[40] Even before exit day, Parliament routinely approved hundreds of Brexit-related SIs that cover a broad array of matters, including food safety, fisheries management, animal and plant health, and pesticide use.[41] Some were not mere changes in nomenclature. For instance, although EU law requires that new pesticides be approved subject to independent scientific advice from the European Food Safety Authority, the superseding SI only requires the relevant minister of state to consider scientific advice.[42] The European Union

(Withdrawal Agreement) Act of 2020 took the UK out of the EU on January 31, but instituted an interim period when EU directives and regulations would continue to apply until a final agreement has been reached. The 2020 act removed the role of Parliament in overseeing the negotiations of the UK with the EU-27 on the future relationship. Neither the 2018 nor the 2020 act placed any emphasis on enhancing public consultation.[43]

At a Meeting of Parties to the Aarhus Convention, Friends of the Earth (FoE), an environmental advocacy organization, challenged the lack of consultation on the drafting of both the European Union (Withdrawal) Act of 2018 and the corresponding SIs. FoE sought an interpretation of the treaty that would extend public-consultation requirements to SIs. It questioned the democratic legitimacy of the government's drafting activities and the promulgation of SIs. The government strongly resisted, and in the end, the Aarhus Convention Compliance Committee ruled that FoE's challenge to the SIs was inadmissible.[44] Although FoE's efforts failed, the values expressed in its lawsuit are exactly the ones that I am trying to defend.

To conclude, although UK practice includes parliamentary oversight of most secondary legislation, in reality there is little rigorous review. Although limited parliamentary time and staff are contributing factors, the basic explanation is the unitary Westminster system of government that gives the parliamentary majority little incentive routinely to second-guess the sitting government. The House of Lords faces no such constraint, but it lacks democratic legitimacy. Thus, even if calls for greater parliamentary involvement succeed, there will continue to be an argument for greater public consultation and deliberation in the drafting of government regulations. The government's interest in streamlining the Brexit process highlights the tension between prompt action and consultations with ordinary citizens that can give more democratic accountability to the resulting policy choices. Developments in environmental policymaking and in the approval of large infrastructure projects demonstrate that members of the public and of environmental advocacy groups have an interest in public participation and hope to encourage reason-giving from public bodies as part of their decision-making processes.

Germany

In Germany, secondary norms or rules with legal force (*Rechtsverordnungen*) are promulgated by political appointees, assisted by expert career bureaucrats.

The ministries may consult the public or key stakeholders, but consultation is seldom a legal requirement. In contrast, public hearings or consultations are legally required for many individual licensing and public-investment decisions. Some legally binding rules result from stakeholder bargaining that originally arose in the field of labor–management relations. This negotiation model and its variants have been applied to other policy areas such as pensions, worker health and safety, and education policy.

The debate over public participation mainly concerns legislative drafts, not government rules. However, as in the UK, increased public involvement in environmental rulemaking by government ministries and agencies arises from civil-society pressure, aided by the Aarhus Convention and EU directives that apply to member states.[45] In addition, echoing the distribution of authority in the German federal system, public input is widespread at the state and local levels under a federal law requiring public participation in the drafting of development plans.[46]

When Germany privatized firms in network industries, such as electricity, gas, and telecoms, it faced new public-law issues related to their regulation. The state shifted from the management of state-owned firms to the steering (*Steuerung*) of private businesses.[47] The policy change led to both formal regulations and programs that encourage firms to self-organize to comply with regulatory goals. Professors Wolfgang Hoffmann-Riem and Eberhard Schmidt-Aßmann edited ten books that urged a "new science of administrative law" (*neue Verwaltungsrechtswissenschaft*) to incorporate principles from social science and to support the regulation of newly privatized industries and of the environment.[48] They argued that public law should further market efficiency, control externalities, and enhance distributive justice in sectors where private firms are now dominant. Government officials were urged to consider the values behind the statutes they implement, not just the legal texts.[49] Their proposed reforms have not been codified into law. As Matthias Ruffert writes: "Generally, politics may be quite immune to generally accepted proposals of administrative reform, e.g., in evaluating the importance of procedural rules, which is too often denied."[50] However, the courts have made various efforts to accommodate the new reality, especially in environmental matters.[51] Furthermore, the EU has made an effort to encourage Germany, along with other member states, to include more public participation in policymaking.[52]

Under the German Basic Law, statutes must delegate rulemaking authority explicitly.[53] Except for emergencies, the government has no inherent power to act without statutory authorization.[54] In 1979, in a case involving nuclear power, the Constitutional Court held that administrative rulemaking is a legitimate way to protect individual rights. The justices argued that a rule, by setting general standards, could serve this purpose better than reliance on case-by-case adjudication.[55] The decision, therefore, marks a significant step in the direction of policymaking accountability. If a government department engages in rulemaking, the civil service plays an important role, operating below the thin layer of political appointees. Politicians inside the government manage the administrative hierarchy and work together with career bureaucrats to ensure performance accountability. Of course, politics has not been banished from administration, but the managerial, Weberian model has deep historical roots.[56] Ministers are responsible to parliament, and their subordinates are accountable up the chain of command. The chancellor is both a chief executive managing the bureaucracy and a politically responsible leader. As Eberhardt Schmidt-Aßmann and Christoph Möllers explain, "subjecting both the political and the administrative parts of the executive to the law was a principal goal of the authors of the 1949 Constitution."[57] "The law," here, represents rights-based accountability, that is, the uniform application of constitutional rights by officials who do not engage in interpretation.

Two countervailing factors operate against a strict hierarchy in the public sector. First, Germany hives off certain issues from national government control, placing the implementation of many federal statutes (*Bundessatzungen*) with the states (Länder) or in quasi-independent bodies.[58] Second, corporatist regulation of industrial relations insulates some matters from central-government regulation, although the boundaries are sometimes contested. Corporatist organizations and professional self-regulatory bodies, some with long pedigrees, exist largely outside the state hierarchy.[59]

In areas of shared competence, the federal government may issue Rechtsverordnungen that the states must implement. The upper house of parliament (the *Bundesrat*), representing the states, must generally approve such rules. Its party composition routinely differs from that of the lower house (*Bundestag*) because members are selected by the ruling parties in each state, not by direct election.[60] Furthermore, even with no party divergence, the state governments have distinct concerns. They typically want to avoid federal mandates with high budgetary costs or complex procedures.[61] In practice, the upper house seldom turns down secondary norms proposed by the national government, but its members may negotiate with the government to avoid confrontations.[62] Some statutes require the Bundestag to approve Rechtsverordnungen; others give parliament the option of voting down a rule within a given time period.[63] Given the parliamentary nature of the German system, disapproval is unlikely. However, the review process provides the opposition a platform to voice complaints and could reveal cracks in a coalition government.

The German Administrative Procedures Act (*Verwaltungsverfahrensgesetz*, VwVfG) applies to individual "administrative acts," not to general rules.[64] The chain of legitimacy is believed to ensure the public legitimacy of the government's actions. Legal requirements for public input into executive or agency rulemaking are limited to a few statutes and mostly apply to individual projects.[65] The statute governing the approval of large infrastructure projects includes explicit consultation requirements, suggesting that German law recognizes that public consultation can enhance the public acceptance of government action. However, executive rules setting general policy are not subject to such requirements, although officials may voluntarily engage in public consultations to give a decision more political legitimacy.[66]

The environmental area has been more open to civil-society participation than other regulatory fields. Public officials and courts have largely accepted the incorporation of public consultations into environmental decision-making for major projects, and even for rules and regulations.[67] These developments are an outgrowth of the Aarhus Convention as enforced by the European Court of Justice and supported by environmental groups. The convention's provisions for general regulations are much weaker.[68]

Certain public choices have no clearly identifiable individuals or firms that suffer significant harms, even though the overall social costs are large. Hence, no one may have an individual motivation to influence government decisions or to seek redress in court. In such cases, cause-based groups may bring neglected issues to the attention of the government and provide fact-based arguments that reflect their policy goals. They are also well positioned to bring court challenges to administrative procedures.[69] Government officials will not necessarily accept the point of view of such intervenors, but they can learn about both facts and public values that might otherwise be overlooked.

Nevertheless, some worry about adding time and hassle to bureaucratic procedures. After German reunification, several "speeding-up laws" were passed to expedite the construction of infrastructure in the east, some as recently as 2006–2007. German courts are quite generous in excusing procedural errors. As Hermann Pünder writes, these laws "might lead the administration to take a lax cavalier approach to procedure . . . [In] light of the irrelevancy of certain procedural errors, some administrative bodies [might] purposefully deny citizens the possibility to state their arguments."[70]

To provide further context, consider the move toward renewable energy over the last decade. It is known as the *Energiewende*, to bring to mind the *Wende*, or fundamental turning point that took place with reunification in 1989.[71] The country's policy on renewables illustrates the tension between public participation in policymaking, on the one hand, and the resolution of local conflicts with clear winners and losers, on the other. Divide-the-pie choices differ from those where public dialogue and compromise could convert seemingly zero-sum choices into win-win situations.[72]

The policy arose in reaction to the 2011 earthquake and tsunami that destroyed the Fukushima nuclear power plant in Japan. The German legislature voted 513 to 79 to phase out nuclear power and to speed up the development of renewable sources of electric power.[73] This vote followed decades of controversy over nuclear power that began during the Cold War.[74] German interest in non-nuclear renewable energy as a substitute for electricity generated by coal, oil, gas, and nuclear pre-dated Fukushima. But this tragedy mobilized public concern and undermined industry claims for nuclear power as an effective response to climate change.

Public opinion strongly supported the phase-out, and political parties from the Greens through the Social Democrats to the Christian Democrats favored it. The statute stepped up the commitment to renewables and provided for expansion of the electrical grid to transport this power source. The law set a goal of generating at least 35 percent of electricity from renewables by 2020, with continuous increases to 80 percent by 2050.[75] In the first nine months of 2020, renewables accounted for almost 50 percent of electrical energy supply.[76]

The rapid enactment of the policy avoided confrontation with the costs as well as the benefits of such a major shift. The cost of electricity has risen for households,[77] but some heavy industrial users of power are exempt, and the owners of closed nuclear power plants are obtaining compensation.[78] The statute did not confront the disparate impact on citizens from land-based wind farms or the high-tension power lines needed to transport wind power across the country. Providing for public involvement in the rules and guidelines needed to put the energy transition into effect might have reduced subsequent opposition. As Armin Grunwald argues, politicians should have explained to the public that the policy would have winners and losers.[79] Supporters should have articulated the costs and benefits of that shift as part of the debate over the policy's value.

This critique may seem unfair because the statute does include multiple opportunities for public input. But participation occurred when most of the remaining decisions were divide-the-pie decisions—the most difficult to resolve through public debate and dialogue.

Statutory law set out a multi-stage process for new transmission lines from the windy North and Baltic Seas to the industrial South. Planners first determined the termini of power lines based on plans submitted by the grid operators and after consultation with other stakeholders. The Bundestag enacted these plans into law. The next step was determining the routes of the three grids in detail, and here, public opposition arose. Residents complained about power lines going over their towns and villages, and environmentalists objected to the lines' passage over nature protection areas. Those supporting the federal policy on renewables, both environmentalists and producers of such energy, argue that the basic choice to build grid lines already had been made.[80]

Opposition to proposed grid routes and wind farms is not, at least overtly, about broad principles related to energy policy. Instead, it concerns the details of where these facilities will be built. The law mandating new high-tension power lines includes multiple decision nodes that require public input, but the emphasis is on strictly local issues dealing with the location, possible health risks, and the aesthetics of route choices.[81] For example, the consultations following the announcement of a fourth grid line only heard from affected local residents (*betroffene Anwohner*).[82]

The government has responded to local opposition with costly fixes, such as burying some grid lines, but, as a result, the falling cost of producing renewable electric power may be canceled out by the increased cost of its transportation. The 2016 Law on the Burial of Cables (*Erdkabelgesetz*) prioritizes placing lines underground, especially near inhabited areas. A 2016 report estimates that burial will increase the cost of the grid expansion by 3–8 billion euros.[83] The dispute over the details of the routes is a classic example of NIMBYism ("not in my backyard"), supplemented by efforts to keep natural landscapes free of power lines and wind farms. These extra costs were not part of the original debate over the shift to renewables. The "public opposition" being overcome is from the residents of the particular towns affected, not the broader public who will bear most of the extra cost. Related disputes have arisen over the siting of land-based windmills close to inhabited areas. Landowners are compensated for leasing their land, but neighbors complain about the noise and appearance of windmills and their effect on wildlife. The result has been a slowdown in the expected rollout of wind farms, an issue that has become politically salient.[84]

These disputes over transition costs illustrate a fundamental problem at the interface between public input and technocratic knowledge. Policy is made at one government level—here, through a statute passed quickly, without sustained analysis of its costs and benefits. Although both the phase-out of nuclear power and the shift to renewables were broadly popular with voters, there was no focused debate on the law's long-term implications. The costs for consumers and citizens only became more salient because of subsidies paid to renewable providers, exemptions for some industries, and compensation paid to owners of shuttered nuclear plants. Some are now discussing retaining nuclear power as part of the energy mix.[85]

In spite of their limited reach, local consultations are a positive step, demonstrating officials' openness to the concerns of ordinary citizens. They may also serve as a steppingstone to more wide-ranging consultations with the general public over broader policies. A consortium of private and public actors, Citizen Dialogue on the Power Grid (*Bürgerdialog Stromnetz*), suggests one way forward. It aims to foster acceptance of the energy transition and to involve the public in a "transparent, inclusive and independent manner."[86] The program invites public input in several cities affected by the transition. The initiative also offers mobile Citizen Bureaus (*Bürgerbüros*) that tour the country to inform and interact with the public. It hosts talks and open discussions and provides mediators who may be consulted in case of conflicts related to the energy transition. It offers on-line information and a hotline for the public to receive information and raise suggestions or make complaints.[87] Its efforts are purely advisory, and it is unclear whether it has had any concrete policy effects. Nevertheless, its model could be a route to a more informed public debate over policy.[88]

Thus, as in the UK, there are a multitude of efforts to engage German citizens and civil-society groups during policymaking processes. Environmental policy is once again a particular locus of activism, and some public agencies have responded with consultation efforts. Large infrastructure projects, especially in the energy sector, must include several layers of consultation. Nevertheless, there is considerable resistance among officials to engaging in open-ended consultations or to supporting legal mandates for executive rules that require hearings and reason-giving. A tension remains between law as a formal set of rules to be implemented by officials and law as a policy framework that must balance technical imperatives with citizen input, over and above the casting of electoral ballots.

France

French civil-society groups, many with an environmental focus, have recently campaigned for enhanced public participation and public accountability in executive policymaking. Mass demonstrations and other forms of direct action have a long history in France, but organized efforts to manage public debate are more recent. The Constitution broadly supports citizen involvement in policymaking. The 1789 Declaration of the Rights of Man and of the Citizen, article 15, states that: "Society has the right to require of any public agent an account of his administration." That language, however, does not translate into a specific set of institutions and legal requirements.[89]

Ideally, career civil servants embody the "general will." Given this strong commitment to a particular model of responsible government, public participation may be seen not only as unnecessary but also as biased and pernicious if narrow, well-organized groups dominate the discussion and fail to represent the public interest. Participation, if it occurs, would then seek to promote performance accountability through competent choices based on expertise, not to further democratic accountability. In France, due process protects the rights of individuals in adjudications, but does not extend to democratic efforts to justify executive-branch policymaking.

Nevertheless, there are signs of change. The Conseil Constitutionnel (CC) reads the Constitution's Charter for the Environment to require public input into regulatory policymaking, and the Conseil d'État (CE) implements that decision. After a period of resistance to the efforts of the European Court of Human Rights,[90] the CE has both modified its own practices and demonstrated an interest in public participation, agency independence, and impact assessment. The CE's 2011 annual public report argued for a deliberative administration (*administration délibérative*), similar to what I call policymaking accountability; it recommended open public participation and the systematic evaluation of policies compared to alternatives.[91]

In 2015 France promulgated its first Code of Administrative Procedure that largely codifies the jurisprudence of the CE and focuses on adjudication, not rulemaking.[92] Public consultations are either "purely" optional or can substitute for existing stakeholder consultations. The provisions are much less robust than US notice-and-comment procedures discussed below; in particular, the government need not give public reasons, and the extent of judicial review is unclear. Nevertheless, the code suggests a growing openness to reform.[93] These judicial and legislative developments parallel other politically motivated efforts, discussed below, that bring the public into discussions of public policy.

But first, one needs to understand how the executive makes policy under the French Constitution to see where the possibility for outside input can arise. Once elected with the political support of the electorate, the president "is not politically accountable except when he [or she] decides to become so."[94] The executive has considerable leeway to issue decrees (*décrets*) and ordinances (*ordonnances*) under statutory delegations that allow it to modify (*modifier*) or "amend" statutes under the residual powers of the executive if no statute exists. The president must sign decrees that were deliberated in the Council of Ministers,[95] but unlike in Britain and Germany, decrees do not need legislative approval. Ordinances lapse unless approved by the legislature within a fixed time period.[96]

The Constitution specifies subject areas where statutes passed by parliament "shall determine the rules" and then adds other areas where statutes "shall determine the fundamental principles" of regulation in fields like the environment, education, and labor law.[97] It also empowers the prime minister to promulgate decrees on matters that do not fall within the ambit of a statute.[98] In exceptional circumstances, the president has the authority to issue decrees with the force of law without any parliamentary authorization whatsoever.[99]

Most decrees must be submitted to the Conseil d'État before approval, but it has been permissive in signing off on the legality of proposed rules. Its review, moreover, is not open to public scrutiny, so it is difficult to know how it evaluates proposals and whether preliminary negotiations occur between the CE and government officials.[100] High-level professional bureaucrats staff the CE, and their review concentrates on performance and rights-based accountability, not policymaking accountability. The CE is the guardian of French legality, and it looks for technical legal and drafting mistakes that would make regulations difficult to implement.[101] Panels also sit as adjudicatory bodies and may hear challenges to a decree arising long after it goes into effect. But these decisions provide little policymaking accountability to concerned citizens and stakeholders at the time of the rule's promulgation. The same is true of the annual reports on specific topics published by the CE.

The Constitution does not require the government to engage in notice, public comment, or reason-giving before it issues decrees or ordinances, although ordinances need parliamentary approval to remain in force. However, a 2008 constitutional amendment gave the Conseil Constitutionnel the ability to rule on rights violations in cases brought by individuals and organizations. Previously, it could only review statutes before their promulgation to check their constitutionality. Now, both the Cour de Cassation, the highest civil court, and the Conseil d'État can refer claimed violations of constitutional rights to the Conseil Constitutionnel.[102] Invoking this constitutional change, the Conseil Constitutionnel held that an umbrella environmental group could have access to the courts to argue for its right to be consulted about the implementation of the air pollution law.[103] The Conseil then held that the lack of consultation violated the Constitution's Charter for the Environment. The broadened jurisdiction of the Conseil Constitutionnel is significant and will be discussed in Chapter 7. However, because the environment has special constitutional status, the decision may have a limited effect on general rulemaking procedures.

These relatively recent legal developments need to be understood against the overall landscape for public input. Building on my work with Thomas Perroud, I begin with the traditional inquest, followed by consultations with stakeholders, moving on to broader *concertations* for large projects, and a form of consultation called a *Grenelle*. I conclude by introducing the Citizens' Assembly on Climate (*Convention Citoyenne pour le Climat*) organized by the government to debate climate-change policy in reaction to the mass protests of the "yellow vests" (*gilets jaunes*) in 2019.

The inquest: Traditional French law limited public input to the inquest. The *préfet*, who is the representative of the national government in each *département*, organizes the procedure. The inquest informs the population about local and regional projects, both public and private, and assists the préfet in making the final decision. An inquest is compulsory for projects that will involve the taking of private property by eminent domain, and a 2011 law expanded its coverage to include projects with an impact on the environment.[104] The process originated 150 to 200 years ago, but recently it has become more open and transparent. These changes are partly the result of EU pressure and partly due to environmental protests against big projects, such as nuclear plants or the extraction of shale gas in undeveloped natural areas.[105]

The inquest occurs at the end of the project planning cycle, based on a fully developed plan. The préfet appoints a single *commissaire* or a small committee on the basis of recommendations from the president of the Regional Administrative Court. The nominees are primarily high national civil servants, often with engineering backgrounds. A committee usually has two or three generalists and two or three specialists knowledgeable about the type of project at issue. Even if committee members are civil servants, the process can be politicized because selection is in the hands of the préfet, a political official.

The inquest evaluates whether a proposed project is in the public interest, but it is not a forum for balancing and debating multiple alternatives. The developer—whether the government, a local authority, or a private firm—prepares a detailed dossier and presents it to the préfet. Domestic law, reinforced by EU pressure for more transparency, requires environmental and social impact assessments.[106] The project must be presented in a nontechnical way that includes both an impact assessment (IA) financed by the developer and the opinion of the Ministry for Ecological Transition, which includes environmental impacts. The dossier is available for a fixed period in town halls and other places—and sometimes on the internet. Anyone can obtain the dossier and make comments. The commissaire can also request the opinion of those with relevant information or expertise. Since the 2011 reforms, the report must explain how the committee assessed the comments, and must communicate the public's observations to the developer.[107] The inquest only invites the public to comment on a particular proposal, not to debate alternatives.[108]

Once comments are recorded and opinions heard, there are three choices: to recommend that the project be approved, that it be abandoned, or that approval be conditioned on certain reservations. The opinion must contain a statement of reasons to inform the préfet and the developer, but it need not respond directly to public comments, and the opinion is not automatically made public. However, if there is litigation challenging the final decision, the opinion will become part of the public record. The inquest usually recommends approval of the project, and the préfet generally follows its recommendation, but it is not a rubber stamp. Project planners are likely to take account of the objections raised by the civil servants who typically serve on inquest committees. Projects are sometimes rejected if they would have had adverse environmental or social effects.[109] If such negative decisions begin to pose a significant risk to developers, planners can be expected to incorporate these values up front.

After a favorable decision, a project can go ahead. However, opponents can bring a case before the administrative courts to have it quashed, and the courts can issue an injunction to put the project on hold while the court deliberates.[110] Such court cases provide another route for public input, but, once again, the decision will only concern whether or not a particular project ought to go forward.

In short, the inquest includes a form of public consultation that, since a 1983 reform,[111] has been open to all, but that does not include public debate. The process essentially allows the national government to exert some control over spending priorities and economic development at the local and regional levels. Many criticize the inquest as being too closed and ineffective, and for coming too late in the process.[112] In response, French law and practice have not only expanded the factors considered by the inquest, but also moved toward increasing public participation through other initiatives.

Consultation and concertation: The French distinguish between *consultation* and *concertation*. The first term refers to consultations with bodies representing various interests—called the consultative administration (*administration consultative*). These bodies have a closed membership and usually have no final decision-making power. Closely related are ad hoc commissions organized to advise particular ministries. The Conseil d'État criticized the proliferation of these bodies, especially the permanent commissions.[113] In contrast, concertation refers to open-ended processes in which there is give and take that permits a discussion with concerned citizens and organized groups. In recent years, they have become more frequent, especially for local and regional projects.[114]

One important example of consultation is the National Consultative Ethics Committee for Health and Life Sciences. The government consults it on such issues as organ harvesting, donations for transplant, research on human embryos, euthanasia, the treatment of personal medical records and problems associated with the computerization of health-related data, and the commercialization of human stem cells. The body, often called the "wise men committee," is made up of experts from various scientific and philosophical backgrounds, such as representatives belonging to the "main philosophical and spiritual families," chosen for their "qualifications and interest in ethical problems" (prominent philosophers and intellectuals), and experts from the field of research.[115] This elite group is supposed to tell the government what is ethical. Its opinions on surrogacy or assisted suicide, for example, claim to represent a consensus view based on present knowledge. Such decisions are also meant to reflect socially acceptable standards, but they are not subject to an electoral or public-opinion test.

The government also organizes consultations where it both learns from participants and gives them information to prepare the way for introduction of a new policy. Ministries consult groups with a stake in the outcome such as unions, professional organizations, and councils, but even if these consultations provide advice to decision-makers, they do not involve the broader public. On the contrary, they act as intermediaries between the public and the government.

Turn next to concertation. Although the practice dates from the times of French central economic planning, it was extended during the 1970s and 1980s to include environmental policymaking and culminated in the enactment of the 1995 Barnier law.[116] The motivation for the law's passage was a fifteen-year controversy, between 1978 and 1992, over the high-speed train from Paris to Marseilles, during which public protests delayed the project.[117] The law created a National Commission on Public Debate (*Commission Nationale du Débat Public*, CNDP) to organize debates on the environmental impacts of major infrastructure projects.[118] In 2002 its mandate was broadened to include socio-economic and development impacts as well.[119] CNDP debates can be compulsory or discretionary, depending on the nature and importance of the project. For compulsory debates, the private developer and the public body responsible for the project must ask the CNDP to organize a debate. For other projects, the request is not compulsory but can come from a local government, ten members of the National Assembly, environmental associations, the private developer, the public body in charge, or the relevant ministry. About two-thirds of requests come from a ministry.[120]

Unlike the inquest, the debates occur at an early stage, before the developer has prepared a final plan. The CNDP seeks to apply principles of inclusion, discussion, and openness. The aim is to permit a broad range of public concerns to be vetted and discussed before the government settles on a particular plan. The ministries request debates for two different reasons: they may hope to get broad public support for a project, or conversely, they may want to highlight opposition to a local plan that national politicians or officials oppose or want modified.

CNDP debates are routine for large projects, meaning that project planners must open their decision-making activities to outside input. Any document produced by the public debate takes the form of advice to the relevant authorities. Even an excellent concertation may not produce a unified recommendation, and even if it does, the advice has no binding force. However, if a proposal obtains strong support in the debate and is then completely ignored, government unresponsiveness could spur public protests or lead to lawsuits down the line.

The quality of the debates varies. Some provide excellent input to subsequent stages, but others are merely talking shops; still others provoke little interest beyond the firms and the government. Most participants are existing associations and groups, not the broader public. The CNDP acknowledges the variability in debate quality, pointing especially to the lack of participation in some processes.[121] The legal rights created by the process are limited. The Conseil d'État reviews the CNDP's decisions concerning whether or not to require a public debate. However, once the CNDP has decided to go ahead, the CE will not evaluate the adequacy of the process.[122]

A **Grenelle** is another type of large consultation, named after the Rue de Grenelle in Paris, where many government ministries are located. The term refers to any large-scale, government-organized consultation process with an agenda and a time limit that focuses on a particular policy issue.[123] The core group consists of stakeholders, other than political parties, that provides advice to the government but does not make binding decisions. The government organized the first such gathering in June 1968, bringing labor union leaders and rank-and-file members together with government and business representatives, and produced an agreement that ended massive and disruptive strikes. Recent examples have dealt with: health (2001), the environment (2007),[124] minimum wages (*le Grenelle de l'insertion*, 2007), advertising on public television, life-long job training (*le Grenelle de la formation*,

2007), access to the high-speed internet (2008), the use of the sea (2009), radio waves from mobile phones (*le Grenelle des ondes*, 2009), and urban security (2010).[125]

The 2007 *Grenelle de l'environnement* provides an example. Soon after Nicolas Sarkozy was elected president, a Grenelle took place over several months in the summer and fall of 2007. The incoming government saw the process as a way to enhance its rather shaky environmental credentials.[126] The consultations involved almost 2,000 people and drew from a wide spectrum of interests. Six working groups included representatives from five types of participants: local authorities, the central government, environmental organizations, employers, and employees. The working-group proposals were discussed in public meetings throughout the country, followed by four roundtables that included representatives of the same five groups. Official political parties were excluded from the working group, but otherwise there were no explicit quotas on who could participate. However, some groups were not certified to participate either because they worked on issues that the organizers excluded from the agenda, such as nuclear power, or because the organizers determined that they were not environmental groups.[127] Some agonized over whether to be part of the process or to maintain a critical stance. A few groups established a counter-Grenelle, arguing that the environmental participants had sold out and labeling the Grenelle a "Munich of ecology."[128]

The Grenelle sought input from a wide range of opinions and interests, although the broad range of the participants resulted in final recommendations that were moderate compromises. Thirty-three follow-up committees were set up in order to implement the recommended program.[129] The government did not move immediately to draft a bill based on the Grenelle's recommendations. Rather, reverting to standard practice, the minister for Environment and Sustainable Development appointed a twenty-four-member commission that produced a report with eighty-eight proposed legal changes. The chair was a member of the Conseil d'État, and members had a range of expertise and political associations. In short, the familiar pattern of government consultation with an elite commission persisted. In practice, the Grenelle was an advisory body to another advisory body.[130]

Despite its limitations, the exercise was the first formal effort by the national government to include environmental groups explicitly in the legislative drafting process, placing business, labor, and environmental groups together around a single negotiating table. This created tensions, but led some large firms voluntarily to adopt environmentally friendly policies, perhaps to stave off more restrictive laws. Some of these agreements have been codified into law.[131] Eventually, two laws were enacted, Grenelle I (2009) and Grenelle II (2010), that built on some of the policies proposed at the original meeting.[132] However, they are mostly aspirational, framework laws with few concrete effects, and a 2012 report to the Economic, Social and Environmental Counsel (*Conseil Économique Social et Environnemental*, CESE), France's third, advisory chamber, argues that the process produced few results.[133]

Another example is the Estates General of Bioethics (*États Généraux de la Bioéthique*).[134] A public debate in the form of an estates general precedes any reform project dealing with ethical and societal issues raised by advances in the fields of biology, medicine, and health. The estates general convenes citizens chosen to represent diverse groups in society. They receive specific training, and then discuss and issue public recommendations. The experts involved in the training are chosen according to criteria of independence and pluralism.

Jacques Chevallier points out the shortcomings of public debates generated by Grenelles or estates general.[135] The participants are mainly professionals and beneficiaries of the sector concerned: doctors and patients for health, teachers and students for education—even though the number of participants has been very large (200,000 for the Health États Généraux and more than 1 million for the debate on the future of education). He argues that the two principles guiding public debates—the principle of equivalence (each participant should be treated equally) and the existence of an independent organizing third party—are not sufficient to guarantee the serious involvement of ordinary citizens. These consultations are more inclusive than more traditional forms of consultation, but the established hierarchy of actors often reappears because some actors are more experienced and informed than others. Nevertheless, they are a step toward a more open process of deliberation over broad national policies.

Open-ended debates: Recently, the French government has moved beyond statutory requirements and past practice to launch new initiatives in public accountability. For example, in 2016 François Hollande's government proposed a statute for a "Digital Republic" and organized an open process that invited public comment from anyone, including both individuals and organizations.[136] The on-line portal attracted 21,472 contributors, who cast nearly 150,000 ballots in favor or against the proposal, and submitted almost 8,500 comments, amendments, and proposals.[137] The site allowed participants to vote for, against, or "maybe," and the government responded by altering some features of the draft law.[138] Although there were deficiencies in the organization of this massive effort, it nevertheless set the stage for future initiatives.

The Citizens' Assembly on Climate is particularly noteworthy. The government's effort to respond to climate change by raising the tax on gasoline produced an aggressive and sometimes disruptive response called the yellow-vests (*gilets-jaunes*) movement. President Emmanuel Macron initially organized a Grand Debate that was actually an informal "listening tour" to gauge public opinion.[139] He subsequently organized a Citizens' Assembly as a systematic attempt to produce specific policy recommendations. The government initially asked the CNDP to organize a debate of French citizens. However, the CNDP's slow-moving protocols were not fast enough for a president facing a public-relations emergency. Macron turned to his own ministers. Their speedy response had significant defects, but it did adopt many of the practices used by the CNDP in its own concertations.[140] Eventually, in the midst of the coronavirus pandemic, the Assembly produced a report with hundreds of policy recommendations. I return to this effort and its aftermath in the context of my general discussion of public participation in Chapter 6.

Environmental rulemaking: Neither a Grenelle nor a public debate is legally required for the promulgation of decrees or ordinances. In contrast, inquests are statutory mandates, as are some consultation processes for infrastructure and development. In the environmental area, additional legal support for public participation arises from the French Constitution itself.

The Constitution includes a Charter for the Environment, promulgated in 2005 as a result of the ratification of the Aarhus Convention and incorporated by reference into the Constitution.[141] Article 7 states: "Each person has the right, in the conditions and to the extent provided by law . . . to participate in the public decision-making process likely to affect the environment."[142] An environmental advocacy organization then invoked the Charter to challenge the existing air pollution statute's failure to provide for public input. The relevant minister had issued a decree after hearing the advice of the Conseil d'État and of an expert body that must be consulted by law. It did not engage in public consultation.[143] The Conseil Constitutionnel held that the charter's participatory requirement created a constitutional duty for the relevant ministry to balance legal and environmental expertise, on the one hand, with public consultation, on the other.[144] Thus, whenever parliament takes measures that affect the environment, it must incorporate public participation into executive regulatory procedures. However, the decision was not explicit about what types of participation would satisfy the constitutional provision. The CC only set a time limit for a legislative response.

The legislature responded to the decision by amending the air pollution statute, and it adopted a soft version of US-style notice-and-comment rulemaking.[145] The amended statute requires the relevant ministry to publish a list of forthcoming policy decisions every three months, and draft regulations must be available electronically to the public along with their context and objectives. The public must have at least twenty-one days to respond. During that period, the comments are not publicly available. At the close of the comment period, the government must wait at least four days before issuing the final rule. Along with the final rule, it must provide a statement of reasons, a response to the comments, and a synopsis of the comments. The comments must remain on the ministry website for three months, but can then be removed.[146] One provision sets up an experiment that asks a neutral person to summarize the comments.[147]

This formulation represents a bare minimum. The time periods for comments and for government review of the comments are very short, and the government can decide how it wishes to summarize them.[148] The law represents a modest move toward greater public input, but it risks being a merely symbolic gesture that may satisfy the CC but do little to enhance the public accountability of environmental policymaking.

In practice, the Conseil d'État seems ready to enforce its provisions. In 2019 it invalidated a ministerial action for failing sufficiently to engage the public under the statute's specific requirements. The CE voided an order by the Ministry for Ecological and Inclusive Development (*Ministère de la Transition Écologique et Solidaire*) that prohibited the hunting of two endangered species of shore birds in certain regions of France. An association of hunters complained that the ministry issued its order one day after the close of the comment period, without waiting for the minimum four days required by the statute. The CE held in favor of the association, suspended the order, and awarded the association €3,000 to cover some of its legal fees. The ministry could provide no extraordinary reason for ignoring the requirement, and it failed to respond to the comments received.[149]

Overall, France is moving toward more public participation in executive rulemaking. Although the constitutional text provides a clear mandate only for environmental matters, the Conseil Constitutionnel's intervention may encourage advocates in other policy areas to claim expanded participatory rights. In non-environmental matters, if the administration must consult expert committees prior to making a decision, it may also, at its own discretion, organize an open on-line consultation to collect comments.[150] The Conseil d'État has held that, even if consultation is optional, the agency must provide procedural guarantees for citizens. It cannot merely engage in a superficial exercise in public relations.[151] Going forward, France must confront the tension between open-ended consultations, on the one hand, and established bodies with limited membership, on the other. The members of these bodies represent the interests of specific groups, for example, business, labor, consumers, or the scientific community. Even if the members are selected by the groups they represent, other interests may not be acknowledged and may lack the resources to demand access.[152] Similarly, the process of selecting "representatives" may itself be biased against new or dissident members of recognized interest groups.

Backed by the new administrative code, recent decisions of the high courts, and even President Macron's Citizens' Assembly, all combine to demonstrate that France is making a serious effort to improve the policymaking accountability of its administrative rulemaking processes. These developments suggest a move toward more participatory administrative processes. More open policymaking may be in the offing. It will be important to discover if efforts to involve the public, such as the Citizens' Assembly, have an impact not only on newly proposed legislation but also on the way any new laws are implemented. It is not sufficient to pass laws that reflect public concerns. The next step is a policymaking process inside government that continues to engage with citizens. France appears to be moving in a direction that invites public input and can complement its historical commitment to the *service publique* ethic of its public officials.

The United States

Unlike French presidents, US presidents have little independent authority to issue decrees with the force of law, even on a time-limited basis. They can, however, issue executive orders, guidance documents, policy statements, and memoranda with no formal legal force but with de facto effects on the operation of government.

The president must "take care that the Laws be faithfully executed,"[153] and, thus, the executive implements statutes that have delegated authority to the president or to a cabinet secretary. This authority may be implicit in the broad wording of a statute, but it must exist. Absent explicit statutory language, executive departments can choose whether to issue rules or act case by case.[154] A permissive non-delegation doctrine places few limits on the ability of Congress to delegate, and Congress has considerable drafting freedom, except in areas that may violate constitutional rights or challenge the federal structure.[155] However, in spite of that freedom, laws are often difficult to pass. A president has less ability than a prime minister to get the executive's legislative agenda passed into law. The House and Senate may have differing party compositions, and single-member districts give individual legislators some independence from party platforms and from the president's agenda. A president must bargain with the legislature at the drafting stage, even if his or her party controls Congress.

Some issues may be politically difficult to codify into statutes, prompting the executive to take unilateral action rather than seek new legislation. All recent presidents have issued multiple executive orders and other types of documents that have gone into effect without judicial resistance.[156] For example, President Barack Obama tested the limits of his authority through policy memoranda issued by a cabinet secretary that set enforcement priorities for immigrants lacking legal status. The policy of Deferred Action for Childhood Arrivals (DACA) stated a general policy that permitted undocumented young adults to attend school and work without fear of deportation for a two-year period, which was later extended. The Trump administration summarily voided DACA through a memorandum from the same cabinet department. However, as I discuss in Chapter 7, that effort was rebuffed by the Supreme Court for faulty administrative procedures, and President Biden issued a memorandum on his first day in office to "preserve and fortify DACA."[157]

In ordinary times, the US system cannot quickly overturn policies embodied in either statutes or legislative rules. Statutes can be repealed only by a vote of both houses and a presidential signature or, in case of a presidential veto, by a two-thirds vote in each house. The legislative process is more contested than in my other cases, especially if one or both houses are not controlled by the president's party. Outside of an emergency situation, such as a pandemic, it would be very unusual to pass a statute within two months, as occurred in the UK after the *Miller I* decision.[158] Partly as a result of divided government and relatively weak party discipline, enacted statutes may be vague or internally inconsistent as a result of the compromises needed to obtain passage.[159] Presidents interpret statutes to accord with their own priorities, urging their cabinet secretaries to enact rules that fit the president's agenda.[160] For example, an administration may interpret an existing statute to permit new regulatory initiatives, such as the Food and Drug Administration's failed attempts to regulate cigarettes under President Bill Clinton or efforts by the Reagan and Trump administrations to cut back existing regulations.[161] Congress cannot vote down executive or agency rules with the force of law unless the repeal takes the form of a statute signed by the president or passed over his veto.[162]

Presidents cannot order officials to issue rules that suit their policy priorities, full stop. Statutes that delegate policymaking authority to the executive often name cabinet departments or agencies, not the president. However, the Executive Office of the President (EOP) seeks to manage the regulatory agenda and claim credit for agency action. Putting this power in the hands of the president can erode the importance of agency expertise and deliberation on policy. According to Peter Shane and Peter Strauss, the president ought to be the overseer, not the decider, in most regulatory areas, excluding some aspects of national security and foreign policy.[163] Shane outlines and critiques presidential efforts to be the "decider" from Presidents Richard Nixon through George W. Bush.[164] The Donald Trump administration continued this trend with its strong assertions of presidential authority.[165] The Joseph Biden administration faces the same incentives, although likely with more respect for civil service and agency expertise.

Countering presidential efforts to assert dominance, the rulemaking process operates under the constraints of the Administrative Procedure Act for the issuance (and repeal) of rules with the force of law.[166] This act extends the US system of checks and balances to include policymaking delegation to the executive. The rulemaking process must accord with the democratic safeguards of notice-and-comment rulemaking, that is, public notice, open-ended public participation, and a published statement of reasons. Judicial review can check that a rule is consistent with the substance of the authorizing statute and is not "arbitrary, capricious, an abuse of discretion, or otherwise not in accordance with law."[167] The APA exempts certain types of actions and substantive areas from the notice-and-comment process.[168] However, judicial review is not so limited; it also covers many other agency actions.[169]

The rulemaking process has evolved over the decades,[170] although the Supreme Court halted the DC Circuit Court's efforts to enhance administrative procedures in an important 1978 case.[171] Nevertheless, the core remains. Unlike the act's provisions governing adjudication, the rulemaking procedures do not primarily protect individual rights against state overreaching. Instead, they further the democratic legitimacy and competence of executive policymaking in a regulatory state that relies on technocratic expertise to make policy. The APA is an instrument of both policymaking and performance accountability. Some commentators label it a "landmark" or "super" statute with quasi-constitutional stature,[172] and it is a foundational aspect of government policymaking. Nevertheless, like any other statute, it can be repealed or amended.

Some deny that notice-and-comment rulemaking furthers performance or policymaking accountability. They describe it as "kabuki theatre" or as an "ossified" process.[173] Careful empirical studies demonstrate that these critiques go too far.[174] At the same time, the critics do raise important questions that I discuss further in Chapter 6. First, does notice-and-comment rulemaking provide important input to executive departments? Second, if it does influence the substance of regulations, is there a bias toward input from organized business interests? Not surprisingly, business groups are very active, both in seeking to influence draft proposals and in submitting comments. Jason Webb Yackee and Susan Webb Yackee provide evidence of business influence but conclude that the process does allow open-ended participation and furthers the goal of "limiting the ability of federal agencies to regulate with impunity."[175] In other words, the process matters, and even if commercial bodies are central participants, it is preferable to put their input into the public rulemaking record. That way it can be countered by others, limiting the ability of insiders to influence policy choices out of the public eye. The importance of the comment period, then, does not turn on whether the final rule is appreciably different from the proposal. The agency's knowledge that it must accept and respond to public comments implies that the drafters of the proposed rule will try to anticipate comments and will respond to them in the posted draft.[176]

The third critique has the greatest substance. Many observers argue that APA rulemaking processes have become less important as the White House has become more assertive.[177] If policy is made outside of APA requirements, the notice-and-comment process risks irrelevance. The real action occurs between cabinet departments, the EOP, and those with privileged access to the president. Other interested parties are effectively excluded. The rise of the Executive Office of the President is a threat to the principles of policymaking accountability expressed by the Administrative Procedure Act.

Critiques of efforts by both president and Congress to limit the APA are complementary. If policymaking is concentrated in the White House staff, presidents may abuse their power in illegal and opaque ways that are beyond the control of countervailing power centers. Similarly, if the APA is amended, as some propose, to authorize new forms of congressional intervention, this will also represent an assault on its core values—the generation of rules that are both technically competent and democratically legitimate. Policymaking accountability in the executive requires both the faithful interpretation of statutory mandates and public participation by citizens and interest groups in the process by which the legislation is converted into workable programs. Business should be part of the process, but not dominate it. Officials need to balance the pros and cons of policy options and to do this in a transparent and reasoned way.

Consider, first, the ways in which the White House, under both Democratic and Republican control, has undermined the APA's notice-and-comment procedures. Beginning with an executive order (EO) issued by the Reagan administration in 1981, cabinet departments must submit their annual regulatory plans and their "significant" rules to the Office of Information and Regulatory Affairs (OIRA) in the White House Office of Management and Budget. The Senate must confirm the head of OIRA, but the office itself depends only on the president's willingness to support the institution.

Although the details of the relevant EOs have changed over time, the basic framework has remained constant, as reflected in EO 12866—issued by the Clinton White House but still in force at the end of the Trump administration. Agencies have to prepare cost-benefit analyses for "economically significant rules" with an annual effect on the economy of $100 million or more. Independent regulatory commissions are not subject to such review, but they must submit regulatory plans to the White House.[178] In addition to systematic analysis, the EO instructs agencies to take the president's priorities into account but also asserts that it shall not be "construed as displacing the agencies' authority or responsibilities as authorized by law."[179] President Biden issued a memorandum on his first day in office that "reaffirms the basic principles" set forth in EO 12866. At the same time, it stresses that OIRA should consider difficult-to-quantity benefits and take account of distributive consequences, especially burdens on "disadvantaged, vulnerable, or marginalized communities."[180] Thus, the Biden administration may issue EOs that differ significantly from prior presidential actions, but it seems clear that it will retain a commitment to White House oversight of regulatory initiatives in the core executive.

One can defend OIRA review as a presidential effort to manage a complex bureaucratic hierarchy through centralized directives, or critique it as an attempt to exert undue influence on policymaking in agencies with delegated authority to implement statutes.[181] Former heads of OIRA defend their actions, but two empirical studies argue that presidential involvement in rulemaking may neither enhance political accountability nor achieve regulatory efficiency.[182] OIRA's close link to the White House may be inconsistent with impartial analytic review. Such review should take place in a separate expert agency whose mission is to recommend ways to rationalize regulatory policy across programs that regulate risk.[183]

Conflicts between technocratic advice and presidential priorities are a familiar feature of executive policymaking. The value of a competent, unbiased bureaucracy for both policymaking and case-by-case implementation is foundational to the field of public administration.[184] Strong oversight by the White House could work against a bureaucratic model that places policy choices in the hands of knowledgeable officials. Models based either on hierarchy or on expertise stress competence and efficiency, that is, performance accountability, rather than policymaking accountability. The APA notice-and-comment process adds a layer of policymaking accountability that may be in tension both with bureaucratic imperatives and with the president's political priorities. Similarly, tensions arise, not just between technocrats and the White House, but also between the political and policy communities associated with different cabinet departments. Presidents claim credit ex post for departmental rules and the policies that they implement, and push those same departments to further their agenda. The notice-and-comment process may seem a time-consuming bother to chief executives, leading them to try to make policy outside its requirements.

Furthermore, the APA says nothing about how the executive sets the policy agenda; it only operates after a rulemaking is set in motion with a notice of proposed rulemaking that includes a draft rule. Procedural provisions are pointless if no rules are proposed or if the president and the cabinet only issue guidelines and policy statements that do not require APA procedures. The APA permits outsiders to petition agencies to begin a rulemaking, but, in practice, the option is seldom used, and few agencies have procedures in place to process petitions.[185]

Credit-claiming by presidents is common, and Elena Kagan illustrates its operation during the Clinton administration.[186] Presidents use their position to highlight the successful promulgation or repeal of rules, upstaging their cabinet members. On the deregulatory side of the ledger, if OIRA review emphasizes cost-benefit criterion, it can limit the issuance of rules if its staff finds violations of that criterion or delays its own assessments.[187] It can have this effect even if the legal authority lies with the department, not the White House.[188] The White House can also help determine agency priorities when it negotiates over the regulatory agenda with government departments. Seeking to limit the reach of the presidency, Congress sometimes enacts clear regulatory mandates and includes time limits or backup standards that will apply if the government does not regulate.[189] Alternatively, agency officials may avoid OIRA review by, for example, staying below the dollar thresholds for stringent review or using case-by-case adjudication instead of rulemaking.[190]

The Trump administration took advantage of the leeway in many regulatory statutes. Without actually seeking to repeal these statutes, it issued executive orders to blunt their effects.[191] For example, EO 13771 on Reducing Regulation and Controlling Regulatory Costs required executive departments and agencies to repeal two rules for every new one they propose. It was voided as soon as the Biden administration took office.[192] Under EO 13771, the costs of new regulations were to be balanced by the cost savings from the eliminated rules. The text ignored the social benefits of regulations. Reducing compliance costs was all that mattered. Officials were to eliminate rules, not respond to substantive regulatory challenges. As one author points out, the executive order gave officials an incentive to void rules that were dead letters and to find ways to streamline existing programs—all to the good, but hardly a revolution.[193] Over time, the repeal of rules with real effects on people's lives started to take effect. Even some businesses became alarmed by the Trump administration's deregulatory zeal. For example, although the coal industry supported the administration's proposal to weaken the national targets for curbing mercury and air toxics from power plants, several energy groups and labor unions in the energy industry opposed the plan.[194] The electric power industry had already spent over $18 billion to comply with the Obama-era rule, and the affected firms wanted to retain it to preserve the value of their investment in compliance.[195]

The Trump administration sought to roll back almost 100 different environmental rules, but many faced court challenges. In a few cases, the administration reversed course and reinstated a rule it had sought to repeal.[196] The career bureaucracy could not do much to push back, even though they had civil service protections and could not simply be fired.[197] Nevertheless, its members are aging, with a wave of retirements taking place and little effort made to recruit a new cadre of committed public servants. Although attrition in the civil service overall was not extreme, one study documents sharp declines in the number of high-level members of the Senior Executive Service, career officials who are essential to government policymaking.[198]

The decline of the civil service during the Trump administration was partly the result of budget cutbacks and unsympathetic agency heads, but it was exacerbated by two developments that pre-date the Trump administration and will continue into the Biden administration and beyond: the increase in the number of political appointees and the use of contractors and grantees in the private sector. The former contrasts sharply with my other cases, where the layer of political appointees is much thinner, giving the public administration more continuity whatever party or coalition is in power.[199] The latter is a contested issue. Sometimes out-sourcing can be desirable for tasks with proven private-sector counterparts, but over the long haul it can hollow out the civil service, making it unable to control its own contractors and grantees or to respond competently to new programs and challenges. Paul Verkuil and Paul Light have sounded the alarm, and they make the case for reinvigorating the professional US civil service.[200] This argument has prompted a lively debate between those advocating reform and those who argue that reform is no longer tenable given a history of underinvestment in the civil service that goes back decades.[201]

At a more basic level, the repeal of a rule with the force of law must follow the same APA procedures as a new rule, slowing down attempts to revise or eliminate rules.[202] That process must permit input from those who favor the old rule—not just direct beneficiaries, but also citizens, civil-society groups, and business interests. Rushing through a rule suspension can lead to judicial push-back.[203] Thus, a US president faces more obstacles than similarly committed heads of government in my other cases, who can repeal executive regulations, subject, at most, to pro forma parliamentary acceptance.

One option is to repeal an old rule and then begin a new process to issue a new rule, but both processes take time. For example, consider the Waters of the United States (WOTUS) Rule, issued in 2015 by the Obama administration to control water pollution. The underlying legal issue was the applicability of the Clean Water Act to intrastate and seasonal bodies of water. The courts had not settled this contested issue prior to the issuance of the rule; hence, it faced multiple legal challenges, and it had not gone into effect by the time President Trump took office in 2017. Arguing for a narrow definition of WOTUS, the new administration issued an executive order directing the EPA and US Army Corps of Engineers to review and potentially rescind the rule.[204] The EPA initially proposed a two-year implementation delay, presumably to leave time to repeal and replace the rule following the notice-and-comment process. Amid numerous legal challenges, the administration eventually repealed the rule in October 2019, and in January 2020 it issued a replacement called the Navigable Waters Protection Rule that took effect in June 2020. The new rule limits the wetlands and small waterways that are covered by the Clean Water Act, but it too is subject to multiple court challenges. The new administration arriving in 2021 will experience similar delays if it seeks to replace that rule. As one commentator wrote: "Replacing that water rule will take time, and they won't want to rescind the Trump rule while they are working on the new rule, because then the waterways would be left with no protection."[205]

During the Trump administration, when repeal of a rule proved too cumbersome, the administration employed other strategies, including lax enforcement with reduced inspections and limited reporting requirements. If the Biden administration wants to strengthen regulations, it must initiate rulemaking processes to reverse rules promulgated by the Trump administration. A legally binding rule, however, is not the only way to make policy. As noted above, cabinet secretaries may issue memoranda, "interpretative rules, . . . [and] general statements of policy" without engaging in notice-and-comment rulemaking.[206] If a statute leaves room for interpretation, officials in the executive branch can set their own priorities, even if they arguably conflict with statutory purposes. The federal courts may eventually strike down such efforts, but even so, administrators have considerable leeway. The legislature can also starve an agency of the budget needed to implement the law and set priorities through explicit language in budget bills that contravene the original purpose of a law.

In promulgating rules with the force of law under the APA, agencies must combine input from civil servants, expert consultants, and political appointees with a time-limited but open-ended call for comments from anyone outside the federal government. After considering the public's views, along with comments from the affected industry, lower-level governments, and others, the agency must deliberate and then justify its final rule with a public statement of reasons. Although the agency may consult members of Congress,[207] the legislature is not legally involved in the promulgation or the repeal of rules, except under the limited reach of the Congressional Review Act.[208] Interested parties with standing can challenge the rule in court, with judicial review taking the agency's expertise and political legitimacy into account.[209]

This system is by no means perfect, and I have outlined ways in which presidents can undermine its effectiveness. There is room for reform, but the notice-and-comment process has retained its key role in executive policy-making because rules with the force of law are central to the administration of the modern regulatory/welfare state. I turn now to the second threat to that process: legislative proposals that would undermine executive rulemaking's effort to combine expertise and public accountability. Although the proposals are unlikely to be revived in the near future, their motivations need to be understood. Two bills passed the Republican-controlled House in 2017, but did not advance in the Senate. The first act, titled Regulations from the Executive in Need of Scrutiny (REINS), would have prevented major rules from going into effect unless explicitly approved by a joint resolution of Congress signed by the president.[210] According to the statement of purpose, REINS would result in a "legislative branch that is truly accountable to the American people for the laws imposed upon them."[211] Each major regulation would be considered under an expedited procedure in Congress with limited debate; if it did not win a majority in each house, the rule would die and could not be reconsidered or reissued in the near future. Notice the similarity to the up-or-down votes on statutory instruments in the UK and to approval of rules by the upper house in Germany. As I argued above, the UK and the German processes seldom produce real debate on the merits and usually lead to pro forma approval. Under REINS with divided government, the result could be just the reverse—pro forma debate with many rules voided. A hostile Congress could void rules that resulted from an agency's considered balance of expertise and public input.[212] Faced with such arbitrary second-guessing, agencies might decide to abandon rulemaking altogether in favor of case-by-case adjudications that are likely to be less fair, less well grounded in expertise, and less transparent.[213] That strategy would reduce agencies' incentives to deliberate carefully on the society-wide implications of their actions.

The second bill, the Regulatory Accountability Act (RAA), aimed to make the rulemaking process in the executive more procedurally difficult and would limit judicial deference to agencies' statutory interpretations and their use of delegated powers.[214] The bill would have replaced the notice-and-comment provisions of the APA with detailed requirements imposing a very high burden of proof on agencies seeking to issue rules. The bill mandates burdensome fact-finding and cost-benefit analyses, even for rules that do not aim to correct market failures. The bill sought to revive "formal rulemaking" with its court-like procedures—procedures permitted under the APA that have become all but a dead letter.[215] Under the RAA, interested parties could petition for oral hearings covering technical matters that would use judicialized procedures, requiring cross-examination and "on-the-record" decisions. At first glance, lawyers might support such court-like procedures, but their superficial appeal is misleading. Adversarial judicial procedures are a poor way to judge the truth value of technical material or balance multifaceted policy options. In science, there are no "parties" in the sense of a court case, but rather debates over the quality of evidence and standards of proof based on scientific, not legal, norms. The agency's expert personnel ought to be involved in that debate, not pose as neutral observers of a "trial" that produces a record of the arguments pro and con submitted by advocates for each "side." The agency should justify the content of its rules in legal and policy terms, as it must do under the reason-giving requirements of the APA. However, this portion of the RAA would make it difficult to issue rules whenever there is controversy over the facts. Yet, the proposed judicialized response fits awkwardly with calls for use of the scientific method and seems to misunderstand the nature of scientific proof.

The RAA also sought to tighten judicial review, with the courts required to apply a "substantial evidence" test in reviewing "high-impact rules" with over a billion dollars of effect annually, presumably an effort to limit deference to agencies' legal and policy interpretations.[216] This contrasts with the more deferential "arbitrary and capricious" test. Once again, as with REINS, the result would likely be less rulemaking and more use of case-by-case adjudication. Although neither bill advanced far in the legislative process, public lawyers concerned with encouraging competent, accountable rulemaking procedures need to be alert for any revived interest in these so-called reforms.

Notice-and-comment rulemaking procedures express two aspects of democratic accountability. They require both open-ended outside input into executive policymaking and public justifications for rules when they are promulgated. Neither of these factors is a widespread legal requirement in my other cases. My basic claim is that presidential regulatory priorities need to be constrained and tested through outreach to the public and to organized groups. Invoking a popular electoral mandate from "the people" may have little relationship to the costs and benefits of particular policy choices facing a regulatory body. Similarly, legislative oversight may be only weakly related to public concerns. The notice-and-comment process, if it works well, balances public involvement with agency expertise to implement statutory mandates.

Thus, the task for reformers is to seek ways to improve that process, not replace it. There are two contrasting problems. First, the process itself has weaknesses. The main barriers to broader-based participation by members of the public are lack of awareness that rulemakings are occurring, lack of knowledge that participation is possible, lack of understanding about how to participate effectively, and—for those who overcome these initial barriers to participation—information overload from the length and complexity of rulemaking documents.[217] For certain controversial rules, agencies must analyze thousands of submissions of varying types. Wendy Wagner suggests that the sheer volume of submissions tends to overload agencies and prevent meaningful information from reaching key decision-makers.[218] Some argue that on-line platforms for posting comments will revolutionize the comment process. However, Cary Coglianese found that despite the ease of electronic filing, "commenters remain deterred by the highly technical knowledge necessary to understand and comment intelligently in an agency proceeding."[219]

Additionally, e-governance introduces new risks and challenges to the notice-and-comment process. The increasing use of bots and other artificial intelligence techniques to skew agency rulemaking has generated concern for the integrity of on-line participation.[220] Second, the increasing involvement of the White House in the regulatory activities of executive departments and agencies risks sidelining the notice-and-comment process, reducing it to a pro forma exercise. Reformers who accept the underlying value of broad public input must respond to these concerns in ways that support the democratic value of public input. In Chapter 6 I revisit these concerns after introducing other methods for incorporating public input into executive policymaking.

Conclusions

Powerful elected presidents and prime ministers serve dual roles; they are both managers of the public administration and the government's chief political officials. They must endeavor to ensure both performance and policymaking accountability to the public for their actions and choices. They may prefer to make partisan or inspirational speeches, but their job includes coordinating and overseeing the operation of the cabinet departments. Civil service professionals can relieve heads of government from immersion in the day-to-day operation of the public sector, but the public's evaluation of politicians' performance will depend both on the fairness and efficiency of service delivery to individuals and firms, and on the policies behind both the delivery of services and the implementation of statutory mandates. Cabinet ministers cannot be merely managers or technocratic administrators, and most would not want such a limited role. Rather, they participate in making policy—efforts that will determine their political legacy and that of their president or prime minister. Part of that legacy involves drafting bills and politicking for new legislation, but much policy-relevant activity occurs inside government ministries, including the promulgation of rules with legal force. Executive-branch policymaking is especially important for US presidents facing a hostile Congress and for French presidents interacting with a weak or even hostile legislature. However, prime ministers also implement legislation in ways that combine technical competence and policymaking. Policymaking is integral to executive-branch activity in all four cases.

Comparison of the UK, Germany, France, and the US illustrates basic weaknesses in the way each polity takes account of public input in the drafting of executive rules and policies. In the UK and Germany, constitutional structures give legislators little incentive to include public-participation mandates in statutes. Furthermore, to the extent that lawmakers defend the chain of legitimacy, such participation may seem anti-democratic. In France the separately elected president generally operates with a politically supportive National Assembly because of the close alignment of the electoral dates for the presidency and the legislature. Thus, statutory constraints on rulemaking seem unlikely there as well, absent a constitutional mandate. However, led by environmental groups, France seems to be moving toward more public consultations on government policy. The UK and Germany also carry out increasing numbers of public consultations, but most involve large infrastructure projects, not general rules. These three democracies are struggling to reconcile popular pressure to increase public participation with democratic models that see direct public input into rulemaking as problematic.

Public values related to the legitimacy of democratic institutions, such as voting or representation, do not easily map onto standard administrative-law categories that stress the violation of individual rights. Furthermore, neither elected politicians nor civil servants may have an incentive to further participatory values. Yet, civil servants and their cabinet superiors need to hear from those outside of government through procedures that supplement periodic elections. Many policymakers in my case-study countries recognize the value of such input, but they have not codified such procedures or made them subject to judicial review beyond a few limited applications. Nevertheless, there is some movement toward more accountable executive policy-making, led by French experiments and lively public debates in both the UK and Germany. I explore these developments in subsequent chapters.

In contrast, the US does have a robust legal regime for public participation, reason-giving, and judicial review that embodies the democratic value of such input, along with its technocratic benefits. However, it is under strain from both inside and outside the executive. OIRA, in the Executive Office of the President, threatens to go beyond pure performance accountability to undermine legislative policy mandates that delegate rulemaking to executive departments. Faced with a divided and fractious Congress, presidents are increasingly acting on their own authority, outside of APA notice-and-comment processes, to make policy and direct agency actions. This may be true even of the Biden administration as it seeks to make progress on its policy goals. Neverthelss, the actions of the Trump administration were especially antagonistic to and detached from the stated purposes of many regulatory statutes. If presidents seek to increase their control over the administration, the democratic value of public participation in US rulemaking procedures may weaken over time. Those who critique the notice-and-comment process for being biased and cumbersome must ask if they would prefer a process closer to executive rulemaking in Europe that lacks legal participation mandates, relying only on the incumbents' political expediency to manage the process.

4. *Why Independent Agencies Should Be Independent*

The threefold separation of powers no longer describes the organizational framework of modern states. Most have experimented with institutional forms that have significant autonomy from the other branches of government.[1] Some have specialized mandates to regulate the private sector. They decide individual cases, and some can issue rules with legal force. All my case-study countries have created innovative regulatory bodies, either explicitly authorized in constitutional texts or operating under statutory authority.

My primary focus is on public agencies that regulate particular industries or sectors and are more or less independent of the cabinet. After comparing the role of such agencies in my cases, I examine private or quasi-public institutions that set standards or control entry for an industry or profession. The chapter concludes with agencies, such as audit bodies, ombudsmen, and electoral institutes, that provide oversight of the executive itself.

Some independent bodies are labeled "courts," although they differ from ordinary courts in important respects. The traditional third branch of government—the judiciary—is a classic example, but I defer discussion of the courts to Chapter 7.[2]

Begin, then, with agencies or commissions that carry out regulatory functions. In the US, the so-called "independent" agencies operate under statutory frameworks that provide a degree of insulation from the political branches. However, the word "independent" is in quotes here to signal that in all countries these bodies are not completely detached from the rest of government. The most independent do not take directions from the political executive, but they may cooperate with public ministries on shared responsibilities. They are accountable to the legislature or the governing coalition through the appointment of commissioners, budgetary appropriations, and threats to repeal their governing statutes. In France and Germany, a few such agencies have constitutional status, giving them a more secure position. Agencies generally make periodic reports to the legislature or the cabinet, but neither political body can overrule decisions in individual cases, although they may be able to make life difficult with budget cutbacks and efforts to pack the commission with political allies.

Outside of the United States, most regulatory agencies are nominally accountable to a particular minister or to the cabinet. Parliamentary systems, in particular, have a unitary theory of executive power that makes fully independent regulators seem incompatible with democratic accountability. In practice, however, institutional realities defy dogmatic legalisms.

US agencies can make rules with the force of law, but such authority is uncommon across the Atlantic. Nevertheless, established practice has evolved to the point where executive departments consult these agencies on policy initiatives in their areas of expertise. Even if an agency is formally under ministerial oversight, it may be quite independent in practice.[3] Weak formal legal control by ministers or the legislature, however, can translate into high levels of de facto control if the enabling statute gives politicians leverage. Even legal independence can erode through aggressive executive efforts.

The mandates of regulatory agencies differ. If agencies serve an adjudicatory, court-like role, they may be free of executive oversight by analogy with the status of the courts. Unlike litigation before the classical judiciary, however, most agencies need not wait for cases to come to them but can act to regulate industries or sectors in the public interest. Nevertheless, to the extent that they make individual decisions—for example, to set rates, license firms, or apply standards in particular cases—the analogy to courts seems apt.

I will emphasize other arguments for independence. First, it can be a guarantee to private firms, especially newly privatized ones, that the government will keep its bargain to further market efficiency and avoid micromanagement. Second, impartial, expert policy may be more likely if agencies are independent of the rest of the government and isolated from political pressures. There is nothing inherently undemocratic about delegating policymaking to such agencies so long as there are checks against capture by the regulated industry and so long as they are subject to oversight by the legislature and the courts. An independent agency may enhance its status through apolitical decisions that rely on an expert staff. Furthermore, it can make its decisions transparently and with input from citizens and other stakeholders, not just from the regulated industry.

Judicial review can assess the conformity of agency actions with statutory law and the constitution. The law may create structural barriers to short-term political influence and impose procedural requirements on policymaking in agencies that mandate transparent, well-justified choices, subject to court review. Thus, in the US, the Administrative Procedure Act's notice-and-comment rulemaking procedures apply to both cabinet departments and independent agencies. Both substantive and procedural violations can lead the courts to void an agency's rule.[4]

Justifications for independent agencies depend upon the public purpose served by independence. Is it mainly to promote impartial individual adjudications, or is independence a condition for effective policymaking? Is the agency meant to be independent of the industry it regulates, of the rest of government, or of both? If the government owns or partly owns some of the regulated firms, does agency independence facilitate impartial, effective regulation?

Agency independence from the executive and the legislature raises particular problems for democratic legitimacy. As a result, in line with my stress on policymaking accountability, agencies have a greater obligation than cabinet departments to consult broadly beyond the regulated industry, to use transparent procedures, and to make their decisions public. Lacking strong oversight from the political branches, agencies should seek democratic legitimacy through participatory processes that include public-interest groups as well as those with narrower economic concerns. Unfortunately, this is not always the case, but I point to some positive developments.

Independent commissions have been a feature of the American system since the late nineteenth century.[5] In Europe, the past half-century has produced an increasing number of regulatory agencies with some measure of independence, although most are formally accountable to cabinet departments.[6] Urged on by the EU, these agencies reflect the changing role of the state vis-à-vis the private sector in the regulation of electric and gas utilities, telecommunications, financial markets, market competition, and the media. State-owned public utilities have been privatized, although the state often retains a "golden share" that gives it certain control rights. These rights have been the subject of extensive litigation, with the European Court of Justice generally disfavoring them as contrary to the free movement of capital.[7] Because privatized industries seldom conform to the free-market ideal, the EU has pushed member states to create regulatory agencies to ensure efficient service provision and to reflect other public values.[8]

Independence from ministerial control (*Ministerialfreiheit* in German) is a contested value in Europe. On the one hand, some claim that a specialized, expert agency will make better policy choices if it is insulated from the executive. It is able credibly to commit to socially beneficial policies that face political opposition.[9] Giandomenico Majone, in supporting such independence, uses the term "trustee" to refer to an agent that makes policies under delegated power.[10] On the other hand, critics condemn independence as an illegitimate break in the chain of legitimacy. They argue that unelected appointees should not make policy without political oversight, and that even the availability of judicial review cannot fill the legitimacy gap.[11]

The debate goes deeper and implicates the very definition of agency responsibilities. At one extreme, an agency might have a mandate to regulate in accord with the best scientific knowledge, leaving political decisions to the legislature and the cabinet. At the other, the statute might use open-ended language, leaving it to the agency to define "the public interest."[12] In these cases regulators must confront the challenge of finding an appropriate balance between facts, norms, and political reality.[13] Is the agency charged with satisfying the industry's customers by promoting competition and assuring reliable service and reasonable prices, or is it meant to facilitate citizen empowerment through deliberative consultations and public involvement? In addition to furthering efficiency, should the agency also promote human rights and democratic values?[14] If it encourages consultation and dialogue, how should it balance submissions from the regulated industry against input from customers, concerned citizens, and organized civil society?

The tension between satisfying customers and empowering citizens has led to a range of responses. Agencies differ in the extent of their powers, in the level of oversight by the cabinet and the courts, in the ease of reversal by the government, in their decree of budgetary control, and in the legislature's ability to change an agency's structure or to vote it out of existence.[15]

I begin with the United States, whose independent agencies often require partisan balance on agency boards. The UK parliamentary system is resistant to fully independent agencies as a violation of the fundamental Westminster principle of unitary government. Nevertheless, in the process of privatizing public firms, it has established regulatory agencies with considerable freedom of action. The German version of parliamentarianism also experiences discomfort in the face of functional demands for independence. France has both a popularly elected president and a prime minister, but, in practice, the president usually shares the political orientation of the National Assembly, and regulatory agencies have, at least, a formal link to a relevant ministry. The notion of a hierarchical public administration maintains its hold on my European cases even though some arguments for independent regulatory bodies are especially strong in those countries.

The United States

A tradition of independent agencies is most firmly entrenched in the United States.[16] The Interstate Commerce Commission (ICC), the first national independent commission, was established in 1887 to regulate railroad rates. Independent agencies expanded in number during the first half of the twentieth century, especially under President Franklin Roosevelt's New Deal. Such commissions regulate, for example, communications, energy, labor relations, and securities markets. Since the "Reagan Revolution," these agencies have been the object of sustained political critique. The ICC itself was abolished in 1996, as was the Civil Aeronautics Administration in 1985. However, many commissions remain, and Congress created a few new independent agencies, such as the Consumer Product Safety Commission (CPSC) and the Federal Election Commission (FEC).[17]

Independent agencies make legally binding rules and adjudicate individual cases. Originally, they only made decisions concerning particular firms or adjudicated disputes. At its inception, the ICC had to obtain court orders to set individual railroad rates. This requirement proved cumbersome and was overturned by statute with Supreme Court approval.[18] In 1943, the Supreme Court upheld independent agencies' power to make rules with the force of law.[19] In subsequent decades, they followed the rest of government in moving toward greater reliance on rulemaking without resistance from the courts.[20] At present, there is no concerted judicial resistance to their rulemaking authority, although recent Supreme Court appointments have raised questions about the "headless fourth branch of government."[21] Legal challenges, instead, involve the appointment and removal processes for top agency officials and independent agencies' organizational form.[22]

The policymaking reach of US independent commissions is broad under open-ended statutory grants of authority. Most statutes do not mandate particular expertise, although, in practice, appointees are often knowledgeable in the agency's regulatory areas. Because they do not report to a cabinet department subject to direct presidential control, their public accountability depends upon other mechanisms.

Most independent agencies are multi-member bodies that must have partisan balance, although a range of other forms exist.[23] In a common variant, the commission consists of five members, no more than three of whom can be affiliated with a single political party.[24] Political balance is justified as a route to impartiality. The president forwards the names of proposed appointees to the Senate for confirmation and often has the authority to appoint the chair from among the members. If removal is only "for cause," a new administration cannot dismiss commissioners at will but only after a finding of incapacity, neglect of duty, malfeasance, or a similar offense.[25] Terms are staggered and usually are longer than the president's term. However, staggered terms create a special problem. If a single seat becomes vacant, the political party that cannot fill the seat may prefer not to approve anyone, potentially producing deadlock. In addition, if the agency cannot operate without a quorum, opponents of agency action may reject all appointments, even those of their own party. The appointment process may stall if the Senate majority is of a different party from the president.[26] As a consequence, the president may fail to submit names to the Senate or seek to score political points by submitting names that are so controversial as to ensure defeat.[27]

Congress exercises external control indirectly through budgetary appropriations, oversight hearings, the Senate's role in approving appointees, and amending or repealing the underlying statute.[28] Political science research suggests that independent commissions are, in practice, politically accountable to Congress and the president.[29] However, neither branch can intervene to determine the outcome in particular rulemakings or adjudications although lobbying by politicians and politically connected individuals is common.[30]

There are several downside risks. The first is capture by the regulated industry. This might occur up front if the industry can influence the legislature and obtain a favorable regulatory regime. Alternatively, the industry might capture the agency ex post because its firms have a strong incentive to monitor and to seek influence over agency decisions.[31] In the aftermath of World War II, these concerns led to legislative responses. Old agencies obtained new consumer-friendly mandates; new agencies were created, while others were abolished.[32] One response was the creation of single-headed regulatory agencies inside the core executive that are responsible to the president, such as the Environmental Protection Agency.[33] Others are inside cabinet departments, such as the Occupational Safety and Health Administration in the Department of Labor and the National Highway Traffic Safety Administration in the Department of Transportation.

Although multi-member commissions are a familiar feature of the US government, one should not over-emphasize their role. Except for their greater policy discretion, they operate much like cabinet departments and agencies. Court review of their rules is not substantially different from review of rules issued by cabinet departments, although a judicial opinion, for example, *FCC v. Fox*, does occasionally suggest that such agencies are agents of Congress.[34] Supreme Court opinions in the 1980s focused on their organizational forms, upholding, for example, the constitutionality of the Sentencing Commission and the Independent Counsel Act as consistent with the separation of powers.[35] In contrast, the Trump administration argued in favor of subjecting commission rules to White House oversight. In addition, the Congressional Review Act gives Congress and the president a limited period of time to void newly issued agency rules.[36] Recent judicial opinions have shattered precedents that upheld agencies' independence and organizational form.

The challenge began with the Supreme Court's 2010 decision in *Free Enterprise Fund v. PCAOB*.[37] In response to the financial crisis of 2008–2009, a statute created the Public Company Accounting Oversight Board (PCAOB) and authorized the Securities and Exchange Commission (SEC)—an independent agency—to appoint the PCAOB's members.[38] The SEC commissioners can only be removed for cause by the president, but the act refused to grant the White House this direct authority over the PCAOB. Instead, the SEC had the power to remove PCAOB members, but only for cause.[39]

A sharply divided Supreme Court found that this delegation of power was unconstitutional. The justices unanimously agreed that the members of the PCAOB were inferior officers who did not need Senate confirmation. But a bare majority held that because members of the SEC can themselves only be removed for cause, PCAOB members cannot also be insulated through for-cause discharge protection.[40] Justice Stephen Breyer, in dissent, argued that the Court should have deferred to Congress and the president because "the Judiciary possesses an inferior understanding of the realities of administration, and the manner in which power, including and more especially political power, operates in context."[41] He went on to enumerate the variety of removal provisions in existing statutes, including examples of two-layer provisions comparable to the one the majority repudiated.[42]

Free Enterprise set the stage for a decision in 2020 that calls into question the constitutional future of "independence" in American constitutional law. *Seila Law LLC v. Consumer Financial Protection Bureau* (CFPB) once again confronted the freedom of Congress and the sitting president to design independent commissions to fit the regulatory problems at hand.[43] The CFPB is an independent agency, operating within the Federal Reserve System. Its statute authorized the president to appoint a single official to head the agency, after gaining the advice and consent of the Senate. The agency head would serve a fixed term and be subject only to for-cause removal.[44] A bare majority of the Supreme Court held that this structure was unconstitutional, holding that the head must be removable at will by the president.[45]

The Court's opinion as well as the concurrence by Justice Clarence Thomas express a strong version of the "unitary executive theory" that requires all parts of the executive branch to be under the direct control of the chief executive.[46] Thus, although ostensibly only dealing with the issue of a single-headed independent bureau, some of the opinion's language invites efforts to overturn *Humphrey's Executor v. United States*, a case that upheld the constitutionality of for-cause removal provisions as applied to independent multi-member commissions.[47] If these arguments are taken seriously in future cases, they will dramatically undermine American legal developments that seek to accommodate modern political and policy realities with the practical need for impartial expertise.

There is an irony in the Court's supposedly conservative majority in *Seila* advocating for an activist judicial role in restricting creative statutory responses to modern problems. As Justice Elena Kagan wrote in dissent, the Constitution "mostly leaves disagreements about administrative structure to Congress and the President, who have the knowledge and experience needed to address them. Within broad bounds, it keeps the courts—who do not—out of the picture." She worries that the majority "commits the Nation to a static version of governance, incapable of responding to new conditions and challenges." In her understanding of the Constitution and of "the need for sound and adaptable governance," Congress has "wide leeway to limit the President's removal power in the interest of enhancing independence from politics in regulatory bodies."[48]

Breyer and Kagan are right. If the Supreme Court continues down its recent path, it will undermine the country's commitment to the principle of political accountability. But there may be room for an accommodation that could modulate the Supreme Court's hostility. In constructing new forms of agency independence, Congress should follow past practice and favor the use of multi-member commissions.[49] As a functional matter, this structure encourages the selection of commissioners with a range of views and backgrounds. Indeed, a long statutory tradition explicitly requires the representation of both political parties on commissions. These provisions build partisan balance into the initial appointment process, and they guarantee all commission members a fixed tenure by allowing presidents to dismiss them only for cause. This protects political appointees against summary removal by presidents from the opposing party, and it promotes thoughtful policymaking over time. Of course, this system can be subject to abuse; future legislation should seek creative ways of responding to potential abuses that could receive constructive responses from the Roberts Court.

The United Kingdom

Although "Britain does not have a legal doctrine of independent agencies," Mark Thatcher shows that, in practice, "independent" regulatory agencies date from the regulation of railways in the nineteenth century.[50] Especially since the end of World War II, practice has trumped doctrine, making it relatively easy to create agencies with a significant degree of decision-making autonomy. Even before the EU began to push for the liberalization of public-utility sectors, the UK started to privatize its state-owned firms, aiming for productive efficiency and customer satisfaction.[51] Quasi-independent agencies regulate a number of sectors, including the competitive environment, the financial sector, and industries with privatized firms, for example: gas and electricity (Ofgem), water (Ofwat), communications (Ofcom), and rail and roads (ORR), often labeled the "Ofdogs."[52]

However, the Westminster system of strong cabinet government limits the attractiveness of agencies that operate free from the influence of the party in power. In most cases, the responsible minister provides at least nominal supervision and makes top-level appointments without seeking parliamentary approval. At first, these agencies were headed by a single official, and their mandate did not require political or ideological balance. Instead, the top appointees were drawn from the highest echelons of the governing class—what the British call "the great and the good."[53] More recently, however, there has been a trend toward multi-member boards—including bodies for the protection of human rights, the regulation of particular industries (the Ofdogs), and the larger system of market competition.[54] Most agencies must report annually to Parliament and depend upon it for budgetary appropriations.[55] Adam Tomkins argues, however, that even the "detailed and expert reports" submitted by key agencies are not used in any systematic way by Parliament, so there is a compelling need for "co-ordination and effective channeling of scrutiny."[56] Furthermore, a few agencies, such as the Civil Aviation Authority, are self-funded through user fees, further reducing the legislature's role. Parliamentary oversight rivals review of statutory instruments in its superficiality.[57] A more effective check comes from the courts. Given the UK's common-law background, however, judges only intervene on a case-by-case basis, and do not usually scrutinize rule-making activities.

The functional reasons for independence combine with limited oversight to support those who advocate for greater public input and agency transparency. Despite the absence of pressure from the government, Parliament, or the courts, some independent commissions are indeed moving in that direction. The Ofdogs are experimenting with public participation in their regulation of privatized government enterprises. But these "public consultations" were not initially designed to elicit the political or normative concerns of the UK's citizens. They were basically forms of market research, which attempted to assess consumer demand. The results were then used in the technocratic cost-benefit analyses required by the relevant statutes governing the privatized industries. However, presently, even consultations with a consumer focus have touched on broader issues of social welfare. Ofcom, the British telecoms regulator, has been in the forefront. As Athanasios Psygkas shows in his study of Ofcom, EU pressure moved that agency in the direction of formal, open public consultation.[58] Ofgem, which regulates electricity markets, has taken a proactive approach to getting citizen feedback. Using a private consulting firm, it invites 100 citizens to participate in a Consumer First Panel that meets throughout Britain to discuss issues of electricity supply and pricing. Although the emphasis is on participants as consumers of electricity, recent deliberations also touched on broader policy issues, such as subsidies for those with medical conditions and the possibility of charging more to consumers in remote locations.[59]

Thus, compared to rulemaking processes in US independent agencies, the British agencies are only beginning to invite broad public input from citizens that goes beyond their role as consumers. In some UK independent agencies, the public is invited not only to express views on the services that they consume, but also to weigh in on the broader policy implications of agency choices. These innovative efforts reflect the awkward fit between these agencies and the UK's Westminster system of unitary government. Their anomalous status may have freed them up to experiment with alternative forms of public input. Independence is a functional necessity for effective industrial regulation, resulting in only a weak link to Parliament. Germany and France are also struggling with the same tension between sovereignty as a unity concept, on the one hand, and functional arguments for allowing certain bodies to operate independent of cabinet control, on the other. They have taken steps to use direct public consultations as a substitute for or supplement to a chain of accountability through the cabinet.

Germany

The German Basic Law (Grundgesetz) guarantees that "[a]ll state authority . . . shall be exercised by the people through elections."[60] Under the chain of legitimacy, the political legitimacy of officials derives from their appointment by a minister, who was chosen by the chancellor, who was elected by the parliament that was elected by the people.[61] The German bureaucracy, moreover, is "rule-based and hierarchical,"[62] giving credibility to the chain of legitimacy and casting doubt on assertions of independent regulatory authority. Although many institutions are called independent federal ministries (*selbstständige Bundesoberbehörden*), statutes put each of them under the supervision of a cabinet department.[63]

There are, however, exceptions. The first involves the EU. Even though the Federal Network Agency (*Bundesnetzagentur*) is nominally supervised by two German ministries, EU law requires it to be independent with respect to the companies it regulates, including those owned in part by the state.[64] The Federal Cartel Office (*Bundeskartellamt*), charged with promoting competition, has a similar status—although, in this case, its independence is only based on a customary right (*Gewohnheitsrecht*), not a statutory guarantee.[65] Both scholars and jurists struggle with the tensions between EU mandates and the nation's commitment to the chain of legitimacy.

The second is the quasi-judicial nature of agency mandates. For example, the Federal Patent Office and the Federal Insurance Oversight Agency are independent adjudicatory bodies.[66] Similarly, the statute establishing the Cartel Office limits government oversight of its enforcement priorities.[67]

The third depends upon the decentralized character of the German system. Under its federal structure, provincial governments take a leading role in many areas of regulatory policy. In the economic realm, the country's long-standing corporatist tradition permits "private" professional associations or "quasi-public" expert bodies to regulate themselves or to gain privileged access to the ministries authorized to draft secondary norms.

The functional case for independence stresses apolitical decision-making and impartial technical expertise. This argument applies to industry regulators and the Cartel Office and to the Bundesbank, which is exempt from cabinet control to enable it to make monetary policy without favoring the political parties in power.[68] In Germany, there is scholarly support for independence in technical areas, such as the regulation of banks and data transmission. Armin Steinbach, for example, persuasively argues that neither ministers nor judges have the competence to assess the specialized expertise required for intelligent regulation in these fields.[69]

Views that favor independent regulators are affecting the design of public institutions, especially when backed up by the EU. The most clear-cut recent case involved the Federal Commissioner for Data Protection and Freedom of Information.[70] This office was under the Ministry of the Interior, but that arrangement became problematic when the EU issued a directive requiring data-protection agencies to operate with "complete independence."[71] When the issue came before the European Court of Justice, Germany argued that it was appropriate for the agency to be supervised by the country's provincial (Länder) governments, invoking the chain of legitimacy on their behalf. The European Court of Justice in *European Commission v. Germany* rejected this claim and held that only the national government could be involved, but with its role narrowly restricted to the selection of the commissioner.[72]

A similar dynamic is unraveling traditional approaches to regulatory authorities that oversee markets where the state holds an ownership stake in key firms. German statutes simultaneously create specialized agencies and retain nominal ministerial oversight. Agency independence is justified by analogizing their activities to case-by-case adjudication in the courts.[73] But, in practice, key agencies do more than resolve individual cases under statutory authority. They also make industrywide policies. If they do, their claims of independence will be under strain if they conflict with government priorities.

Of central importance is the Federal Network Agency, which has a broad mandate covering electricity, gas, telecoms, postal services, and railroads, now extended to the regulation of information technology and the expansion of the electrical grid.[74] It is formally under the supervision of the Federal Ministry for Economic Affairs and Energy and, for telecommunications, also the Federal Ministry of Transport and Digital Infrastructure.[75] However, it operates independently, so that, as a practical matter, it breaks the chain of legitimacy. The Network Agency's relationship to EU mandates accounts for this anomalous state of affairs because it must coordinate national, supernational, and international law in carrying out its regulatory efforts.[76]

The agency's governing statute illuminates its broad-based operational independence. Sixteen members from each house of parliament sit on the agency's Advisory Council to provide guidance on policy—but its pronouncements are strictly advisory. In practice, the council does play a monitoring role, and the agency is required to consult with it under some circumstances.[77] The council also proposes candidates to serve as the agency's president and two vice presidents.[78] Although the Network Agency is obviously alert to the political consequences of its actions, direct political control is exclusively exercised by the appointments of these three officials to fixed terms in office.

What is more, the Network Agency has separate divisions for each regulated sector, and the expert civil servants in each division can make binding decisions in individual cases. The companies directly concerned may participate in these proceedings, and business groups may be invited to attend. There seems to be no regularized practice of involving civil-society groups, except for decisions on new long-distance electric cables, where the law requires public consultation.[79] The Economic Ministry cannot overturn individual agency decisions, but agency rulings can be subject to court challenges.[80] The Constitutional Court, on one occasion, struck down a provision of the Telecommunications Act because it gave the agency too much power to restrict private parties' access to justice.[81] The court-like nature of most Network Agency decisions supports its independence from the cabinet, but the broad implications that follow from some of its pronouncements highlight the agency's awkward fit with conventional German notions of democratic institutions.[82]

The Network Agency operates under a "customer satisfaction" model rather than a "citizen empowerment" model in regulating network industries. Its goal has been the efficient provision of reliable services under fair prices that limit monopoly gains. Recently, however, the regulation of both electricity and telecoms has taken the agency out of its comfort zone. The regulator's attenuated links to the cabinet have opened up a space for experiments in policymaking accountability. It is no longer sufficient to justify independence by stressing the case-by-case nature of its actions.

In the field of telecoms, the Network Agency has no mandate to regulate media content, which is a responsibility of the Länder.[83] However, the internet has made state-level regulation less feasible and thrust the Network Agency into discussions over content regulation.[84] In the electricity sector, the agency responded to its leading role in the oversight of environmentally friendly electricity generation by improving public accountability. In 2017, it conducted a "feedback" exercise to get the public's views on "man and nature" as it reviewed plans to lay cables to transport wind power from the Baltic and North Seas to southern Germany.[85] In 2018 and 2019 it invited interested individuals and groups to comment on the environmental impact of its plan to bury some cables underground.[86] Although these consultations were limited in scope and did not invite the public to balance environmental values with efficiency, they could open the way for more ambitious experiments in the future. As in the UK, the independence of the Network Agency and its de facto operation outside the chain of legitimacy provides an opportunity for alternative forms of policymaking accountability through more open and consultative processes. Thus, in both the UK and Germany, policymaking accountability to a nation's citizens is arising through the actions of regulatory agencies that operate with some independence from the legislature and the cabinet. These agencies, which lack a strong democratic pedigree through the chain of legitimacy, have begun to counteract that difficulty with direct efforts to engage the public. True, many of these efforts treat the public as consumers rather than citizens, but even then, broader policy issues do get onto the table. In spite of their different legal traditions, arising from the civil and the common law, their independent regulatory bodies seem to be heading in the same direction.

France

France shares with Germany a hierarchical view of administration. Traditionally, "ministers have the power to give instructions to civil servants and also can revise decisions made by civil servants, subject to the law and regulations governing their behavior."[87] As a consequence, Mark Thatcher claims, "there existed a long-standing suspicion of 'independent' agencies that would either not be properly independent or which fragmented the unity of the state."[88]

Contemporary French doctrine distinguishes "between independent authorities (*autorités administratives indépendantes*), most of which are regulatory bodies, and autonomous agencies (*établissements publics*), which are not integrated into the hierarchy of ministerial departments but are not fully independent either."[89] Autonomous agencies are service-providing bodies such as universities, hospitals, and museums. I leave them to one side to focus on the role of independent authorities with regulatory functions.[90]

The awkward fit between independent authorities and French democratic theory leads, in practice, to limits on their power. Some can only make recommendations, which do not have the force of law. Others possess decision-making authority, but it is often limited to individual administrative acts and excludes legally binding rules.[91] Many independent agencies serve one of two missions. Either they seek to protect the individual against state overreaching or they regulate firms in partly privatized industries, where the state retains an ownership stake in key firms. Separating ownership from regulatory authority helps to ensure that all firms are treated fairly.

The balance between government control and the value of independence is resolved in a number of different ways. Sometimes the government or the parliament appoints the members of the regulatory board. In others, appointment is by the high courts, cultural organizations, or "a committee of wise men." Some have mixed boards appointed by both governmental and nongovernmental institutions. After appointment, independence is frequently enhanced by familiar devices such as "long terms, strict conflict of interest rules, guarantees of irremovability and immunity."[92] Some commentators argue that such arrangements are broadly consistent with public opinion; thus, Marco D'Alberti claims, the French are willing "to leave the details of government to experts" so long as the government does not interfere in their private affairs.[93]

Ex post accountability is achieved through judicial review of agency "decisions and regulations" by the administrative courts (or in a few cases by the Paris Court of Appeal [*Cour d'Appel de Paris*], a civil court) and by parliament's threat to amend the underlying statutes to limit independence. Review by the Conseil d'État typically respects agencies' independence by subjecting their decisions to "less penetrating" review than it accords to the actions of government ministries—satisfying itself with only a minimal scrutiny of the facts.[94] But, as in the case of Germany, intervention by the EU has provoked a renewed struggle over the proper scope and nature of "independence" and its implications for interventions from business and civil society.[95]

The debate over the role of independent authorities focuses both on agencies with broad mandates, such as the Competition Authority (*Autorité de la Concurrence*) that regulates monopolies, takeovers, and restrictive practices, and on more specialized authorities that focus on particular economic sectors.[96] As in my other European cases, the EU has pushed for the creation of independent regulatory authorities to accompany the privatization of public utilities. Once created, both private groups and privatized firms have brought lawsuits before the French courts to demand stronger roles in these bodies' decision-making processes.

A fundamental issue, as in the UK and Germany, is the problematic legality of delegating policymaking outside the conventional structure of government. Both the legislature and the government have lawmaking authority, but the French Constitution does not explicitly mention independent authorities.[97] This raises three related questions. First, does the Constitution permit the creation of such authorities? Second, if it does, how much detail must be included in the statute that establishes the regulatory body? Third, how independent can agencies be from the rest of government? Can they issue decrees on their own authority without the participation of the president or a member of the cabinet?

The Conseil Constitutionnel answered the first question in the affirmative. The French Constitution, in articles 20 and 21, places the government under the control of the prime minister. The CC could have read this language narrowly and denied parliament the right to create independent regulatory authorities. Instead, with a few caveats, it refused to take that step and affirmed the constitutionality of statutes establishing agencies with institutional independence.[98]

The second question arose in 2010 when the CC upheld a challenge to an individual decision of the French Association for Internet Names (*Association Française pour le Nommage Internet en Coopération*, AFNIC), a state-created, nonprofit body that assigns the domain name ".fr." Under the statute, these decisions must reflect "the general interest, under publicized nondiscriminatory rules designed to ensure compliance by the applicant with intellectual property rights."[99] Even though it upheld the particular decision in question, the CC went on to find that the law was an unconstitutional delegation from the government to the association because the language was too imprecise.[100] The statute permits the minister in charge of electronic communications to determine which bodies have the task of assigning and managing domain addresses, but offers no further guidance on how to accomplish that task.

This decision suggests that France may be developing a "non-delegation doctrine" similar to that advanced by the US Supreme Court in its struggle against the New Deal in the 1930s.[101] Although the US decisions have never been formally overruled, they have not been explicitly reaffirmed and attempts to reanimate the doctrine have not succeeded.[102] The delegation of policymaking authority to ministries and independent commissions continues. This may well be the fate of the French decision as well. The Conseil Constitutionnel suspended its judgment to give the legislature the chance to revise the law, and parliament took advantage of this opportunity.[103] It remains to be seen, however, if the 2010 decision will be applied to future cases. Setting the stage is a decision by the Conseil d'État holding that individual liberties cannot be limited by normative acts; a statute is required.[104]

The third question asks if independent agencies are constitutionally permitted to engage in policymaking activities, building on the French Constitution's explicit provisions for secondary legislation.[105] That issue has been put on the table by members of the Senate. Although the National Assembly is elected by universal suffrage, the Senate is indirectly elected through a process that gives heavy representation to members of municipal councils.[106] This means that some senators support efforts to limit the national government's powers. Along those lines, senators have expressed strong opposition to independent bodies in general, including those with regulatory authority.[107] Although no laws have passed the Assembly, senators have introduced bills that would constrain existing independent bodies and block the creation of new ones.[108]

To further explore the tensions between functional arguments for independence and constitutional requirements, Thomas Perroud and I considered one of the French agencies involved in the regulation of the media and telecommunications: the French Audiovisual Board (*Conseil Supérieur de l'Audiovisuel*, CSA). It grants licenses and regulates content, including political speech.[109] It deals with important policy issues that cannot effectively be resolved through case-by-case adjudication alone. Regulation combines high levels of technical expertise and strong public concern that highlights the tensions between independence and political accountability.[110]

The CSA was founded in 1989 as an independent authority to guarantee freedom of expression in audiovisual communications. It regulates and monitors content, grants licenses, and can revoke them. Its decisions are politically and economically salient and of great interest to ordinary citizens. It seeks to be both independent of politics and responsive to public concerns. The complex interactions between the government, the CSA, and the public broadcaster illustrate some of the challenges of maintaining an independent authority in an industry with prominent, publicly owned firms.

The agency's board has nine members—three appointed by the president, three by the president of the Assembly, and three by the president of the Senate.[111] Each member serves one non-renewable term of six years, with one-third (one from each group) appointed every two years. Unlike the US, where the Senate must confirm presidential nominees, the majority of each body can generally appoint its own preferred candidate. Under the 2008 amendments to the Constitution, the relevant legislative committees can veto individuals nominated by the president (or other appointing authority) if they can muster a three-fifths majority.

Serving as a member of the council is a full-time job, and members cannot be employed in the industry for one year after leaving the board.[112] Journalists have always been well represented, and retired politicians are common. Others are senior civil servants who will return to government ministries after the end of their terms of service. The board and especially the chair are supposed to be above politics, but given the sensitive nature of their responsibilities, their credibility in this regard is a source of ongoing debate and critique.

The Audiovisual Board issues individual decisions (for example, it awards and renews licenses, and sanctions stations for violations). It lacks open-ended authority to issue secondary legislation, but statutes do give it decree authority in particular areas.[113] These statutes set out the general guidelines for CSA processes, but the courts do not use them to review the legality of its rules. One Annual Report discusses a requirement of "public consultation,"[114] but this only involves individual licensing decisions and seems designed to grant a hearing to would-be applicants for a license and other competing firms, not to the public in general. The relevant statute does refer to a decision's impact on the market, a criterion that would seem to invite not only potential competitors but also consumers to take part.[115]

The Board also conducts hearings that invite input from the companies and associations interested in its broad policies, but these are not open to all comers.[116] It has, however, also organized consultations with the general public. Although members of the public can submit written comments, the comments are not public. The CSA merely summarizes them ex post without attribution. It justifies this practice on the ground that it protects privacy and encourages frankness, yet it obviously limits debate because participants cannot respond to each others' arguments. Nevertheless, administrative tribunals have not invalidated the Board's decisions for inadequate participation, although they have occasionally overturned its holdings in individual cases.[117]

There is another important check on the independence of the Audiovisual Board—the government. Because it is a statutorily independent body, the government cannot interfere with individual licenses and sanctioning decisions. But, given its limited decree authority, the CSA can only give advice (*avis*) to government ministries on draft decrees and laws that affect the agency's ongoing regulatory efforts.[118] As a consequence, the agency depends on the government for major policy initiatives.[119] This can be a plus if one worries that the agency is too independent of democratic checks, but it is a minus if one wants the agency to act independently of political pressures to encourage free-flowing political debate and a free media. The latter concern is particularly salient because the government owns or partly owns major providers and has an interest in their financial health and in program content.

In practice, rulemaking is a shared competence.[120] The government includes the agency in task forces that consider overlapping policy issues and asks it for advice with respect to ministry policymaking. Nevertheless, even though the Audiovisual Board and the ministry negotiate over the official text, the ministry has the ultimate authority to issue rules that the independent agency must enforce on a case-by-case basis. Analogous cooperative arrangements exist in the US. The US Department of Justice and the Federal Trade Commission share anti-trust competence, and the Securities and Exchange Commission and the Department of Justice enforce different aspects of the Foreign Corrupt Practices Act. Both pairs frequently collaborate on prosecutions and general policies. The US agencies have more bargaining power than their French counterparts, however, because most can issue rules on their own authority under statutory grants of power.

Unlike regulatory commissions in the US, the agencies that regulate network industries in the UK, Germany, and France lack formal independence from cabinet ministries. The UK began to privatize the telephone sector in the mid-1980s, and in the 1990s the European Union began to push member states to privatize public utilities, sometimes backed up by formal EU directives. The privatization process involved the creation of national regulatory authorities that often faced the reality of states holding a "golden share" of some privatized firms. The agencies aim to promote the efficient operation of the market, and they need independence to avoid conflicts of interest between the state as owner and the state as regulator. In my European cases, however, this functional argument for independence is undermined by each country's hierarchical bureaucratic structure, which places all agencies under political officials. The UK and Germany both have a parliamentary system with an expert, career civil service that creates a chain of legitimacy from bureaucrats back to the electorate. The UK has a tradition of staffing the civil service with generalists responsible to ministers who are members of the cabinet. Germany has respect for professional credentials, a perspective that supports dependence upon experts but does not favor giving them outright policy discretion. Although France has a powerful, directly elected president as well as a prime minister, that complexity has not produced support for regulatory authorities with the independent power to make policy through rules.

The US is an exception. Although the commission founded in 1887 to regulate the railroads initially only engaged in rate-setting, in the twentieth century commissions began to issue rules and make policy. Divided government under the US separation of powers gave Congress a motivation for creating commissions that both were independent of the cabinet structure of government and required political-party balance. Unlike Europe, because of the lack of state-owned firms, conflicts of interest with such firms were not a concern. Rather, the emphasis was on capture by private firms. Rulemaking processes in the US require public comment and published reasons, procedures that I have defended as furthering policymaking accountability. Although none of my other cases requires such procedures as a general matter, a number of regulatory bodies have given the public expanded opportunities for input. Even if many agencies treat people as consumers, rather than citizens, some processes do recognize the value of incorporating public concerns that go beyond views of service quality and price. Agencies can justify their efforts to avoid close supervision by a ministry not just by invoking their own expertise but also by making an effort to achieve policymaking accountability through public consultation and transparent reason-giving.

Private and Quasi-public Standard-Setters and Regulators

I have been focusing thus far on "independent" agencies created by elected governments. But in each of my four countries, non-state institutions discharge important regulatory functions.[121] Private associations regulate the professions, such as law, medicine, engineering, and architecture. They set the rules for entry, training, discipline, and quality.[122] Private bodies also regulate whole sectors of the economy—the US stock markets are notable examples. Others set detailed product specifications, especially for products that are used by firms in many different industries—such as batteries that must be compatible with electrical equipment, or paper that must fit into printers.[123] These private institutions generally adjudicate disputes involving individuals or firms under their jurisdiction.

Across the industrial and professional landscape, private rules and standards often obtain formal legal status when they are codified in statutes or regulation—saving the government from taking on the job itself.[124] Even if these provisions have no formal legal status, compliance may be a condition for contracting with the government or practicing a profession. Courts often will presume their validity in making legally binding decisions.[125]

These privately set rules suffer from a particularly acute legitimacy deficit whenever they essentially substitute for public regulation.[126] Although the institutions' internal decision-making processes involve consultation with their members or other insiders, they usually operate without broad public input and with little transparency.[127] Private regulatory bodies in the US need not follow notice-and-comment procedures, and in Europe, they stand outside the chain of legitimacy. Paradoxically, the case for requiring participatory procedures in such institutions is especially strong if they obtain public funding or have de facto or de jure monopoly control over an industry or profession.[128] If their standards are incorporated by reference into statutes and ordinances, public participation becomes even more essential.[129]

Sometimes a private trade association has regulatory incentives that are compatible with economic efficiency and customer satisfaction. For example, consider the market for used cars. Because buyers cannot easily assess the reliability of particular autos on display, sellers of inferior vehicles could dominate the market and discourage consumers who fear buying a low-quality "lemon." In the extreme, the market might collapse if high-quality sellers are unable to overcome consumers' inability to judge quality.[130] A trade association might respond by granting a "seal of approval" to dealers in cars that meet their standards. This action will benefit both consumers and responsible used-car dealers.

However, such a happy conjunction of self-regulation and customer satisfaction is not inevitable. The used-car business is only one of many in which private standard-setting has become the norm, and this practice may generate its own pathologies.[131] Existing firms may set anti-competitive rules that restrict entry. The body may operate by "raising rivals' costs," that is, using its power over rules to set standards that are cheaper for its members to follow compared with competitors and potential entrants.[132] Rules that further compatibility and standardization can facilitate entry, but these same rules may restrict the use of substitutes in other situations. For example, industry-set standards can have anti-competitive effects in highly regulated sectors, such as construction. Alternatively, a private building-materials association may approve weak safety standards and liability rules that benefit all firms, and then seek to convince government officials that more stringent requirements are unnecessary—when, in fact, they would serve the public interest. In other words, privately set standards can be too strict or too lax depending upon industry conditions. An informed assessment of the private option, then, requires an intensive study of individual cases. For present purposes, it is more important to provide a brief overview of self-regulation in my case-study countries.

German practice is rooted in a very old tradition that relies heavily on private self-regulation.[133] Two different organizational types play crucial roles. The first are "private associations" (*eingetragener Vereinen*) that establish binding standards on the national or European level. The second category includes "private self-governments" consisting of chambers (*Kammern*) in which representatives of a particular profession or economic sector set standards of acceptable conduct.

Private associations include, most importantly, the Standardization Institute (*Deutsches Institut für Normung*, DIN) and the Association of Electrical, Electronic, and Information Technology (*Verband der Elektrotechnik*, VDE). They both set industrial standards, but I concentrate on the broad-based Standardization Institute—outlining its underlying structures and practical importance. It was established in the early nineteenth century to set standards for the manufacturers of steam boilers to reduce the risk of explosions and thereby increase market demand. Over time, these standards were incorporated into binding statutes or regulations—often with little input from cabinet ministers or the parliament.

The contemporary Standardization Institute has moved far beyond its early focus on quality assurance and standard-setting in a few high-risk sectors. Under statutory mandates, it has become a powerful regulatory force in the fields of public health, energy, consumer protection, environmental protection, science and technology, product quality, and the rationalization of production. Its private standards are usually subject to government oversight, and they are frequently backed up with statutes or legally enforceable rules. In cases of disagreement, the responsible ministries have sometimes threatened to use their legal authority to impose different standards to induce the "private" bodies to follow the government's lead.[134]

The institute's members come from the industrial, commercial, and research sectors, as well as from government. It is registered as a private nonprofit association, whose funding comes mostly from industry and its own earnings, but it also receives support from the national government. The government has formally designated it as the representative of German interests in standard-setting organizations operating on the European and international levels.[135]

Institute standards are deployed in a wide variety of legal contexts. Although they are not formally treated as mandatory legal provisions (*zwingende Rechtsvorschriften*), they codify customary standards prevailing in particular areas of activity (*Maßstab verkehrsüblicher Beschaffenheit*). As a consequence, they powerfully shape the application of statutes such as the Product Liability Act. In cases arising under that statute, compliance with institute standards shifts the burden of proof to the injured party.[136]

The Standardization Institute promotes its standards as an "instrument of deregulation." It argues that it reduces the legislative burden on the state so that elected officials can concentrate on overall legal objectives.[137] The institute also highlights its role in helping to establish common EU standards to promote the European internal market, and some of its norms have been adopted by other states, such as France.[138] Its expertise and reputation give weight to its standards.

In addition to its reputation for technical competence, the DIN has taken steps to increase its legitimacy to elected officials and the general public by embracing some aspects of policymaking accountability. Over time, it has increased the transparency of its processes and implemented procedural rules, such as equal representation of stakeholder groups, consumer participation, and the more open provision of information and documentation. However, it regularly charges a fee to those that participate. In contrast, the VDE does not seem to have opened up its consultation processes, at least as indicated by its website.[139] So far, the parliament has not created a coherent framework to govern the processes that private associations must use in revising their customary standards. Given the fact that regulations issued by German ministries need not follow any particular procedures for public input and reason-giving, it is perhaps not surprising that the legislature has not moved to require such processes in these nominally private bodies.

Like private associations, Germany's second category of private self-governments has a long history. Since the late nineteenth century, labor unions and businesses in particular sectors have joined together in "chambers" with the aim of setting standards to govern working conditions within particular industries.[140] Over the course of the twentieth century, these "private" agreements have often served as the basis for legislation. In such cases, the chain of legitimacy linking voters and elected officials to the chambers' actions is so attenuated as to become a mere formality. Nevertheless, chamber-based standard-setting remains an important feature of German business regulation.

The problem raised by self-interested private regulation arises in Britain and France as well. The British Standards Institute, like its German analogue, provides opportunities for comment on standards. It has a Consumer and Public Interest Network made up of volunteers trained in consumer issues who serve on its standards committees. In addition, anyone can comment on a draft standard or suggest ideas on standardization.[141] As in Germany, the British Parliament has not attempted to impose legally binding conditions on these outreach efforts. The same holds true of the processes of the French Standardization Association (*Association Française de Normalisation*, AFNOR). However, the balance between the authority of private and public rules tilts toward the state. The regulation of the professions falls into the category of state action, so professional self-regulation bodies have limited authority to adopt and implement standards. For one commentator, this is so because "[a]s the State became the organizer of public services and a welfare State, it had to organize professional life."[142] Nevertheless, as in the UK and Germany, the French associations overseeing standard-setting and the professions have considerable impact on the state's final rules and standards.

At the EU level, the French and German bodies work with the European Committee for Standardization (CEN), the European Committee for Electrotechnical Standardization (CENELEC), and the European Telecommunications Standards Institute (ETSI), which issue voluntary European-wide standards. Based in Brussels, they cooperate with the European Union, the European Free Trade Area, and member-state standardization bodies. One of their websites pictures puzzle pieces fitting together perfectly. Thus, the underlying model is one in which European businesses and consumers benefit from voluntary standards of quality. These bodies are private nonprofit organizations, but most of their funding comes from the industry, with small contributions from public sources.[143] One website states that "standards are driven by business and made through a transparent, balanced and consensus-based process in which relevant stakeholders are involved." They list among the stakeholders "interest groups representing environmentalists, consumers, trade unions."[144] Standard-setting is presented as a benefit to both business and consumers and also as furthering environmental values. However, the process is funded and heavily influenced by business interests, so it may produce biased standards in sensitive areas that cannot be challenged before public agencies or in court because they have no formal legal force. One need not question the good faith of the participants to observe that the incentives built into this system suggest that caution is warranted.

To conclude, despite cross-country differences, self-regulation in Europe displays four pervasive weaknesses, two concerning process and two that affect substance. On procedures, private standard-setting invites only limited public participation. Although there have been some recent changes for the better that include not only consumers but also environmental groups, the procedures are fundamentally linked to the needs of business. Furthermore, the processes fail to require standard-setters to justify their decisions in a transparent fashion. On substance, private associations may use their authority to monopolize the market and to engage in the self-interested generation of standards that neglect the interests, not only of consumers but also of the general public. Nominally voluntary standards become mandatory strictures when they are incorporated into government regulations.

Two complementary difficulties have arisen in the United States that could create problems elsewhere. They are the special difficulties of regulating a sector with both public and private providers and the private sale of legal texts.

First, several economic sectors include a mixture of public and private firms, along with government regulation. Mail delivery is a classic example: Should regulation favor the US Postal Service because it delivers the mail, at extra cost, to remote residents and businesses? Private firms will argue that a post-office subsidy amounts to unfair competition; the Postal Service will assert that it represents a fair payment for the discharge of its public-service responsibility to provide universal service. However, it does not engage in an accountable APA process as it makes policy; rather, its choices are constrained by the actions of its lightly regulated private competitors. Thus, an evaluation of these arrangements depends upon the benefits and costs of such a competitive environment for both customers and the public at large.

An interesting complexity arose in connection with Amtrak, a passenger railway that is treated by the Supreme Court as a government entity because it receives substantial public subsidies.[145] A statute gave Amtrak authority to work with the Department of Transportation (DOT) to regulate performance standards that control the operation of all railways.[146] Private freight haulers objected, arguing that Amtrak competed with it for access to the tracks and hence should not help the DOT set standards. Is Amtrak trying to further the general public interest, or only the financial health of its passenger rail business? The D.C. Court of Appeals held that, even though Amtrak was a government firm, it was unlawful for "an economically self-interested actor to regulate its competitors."[147]

The second type of public-private interaction arises when government-issued building codes incorporate private standards by reference. In some cases, these codes are under copyright, and private bodies charge for access to updated standards. The body claims that the charges allow it to perform the research needed to provide updates. Builders complain that a private firm is levying a charge for internet access to a public law. The firms respond that paper copies are available in agency libraries and local government reading rooms. In response, others claim that the sale of internet access comes close to the prohibited sale of legal texts. On one side, the private firms arguably benefit the public by monitoring technical and engineering advances and promptly updating building codes. On the other, updates may not only be technical fixes. They may increase (or decrease) costs, shift product quality in ways that are not uniformly positive, and limit the choices of developers and customers. In analyzing this issue, Peter Strauss seeks a middle road. He recommends that the US adopt the EU practice of making private standards presumptively binding subject to a showing that a different standard would be just as effective.[148] That compromise, however, does not fully respond to the worry that private standards may chill competition by signaling preferred product features to builders.

Delegating rulemaking and standard-setting to private bodies raises questions about their ability to further the public interest. However, even in those cases where the advantages of expertise outweigh those concerns, public-law values should be imported to respond to the remaining difficulties. Hence, at the very least, notice-and-comment procedures should apply to the promulgation of private standards with legal or presumptive legal force. Even if the state itself need not hold open hearings and give public reasons when it issues secondary norms with the force of law, such procedures should apply to privately set standards with legal force. The substantive and procedural weaknesses outlined above can undermine the legitimacy of private standard-setting both in the United States and in the European cases.

Horizontal Accountability

The previous section considered the problem of vertical accountability that arises when a private or quasi-public institution takes on a policymaking role. To what extent should it engage in reason-giving and popular participation if it hopes to exercise legitimate regulatory power? In reviewing the institutional landscape, there remains a final dimension to consider. These are independent bodies that monitor the government itself, or what Guillermo O'Donnell called institutions of "horizontal accountability."[149] To be effective, such agencies should not be under the control of either the executive or the legislature. In practice, strong autonomy does not generally prevail in any of my four case-study countries.

To illustrate the cross-country differences, I discuss three oversight bodies: audit offices, electoral commissions, and ombudsmen, highlighting their connection with the rest of government and their degree of effective independence. The UK, Germany, and France all provide some functional autonomy for these bodies while remaining true to their underlying constitutional traditions that see such independence as problematic. In spite of its separation of powers, the US stands out as particularly weak in institutions of horizontal accountability, especially at the national level. The system of checks and balances between the executive, the legislature, and the courts substitutes for other routes to accountability.

Audit Bodies

All four countries have audit bodies with some degree of independence. The US Government Accountability Office (GAO) reports to Congress and evaluates the performance of public programs.[150] Its remit goes beyond monitoring financial integrity to evaluating the effectiveness of programs, and almost all its reports are published openly. Its head, the Comptroller General, is appointed for a fifteen-year, nonrenewable term by the president with the consent of the Senate and can only be removed for cause by a joint resolution of Congress or by impeachment. This official is selected from a list of at least three nominees proposed by a bipartisan committee of both houses of Congress.[151] From a legal point of view, this system establishes a strong form of horizontal accountability, but it has not lived up to its promise in practice. Congressional requests to investigate problems of interest to particular committees leave the GAO with little time to focus on many of the executive programs that need the most intensive oversight.[152] Nevertheless, in contrast to American performance in other functional areas, the GAO represents an advance over comparable efforts in France and Germany.

The UK's National Audit Office (NAO) has a level of autonomy comparable to its American counterpart.[153] Given the unitary nature of the

British Westminster system, such independence seems difficult to explain.[154] How effective can legislative review be if the Commons is controlled by the same political party that runs the government? The NAO currently engages in "value for money" evaluations that, like the GAO's, go beyond financial integrity to assess policy initiatives.[155] NAO staff are not part of the civil service, and the office does not report to any cabinet minister. Its Comptroller General and the chairman of its board are appointed by the prime minister, acting on behalf of the Crown. The rest of the board and the top executives are mostly professional auditors and retired civil servants. Like the GAO, the NAO both responds to requests from individual MPs and initiates its own investigations. It reports its findings to the Public Accounts Committee in the House of Commons, in which the party in power shares control with members of the opposition who put a high value on NAO independence. The result is an audit office with significant independence, without an undue sacrifice of the country's democratic traditions—in this case, parliamentary sovereignty. The British tradition of permitting substantial opposition membership on the Public Accounts Committee supports an independent auditing process that recognizes the risks of a completely unitary government.

France and Germany have bodies called the *Cour des Comptes* and the *Bundesrechnungshof*, respectively, whose names both translate as "audit court" or "audit office." They are not courts as understood in Anglo-Saxon parlance. Both have mandates similar to the GAO and the NAO, but they are less tied to the legislature. They engage both in auditing and in studies of the efficiency and effectiveness of public spending. Unlike conventional courts, they set their own agendas and issue investigative reports.

The German Federal Court of Auditors is mandated by the Basic Law, which states that its members have "judicial independence," distinguishing it from executive-branch agencies, including industrial regulators.[156] The body is headed by a president and vice president selected by the federal president and voted into office without debate by a majority vote of the Bundestag for nonrenewable twelve-year terms. The sixteen-person board is the top management of the office. One-third of the board must be qualified for the judiciary, and others must have economic or technical training. The Court of Auditors stresses its role in generating cost savings in government programs. Although its findings and reports are purely advisory, the body appears well respected by citizens, and its reports are covered in the media.[157] Its court-like features give it the legitimacy to operate outside the chain that connects voters to legislators to the executive. In addition, expert qualifications in law and economics further remove its leadership from day-to-day political pressures. However, the need for the Bundestag to appoint the top leadership indicates ties to the governing majority at the time of appointment.

The reports of the French Cour des Comptes are sent to both houses of parliament as well as to the government.[158] It is an elite body with both auditing and policy-assessment responsibilities. In addition, it adjudicates disputes over public finances. It sits above twenty-seven regional financial courts and hears appeals that can then be appealed to the Conseil d'État. Thus, it is more like a court than its German equivalent. Even though neither institution is formally part of the judiciary, labeling them courts distinguishes them from the governing coalition in Germany and from both the president and the prime minister and their coalition in France.

Electoral Commissions

Independent bodies oversee elections and campaign finance in all my cases, although the US federal agency is particularly weak. The US Federal Election Commission (FEC) has oversight only over campaign spending, not the organization of elections, which is a state and local responsibility. It is one of the few federal commissions with an even number of members. That means that four of its six members must agree to take any action. The voting rule is de facto two-thirds. The FEC has not been a strong force for the control of private funds in elections, a result that arises from its structure, the weakness of the underlying statute, and Supreme Court rulings.[159]

The UK has an independent Electoral Commission that oversees both elections and the rules governing political finance.[160] Elections are organized by local officials in each constituency, but the Commission provides advice and guidance.[161] It also oversees compliance with campaign spending rules for parties, individual candidates, and other groups, such as civil-society organizations, and it publishes extensive data on campaign spending. There are ten commissioners, most of whom have experience as elected politicians or civil servants. The management and staff are not subject to the civil service pay scale and rules, and it seems to operate much like a US independent agency.[162] However, because the actual organization of elections is in the hands of officials closely linked to local politics, the Commission may face conflicts between its goal of impartial elections and the political ties of those who actually organize elections locally.[163]

Germany has an unusual hybrid system. A Federal Returning Officer (*Bundeswahlleiter*, BWL) is appointed by the minister of the interior to an indefinite term; in practice, the head of the Federal Statistical Office, a federal self-governing body reporting to the Interior Ministry, usually has held that office.[164] This official is aided by the Federal Electoral Committee that oversees elections and announces the results.[165] It includes eight people appointed by the Returning Officer plus two judges of the Federal Administrative Court. It oversees a particular Bundestag election, and the eight members only serve until the end of the legislative session after that election. The organization of elections rests with non-party "electoral bodies" at the state and local levels. They are described as "self-organising societal institutions and not bound by any instructions." Disputes directed at the Committee go directly to the Constitutional Court.[166] The structure seems designed to be independent of the political party composition of the sitting government, but it is tied to the cabinet structure of government through the Interior Ministry. However, this framework only manages elections; it does not oversee campaign funding, which depends upon both public funds and private donations subject to Bundestag oversight.[167]

In France, elections to the parliament are organized and monitored in a decentralized fashion under the French Electoral Code. All communities with more than 20,000 inhabitants must have an electoral commission headed by a magistrate who oversees the election.[168] A National Commission for Campaign Accounts and Political Finance (*Commission Nationale des Comptes de Campagne et des Financements Politiques*), established in 1988, oversees the financing of political parties and of electoral campaigns. It is an independent authority with nine members, appointed by the prime minister on recommendations by the Conseil d'État, the Cour de Cassation, and the Court of Auditors. In 2007 it was given the authority to examine the financing of presidential campaigns. However, it has limited investigatory powers and lacks judicial powers.[169] Ultimately, the Conseil Constitutionnel has the responsibility of ensuring "the proper conduct of elections" and proclaiming the results of the vote for presidential elections and referenda.[170] This ex post review appears to be a weak check on electoral-law violations. For example, after the 2017 elections, the Conseil Constitutionnel received 298 complaints by candidates or voters, and 351 submissions by the National Commission. The Conseil Constitutionnel declined to entertain most of these submissions and considered only fifteen. In 2019, two years after the elections, it issued a decision that made only general observations on electoral law, based on the submissions received, in areas such as the use of social media in campaigning, polling stations' hours of operation, and the use of electronic payment systems for campaign contributions.[171]

Ombudsmen

An ombudsman handles individual complaints about government behavior. The office can evaluate the efficacy of public policies, similar to a modern audit office, but its mandate is tied to the concerns of individual citizens, not the financial integrity of public spending. The US does not have a national ombudsman, although a few agencies have ombuds' offices.[172] In France an ombudsman was introduced in 1973, and in 2011 several related offices combined to create the Defender of Rights (*Défenseur des Droits*).[173] The Conseil d'État appoints the head of that body on the recommendation of the prime minister, and that official reports to the National Assembly.[174] Germany has a Parliamentary Petitions Committee (*Petitionsausschuss Deutscher Bundestag*) that accepts individual complaints,[175] and there are also ombudsmen inside the government with specific mandates, for example, the Parliamentary Military-Ombudsman and the Conciliation Body for Public Transportation. The UK follows the pattern of parliamentary responsibility, with one ombudsman to deal with the central government and another for the National Health Service, although the same person held both posts since 2017.[176] The caseload is determined by complaints referred by members of Parliament.[177] These organizational structures may all be helpful ways to relieve members of Parliament of some constituency service, but they are not powerful routes to structural reform in any of my cases. In fact, they could dampen demands for fundamental change by giving satisfaction to squeaky wheels and masking deeper problems.

Independent Monitoring and Democratic Accountability

Institutions of horizontal accountability monitor the government itself. Audit offices, electoral commissions, and ombudsmen are windows through which to consider the puzzling problem of combining independent monitoring of government with a commitment to democratic input from the citizenry. In practice, some bodies report either to the parliament or to a cabinet minister, raising questions about their ability to exercise impartial judgment. To help ensure independence, a few have independent sources of funds outside the ordinary budget process. Others have access to the courts to carry out their oversight missions, and in some cases specialized courts review their decisions, especially if ordinary courts cannot be trusted to review the government impartially.

In the US separation-of-powers system, the creation of an audit or other oversight body that reports to the Congress fits well with the overall structure of government. In contrast, in the parliamentary systems of the UK and Germany, and in France with its strong executive, a monitor of the executive may clash with principles of national sovereignty, even if it could be a valuable check on government. Matching functional imperatives with constitutional frameworks leads the European cases to call these bodies "courts," stressing their technical outlook or their direct link to individual citizens. They often have the structure of independent regulatory agencies, with multi-member boards and long, overlapping terms. At the same time, these monitoring bodies maintain links to the legislature and/or the executive; hence, they are not entirely independent of the rest of the public sector. In the UK and Germany, the main difficulty with independent oversight is the congruence between the legislative majority and the executive. In France, the problem is the strength of the president. Oversight is linked to the parliament in all three countries, but parliament is unlikely to challenge government incompetence or malfeasance effectively if it is controlled by the same party or party coalition as the executive. Restive coalition partners and the opposition have an incentive to monitor the executive, but may not have the power to do so. Even France, with its separately elected president, lacks institutions of horizontal accountability that can provide checks. Particularly in Germany and France, however, traditions of civil-service professionalism help produce checks on executive power operating both inside the core executive and in their auditing institutions.

Outside of the auditing and policy review of the GAO, the United States is a laggard in specialized oversight institutions. The Federal Election Commission is a weak agency with a limited mandate, and there are only a few ombudsmen scattered through the federal government. The lack of these intermediate bodies places an extra burden on the courts because cases come directly to them unfiltered by an intermediate body. The federal courts are poorly equipped to evaluate internal failures of the government bureaucracy that concern information availability or bureaucratic derelictions of duty. The US tradition of independent regulatory agencies has not produced powerful independent oversight bodies that concentrate on the government itself. Even the US inspectors general, who are meant to impartially investigate fraud, waste, abuse, and mismanagement, are political appointees.[178] Part of the reason for this is the oversight provided by congressional committees and congressional "casework" that helps individual constituents in their dealings with public bodies. Thus, there is likely to be little enthusiasm in Congress either for strong outside electoral oversight or for an ombudsman who could substitute for the members' own casework. As with independent regulatory commissions, a key issue is whether such bodies should be staffed by impartial experts and generalists or should reflect the partisan composition of those holding elected office.

Monitoring institutions established by politicians are not the place to look for improvements in policymaking accountability. They may prevent fraud and self-dealing and provide ex post reviews of government choices, but they are not likely to further public participation in policymaking. Powerful political players have little incentive to establish strong checks on their own behavior. Agencies of horizontal accountability reflect the tug of war between political control and independent oversight. Institutions that respond to individual complaints are a poor basis for structural reform. An ombudsman might be allowed to investigate particular policies and propose reforms, but he or she would need sufficient funding and political leverage to resist the pressure of individual complainants.[179] Independent audit offices such as the US GAO and the French Cour des Comptes are a more promising route, but they may concentrate only on economic efficiency and financial integrity. An effective electoral commission may need a constitutional pedigree because incumbent politicians are unlikely to support such a body absent a crisis of democratic legitimacy.

Conclusions

The puzzle of balancing functional independence with political accountability confronts all bodies with some independence from the core executive. My four case-study countries face this conundrum in distinctive ways, but independence, however achieved, ought not to push public accountability off the stage. Public hearings and consultations along with published reasons are especially important in bodies with some degree of independence because they cannot rely on the chain of legitimacy to justify their actions.

Of my four cases, the United States has the longest experience with independent regulatory agencies, and the notice-and-comment rulemaking process under the Administrative Procedure Act applies to them. The US multi-member commission model has been widely copied elsewhere, especially when state-owned enterprises were privatized and subject to regulation. However, the US administrative law of rulemaking did not follow. That difference reflects the differences in constitutional structure. Independence is difficult to achieve or to justify in a regime with strong traditions of parliamentary sovereignty based on the chain of legitimacy, such as the UK and Germany.[180] Such systems struggle to balance independence with political control. France's strong presidential system is similarly reluctant to grant independent policymaking power to regulators. Hence, regulatory agencies in these countries are not as separate from the core executive as in the United States, at least in their policymaking role.

In spite of these different constitutional frameworks, the functional justification for independent regulators is very strong in the European cases because the state often retains an ownership stake in its legacy firms. Thus, it is necessary to break the chain of legitimacy to achieve an effective regulatory environment. To make up for the legitimacy lost in the process, the agency should remedy that defect by engaging in open, inclusive, and transparent processes and public reason-giving.

In recent years, US independent regulatory agencies have confronted skeptics in the White House, in Congress, and in the courts. That skepticism could result in the loss of agency independence. That would be an ironic result given that the original worry was capture by the regulated industry. US industries where such capture was the most salient—trucking, airlines, and railroads—were deregulated decades ago. At present, some argue that the Federal Communications Commission is too deferential to the industries it regulates, but incorporating it into the core executive would not solve that problem if the president has a deregulatory agenda. Keeping regulators isolated from day-to-day political pressures and from industry capture remains a valid reason for their existence. However, that independence should go along with a strong commitment to open and transparent procedures with public involvement in consultations, not just as customers but also as citizens.

Private standard-setters and regulators may engage in self-serving behavior either in setting standards or in limiting entry. Whenever their actions affect the public interest, even if only indirectly, the law should require them to carry out open and transparent processes and to make their standards and rules freely available to the public. These protections, which I defend for rulemaking inside government, are even more necessary for rule-making that occurs outside in quasi-public bodies. At a minimum, even if the government is not required to engage in open-ended hearings and public reason-giving, private bodies should do so because of their lack of political legitimacy.

Agencies that monitor government itself are in a special category. They cannot responsibly carry out their mandates unless they are isolated from political influence. Labeling them as "courts" in Germany and France is one solution, but only if the body has investigative and oversight powers that allow it to generate its own caseload. Oversight agencies need to be able to set at least part of their agenda. Once again, engagement with the public should be part of their mandate.

Building on my overview of policymaking processes in the core executive and in regulatory agencies in Chapters 3 and 4, Chapter 5 considers the value and limits of technocratic analysis, and Chapter 6 asks how public participation can contribute to responsible executive policymaking. Chapter 7 considers the courts, the ultimate independent oversight body in each of my cases.

5. *Policymaking Norms*

The Value and Limits of Cost-Benefit Analysis and Impact Assessment

Despite the significant differences in policymaking institutions and practices outlined in previous chapters, the US, the UK, Germany, and France have one thing in common: The executive in each country increasingly uses technocratic techniques to resolve policy issues left open in statutory texts. In the United States, the dominant method is cost-benefit analysis (CBA). Although this technique is increasingly used across the Atlantic, impact assessment (IA) provides a common baseline.

Although these techniques are defensible in some contexts, their sweeping, uncritical use is deeply flawed.[1] This chapter first focuses on the normative assumptions underpinning CBA and IA, and then argues that these techniques are useful in resolving the relatively well-defined tradeoffs generated by short- and medium-term market failures. In addition, the systematic measurement of social costs can help clarify the best ways to aid victims of injustice. Cost-effectiveness studies can improve bureaucratic practices, even if benefits are intangible and difficult to measure. After exploring these applications, I turn to policies whose costs and benefits extend into the distant future—generating consequences that are large, uncertain, and unequally distributed. The standard technocratic techniques cannot do justice to value tradeoffs behind these initiatives in areas such as climate change and intergenerational justice.

The chapter concludes with a review of recent developments that have escalated the role of technocratic analysis in all four countries. The expansion of technocratic input is occurring at the same time as politicians have endorsed important new experiments in political accountability. Chapter 6 thus explores how public participation in executive-branch policymaking can be consistent with democratic ideals. The basic question is: Can technocratic expertise interact with public participation in executive policymaking in ways that further democratic values? These two chapters set the stage for an assessment of judicial review of executive policymaking as a way to help fill the "legitimacy gap" in Chapter 7.

A Primer on Policy Analysis

Technocratic analysis attempts to provide a quantitative measurement of the costs and benefits of public programs. The technique permits comparisons across policies so that scarce resources can efficiently further public goals. It measures overall social costs and benefits, not just a program's implications for the public budget. The economist's notion of opportunity cost is central; the analyst seeks to measure the value of economic activities forgone if resources, both public and private, are used to carry out a policy.

Begin with impact assessment. The European Commission and the Organization for Economic Cooperation and Development (OECD) present IA as a systematic technique for sorting out good from bad policies—in drafting statutes, in implementing spending programs, and in promulgating executive rules and regulations. The use of IA signals an interest not only in the formal properties of the law but also in how it operates in the real world. Neatness, clear drafting, and consistency are valuable only as means to an end, not as ends in themselves.[2]

IA evaluates the effects of government policies on human behavior and private markets as well as on public institutions. It itemizes and measures the costs and benefits of a policy, but it is not always clear how one should conduct an IA. Is it merely a way to highlight the tradeoffs involved in policymaking? Under that view, IA does not take a stand on how to strike the balance. Rather, it sets up the decision-making problem in a clear and well-informed way so officials can proceed in a logical manner and the public can see what is at stake. If that is its goal, it seems unproblematic and counters both officials who wish to make secret, unaccountable choices and politicians who attempt behind-the-scenes deal-making.

The OECD's publications express that aim. They argue for open, transparent, and wide-ranging participation by those affected. Decision-makers should canvass a range of options, including doing nothing, and explain why they have selected a particular outcome. EU and OECD documents support public consultation in language that mimics the justifications for notice-and-comment processes under the US Administrative Procedure Act.[3] However, there is a troubling undercurrent in the OECD's reports. They note with approval policies of removing one rule for each new one promulgated, as in Germany, or removing two old for one new, as in France. These problematic principles have little connection to the social value of individual policies. Some OECD rhetoric puts the burden of proof on those who seek new regulations. "Impact" in that discussion is impact on economic interests, not impact on the environment, on poor or marginalized communities, or on households. In some versions, impact assessment reflects a libertarian philosophy that seeks less state intervention. Concerned about giving prominence to economic effects, advocates for particular values have redefined impact assessment to focus on certain aspects of policy. For example, environmental impact assessments (EIAs) are an established aspect of the policy process in all my cases.

In the US, since the enactment of the National Environmental Policy Act (NEPA) in 1970, all public projects that affect the natural environment must perform an EIA.[4] The reports are public, but they are only advisory; if the government has carried out a satisfactory assessment, the project can go forward.[5] Nevertheless, the law creates background procedural requirements that highlight environmental impacts. The government has prevailed in the NEPA cases reviewed by the Supreme Court,[6] and the courts have delayed projects when the EIAs were inadequate or nonexistent. NEPA has affected the incorporation of environmental values into policymaking. The Trump administration reduced the scope of NEPA by changing the rules implementing the statute. These rules are unlikely to survive the transition to the Biden presidency, but their replacement will take time because the EPA must organize a notice-and-comment process.[7]

In enforcing the Aarhus Convention, discussed in Chapter 3, the EU requires member states to carry out both EIAs and strategic environmental assessments (SEAs). The former apply to specific infrastructure projects, such as a power plant or a bridge; the latter apply to plans and programs, usually local or regional development plans.[8] There are no such requirements for environmental rules, where the convention's language is much weaker.

Overall, the EU Commission performs IAs of its own legislative and rulemaking proposals in all subject areas, not just those with environmental effects.[9] In spite of advocacy by the EU and the OECD, the incorporation of IA into policymaking in Europe is still under development. One fundamental issue is whether such assessments will evolve toward a formal CBA requirement. In contrast, some want to tilt choices in the direction of environmental values or preserving certain rights. Others seek to further distributive justice through policies that aid poor and marginalized groups. Still others believe that economic growth measured in terms of GDP should trump other concerns.

Now consider cost-benefit analysis. IA is an open-ended concept that can encompass a range of values and processes, but taken by itself, it provides little guidance about how to make tradeoffs. CBA, in contrast, is clear about the method of balancing. The common metric is money, and the aim is to maximize net benefits. Policy-oriented economists have long promoted CBA. A canonical statement by a group of leading American economists in 1996 argued that all major regulatory decisions should be subject to a cost-benefit test. They wrote that CBA "has a potentially important role to play in policymaking, although it should not be the sole basis of such decision-making."[10] If the costs of a policy are out of line with the benefits, an agency ought, at least, to justify its choice.

CBA embodies a specific way of managing conflicts over values. Its methodology originated in public-finance economics, and it resolves trade-offs in a systematic way. The technique shares with democratic elections a focus on aggregating individual preferences using a common metric. Democratic elections give each person a single vote, and under majority rule with two options, the one with the most votes wins.[11] Policy analysis is similarly individualistic, but, instead of giving everyone a single vote, the technique measures each person's benefits and costs and adds them up. CBA expresses benefits and costs in monetary equivalents and selects the policy that maximizes the difference between the two. The technique seeks to include benefits and costs that are not traded in markets, such as levels of mortality and morbidity and aesthetic values. The analyst converts these sources of pleasure or pain into dollar equivalents to permit an overall balancing of the pluses and minuses of a policy.

In maximizing net benefits, a dollar of costs and a dollar of benefits have equal weight, with the signs reversed. Just as a secret ballot determines who wins an election, CBA is uninterested in the personal identities of those receiving the benefits and bearing the costs. Unlike majority voting, a person who experiences a large benefit or bears a large cost in monetary equivalents has more impact on the outcome than another who experiences only small monetary benefits or costs. As with majority voting, the beneficiaries do not need to compensate the losers. Everyone need not be better off under the proposed policy, and willingness to pay depends on individual endowments as well as preferences.[12]

The early utilitarians thought that utility was a cardinal, interpersonally comparable "entity" that could be maximized across the population. If marginal benefits to society fall as the scale of the policy increases and if marginal costs rise, then welfare maximization occurs where the marginal benefits of the policy equal the marginal costs. Unfortunately, no one knows how to measure utility in units like inches and pounds that permit interpersonal comparisons.[13] The Marginalist Revolution in economics at the end of the nineteenth century showed that economic theory could do away with cardinal, interpersonally comparable utility and posit only that people could order their options in a consistent way. Eventually, revealed-preference theory derived consistent preference relations from studying the choices that individuals make in the market.[14] However, those theoretical developments did away with the ability to measure social welfare in utilitarian terms. In response, Nicolas Kaldor and John Hicks proposed the metric of money as a substitute for utility, and cost-benefit analysis was born.[15] However, this apparent solution contains deep problems as a measure of welfare.

Using money as a metric implies two things. First, if individuals have approximately the same income, differences in willingness to pay for a benefit or to avoid a cost mirror their underlying gains and losses in satisfaction. Even if underlying levels of satisfaction are not measurable, one can infer that giving a benefit to the person who values it the most in dollar terms increases total utility. Given pervasive income inequality, this conclusion no longer follows. Poor people may suffer major losses in utility if they suffer a loss or fail to obtain a benefit, but their preferences have little weight in the CBA. Their ability to pay is low compared with the rich, just as it is in the marketplace. An exercise in public accountability can help ameliorate that problem. Pollsters could target an appropriate sample and ask how much money individuals would be willing to accept to forgo a benefit or to accept a cost. Nevertheless, even in this variant, a poor person's dollars will signify far higher utility gains or losses than will those of the top 10 percent. In practice, the greater number of low-income people may partly compensate for the low weight of each one in the calculation. But it remains true that, at the individual level, the preferences of the rich have a greater weight, just as they do in the market. Even a committed utilitarian, interested only in maximizing total happiness, would reject the cost-benefit answer.[16]

Second, maximizing net monetary benefits does not inevitably make everyone better off relative to the status quo. It imposes costs on some and benefits on others; only total net benefits matter. Yet, cost-benefit analysis has no built-in metric for evaluating distributive consequences. Giving the preferences of the poor greater weight is one response, but that technique brings to the fore CBA's lack of distributive-justice principles. One alternative is only to consider win-win policies, but that option is unsatisfactory because it places a huge normative weight on the status quo distribution of resources. It implies that the status quo is fair and just, so that regulatory changes are appropriate only if everyone is at least as well off as they were in the status quo. Rather than either burying distribution effects inside a CBA or refusing to engage in redistributive policies, policymakers should face these tradeoffs straightforwardly.

Fundamentally, the cost-benefit test is not suitable for making large-scale policy choices at the societal level. Conventional CBA assumes that the prices for inputs and outputs are fixed. However, for society as a whole, prices are a function of the way resources are used. For a given resource constraint and set of production possibilities, there are many possible ways to allocate resources, each implying a different set of prices. The "best" allocation of resources requires one to combine efficiency and equity to select a distribution that both avoids waste and satisfies society's distributional concerns.

To understand the value and limitations of CBA, I begin with situations where cost-benefit criteria seem relatively unproblematic—that is, government efforts to correct market failures that produce inefficiencies. I next proceed to more complex programs, whose goals cannot be reduced to net-dollar-benefit maximization. These two types of programs set the stage for consideration of large-scale multi-generational problems, such as climate change.

Correcting Market Failures

Markets are not always efficient—so much is conventional wisdom. Externalities, such as air and water pollution, impose costs that profit-maximizing firms ordinarily will not take into account unless regulatory laws or threats of legal liability induce them to do so. Firms may exercise monopoly power, and high entry barriers can make competition unlikely. Information about risks and harms may be unavailable or poorly processed by busy people who lack expertise. For such policies, the problem is one of measurement, not principle.

However, performing an adequate CBA for regulations is not always straightforward. Market prices are not available for many benefits and costs, and attempts to mimic the market are fraught with uncertainty. One thing, however, is clear: All the benefits and costs of the options should be measured, including so-called co-benefits, that is, bonus gains that occur in tandem with the primary purpose of a program. Unfortunately, the US Supreme Court disallowed such benefits in an opinion that falsely claimed to be applying rigorous economic analysis.[17]

Over and above such obvious mistakes, CBA faces a fundamental measurement problem. Analysts need to select an interest rate to discount future costs and benefits. Because costs tend to be concentrated in the present and benefits in the future, the choice of a rate can have important implications for policy choice, with lower rates making more policies look justified.[18] One possible discount rate is the opportunity cost of capital, but another is the consumers' rate of time preference—rates that, in our imperfect world, need not be equivalent. Using the opportunity cost of capital ensures that the capital-labor ratio for government programs is in line with private investment incentives so that capital is not over- or underused by the government. Using the rate of time preference requires information on how citizens trade off present and future benefits and costs.[19] The controversy over the appropriate discount rate affects both the weight given to future generations and the most efficient mixture of capital and other inputs.

If the benefits of correcting a market failure extend far into the future, the policy must incorporate the preferences of future generations. The logic of discounting means that these preferences are given little weight beyond fifty years or so at any discount rate close to the long-run rate of return on capital. For most conventional regulatory and spending programs, this does not raise particular problems. The policies correct market failures that will benefit people in the relatively short run, and, most important, there are no irreversibilities. The effects do not threaten future generations with catastrophic outcomes. Future generations can decide whether or not to pursue these policies if they have failed or if they conflict with other goals. William Nordhaus expresses this thought well:

> As parents, we naturally feel intense concern for our children, worrying about their safety, well-being, health, and happiness. We also care deeply about our grandchildren, but our anxieties are mediated by the knowledge that their parents—our children—are also caring for them. Similarly, our great-grandchildren and great-great-grandchildren are more remote from our anxieties. In a sense, they have an "anxiety discount" because we cannot judge the circumstances in which they will live, and because our children and grandchildren will be there to care for them after we are gone.[20]

Once one accepts the necessity of discounting, policymakers still need to determine what rate to use. Policy proposals that seek to correct imperfections in particular markets ought "to use a discount rate that reflects the actual market opportunities that societies face, not an abstract definition of equity taken out of the context of market realities."[21] In practice, because there are many different "market" rates, analysts ought to consider how their policy choices would vary depending upon the discount rate that they use. The basic point is that new policies ought to compete with other productive investments in both the public and private sectors. Sectoral policies of this type are not appropriate places to solve problems of distributive justice.

In general, policies that make the economy more efficient and less subject to negative externalities will be ones that future generations will want to continue. However, future generations can make that decision themselves. Today's policymakers need to set a discount rate, but the problem of setting one arises from market imperfections, not deep philosophical controversies. A key condition is that the policy is reversible. Future governments are not locked in and do not face irreversible, catastrophic risks. "The dictatorship of the present" is not a serious problem for such policy choices.[22]

A second measurement issue is the treatment of risk. Many policies, especially in the area of health and safety, have uncertain net benefits. They reduce the risk of cancer or lung disease, say, but with a large margin of error. Furthermore, even if the actual number of cases is known with a high level of certainty, no one may know ex ante who will actually get sick. These two kinds of risk raise different, but linked, issues.

The easiest case is one where the risk is distributed broadly and equally across the population, and the regulation reduces everyone's risk by an equal amount. Then, the expected benefit is the fall in risk multiplied by the average harm. If the harm is measurable, a remaining issue is the possibility that people have different attitudes toward risk. Should one use expected values, which assume risk neutrality, or assume that people are generally risk-averse? This is an issue either of predicting preferences or of arguing that government policy ought to adopt a particular attitude toward risk independent of the views of citizens. Some scholars argue that the state should be risk-neutral whatever the underlying preferences of current citizens.[23] More difficult cases arise when the science does not provide good estimates of the risk avoided. Then risk is not limited to the identity of the victims but includes uncertainty about the actual level of harm avoided. How precautionary should the regulation be when estimates of the harm are uncertain? Should this depend upon estimates of risk aversion or, alternatively, on potential victims' fear of being harmed? For example, a dispute erupted in the early 2000s over levels of arsenic in drinking water, and controversy over the steps to control the corona virus raise these issues.[24]

Furthermore, people misperceive the relative risk of low-probability events as well as the harm that each produces. They underestimate risks they can partially control (skiing, automobile, and bicycle accidents) and overestimate those they cannot (nuclear power plant meltdowns, food contaminants, terrorism).[25] The public is apparently concerned with the extinctions of species but not very worried about those whose numbers simply decline sharply. A study of the extreme reduction in North American duck populations found that "it appears that the public loses interest in preserving species when they move from endangered to the marginal category."[26]

A policy may be harder to put in place if the state knows the identities of the victims, some of whom can be saved depending upon the stringency of the policy. Most receive no benefits, but a few receive very large benefits in extra years of life or enhanced quality of life. There is no reason to think that people value life and health in a linear fashion. Perhaps you will pay a small amount to improve the safety of your automobile so that the risk of a fatal car crash is reduced, say, from 2 percent to 1 percent, but one cannot multiply that number by 100 to determine the amount you must be paid to be killed for sure. This poses a familiar conundrum where society spends large amounts to rescue particular individuals trapped in coal mines or under earthquake rubble but does not spend much to prevent such accidents in the first place. This can happen even when the overall life-saving benefits are higher for preventive measures.

Furthermore, one can argue that the state ought not to determine the value of a statistical life by aggregating the risk preferences of the population related to individuals' own mortality and morbidity. For example, although survey evidence shows that older people value extra life years the same as younger people, it does not follow that the state should equate a policy that prevents the premature death of young people with one that extends the lives of the same number of people in their seventies.[27]

Finally, the market does not price all benefits and costs. The most important examples are risks and benefits to human life and health, aesthetic and recreational benefits and harms, and benefits and costs to wildlife and natural sites. None of these has an unproblematic monetary equivalent, and indirect estimates are imprecise. It is the responsibility of experts to try to educate citizens on relative risks and benefits, not to assert that they necessarily have the correct answers. Jonathan Wiener makes a distinction between "cold" and "warm" analysis. The former includes only benefits and costs that can be quantified in unproblematic dollar terms. The latter attempts to include the kind of benefits and costs outlined here. Wiener rejects "cold" CBA, but that is an easy choice.[28] Even to a committed cost-benefit proponent, "cold" analysis is simply incompetent.

CBA has the strongest claim if policies seek to correct market failures—such as externalities and information failures—that are small relative to the overall economy.[29] Even if a market failure justifies regulation, political pressures in the legislature may push drafters toward the provision of special-interest benefits. When the government makes rules, it may favor concentrated, well-organized groups. Special-interest legislation is not unconstitutional or illegal; but efforts to benefit narrow groups should be transparent to voters. A presumption in favor of net benefit maximization increases the political costs for narrow groups, which must obtain explicit statutory language in order to have their interests recognized by courts and agencies. Non-transparent efforts to induce agencies to benefit narrow interests would be off limits.[30]

Even in these best-case scenarios, cost-benefit analysis faces at least four challenges: the problematic link between dollar totals and overall utility or net benefits; the choice of a discount rate; the treatment of risk and uncertainty; and the valuation of life, health, and other non-market values.

Economic experts can highlight the wrong way to deal with these difficult problems, but they cannot ultimately solve these problems within the CBA paradigm. Nevertheless, if analysts admit these difficulties and carry out sensitivity analyses to see if the choice of discount rate or the use of proxies for non-market values matters to the outcome, a cost-benefit framework can help structure the policy debate. It can highlight the areas where one needs judgments from outside that paradigm to make the final decision.[31]

Other Values

Many policies incorporate values other than economic efficiency. They guide transfer programs, such as social security, disability, or welfare. They administer subsidy programs, such as those that aid agriculture or public housing. They are concerned with the fairness and equity of markets. They take on ethical issues, such as free speech. A pure cost-benefit test, with its omission of distributive justice, fairness, and procedural concerns, would not encompass the purposes of these statutory mandates. Pure transfers from taxpayers to beneficiaries cancel out in a CBA. Furthermore, cost-benefit analysts balance risks to health and safety against other values, but others believe in risk minimization regardless of the costs.

Especially in Europe, the concepts of precaution and proportionality compete with CBA and IA for primacy. Proportionality applies if a policy goal violates rights. To summarize a vast and contested literature, the action proposed must be suitable for the stated goal; necessary, in the sense that no less-restrictive option is available, and (in the strict sense) not disproportionate to the restrictions imposed.[32] This third criterion, which looks like balancing, leads to the claim that proportionality is analogous to CBA, but efficiency is not the only value at stake. Moshe Cohen-Eliya and Iddo Porat's analysis of proportionality in German law and of American-style balancing in the courts stresses their different starting points. They conclude that "proportionality . . . was a way to guarantee that rights were not harmed unnecessarily, [while] balancing was a way to ensure that rights were not protected unnecessarily."[33] The two principles could end up at the same place because both recognize the need for tradeoffs, but given their lack of clarity in many applications, that will not invariably be true.

The precautionary principle is a risk-benefit tradeoff with a thumb on the scale for protective policies.[34] It places the burden of proof on opponents of regulation, making stringent protections easier. That principle states that regulators should err on the side of protecting health and safety even if the evidence is not completely clear.[35] The principle does not mean that no tradeoffs occur or that zero risk is the goal. However, it tilts decisions in a protective direction. If we presume that the average citizen supports stringent regulations, then the precautionary principle is a rough substitute for a participatory process. That presumption, however, might not be true across either issues or citizens. One could imagine a mixed system with the precautionary principle as a baseline that allows tradeoffs where the policymaker accepts greater risk in return for greater benefits along other dimensions. Consistent with that possibility, a careful comparison of US and European risk regulation in specific areas demonstrates considerable variation both over issues and over jurisdictions, with the US more "precautionary" in some areas than Europe.[36]

Where values other than economic efficiency are in the forefront, economic analysis can still assist policymakers. It can complement traditional public-administration solutions by introducing economic incentives into bureaucratic performance.

In short, for a range of policy choices, cost-benefit analysis is not a useful tool. It involves too many assumptions either about individual components or about how to aggregate them. In such cases, the principle of itemizing costs and benefits remains, but aggregation using the metric of money hides too many contested assumptions. Then, a sister technique called cost-effectiveness analysis may be helpful. This involves setting a goal, say, reducing the level of workplace injuries of a particular type by a certain amount in a certain time period. The analyst then evaluates the costs of alternative routes to that goal, and selects the most cost-effective. Real-world cases may have multiple goals that require tradeoffs, and the costs may include imponderables, such as health and safety risks. Thus, cost-effectiveness estimates may narrow the range of viable choices but still require an exercise of judgment.

Cass Sunstein recommends considering risk-risk tradeoffs. In other words, one would compare the expected loss of life and morbidity from alternative policies without assigning monetary values to the options.[37] His proposal recognizes that risks exist on both sides of many policies, but his focus on risk alone is too narrow. Even if human health and safety are involved, monetary costs matter not only because poorer people are less healthy but also because they are poor. Such tradeoffs between health risks and economic hardships have been central to the debates over responses to the coronavirus.

Sunstein's proposal to balance risks relates to another policy analytic technique—risk assessment. In the popular and political discourse, some commentators conflate this technique with cost-benefit analysis, but it is quite different. It emerged from the fields of engineering and public health, where policy involves a tradeoff among risks. Sometimes a policy is framed as designed to "minimize risks." Of course, one way to minimize risks is never to open oneself up to risk by sitting quietly at home, but most people do not act as if their goal were to minimize risks. There is always a risk/benefit tradeoff, as the world has faced during the corona-virus pandemic. Government must decide how to react when some impose risks on others without their consent and when individuals are unable accurately to assess the risks they face themselves and impose on others.

Even worse, those who benefit from a risky situation may try to manipulate the information available to others, hiding the dangers. Limiting the externalization of risk is one goal of many public policies by, for example, providing better information or limiting people's choices. However, risk assessment as an analytic technique tends to focus on risk to the exclusion of all else. Even when it implicitly assesses costs, it does so in a very simplistic way. For example, some recommend setting standards at the "knee of the curve," where a dose-response curve shifts from a slow increase as the dose increases to a steep upward slope. Such policies take no account of the marginal cost of reducing the dose. Perhaps costs are so low that policymakers should consider more stringent protections; or perhaps they are so high that lower standards are optimal. Alternatively, in some cases the substance should simply be banned, not set at the "knee."

Large-Scale, Multi-Generation Problems: Irreversibilities and Catastrophes

For long-run macroeconomic policies, nothing is held constant. Policymakers traditionally aimed to maximize the sustainable rate of economic growth, a policy position that calls for the present generation to give up consumption in the interest of long-run economic growth.[38] Others have pointed out that there is no sound philosophical reason to favor the future over the present, so that the goal should be to maximize the steady-state level of per capita income over time.[39] Many growth models assume a population that can save and invest at different rates over time. If we add in the possibility that the present can impose large, irreversible, and possibly catastrophic costs on the distant future, the question of inter-generational obligation arises with particular salience.

To see the problem, consider the issue of climate change. Society will experience many of the benefits of climate-change policy far in the future. Using a discount rate of 5 percent implies that a $1 benefit obtained fifty years in the future has a present value of 9 cents. At 3 percent, the present value is 23 cents, and at 6 percent, it is 5 cents. Suppose, to keep things simple, that all the benefits will accrue in year 50 and that they will be $5 billion. At 5 percent, the discounted present value of these benefits is $450,000, but it could be much higher or lower depending upon the rate chosen. Should the choice of a rate determine global policy on climate change?

In addition to the way compound interest determines the present valuation of future effects, estimates become less and less certain the farther one looks into the future. If we assume risk aversion, then society should save more in the present as future outcomes become more uncertain—that is, one should discount the distant future at a lower rate than the near term. Furthermore, if results are correlated between periods, expectations will further depress the discount rate.[40] As a result, some analysts argue that the social rate of discount should fall toward zero as one looks farther and farther into the future.[41] This does not mean that one values the future more highly than the present. It is rather a response to the uncertainty of outcomes in distant time periods. It operates within the utilitarian values behind conventional CBA; utility maximization requires more savings today to compensate for future uncertainty. With a declining discount rate, climate-change policy will then appear more attractive in CBA terms than with a constant rate. However, adopting such a perspective does not deal with the fundamental issue of whether utilitarianism is broadly acceptable to citizens as a measure of value across long periods of time.

The value-laden decisions that society must make in the present ought not to hide in the seemingly technical choice of a discount rate. This is perhaps behind the claim that society ought to be impartial about the time when benefits and costs accrue. According to Christian Gollier: "If one treats different generations equally, the only argument in favor of a positive rate of pure preference for the present is the possibility of extinction." However, one still needs to select a discount rate to reflect the "price of time that is compatible with a given consumption plan."[42]

Two further problems raise fundamental challenges to CBA: converting well-being to a measurable metric across people and dealing with the possibility of catastrophic, irreversible downside risks. Models that distinguish between market and non-market goods are promising responses to the first problem, but they rely on arbitrary assumptions about how each type of good enters individuals' utility functions. They posit that the value of non-market goods should rise over time because these goods will become scarcer as climate change progresses.[43] This effect will give these goods a larger weight in total output over time, depending upon how easy it is for people to substitute market for non-market goods. If substitutability is low, events that have large effects on non-market goods are more likely to produce a discontinuity (that is, a disaster), and the cost of the disaster in subsequent periods will be high. One study performs a number of simulations that justify a high tax on global carbon emissions.[44] Providing more structure to the utility function is a contribution, but this work retains the underlying utilitarian framework.

The second problem of catastrophic, irreversible harms raises special difficulties for conventional cost-benefit analysis. A classic article by Kenneth Arrow and A. C. Fisher argues for giving options to future generations instead of locking in present-day choices that are irreversible and limit choice.[45] In this model, the options are not necessarily discontinuous; they are just irreversible. Options can be valuable because present-day policymakers have imperfect knowledge of future preferences, and also because technological and resource constraints are uncertain. Future generations benefit from present-day policies that do not lock them in. The application to disasters is straightforward if we assume that the definition of a disaster is clear—for example, the present generation believes that future humans will also view large-scale, irreversible global warming as a bad outcome—and that major disasters limit the options available to humankind. Climate-change policy is, in part, an effort to keep a wider range of options open to future generations.

Some models take account of one-time events that affect future growth trajectories and cannot reoccur.[46] These events limit human options by moving the global economy to a lower baseline. In addition, if the harm has not yet occurred, the chance of its occurrence rises over time or, for climate change, as the average global temperature rises. Discontinuities, such as the melting of the Greenland ice cap or the reversal in directions of some ocean currents, are analogous to the end of an individual human life. They only happen once and the chance of their occurrence rises over time—although perhaps not to 100 percent.

These models are an advance, but they do not resolve the basic underlying problem of cost-benefit analysis. Underlying risks that increase with time counsel the use of a declining discount rate. However, if proposed long-term mitigating projects have uncertain payoffs compared to other short-term options, risky long-term projects become relatively less attractive, and one can justify using a higher discount rate for such projects.

Some proposals for dealing with climate change violate the basic assumption of CBA that the policy problem is "small" relative to the overall world economy. If disasters are large, discontinuous, and irreversible, and if appropriate policies might reduce those risks or push them farther into the future, CBA does not fit the underlying problem.[47] CBA assumes that equilibrium prices are given, but if our present actions increase the chances of a global disaster, this behavior will show up in the long-run rate of interest. Under some conditions, the supply of funds for projects that will only pay off in the distant future will shrink. Those shifts might be sufficient to persuade the government to initiate policies to limit those risks, but, because of the logic of discounting, very long-run harms will have little impact on current markets.

The fundamental issue is the obligation of the present toward the future. Those living today wield absolute authority over future generations.[48] Some economic analysts have dismissed this concern with the claim that future generations will be richer than we are and so we need not worry about them, beyond the incentives for saving and investment given by market interest rates and inter-family affection. Today, the ground has shifted as climate change and other risks appear to threaten future generations' hold on prosperity. We can still use economics to discuss cost-effective ways to deal with climate change, but it will not resolve the basic issues.

Even the most sophisticated modeling exercises cannot work without making normative and empirical claims. CBA includes the interests of all citizens, not just those with political clout, and thus, CBA may produce better policies than special-interest politics, but that ought not to be the end of the debate. If a policy choice can have massive, discontinuous, irreversible effects on the quality and quantity of human life in the distant future, the net-benefit calculations of CBA are not sufficient. The critiques of utilitarianism as a political philosophy and of CBA as an imperfect reflection even of utilitarian values come into play. Analytic efforts to demonstrate how sensitive CBA can be to the harm suffered by future generations may help dampen some criticisms of climate-change policy, but they cannot deal with the basic value judgments that nation states and the international community must make.

Debate over the obligations of the present to the distant human future needs to be part of the public debate, not viewed as side issues subordinate to the CBA enterprise. Climate change and similar problems with long-term effects should not be delegated to technocrats alone. Scientists and social scientists bring much of value to the table, but their input should not replace the responsibility of political bodies to consider the obligations of the present generation toward future generations.

Policy Analysis and Democratic Accountability: Back to the Cases

Cost-benefit analysis and, especially, regulatory impact assessment (RIA) have spread throughout the world, including to all my case-study countries. Both techniques require the drafters of statutes and regulations to consider the real-world effects of their proposals on individuals and businesses. Laws are not simply free-standing documents demanding obedience; rather, they should help solve pressing social problems in a cost-effective manner. However, as this chapter has argued, rigorous CBA has serious limitations as the primary technique for evaluating policy options, and RIAs share many of these downsides. These limitations include both their narrow normative framework and measurement difficulties. As the experiences of the US, the UK, Germany, and France demonstrate, some RIAs help promote better policymaking, while others merely relieve the regulatory burdens on business, without considering what may be lost in the process.

Policy analysis has developed unevenly in my case-study countries. At first glance, a scholar of comparative administrative law might guess that the use of analytic techniques in executive rulemaking would arise and predominate in France and Germany, with their strong bureaucratic traditions based on a public-service ethic. However, that guess would be wrong. Instead, the application of economic analysis to policymaking originated in academic circles in the US and UK based on utilitarian concepts dating to the nineteenth century.[49] The US government was the first to apply CBA and Impact Assessment to government decisions, based on methodologies used by the Army Corps of Engineers in the design of infrastructure. Government agencies applied these techniques across the US government during the administration of President Lyndon Johnson in the 1960s for all types of public programs. These analyses continue in most cabinet departments, and the 2018 Evidence Act further supports such efforts.[50] For spending programs, much of the cost shows up in government budgets, with citizens and businesses receiving the benefits.

In contrast, for regulations neither the costs nor the benefits are included in the budget, except for the administrative costs of issuing and enforcing the regulations themselves. Concerned that regulations were proving excessively costly, President Ronald Reagan issued an executive order in 1981 that required executive departments to prepare cost-benefit analyses of major rules and to submit them for review to the Office of Information and Regulatory Affairs (OIRA) in the Office of Management and Budget. The order does not apply to the rules issued by independent commissions. Even though executive rules are formally issued by cabinet departments, OIRA has centralized the rulemaking process and put it under closer presidential control. The Biden administration will maintain such presidential oversight, but it is reexamining the substantive principles that OIRA applies to regulatory review. A presidential memorandum, issued on the new president's first day in office, seeks "concrete suggestions on how the regulatory review process can promote public health and safety, economic growth, social welfare, racial justice, environmental stewardship, human dignity, equity, and the interests of future generations."[51]

Although the US executive branch took the lead in performing CBA for spending programs and for major executive rules, neither CBA nor IA is required for legislation. The Congressional Budget Office must "score" the federal budgetary impact of legislative proposals, and it estimates the costs of mandates that affect other governments and the private sector. That exercise, however, does not consider the overall costs and benefits to society.[52] Technocratic studies influence legislative drafting, but the US separation of powers and the complex interplay between and within the branches mean that the statutory drafting process faces few technocratic constraints. The

Constitution, as interpreted by the courts, imposes a weak rationality condition and incorporates a permissive non-delegation doctrine. Outside of issues related to the protection of rights, the Constitution does not require that statutes provide the means adequate to pursue their ends.[53]

The UK introduced RIA techniques into policymaking under Prime Minister Margaret Thatcher in the 1980s, and in 2004 the government created a centralized IA system called the Better Regulation Executive.[54] IAs should, at a minimum, identify "losers and winners" and provide a qualitative description of costs and benefits, although quantifiable impacts are preferred.[55] Some critical studies claim that these analyses emphasized economic costs over social and environmental considerations. Conversely, others argue that IAs are conducted too late in the policy process to have much effect.[56] These are familiar criticisms: CBA and IA either are incomplete guides to policy, on the one hand, or do not actually guide choices in spite of enthusiastic rhetoric, on the other.

The use of RIA in the UK, Germany, France, and the EU needs to be understood in the context of changes in the ownership and regulation of network industries such as electricity, gas, and telecoms. EU member states have shifted from directly managing to steering (*Steuerung*) the economy.[57] As discussed in Chapter 4, the European cases have histories of public ownership of firms in network industries. Eventually, the neo-liberal, pro-market agenda of the EU pushed member states to privatize and then regulate public-utility firms. The widespread conversion of public firms into private corporations changed the role of the state. As the privatization of these firms proceeded, the regulation of these private-law corporations has become a subject for administrative law, pushing officials to consider the social and economic implications of their actions. These new regulatory agencies drew on a long history of the application of economic analysis to network industries under state ownership. When public utilities were state-owned firms, their managers applied systematic economic analysis to their operation. For example, the French electricity company saw efficient energy pricing as a public responsibility. Trained engineers used advanced public-finance concepts to price services. US economists learned from their work, translated a key publication from 1956, and published it in a leading journal in 1971.[58] The use of public-finance economics within the state-owned sector was a technocratic effort that did not involve the general public or even the rest of government. However, its practitioners understood themselves as acting in the public interest.

In contrast, public ownership of utilities was never widespread in the US, but the government has long sought to constrain private monopolies, using economics as part of the justification for its actions. Federal statutes governing pollution, health, safety, and so on proliferated in the second half of the twentieth century, and economic analysts moved from constraining the inefficiencies of monopoly supply to confronting other market failures. Thus, in the US the broad application of CBA to all types of government regulatory activity was an extension of existing practice, not a paradigm shift.

Following the lead of the US and the UK, the European Commission, supported by the OECD, advocated for "better regulation" in the 1980s and 1990s. They supported RIAs for both draft legislation and executive rules, setting in motion a bandwagon that needs to be subject to critical scrutiny before it acquires the status of conventional wisdom.[59] A recent OECD report shows the trend in RIA adoption across the thirty-four member countries from one in 1974 to all members in 2015. However, for secondary regulations, only about half of the member states require them for all regulations. Furthermore, the quality of assessments varies widely, with the UK and EU higher in the OECD's ranking than Germany and France.[60]

The EU introduced a formal Better Regulation initiative in 2001, issued guidelines for impact assessment in 2003, and created an Impact Assessment Board to review European Commission legislative proposals. That board, renamed the Regulatory Scrutiny Board in 2015, is a multi-member body that must give a positive report on a legislative proposal before the commission can put it on the agenda of the European Council and Parliament.[61] Recently, that board has been quite active in disapproving proposed laws and returning them to commission officials. The Better Regulation initiative has a libertarian gloss that its technocratic language obscures by implying that these methods are neutral, impartial, and not subject to debate. However, its mandate, unlike OIRA in the US, does not include executive rules, what the EU calls "tertiary legislation."[62]

The EU, along with the UK, Germany, and France, has participated in the troubling recent spread of a technique called the standard cost model (SCM), a label implying that it is an unproblematic "standard." In practice, it will exacerbate the built-in weaknesses of CBA and RIA as policymaking tools. The European Commission has announced that it seeks to cut the administrative costs imposed on business by 25 percent by using the SCM to cut red tape without affecting substantive standards. The UK, Germany, and

France introduced similar rhetorical commitments to cost-cutting, expressed as "one-in-N-out," that is, for every new regulation, one or more old regulations must be repealed. France and Germany have one-in-one-out policies, and the UK moved from one-in-one-out in 2010 to one-in-three-out in 2016. In the US, President Trump issued an executive order in 2017 that instructed government officials to eliminate two rules for every new one they put in place. That EO was voided by President Biden in 2021.

These policies do not make sense as analytic tools because they ignore benefits. Supporters of the SCM claim to be eliminating pure red tape with no effect on substance, but that is generally an absurd claim.[63] Administrative burdens are a necessary part of policy implementation. Policies can often be made more cost-effective, but reforms that cut red tape should only occur after a careful consideration of their impact on a program's regulatory goals. As a cross-country study concludes, one-in-N-out programs are usually no more than rhetorical commitments that put down a marker in favor of less regulation.[64] The risk is that the implementation, even of a largely symbolic policy, can do real damage to regulatory goals. That is particularly likely in the case of executive actions that instruct officials to take account of all the opportunity costs to society and none of the benefits. A program that focuses on direct costs to business neglects broader social effects. At least in the US, a rule with the force of law cannot be voided without going through a notice-and-comment process that requires public input and reason-giving. The European processes rely on bureaucratic competence and could lead to the rescission of rules with important social benefits without a chance for public input.

For example, Germany has embraced the standard cost model. The government requires Regulatory Impact Assessments for all laws and regulations originating in the executive, and a National Regulatory Reform Council reviews draft laws before adoption by the federal cabinet.[65] Draft regulations must be submitted to this council before the start of the coordination process within the federal government.[66] The council primarily reviews ministry estimates of compliance costs and publishes a guide for preparing RIAs. Since 2011, the German government has committed itself to limiting the compliance costs of new regulations, including the costs imposed on citizens, businesses, and public authorities.[67] Its policy states that "for every additional burden created by new regulatory proposals, an equivalent portion of the existing burden is reduced."[68] German officials posit that the government can reduce red tape using the SCM with no impact on "political projects." Unlike OIRA, however, the German Council cannot return a costly regulation to a government ministry to be redrafted,[69] and the OECD has critiqued Germany's relatively limited progress.[70] Given the weaknesses of the techniques it uses, the claimed "limits" may actually imply that officials are not mechanically seeking mere cost reductions but do consider social benefits as well.

France initially opposed expanding the application of economic analysis to regulatory bodies and to policymaking in general. In 2004, the OECD observed that "[w]hile France conducts some ex ante assessments, these are often un-coordinated and do not systematically take into account the overall costs and benefits of regulations from a social and economic perspective, and they are drafted prior to the RIAs, which are often no more than a formal exercise. . . ."[71] Documents were considered a formality and generally were compiled after the conclusion of the decision-making process.[72] Nevertheless, following the adoption of the Constitutional Act of 2008, France changed tack. It enacted a Framework Act in 2009 that implemented article 39 of the amended Constitution requiring IAs for most government legislative proposals. The act provides that "[d]raft legislation shall be the subject of an impact assessment," which must include a cost-benefit analysis.[73] The act, however, does not apply to secondary legislation, including rules that implement regulatory statutes. Ministries develop their own IAs with the General Secretariat providing guidance, which, as in Germany, is based on the Standard Cost Model.[74] IAs must be appended to draft bills submitted to the Conseil d'État, which reviews their quality before submission to the parliament. However, the Conseil's review is legal rather than economic.[75] Disagreements on the quality of impact studies between the executive and legislative branches are settled by the Constitutional Council.[76] The OECD continues to note an overall lack of oversight of the French IA process. The potential first line of defense, the government's General Secretariat, is only responsible for ensuring that an IA is executed; it does not evaluate quality and consistency.[77]

In acknowledging the new reality of the regulatory state, the UK, Germany, and France, pushed by the EU and the OECD, carry out Regulatory Impact Assessments. However, many such exercises focus too heavily on cost reduction, not on balancing costs and benefits. At least, the IA process has moved beyond a formalistic view of law to recognize the functional impact of executive rules and secondary norms. Nevertheless, except for environmental policy and some aspects of planning law, these assessments frequently ignore the important social benefits and the distributive consequences of regulatory policies.[78] The focus on technical competence goes along with doubts about the value of public input for complex technical decisions.

Conclusions

Cost-benefit studies and impact assessments pervade the regulatory environment in the US and Europe.[79] But their limitations need to be better understood. Quantifying costs and benefits is necessary but not sufficient. Executive policymakers should seek input both from those subject to the direct effects of a policy and from those with strong, principled policy positions.

Policymakers should discount the future benefits and costs of regulatory and spending programs that correct market failures. They should be transparent about modeling and measurement choices that bring in noneconomic judgments, and they should perform a sensitivity analysis to see if decisions based on these judgments matter to the final outcome. However, they should not force CBA to perform tasks for which it is, in principle, not suited. Those include policies that serve other goals, such as fairness or poverty alleviation, and those with macroeconomic consequences that are large, multi-generational, and potentially irreversible, such as climate change or the extinction of species. Even there, economic analysts can perform cost-effectiveness studies and help policymakers consider opportunity costs and secondary benefits. They can outline options, highlighting uncertainties and value judgments. These analytic exercises ought to be an input into the political debate, not a source of definitive answers. Policymakers must make the ultimate choices on grounds that frequently cannot be expressed by CBA. Those with training in economics and policy analysis need to step back and cede the floor to those concerned with both educating citizens about complex problems and listening to their responses. A democracy may make choices that do not jibe with those supported by technically trained analysts, but that is a problem for the analysts, not a critique of democracy.

I do not wish to be misunderstood. I favor analyses that measure costs and benefits in the most accurate way possible and that use these data to make intelligent policy choices. Clearly, techniques that just measure cost savings are deeply inadequate. At the same time, the responsible use of CBA requires institutional reforms in both the US and Europe. Cost-benefit analysis and majoritarian democracy can conflict. A search for a single "best" policy may lead analysts to make controversial assumptions simply to produce an answer that "maximizes" social welfare. CBA and IA must complement democratically accountable decision-making processes, not substitute for them.[80]

Some supporters of CBA and IA take a dim view of public participation, emphasizing that it can legitimate special interests with political clout, such as oil companies, farmers, or medical doctors. The most pessimistic conclude that narrow interests invariably capture sitting governments, leading to the conclusion that constitutions should limit taxation powers and prevent elected governments from engaging in regulatory activity.[81] My approach is more balanced. I recognize that interest-group capture does occur inside ministries and agencies as well as in the legislature. The solution, however, is not to impose draconian limits on government. Rather, the systematic adoption of principles of public accountability can create institutional checks on executive power that will better serve democratic values.

The defenders of CBA and IA agree on the importance of improving government performance.[82] They argue that technocratic techniques can further the national interest better than the direct pursuit of public accountability through citizen involvement. Frequently, there is no stark choice between the two options. In some contexts, technocracy and public accountability complement rather than substitute for each other. But there are contexts in which CBA and IA trivialize the values that underlie statutory programs enacted by the governing majority.[83] Thus, it is important to ask if there are ways to encourage citizen participation and consultation without giving up on the value of fact-based, technically competent executive policymaking.

Both CBA and IA are rooted in individual preferences, but if reduced to purely technocratic exercises, they risk losing the connection to citizens necessary for legitimate government. A government that justifies a policy through the invocation of a cost-benefit study, standing alone, risks backlash from those on the cost side of the ledger, who may be far more numerous and better organized than the beneficiaries. Costs may occur today that provide benefits to unborn future generations. If the state asks its citizens to sacrifice for the common good, they need to be included in the debate and to be listened to by those who have ultimate decision-making authority.

6. *Public Participation*

Cost-benefit analysis and impact assessment help frame executive-branch policymaking in my case-study countries, but they can mask the complex value tradeoffs that pervade government decision-making. Hence, Chapter 5 took a fundamentally critical stance toward their currently dominant role in executive decision-making. The present chapter reverses these priorities. It explores the strengths and weaknesses of recent efforts to involve citizens in developing politically accountable policies. There are no easy answers, but this assessment will, I hope, help define more constructive forms of political accountability that also recognize the importance of technocratic analysis. It will also set the stage for the next chapter's consideration of the judiciary's role in monitoring executive efforts to move beyond narrow partisan politics to a more sustained pursuit of the public interest.

The chapter begins by distinguishing my view of public accountability from other rationales for broad involvement. Although these rationales may play a positive role, they are distinct from my central concern with involving the public in framing executive policy choices. I use the following definition of public participation: "forums of exchange that are organised for the purpose of facilitating communication between government, citizens, stakeholders and interest groups, and businesses regarding a specific decision or problem."[1] The definition excludes protests, expert workshops, and government service, and includes public hearings, public meetings, focus groups, surveys, citizen advisory councils, civic forums, negotiations, referenda, and initiatives. It includes efforts by individuals and organizations to inform the government of their views without engaging in any give and take. I accept

Jürgen Habermas's ideal of "discourse" that implies "equality among participants, holding knowledge claims up to public as well as expert scrutiny, and a bias toward resolving conflicts in consensual rather than adversarial ways."[2] However, moderate- or large-scale polities can seldom achieve that ideal, especially for decisions based on technocratic expertise and probabilistic risk assessments.[3] I ask when public involvement can be valuable in a democracy even though it does not lead everyone to consent to a single policy direction.

The distinction between general policy and individual decisions is central to an assessment of what public participation can accomplish. Local projects are immediately salient to ordinary citizens living, for example, near a power plant applying for a license, a railroad station about to be rebuilt, or a plan to route a high-tension power line over their village. Much public participation involves local grievances over issues such as housing, education, and basic services. The demands for participation are tied to social and economic rights through public input into local infrastructure projects or licensing decisions.[4] These processes express important public values, but they do not respond to the democratic imperative for public involvement in broad-based policy choices. Such policy choices are of overall importance but less immediate salience. Those who focus on rights tend to downplay the value of democratic accountability, but much is lost if rights, however important, are the only frame for analysis.

The following table outlines the loci of public involvement by types of decisions and by the institutions involved. In this volume I focus on the central column and consider tensions between expertise and public involvement in decisions taken by ministries and agencies.[5] In my European cases, there is considerable public participation in individual infrastructure decisions compared with the relative lack of such processes in rulemaking (that is, in the production of secondary norms, statutory instruments, and regulations with the force of law). The US federal government requires public consultations for most rulemakings. However, the impact of notice-and-comment procedures may be limited both by their own deficiencies and by assertions of presidential power that undermine the role of public participation in cabinet departments.

If ministries and agencies seek to reach out to the public in making policy, they face difficult choices in balancing public accountability against feasibility. The best techniques are not obvious. Clearly, not everyone can be

LOCI FOR PUBLIC INVOLVEMENT AND TYPE OF DECISION

	REFERENDA	LEGISLATURE	MINISTRIES AND AGENCIES	COURTS	PRIVATE BODIES OR PPPS
POLICY CHOICES	Binding laws	General statutes	Rules with force of law	Structural injunctions *and* review of other policy processes	Private rules (may be enacted into law)
INDIVIDUAL DECISIONS	Approval or disapproval of infra-structure projects	Approval and funding of particular projects; laws that aid a named individual	Decisions on particular projects or cases; neighborhood-project choices	Adjudications resolving disputes over particular cases *and* review of executive adjudications	Adjudications to resolve disputes, e.g., intra-industry disputes

consulted, and even those willing to provide input may not be knowledgeable or may represent narrow, minority viewpoints. A commitment to representative democracy means that policy ought to be made by politically accountable officials in both presidential and parliamentary systems. As outlined in previous chapters, this can be achieved through cabinet ministries or through agencies that are independent of the executive but accountable to the legislature and overseen by the courts.[6] Nevertheless, the chain of legitimacy is not sufficient. Important questions remain about how to structure executive policymaking to integrate the concerns of citizens, businesses, and other interest groups with the political and technical demands of public programs.

Consider, first, the claim that there is no necessary conflict between political and technocratic choices. Under that view, policymaking processes in the executive ought to be transparent and open to public scrutiny. Analysts should not simply announce a final "best" result but rather present their assumptions, the data used, and the techniques employed. If information is unavailable from published sources, the administrators should consult those who possess expertise. They should take account of public input based on surveys and focus groups. Cabinet ministers and agency heads need not blindly follow public opinion, but it must be considered before issuing the final rule.[7] Under such conditions, consultation with private individuals, civil-society groups, business, and labor permits a more informed analysis and a better result.

That scenario is certainly possible, but it presents too happy a story. The decision remains in the hands of officials who weigh the various factors. Instead, democratic citizens ought to be able to hold the executive to account and ensure that officials consider their values and concerns. Agency technocrats may support the result of a cost-benefit analysis or seek the risk-benefit ratio at the "knee" of the curve. Others, including politicians inside government, as well as interest groups and activists, may weigh the costs and benefits very differently. Under an open and participatory process, those involved may not be content with simply stating their views or submitting documents. They may claim a role in setting the agenda and in balancing conflicting values. They do not wish to be simply an "input" into a technocratic choice based on anonymous surveys and other social-science methods.[8]

There are many critiques of public involvement. The underlying problems are citizens' lack of knowledge and lack of motivation, as well as the challenge of organizing productive deliberations. Expertise may be both time-consuming to obtain and difficult for non-experts to understand, even if they can access the relevant documents and websites. People are busy with their lives, and they may believe that their marginal contributions will not matter—they face a collective-action problem that leads them to free-ride on the actions of others. These conditions support both representative democracy and the delegation of technocratic decisions to the bureaucracy. But those with specialized knowledge cannot be sure that their policy judgments accord with public values and preferences. Experts may disagree on the best course of action based on their understanding of the facts and of the causal mechanisms. Hard scientists may disagree with social scientists, and lawyers may disagree with substantive experts. Issues that seemed settled at the legislative drafting stage may become controversial when analyzed ex post through a technocratic lens. Disagreements about both facts and values leave an opening for public input.

The loci for public involvement may overlap. For example, a civil-society group's access to the courts can supplement its participation in executive rulemaking. Thus, a group may bring a lawsuit to claim that government officials have excluded it from participation in a policymaking forum. Furthermore, even if the government must consult broadly before issuing a rule, it may avoid that requirement through a series of adjudications that add up to a general policy. That option will be especially likely in a legal system based on the common law where judicial precedent operates.[9] Even in the absence of formal precedents, an agency's established case-by-case practices can produce a de facto policy framework.

To proceed, I explore alternative meanings of public participation in executive-branch policymaking. I first critique alternatives that do not include deliberation. I turn next to options explicitly designed to incorporate democratic values—mini-publics or civic forums, consultation with stakeholders, and American-style notice-and-comment rulemaking. The chapter concludes with a return to the practices and principles of participation discussed in Chapter 3 and provides some guidelines for public input.

Participation without Deliberation

The knowledge and interests of citizens can be included in policymaking in ways that, while useful to technocrats, do not enhance democratic legitimacy. They make useful contributions, but they do not respond to the democratic deficit embedded in delegation. I distinguish between three types: participation to find facts, to produce "satisfied customers," and to reach unanimous consent.

Participation to Find Facts

I have already mentioned surveys and focus groups that can help public officials make policy. Going further, some proponents of public participation emphasize the "wisdom of crowds" when the information needed to make policy is widely distributed in the population.[10] In one case, interested citizens were labeled the "18th specialist" to emphasize the compatibility of public involvement with expertise.[11] This view of public input has several variants.

In its purest form, the public is a source of information for determining the facts. In an often-used example, the task is to guess the number of jellybeans in a jar. The logic, first articulated in the Condorcet Jury Theorem,[12] is as follows. Suppose that everyone independently guesses the value of some unknown based on random draws from a distribution that is symmetric about the true value. Each individual has a very small chance of guessing correctly, but if the "crowd" is large enough, then pooling the random draws will reflect the underlying distribution, and the mean of the guesses will be close to the true value. The guesses must be independent and not strategic; thus the participants ought not to discuss their draws with each other because that could bias their guesses. There is no debate and no dialogue to air facts and values and consider consequences. Everyone is indeed treated equally, but the aim is simply to find a fact, not to debate policy options.

In other cases individuals' information is additive or, at least, complementary. In one example, individual mass-transit riders reported on bus routes serving their neighborhoods with times and stops.[13] The city, which lacked that information, combined the reports to produce a citywide bus-route map. The government gathered the information more efficiently through public input than through a top-down study. The method taps into distributed knowledge to produce a predetermined benefit for urban commuters. The goal is not itself controversial; the only task is generating relevant knowledge at least cost.

A third example is a survey designed to elicit opinions to feed into a public-policy decision. Here, the aim is not only to collect information as an input but also to elicit expressions of values and policy preferences. As in the other two cases, there is no deliberation; a survey asks participants a list of questions, and the answers are usually anonymous, although demographic information is collected. People with different characteristics may have different policy preferences, but there is no discussion with participants, and answers are usually multiple-choice. The participants are not "specialists"; they report only their own values and preferences.

These three techniques can answer pre-set questions. What is the value of a variable? Where and when do the buses travel? Which option has the most support and from whom? These types of exercises inform Beth Noveck's study of processes that tap into distributed knowledge to solve problems.[14] She recommends using these techniques to locate hidden expertise in large organizations, such as a federal bureaucracy, the military, or the World Bank.

Important as these innovations are for public policymaking (and for business decisions in the private sector), they are not my primary concern because they do not deal with democratic accountability. They produce information that the bureaucracy can assess along with other types of factual material. Asking questions of the public has no necessary relationship to the democratic legitimacy of government, although such practices may produce more efficient and effective policies. Even autocrats with no need to face the voters may want to tap into information distributed throughout the population.

Participation to Produce Satisfied Customers

The New Public Management (NPM) views citizens as customers whom public officials should accommodate, but it often ignores the mismatch between satisfied customers and good policy.[15] Government agencies ought not to design procedures primarily to produce satisfied participants, analogous to satisfied customers in a market. Of course, a service orientation can be valuable at the implementation stage, and bureaucrats might benefit from consulting beneficiaries and regulated entities to discover how to improve the operation of their programs. Nonetheless, when executive agencies make policy, the aim is good policy, not the satisfaction of those who are actively involved. The criterion of participant satisfaction feeds into critiques of public involvement that stress the unrepresentative character of those who come forward. Biases are built into procedures that only consult direct beneficiaries and neglect others concerned with the policy's overall effects on public welfare.

Cary Coglianese provides a thoughtful critique of studies that judge the value of participatory process by looking at the satisfaction of the participants. He argues that such processes are not the appropriate forums for resolving private grievances.[16] Surveying participants after the fact only reveals how they feel about the process, not whether it led to good policy. The mismatch between satisfied participants and good policy can be especially acute for consensus-building procedures, which I discuss next. Those involved in the process may not be representative of the interests at stake, and some interests may be better at articulating their views and values than others. Thus, an ex post evaluation based on participants' opinions is problematic, and even the unanimous consent of designated stakeholders may have similar legitimacy deficits.[17] The exercise of public power ought to be responsive to the citizens in whose name it is exercised—as citizens, not as customers.

Unanimous Consent

Some advocates of public involvement take unanimous consent as the ideal. This seems utopian and of limited value outside quite homogeneous communities. Some political theorists imagine that if citizens could only take a disinterested, public-regarding perspective when they debate public choices, then everyone would eventually agree on the best way forward. This does occur in some situations, but if nothing can be done unless everyone in the group agrees on the way forward, the process favors the status quo, which may be low on the list of options for most participants. Such procedures do involve deliberation, but to require that everyone agree with the result is usually not a realistic condition. I discuss options that do not make that type of consensus necessary in the next section. Here, I consider options that produce agreement by compensating the losers for accepting a new policy.[18] The gainers give up some of their benefits in order to produce agreement on how to proceed. Everyone is at least as well off with the new policy as he or she was in the status quo. Taking the status quo as the baseline limits the policy options to those that can earn unanimous consent based on private benefits and costs. However, even then, the division of the surplus may be hotly contested. More fundamentally, if taken as the primary guide to policy, it rules out redistributive policies by starting the policy discussion from the existing distribution of wealth. The poor would have to compensate the rich for the cost of welfare payments; the state would have to compensate monopolists if antitrust laws reduced their profits.

There are ways around this status-quo bias. For example, the participants could have a budget to allocate that limits the effect of the status quo on bargained outcomes, but that option is hardly a reasonable option for a large polity unable to engage in face-to-face bargaining. Alternatively, the state might give those who bear the costs an ownership stake in the program, as Germany attempted to do in some auctions for on-shore wind farms.[19]

One problem with efforts to reach agreement is strategic behavior. Some may overstate the harm they will suffer in order to persuade others to compensate them. Others may understate the benefits they receive in order to induce greater sacrifices from others. If everyone realizes that everyone else has those incentives, no one will take others' claims of benefits and harms at face value, and negotiations may break down. Several scholars have developed clever schemes to induce participants to reveal their true valuation of the various options.[20] These schemes, however, are limited by their dependence on the utilitarian values behind cost-benefit analysis.

In short, unanimous consent based on persuasion is too stringent a standard, and an agreement based on payoffs relies on an impoverished normative framework. Representative democracy aims to manage disagreements through votes in which losers accept their losses and try to win the next time around.[21]

I put to one side processes that merely collect data from the public, those that aim for participant satisfaction, and those that seek unanimous agreement. Instead, I turn to options that accept the inevitability of public disagreement over policy and the impossibility of inclusive deliberation in polities larger than a small village. These options build on the policy legitimacy that flows from statutes to the administration that must carry out their mandates. Administrators should recognize the limits to their legitimacy and seek to involve individual citizens and organized groups in discussions with each other and with public bodies. The aim is not to override legislative mandates, but rather to build on legislative texts to produce democratically acceptable policies that recognize the limitations of the chain of legitimacy as a reflection of the values and interests of citizens.

Policymaking Accountability in the Executive: Options for Democracies

The electoral process has its own weaknesses, but I take those limitations as given here and focus on efforts to involve citizens and organized groups in designing policies beyond the ballot box.[22] The issues can range from individual infrastructure projects to national or regional policies. Participatory processes feed into both executive-branch decisions and the legislative process, and much research in this area concerns consultations that inform legislative choices. I concentrate, instead, on policymaking that occurs between elections and may deal with issues that were not salient on election day. Rather than unpack the legislative process, my focus is on public participation in policymaking inside government ministries and agencies.

There are two basic tensions. One is between efforts to increase the participation of organized, not-for-profit groups versus attempts to bring in individual citizens whose involvement with politics centers on the voting booth. In one discussion over the role of citizen input, a speaker stated that in order to "count" as the general public, participants would have to be unorganized.[23] As a matter of practical policymaking, this is an absurd claim. It draws on Rousseau's ideal of each individual expressing his or her informed but unmediated "will" to generate the "general will."[24] That ideal is very far from reality for two reasons. First, it is unrealistic to assume that deliberation and debate between unorganized individuals will generally lead everyone to agree on the best policy. Second, if the government only consults individuals and rules out the participation of organizations, collective-action problems tempt most to free-ride. If people band together out of a moral commitment to promote certain policies or organize to support both private benefits and public values, these groups can help public bodies make choices. Biases will exist, but the task of responsible officials is to take them into account in making policy, not to refuse to accept input.[25] In practice, participatory processes are generally limited, not by too many organizations but by too much free-riding.

A second tension is between the policy positions of political parties and the roles of both cause-based groups and individual citizens. Parties mediate between their supporters and state policymaking institutions. Political parties may oppose alternative routes to incorporating voters' preferences and values into government policies. However, no party provides nuanced analyses of all the items in its platform. In any case, the rules that ultimately result from government processes may be only weakly connected to the views of the ruling party's supporters. Thus, even those who give governing parties a leading role can support efforts by political regimes to connect directly with the voters. However, to claim political legitimacy, that obligation should extend to the views of political opponents as well. The chain of legitimacy that goes back to the ballot box is an essential feature of democracy, but it can be a weak transmission belt for public sentiment and often fails as a deliberative forum.[26] Because delegation is inevitable under modern conditions, public participation should occur at loci of decision-making inside the government and in independent or quasi-public bodies that make binding rules. Yet exactly how to accomplish this goal is not clear. Designers of participatory institutions that aim to assist delegated policymaking must answer the following questions:

- What issues should be aired in a participatory process? Is the aim to develop a general policy or to make a particular project-level decision that is embedded in an existing policy?
- At what stage in the administrative process should public participation occur? What issues have been decided and which are open to debate? How is the agenda set?

- How is technical expertise incorporated into the process? Are experts consulted before the process begins, or do experts participate in the process? Do citizens need basic knowledge of some technical matters in order to participate?
- Is participation open-ended or closed, and if closed, how are participants selected and by whom? How many are involved?
- Does the process occur in a limited time frame, or is it spread over weeks and months? Are potential participants given time to prepare for providing input?
- How costly is the process in time and money? Does the government subsidize the costs of participation, especially for those with few resources? Do the participants have access to staff, over and above the staff of private organizations that participate?
- What role do government officials and consultants play? Are they active participants in dialogue with citizens and groups, or are they simply the recipients of public input?
- What is the role of groups such as civil-society groups, labor unions, political parties, religious groups, business associations, professional groups, and academic associations?
- What form does participation take—for example, hearings or moderated debates?
- Do the discussions occur in public or behind closed doors? Are the relevant documents, testimony, and debates posted on public websites?
- Do participants believe that the process matters to the final result? Is it purely advisory? How does the process mesh with the bureaucratic structure?
- Can the courts review the substantive outcomes and/or the legality of the process?

These questions have many valid answers and can be combined in multiple formats. I consider three familiar options. The first are civic forums or minipublics that call on a small group of ordinary citizens to present their views and deliberate. The process asks if citizens change their views after deliberating on the topic at hand. In more ambitious efforts, the goal is a recommendation to the public agency, which makes the policy choice.

Under the second option, the regulator selects stakeholders who represent the affected interests and organizes them as an advisory group. In these cases, the important issues are the criteria for inclusion and the role of those selected. Both of these options keep participation within manageable bounds. Notice, however, how they differ. The former encourages dialogue and learning to facilitate agreement on the way forward, even if that ultimately proves impossible. The latter is closer to a bargaining session between groups with an interest in the outcome, although learning and dialogue can occur there as well.

Third, the call for public input can be open-ended, as it is under the notice-and-comment provisions of the US Administrative Procedure Act. The government may then face the possible influx of thousands of submissions and must decide how to handle the volume. Are public hearings required, and should the agency hold them throughout the country? How much preparatory work should occur, involving preliminary input from organized stakeholders and technical experts? Should the agency actively seek to encourage participation and provide public resources for underfunded groups and individuals? What time limits should apply, and should comments be publicly posted so others can respond? Is a second round of comments required if the agency revises its proposed rule in response to comments?

Each variant responds in a different way to the infeasibility of involving the mass public in making public choices. In the first two, the state creates a forum for public debate. In the third, the process forces public officials to accept public input, deliberate on what they have learned, and provide public reasons for their policy choices.

Civic Forums or Mini-publics

Civic forums and mini-publics involve small groups of citizens in deliberations over policy. Similar efforts to promote deliberative democracy go by different labels, such as citizen assemblies, citizen juries, participatory governance, deliberative polls, and consensus conferences.[27] In many versions, those who deliberate are chosen through stratified random sampling to obtain a group that roughly reflects the polity's major demographic categories.[28] However, not all efforts have been so careful about identifying participants.

One variant, called a Deliberative Poll, brings together a stratified random sample of the relevant population to deliberate over policy options for several days. The group is informed by experts and politicians, and engages in interpersonal debate and discussion. The participants are provided with information as part of the process itself, a feature that increases the cost of Deliberative Polls, even as it makes them more egalitarian. The process does not necessarily produce policy proposals; rather, in an exit poll participants express informed opinions on the issues under debate. It is up to the political actors to justify their choices in light of the poll's results or to ignore it in favor of other factors, including the voices of uninformed citizens. In some applications, the relevant public body or ministry agrees to abide by the options supported by a majority of the participants.

Other mini-publics or civic forums aim to produce policy recommendations that are submitted to the government. Mini-publics have rarely been relied on to make policy on their own. Nevertheless, they may serve important political functions—namely, informing public debate, "market testing," policy legitimation, constituency-building, and popular oversight. Proponents argue that structured facilitation can address forms of bias, leading to improved decision-making[29] and promoting civic and social learning.[30] There is, however, some ambiguity about who is doing the learning. Are officials learning more about public concerns, or are citizens learning enough about a proposed policy to tolerate its negative consequences?

A review of civic forums by Christopher Karpowitz and Chad Raphael is realistic about what they can accomplish.[31] The authors highlight two normative values. The first is the equality of participants' involvement in the forum; the second is publicity of the results to help the larger public view the forum as a source of legitimacy for policy choices. Because some participants will be less active, depending on, say, education, income, or social class, the authors recommend that civic forums include subgroups or "enclaves" limited to citizens who might not participate actively in more representative forums. Their proposal is a compromise between the ideal of broad citizen dialogue and efforts to hear all views. It is tied to a tension between hearing from a broad range of views and using the forum to produce options that go beyond canvassing policy positions. In the extreme, if a representative forum does not engage in dialogue, a citizen survey would be an adequate substitute. The authors confront the possibility that subgroups or enclaves will produce greater divergence in overall opinions because like-minded individuals in each group debate the policy options. They provide some encouraging evidence linked to techniques that encourage open-mindedness and debate,[32] but the concern remains. The authors put special emphasis on publicity, both of the techniques used to select participants and organize the forums and of the results of the deliberation. Transparency is important to reduce the risk that the broader citizenry will reject the forum's conclusions, seeing them as biased, elitist, or uninformed. Experts and elites, however, may critique the conclusions as not reflective of the best available expertise.

Analysts diverge over whether deliberative processes can be effectively translated from local decisions to the macropolitical level. Several writers point to the apparent tradeoffs between participation and deliberation, arguing that deliberative methods function less well with larger and more diverse groups.[33] For these reasons, Archon Fung has suggested that "effective large-scale public sphere reforms may consist largely in the proliferation of better mini-publics rather than improving the one big public."[34] Other political scientists, however, argue that participation and deliberation go together. They suggest that "large-scale participation is not only feasible, but [can also be attained without forfeiting deliberation]."[35] Thamy Pogrebinschi highlights Brazil's National Public Policy Conferences as an effective, national-level forum with legislative impact.[36]

Some worry that the widespread use of mini-publics could reduce participation in broader democratic institutions and undermine their legitimacy. Critiquing James Fishkin's proposal for deliberative polls, Cristina Lafont writes that "[u]nless the political dialogue in the public sphere itself has some of the required deliberative characteristics [of the polling group] . . . then simply inserting the conclusions of mini-publics . . . would hardly lead to the intended positive effects."[37] One source of divergence is the voters' ignorance of the topics for debate, which may be exacerbated by the media, if it is under state control or, conversely, if it focuses on divisive, sensational stories to drive readership. Hence, some urge that mini-publics be used mainly for research purposes, or as a means to stimulate public debate.[38]

A fundamental problem with the analyses of civic forums and mini-publics is that there is no agreement on what "effectiveness" means. One overview, for example, argues that mini-publics should be judged in terms of both "the extent to which the micro-deliberative forum is inclusive and deliberative" and "the extent to which it contributes to the system's deliberative capacity."[39] These are both worthy goals, but the authors do not explain how to balance these possibly conflicting notions. A meta-analysis of citizens' deliberations at the local level in Germany assessed their policy impact and the participants' feelings of efficacy. The authors found that citizens were more likely to report both an impact on policy and an increase in their own efficacy if the government was committed to citizen participation, had some experience with such procedures, and provided staff assistance for the endeavor.[40]

That result is hardly surprising, but it highlights the fact that mini-publics need governmental support if they are to function well. Participants need resources to organize dialogues, and they must believe that public officials will take their efforts seriously. One study concludes with the platitude that "successful [public engagement] involves right people with right methods and goals, while leaving a big 'footprint' on research, innovation and society."[41]

Others have elaborated more complex frameworks for assessing participatory mechanisms. Archon Fung includes a long list of design choices that may require tradeoffs in practice. They are the degree of civic engagement, participation bias, the quality of deliberation, ability to inform officials, ability to inform citizens, development of democratic skills and socialization, official accountability, the justice of the public policy, the effectiveness of public action, and the extent of popular mobilization resulting from the institutional design.[42] Building on the work of Fung and others, David Beetham condenses these variables into three overarching categories: participatory range, deliberative mode, and degree of impact.[43] Brigette Geissel scrutinizes input-legitimacy, democratic process, effectiveness, and civic education.[44]

Civic forums are most likely to produce agreement if the participants are not too far apart to start with.[45] In a society without deep divisions, civic forums may simply reproduce the policy proposals already supported by elected representatives, so that the forum adds little to the political debate. For example, Denmark is "well known for its tradition of consensus-oriented decision making and direct engagement with citizens."[46] Consensus conferences to discuss specific policies are an accepted part of the policymaking process. Even in this best-case scenario, the impact is often hard to measure because the recommendations tend to be close to current policy.[47] In other words, the ordinary processes of Danish representative democracy appear to work quite well. Civic forums and mini-publics may appear most successful where they make the least difference to the outcome.

In the contrary case where organized political interests support policy choices that diverge from the outcome of a civic forum, the effort may be a waste of time. Thus, one assessment concluded that a citizens' conference organized by the French prime minister's office to discuss the regulation of genetically modified (GM) foods was "not integrated into the established structure in a way that would allow its process and recommendations to be taken seriously."[48] Both top bureaucrats and elected representatives were skeptical about the effort. The exercise was "used as a tool through which key policy makers (who apparently favored some weakening of limits on GM foods) thought they could produce an alternative representation of informed public opinion." In fact, the participants were better informed and more negative about GM foods than originally expected. Nevertheless, as in Denmark, the recommendations were not dramatically different from government policy.[49]

To some extent, the effort to evaluate the benefits of mini-publics and civic forums is a triumph of hope over experience. The techniques promise much to their advocates, but consulting a small, closed group, however cleverly chosen, will always be unrepresentative simply because that group has engaged in an intense effort to understand a particular issue and debate about it with others. Even James Fishkin's carefully structured Deliberative Polls, using stratified random samples, have this problem. Informed participants may change their views on the policies under debate, but the government still needs to convince the citizenry to accept the results as an input into policymaking. This can happen, but it is by no means a foregone conclusion. On a hopeful note, Fishkin and his associates report positive results on their website where Deliberative Polls did influence policy.[50]

To conclude this section, I outline two European efforts in Belgium and France. Each one illustrates the complex interactions between civic forums and established institutions of representative government. The first involves an ongoing effort to transform the political life of a small region; the second was a time-limited, nationwide effort to recommend policies for an issue of global importance.

The first, an experiment in citizen agenda-setting, is taking place in Eupen, the German-speaking region of Belgium. The initiative is funded by the regional government, including a small permanent secretariat. The nonprofit G1000, which has experience in deliberative democracy programs, is providing advice.[51] Eupen has a population of about 20,000, so its experience will not easily apply to larger polities, but it is worth examining. The regional government has set up two bodies, with members drawn by lot in a way that is representative of gender, age, education, and residence. The twenty-four members of the Citizens' Council hold office for eighteen months, with one-third rotating off every six months. They decide the topics for discussion. These are then passed on to Citizens' Assemblies, ad hoc groups of twenty-five to fifty people, also constituted by random selection.

They deliberate over three weekends on a specific topic and make policy recommendations that are passed on to the parliament by the Citizens' Council.[52] As with deliberative polls, the Citizens' Assemblies neither set their own agenda nor make policy themselves. Members receive information on the selected topic and mediators facilitate the discussion. Their work feeds into the institutions of representative government by providing input from ordinary citizens who have debated the issue before them. Once the Eupen program becomes established, members of the Council will be drawn randomly, not from the general population, but rather from those who have participated in a prior Assembly.

The Belgian experiment is described in a publication of the EU Committee of the Regions along with other efforts to promote citizen participation at the local, regional, and national levels.[53] Although these efforts are mostly designed to influence legislative deliberations, a few lessons stand out that are relevant to executive policymaking procedures. First, even if the process is organized by a civil-society organization, politicians must be supportive if it is to have an impact.[54] For administrative rulemaking, the key political actors are ministers, agency commissioners, and other top officials. Second, absent a generous outside funder, the government needs to provide financial and staff support. Third, participants should be chosen randomly in a way that reflects the demographic composition of the population. Fourth, the topics for discussion should be quite specific, and experts should provide information. Fifth, trained facilitators should keep the discussion focused on reaching a concrete policy recommendation within time limits. Sixth, the group's recommendations should be made public, and both participants and the public must learn how the government uses the committee's recommendations and how it deals with opposition from those not part of the group.

This list will not be easy to satisfy within the constraints of time and resources, but all its items seem necessary to produce a final product with a good chance of influencing policy. Nevertheless, the process can only produce incremental results; it cannot confront deeper problems of public accountability. By design, the procedure does not challenge the ultimate authority of elected representatives and government ministers. It does not deal with the overlap between different policy areas, for example, the tensions between job creation and environmental protection, or between poverty alleviation and infrastructure development. As Richard Youngs states, "civic deliberation implicitly gets framed as a tame, consensus-oriented, civilizing phenomenon, devoid of sharp, ideological power contestations." As he concludes, "[t]he challenge will be to design participation in a way that improves other forms of democratic accountability, rather than undermining or overshadowing them."[55]

Sometimes deliberations operate at a very high level of generality, such as the French Citizens' Assembly on Climate, mentioned in Chapter 3, that brought together a small, random sample of the population to propose solutions. The Assembly involved 150 citizens, representing a cross-section of the population who were briefed on the issues and deliberated over several weekends. After the group issued its report in 2020 with 149 recommendations, President Macron used executive orders to implement some of them, proposed related statutory initiatives, accepted some for future study, and rejected a few proposals outright.[56] He has followed the lead of the Citizens' Assembly by proposing to amend Article 1 of the Constitution to require France to guarantee the preservation of biodiversity and the environment and the struggle against climate change. Eventually, the amending language must be approved by a popular referendum of all voters, not just those who deliberated in the Assembly.[57]

The Citizens' Assembly is particularly interesting because, after presenting its recommendations to the government, its members did not disband but instead created a group called *Les 150* to advocate for government and EU action. Rather than diffusing the issue and taking pressure off the government, the process energized some of the participants to become deeply involved in implementation. A dozen members met with the French prime minister in the summer and fall, and participants made a presentation to the environment committee of the EU Parliament. They have not been content only to be an input into established political processes. Instead, they want to build on their newfound knowledge and their deliberative experience to claim legitimacy as political actors. The tension between a mini-public's recommendations and ordinary lawmaking processes is evident in the government's response to the 40 percent of the recommendations that would need to be transposed into legislation to take effect. The government argues that it cannot proceed without expert reports that calculate the economic, social, and environmental effects of each proposal, and it must verify that the proposed measures do not conflict with existing laws.[58]

An important question is whether these participatory techniques can assist executive policymaking activities under statutory delegations.

Statutory and constitutional texts limit the freedom of any administration. Within those parameters, systematic consultations could help in the promulgation of rules. The above list of requirements needs to be met, and even in the best cases, they are "mini-" publics whose recommendations need to be tested against broader political reality.

A fundamental difficulty lies at the heart of the debate over mini-publics. Some see them as the vanguard of a fundamental reorientation of the democratic landscape that would downplay the role of the legislature, the ballot box, and the bureaucracy. A second group, reflective of my view, defends the basic institutions of representative democracy but asks if mini-publics can further the ideals of such democracies. As Éric Buge argues, an invitation to engage in serious deliberation and discussion over policy options can further democratic values. He proposes that citizens should have the legal right to petition to initiate such convocations on particular themes. David Owen and Graham Smith argue: "The systemic question thus becomes one of the role of deliberation *within* democratic systems, rather than whether democratic systems are deliberative in nature. Relevant questions to pose to a democratic system would include: what is the appropriate place of deliberation within a given system and how can it be embedded, protected, and enhanced? What is the requisite balance between deliberation and other modes of interaction and coordination within a given democratic system?" If the issues are phrased in that way, deliberative mini-publics become one option to consider, given a background of representative democratic institutions, including elections, a legislature, political parties, bureaucracies, expert bodies, and organized groups.[59] A second option is participation centered on organized groups with an institutional history. I turn next to that possibility.

Stakeholder Groups

A public agency may limit participation to "stakeholders" and either choose the individual participants itself or ask the relevant groups to select them. In some countries, such as Germany, these processes arose from a model of labor-management relations that goes back to the nineteenth century—a model that has been copied in eastern Europe.[60] In other policy areas, the groups may include those with particular policy agendas, such as environmental organizations, as well as representatives of business, labor, and academia, along with public officials. Often the government agency itself determines which groups to invite.

Notice the sharply different concept of participation compared to a civic forum or mini-public. Here, dialogue among participants may produce agreement on a policy proposal or, at least, clarify areas of disagreement, but the goal is not so much to change minds as to come to a reasonable compromise in light of the positions and interests of the organizations involved. Sometimes the public agency is simply seeking information and support for its own preferred outcome.[61] There can be an inconsistency between a ministry's efforts to sell its preferred policy and efforts to design policy based, in part, on consultation.

Furthermore, in stakeholder negotiations there may be tensions between participants as members of the negotiating committee and as representatives of organized groups. A member of a stakeholder group who compromises too much with other members may be sharply criticized by the organization he or she is supposed to represent.

Studies of stakeholder groups suggest the difficulty of assuring constructive dialogue. For example, a German study of the siting of hazardous-waste facilities surveyed the participants and found that all believed they were weak relative to the other participants. Environmentalists saw themselves as powerless defenders of nature; nearby residents claimed to be disadvantaged victims. Others believed that the environmental advocates were hysterics unwilling to consider practical solutions. Representatives of the waste-disposal industry viewed themselves as weak but reasonable pragmatists; others claimed that industry was a powerful, profit-oriented degrader of the environment. If there are no feasible solutions where everyone gains relative to the status quo, negotiations may collapse because at least one stakeholder group is better off with no deal.[62]

Mark Reed reviews some of the experiences with stakeholder participation in environmental management in the US, supporting such efforts on grounds of "efficiency" compared with engaging the wider public.[63] The processes that he reviewed were mostly site-specific and had widely varying results. The outcomes depended, in part, upon differing definitions of "success," as well as on how the process operated in practice. Reed developed an eightfold list of best practices. The selection of participants is obviously key. In some cases, he recommends that the selection itself be done through a participatory process. One sees an infinite regress looming. Other recommendations involve clarity about goals, education in technical matters, and trained facilitators—all attempts to manage and contain the process.

Reed recommends early and ongoing stakeholder involvement, a proposal that might clash with the need to educate participants.[64] These recommendations mostly echo those voiced by supporters of mini-publics. The difference is that participants in mini-publics reflect the polity's demographics, and they do not consult with others of their "type" before participating.

Given the often fraught relationships between individual participants in stakeholder advisory panels and the groups they represent, organizers must be sure that compromise solutions are actually in the choice set and that members engage in ongoing interactions with their sponsoring organizations to communicate new knowledge and vet the tradeoffs required. Stakeholder groups often do not make decisions themselves but rather highlight areas of both agreement and disagreement so that officials can balance them in making a choice.

For example, France has carried out several organized large-scale *concertations* with stakeholders other than political parties, as discussed in Chapter 3. Called Grenelles or états généraux, they produce legislative proposals, not secondary norms, but the process could cover either.[65] The working groups include stakeholder representatives of business, labor, and the environmental community.[66] Working-group proposals are discussed in public meetings, followed by roundtables with representatives of the same groups. The traditional hierarchy of actors often reappears in the debate because some actors are more experienced and knowledgeable than others.[67] The debates are organized at the discretion of the government; they create no legal rights and are not subject to judicial review.[68] Another French example occurred at the regional level. The Poitou-Charentes region organized a stakeholder process involving school budgets; those invited were students, teachers, other staff, and parents. People participated as individuals, not necessarily as designated spokespeople for their group, but the composition of the group reflected those with a stake in the outcome. After debate, the process concluded with a vote on a range of options to be implemented by the school board. Stakeholder debates differ significantly from the Citizens' Assembly for Climate, whose invited participants reflected the country's demographics, not organized advocacy groups.

Combining Mini-Publics and Stakeholders

Given the strengths and weaknesses of stakeholder groups and mini-publics, perhaps policymakers can combine them to produce a superior model.

Unfortunately, such a merger is not easy to accomplish. To take just one example, consider German efforts to use public input to develop a climate policy in 2016. A "participation-and-dialogue" process fed into the government's Climate Action Plan 2050 that the coalition government approved on November 11, 2016, on the eve of the UN Global Climate Conference in Marrakesh, Morocco.[69] The Environmental Ministry called it a "reversed" process because the ministry did not produce a draft for comment.[70] Rather, "stakeholders and citizen workshops were to suggest climate protection measures that would then be consolidated into the Climate Action Plan by the ministry." The stakeholders were local communities, federal states, associations from industry and the environmental community, and citizens. Ministry officials consolidated the 400 proposals into "measures set 1.0." Each stakeholder group had a representative on a delegates' committee that produced "measures set 2.0." In November 2015, "472 randomly chosen citizens in five German cities participated in workshops" that made nineteen further proposals, with twelve citizens added to the delegates' committee. The groups and the twelve citizens then voted on the measures, leading to "measures set 3.0" that was subject to a final review by the delegates' committee. The report states that "then the political process began"—as if the prior exercise had been apolitical, which it obviously was not. The language, however, echoes the German view of the chain of political legitimacy discussed above. "Politics" here implies the intervention of officials who are part of the chain that goes through the Bundestag to the voters.

Eventually, the German Environmental Ministry published a draft plan that provided a "(non-exhaustive) list"—essentially a wish-list. It included very general proposals, with no specifics or sense of priorities and no explicit tradeoffs. The few specifics, such as coal exit, speed limits on the highways, and road tolls, were very controversial. The participants generally "welcomed" the general idea of a long-term framework, but the process was not set up to produce such a framework. One has to sympathize with the German industry associations that wrote to the Environmental Minister criticizing the process as "highly complex, lacking transparency, and prone to be instrumentalized." Of course, those groups had their own interests in limiting the stringency of the plan, but the basic point is that open-ended public consultations can put the major issues on the table for debate, but they are poor forums for negotiating concrete policies and making practical tradeoffs.

After the Environmental Ministry issued its draft, the political negotiations began with deep involvement of the Economics Ministry and industry.[71] The final plan signed on November 11, 2016, accommodated some of the demands of the ministry; environmental groups criticized it for lacking teeth. Opposition from business was tempered by statements from the government that greenhouse gas targets will "be subject to a comprehensive impact assessment."[72] In other words, the plan allowed Germany to go to the Marrakesh meeting with something in hand, but the effort was not a success either of public participation or of technocratic policymaking. Rather, it was essentially a political compromise, with little concrete effect.

Neither citizen forums nor stakeholder negotiations are an adequate response to demands for public participation in executive-branch policymaking. Each one taken alone or in combination can inform executive policy deliberations, but they ought not to be the only route to public input. The third type of participation, represented by US notice-and-comment rulemaking, is not a complete response either, but it does counteract some of the weaknesses of the other options.

Open-ended Notice and Comment

Consider a third type of participation—US-style notice-and-comment rulemaking. Here, deliberation occurs inside cabinet departments and agencies in light of input from a wide range of outsiders. The government agency must inform the public about its plans, hold hearings where anyone can submit a statement, and provide public reasons for the final policy choice that take account of the comments received. The agency cannot filter who may participate, thus minimizing the chance of an echo chamber in which the agency only hears from those who support its proposals. Agency deliberations must consider the probity of the submitted material. It need not respond to all comments, but only to those of "cogent materiality" to the technical and policy issues raised by the rulemaking.[73] The hearing produces not just factual material, but also policy arguments from outside government that must be considered as the agency deliberates over the text of the final rule.

As we saw in Chapter 3, the notice-and-comment process is foundational to American rulemaking. The US Administrative Procedure Act requires that process for a large share of rules with the force of law. Organized groups representing business, labor, public-interest causes, and nonfederal governments view participation as an important part of their strategy to influence public policymaking. Participation involves the submission of written comments and testimony at oral hearings. Less transparent informal contacts occur before the publication of a proposed rule in the Federal Register.[74] Nevertheless, whatever occurs out of public view, the agency must articulate public reasons for its policy response based on the statute, public comments, and its own analysis of the problem.

The process can be costly and time-consuming for agencies and for participants. In the United States, a major rulemaking at the Environmental Protection Agency averages almost three years and requires many hours of input from bureaucrats, outside experts, and interest groups.[75] As an extreme case, the Occupational Safety and Health Administration (OSHA) proposed a rule limiting the use of beryllium in 1975, but the agency issued the final rule only in 2016, near the end of the Obama administration, after a compromise between unions and employers. The Trump administration sought to weaken the rule just as it was to go into effect.[76] In addition, many rules face court challenges before they are enforced, introducing further delay.

If a rulemaking generates public concern, the number of comments can be very large. When the Forest Service was considering a rule on roadless areas in national forests, it received over 1 million comments.[77] Most, however, were form letters and could be processed quite easily; they expressed opinions but did not need to be treated as equally weighted votes. The possibility of commenting on-line facilitates massive letter-writing campaigns and can open the door to the posting of fake comments. In 2017 the Federal Communications Commission (FCC) invited comments on a proposal to weaken the net-neutrality rule, which requires that any customer should be able to access any internet content at the same speed on any device.[78] The principle would prevent a broadband provider from prioritizing access of an affiliated streaming service or restricting the access of other streaming services. Advocates for net neutrality argue that it is necessary to prevent discrimination and consumer harm. Opponents claim that it would reduce incentives for investment and ultimately harm consumers.[79] On-line participants or “netizens” posted over 22 million comments on the proposed rule, of which an estimated 9.5 million were fake. Studies located mass duplication of posts and stolen identities.[80]

The flood of comments in contested cases highlights that the process is not a referendum on the proposed rule, but rather ought to be a source of thoughtful input that the agency considers before issuing the rule. Agencies need to sort through the comments to determine which ones raise important issues and to establish protocols for dealing with massive comment volumes without ignoring valid public concerns. A first step would be stronger norms of transparency. In the case of the net-neutrality rulemaking, the FCC resisted media requests for a record of the comments, leading to lawsuits under the Freedom of Information Act. In one such case, Judge Lorna Schofield of the Southern District Court of New York wrote:

> If genuine public comment is drowned out by a fraudulent facsimile, then the notice-and-comment process has failed. Disclosing the requested data in this case informs the public understanding of the operations and activities of government in two ways—at the micro level with regard to the integrity of the FCC's repeal of the particular net neutrality rules at issue, and at the macro level with regard to the vulnerability of agency rulemaking in general.[81]

Over and above the simple logistics of managing the open-ended process, the reasons for long delays are unclear. One study of 150 Environmental Protection Agency rules asked if the elapsed time was associated with the number of internal participants and the number of comments. Surprisingly, neither had a positive impact, and the number of internal participants even had a small negative impact—the greater the number of such participants, the shorter the elapsed time. The authors suggest that rulemaking is speeded along by procedures that are more inclusive.[82] Delay may be strategic and may depend upon whether the agency or the White House wants to hold up resolution of an issue and whether members of Congress try to keep the issue from being decided. To examine this question, one would need to compare elapsed time with the hours of staff time spent on particular regulations. The beryllium rulemaking, for example, seems to have been strung out by manufacturers of the product, not by government insiders. Conversely, when an administration risks losing the White House in an oncoming election, it may pressure cabinet departments and agencies to rush rulemakings to conclusion.[83]

Some rulemakings only attract the interest of a few groups. Marissa Martino Golden's review of eleven dockets covered rules that attracted from one to 268 comments.[84] Examination of a random sample of forty-two rulemakings found that the median number of comments was about thirty.[85] Susan Webb Yackee studied thirty-six US Department of Transportation

(DOT) "completed actions" between 2002 and 2005, including final rules and those that were withdrawn.[86] DOT received 2,857 public comments over all the stages of rulemaking, ranging from three to 387 per rule. Based on this research, agencies do not seem to be overwhelmed with comments except in a few especially controversial cases.

Jason Webb Yackee and Susan Webb Yackee studied all federal rulemaking agencies between 1983 and 2006 and all rulemakings in the US Department of the Interior between 1950 and 1999. Their results largely disconfirm the claim of excessive delay, although the time to issuance of rules has increased over time, at least in some agencies. However, they were unable to distinguish between unjustified delays and those that resulted from complexity and public interest in the topics.[87]

Both career bureaucrats and political officials may resist increased participation and transparency on the grounds that they threaten to delay action and to distort choices. Furthermore, the very time and trouble of participation may discourage advocates and citizens with little time and money and weak organizational capacities.[88] Open, participatory processes are broadly acceptable to those who use them,[89] but little hard evidence exists on their marginal impact, either on perceptions of democratic legitimacy or on the quality of substantive policy.

More fundamental than the time and trouble of notice-and-comment rulemaking is the claim that business interests have a disproportionate effect on the outcome. Although the hearings must be open to all, not limited to a closed set of stakeholders, US agencies need not finance input from impecunious groups and need not actively seek out a wide range of voices. They can often avoid the informal rulemaking process entirely by using exempt routes to the same result. Notice-and-comment rulemaking works best when all those affected are able to participate. If a policy will have effects far into the future or if the costs fall on a small fraction of the population who cannot be individually identified ex ante, however, then even an open-ended hearing will miss many of those affected. Concentrated input from industry may not be balanced by well-informed input from workers, nearby residents, consumers, and ordinary citizens. That critique is not an argument for abandoning a procedure that, at least, provides broad access along with transparency and a public record. Rulemaking in most other polities is much less transparent to the public. Nevertheless, the material presented to a US agency in comments may contain biases that public officials have an obligation to counteract in writing their rules. Public officials ought to regulate in the public interest, whatever the biases in the comment process.

The evidence shows heavy business involvement. Golden's study of rulemaking dockets at the EPA, the National Highway Traffic Safety Administration (NHTSA), and the Department of Housing and Urban Development (HUD) found that comments were predominately submitted by business.[90] Two studies by Cornelius Kerwin and by Kay Lehman Schlozman and John T. Tierney documented the heavy participation of Washington-based organizations in rulemaking processes.[91] According to Schlozman and Tierney, these organizations predominantly represent business interests in both their number and their financial resources. They generally also have other contacts with the executive and can advise agencies as they prepare for rulemakings. Jason Webb Yackee and Susan Webb Yackee show that business participates more actively than other interests overall, and that it affects the content of rules when it does.[92] In Europe, Athanasios Psygkas's study of consultations organized by telecoms regulators between 2006 and 2011 reports high industry participation: 77 percent of the comments in France, 91 percent in Greece, and 49 percent in the UK.[93]

Nevertheless, public-interest groups can have an influence if they submit comments.[94] Susan Webb Yackee documents the importance of such groups, along with state governments and business, in DOT hearings, and Golden found that, for HUD rulemakings, most comments were from government agencies, public-interest groups, and citizen advocacy groups.[95] Interagency differences presumably arose because the HUD and DOT rules affect state and local governments and have fewer direct effects on business.

Government departments should exercise independent judgment, using comments as inputs into balanced assessments of the policy options. Wesley A. Magat, Alan J. Krupnick, and Winston Harrington studied EPA rulemakings that determined the "best practical technology currently available" for controlling water pollution on an industry-by-industry basis.[96] At least for their sample time period, the results were encouraging about the ability of EPA officials to resist pressure from regulated industry. Comments that supported weaker standards did not tend to produce weaker standards, and industries with more firms out of compliance with proposed rules did not get weaker standards.[97]

Well-organized industry groups with a consistent message are often able to influence outcomes in their favor.[98] If such groups have a financial advantage, then groups that seek to counter the impact of industry ought to be subsidized to provide input. If civil-society groups do get their message across, they can have an effect. For example, a study of Forest Service roadless areas rulemaking processes during the Clinton administration found that the notice-and-comment period produced modifications in the rule that responded to some comments from those favoring a strong rule.[99] Furthermore, if the draft rule is overtly biased toward the regulated industry, the publicity attendant on the process could provide unfavorable public relations for the agency. This concern will feed back to the agency and affect its willingness to buckle to interest-group pressure from any direction.

Two researchers evaluated public participation in over 200 environmental decisions covering federal, state, local, and regional processes during a thirty-year period.[100] Their data, however, only include thirteen regulation and standard-setting cases, mostly regulatory negotiations. The other cases concern "policy-development cases," most with a limited geographical focus and dealing with implementation in individual cases. The authors conclude that involving the public "not only frequently produces decisions that are responsive to public values and substantially robust, but it also helps to resolve conflict, build trust, and educate and inform the public about the environment."[101] The cases ranked highly by the participants in terms of process also scored highly on measures of success, holding other factors constant. However, the one-third counted as successes turned out on further examination to have worked well either because some particularly divisive interests were kept off the table, or because controversial potential participants were excluded.[102]

Some proposed rules change very little after the end of the comment period.[103] One reason for this is that groups seek access to the agency before the proposed rule is published in the Federal Register. Those contacts are generally less well documented than submissions made during the APA comment period. However, empirical studies concerning air toxics regulation, DOT rules, and the Dodd-Frank Act's "Volcker Rule," which affects financial institutions, provide selective evidence. They show that during pre-APA processes, substantive comments and meetings mainly involved representatives of the regulated industries. Public comments mostly consisted of form-letter campaigns and general expressions of sentiment, without detailed analysis of the technical issues. The same biases exist both before and after the publication of an APA Notice of Proposed Rulemaking.

However, other factors constrained the bias. The statute regulating air toxics includes multiple deadlines for the issuance of rules. Hence, many rulemakings were begun in response to lawsuits by environmental groups that forced the agency's hand when it missed deadlines. The issuance of regulations implementing the Volcker Rule was subject to ongoing oversight by the two senators most involved in its inclusion in the Dodd-Frank Act.[104]

If an agency has locked itself into a particular regulatory approach before the APA process begins, its rigidity can undermine the democratic legitimacy of the subsequent open-ended comment period. Yet, the negative impact of this behavior is limited by the requirement that the agency must be open to other input during the APA process and must publish a statement of reasons when it issues the rule. If it cannot justify its actions, it risks both a loss of public legitimacy and an unfavorable ruling by the courts.

The American experience suggests that the most important problems with participation in rulemaking are delay, bias, irrelevance, displacement to other methods, and curbs on agency implementation. Case studies provide examples of all these problems, but they are mostly the result of poorly designed and biased procedures, not participation per se. Some delay is the inevitable result of expanded participation. Agencies must take the time and trouble to consult. Nevertheless, the extremely long time between initiation and final rules in the US seems to be driven more by strategic considerations than by the cost of the process per se. Still, displacement of agency activity to nonbinding guidelines and to implementation through the adjudication of individual cases occurs, especially if agencies seek to avoid oversight by the Executive Office of the President, which reviews major rules.[105]

In any case, the problem of displacement can be overcome if the legislature includes rulemaking requirements in statutes with deadlines and if the courts do not add incremental demands. If Congress uses procedural hurdles to undermine a statute's stated purposes, this is a special case of narrow interests overcoming broader public goals. For example, the US Toxic Substances Control Act (TSCA) imposed requirements on the Environmental Protection Agency that limited its ability to regulate. Procedural requirements imposed by judicial interpretations of the act further constrained EPA regulatory activity.[106] The weaknesses of the TSCA were partly overcome by an act passed in 2016,[107] but it remains to be seen how implementation will proceed under the Biden administration that took office in 2021.

In a well-functioning notice-and-comment rulemaking, the proposed rule printed in the Federal Register takes account of the forthcoming public-participation process. Even if officials consult with a biased selection of interest groups beforehand, they need to consider how their proposals will be greeted by the public and the media when they are publicly posted in the Federal Register and, later, when they are subject to judicial review. Even if the text of a rule is little changed between the proposed and final texts, that result does not imply that the rulemaking process was irrelevant. Agency officials anticipate that their proposed rules will face public and interest-group scrutiny and try to anticipate objections ex ante. The possibility of subsequent judicial challenges by interested groups on all sides feeds back to the drafting of the initial proposal.[108]

Furthermore, if an agency substantially revises a rule as a result of APA procedures, it may need to organize a second comment period. If the amended rule takes a fundamentally different regulatory approach from the original draft, the courts may require such a process.[109] The aim is not to introduce excessive delay but rather to tap into the expertise, interests, and sentiments of those outside government to produce better rules.

Notice-and-comment rulemaking is quite different from mini-publics that require a few members of the public to engage in focused debate to produce a policy proposal. The informal rulemaking process recognizes the democratic pedigree of statutes but appreciates their limitations as governments put them into effect. Public officials, both political appointees and bureaucrats, manage the notice-and-comment process under delegated statutory and constitutional powers. However, the chain of legitimacy is an insufficient guide. Statutory language may be vague and self-contradictory, and with the passage of time, the factual situation may change. Hence, those who make executive rules must be open to contemporary input from outside government and must explain how promulgated rules have taken that material into account. The reasons given depend, in part, upon expertise and on evidence of a policy's effects on individuals and firms. Over and above these factual matters, public comments can emphasize the values that citizens want to see reflected in the final rule. Rulemakers ought to acknowledge these normative expressions of concern and to explain how they have been taken into account or rejected as inconsistent with the statutory mandate.

Public Participation in Practice and in Principle

Participation in executive policymaking can find facts, seek consensus on a policy recommendation, or enhance the representative character of democracy. Concentrating on the last category, there are many alternative ways to incorporate public input—civic forums, stakeholder groups, and open notice-and-comment processes. Each faces distinct difficulties in furthering democratic values. Advocates of civic forums and mini-publics must justify their composition and deliberative procedures as well as their link to established public-sector institutions. Stakeholder groups must avoid an overly narrow range of membership and provide a balanced forum for debate. Open-ended hearings must confront the diffuse nature of participation and seek to ensure a good balance of opinion.

In the cases that I consider, the ultimate policy choices are in the hands of politically accountable officials. Even though the chain of legitimacy remains in the background, public officials ought to assess public input and balance the comments from the participants with information about the benefits and costs of a rule. Structuring public participation as a constructive aspect of executive-branch policymaking is a key aspect of democratic accountability, but it is often conflated with fights over the allocation of benefits and costs that have a zero-sum character—controversies that are difficult to resolve through reasoned discussion.

Debates over the role of the public need to consider at what stage in the process participation occurs. Are policy options still open, or have most routes been closed so that the decision is essentially a zero-sum game about dividing up benefits and costs or making marginal tweaks? Participatory processes ought to feed into administrative policy decisions that balance overall benefits and costs against their distribution across the population. Policy choices can correct market failures, improve the fairness of the distribution of income and social goods, or explore the content and extent of rights. Debates should encourage participants to rely on principled expressions of values, not on their own individual gains and losses. Narrow self-interest will remain, and principled discourse will not be easy to produce. However, if the goal of a process is to structure a general policy, then encouraging debate over public values should be a key aspect of participatory procedures.[110]

Some claim that public participation in rulemaking is undemocratic because it risks producing policies that flout the will of the legislative majority or of the majority of the electorate. Only a small subset of the population will participate in hearings or post comments, and it is likely to be a biased sample. Furthermore, if the process welcomes input from organized groups—industry associations, large firms, labor unions, professional associations, civil-society advocacy groups—their input may be similarly unbalanced. This has led some to argue against any outside participation in executive or agency policymaking. To them, either executive rulemaking itself should be sharply limited, or career bureaucrats should issue rules using expert advice to design and justify rules. This distrust of outside participation fails to recognize that participatory procedures can improve the democratic legitimacy of the state and of other agencies and bodies that make policy. One can accept the importance of competent and up-to-date technical information without concluding that public input will distort the ultimate policy choices. Those critics who find rulemaking undemocratic and who would require greater detail and specificity in statutes are either opponents of the modern regulatory/welfare state or else idealize the capacity of the legislature. An insistence on detailed statutes would imply either that some issues could not be tackled in any realistic manner or that the statutes that do result are unlikely to incorporate technocratic expertise and will need constant updating.

The ideal of majority rule is a central challenge to public involvement beyond the ballot box. The literature is conflicted over whether participatory processes perfect majority rule or dilute and supersede it.[111] Drawing on both specialized expertise and citizen input can produce policy choices that would not obtain majority support in a referendum. But majority rule ought not to be a litmus test for the acceptable implementation of statutory mandates by the executive. The majority may be very poorly informed—for example, in voting on referenda couched in misleading and over-simplified language. Merely providing better public information to voters is insufficient. Collective-action and free-rider problems imply that individuals have little incentive to learn about complex policy issues. Yet, even so, they should have a way to express their concerns and to be sure that officials will take their views into account, not just as data but also as reflections of citizens' concerns and values. That does not mean that public opinion ought to determine policy, but rather that there should be opportunities for the public to provide input and engage in debate. The public must be given reasoned, public explanations for the policy choices made in their name by the executive and the agencies.[112]

How do my case-study countries stack up in providing policymaking accountability? The US has the longest experience with public consultation in the rulemaking process. The UK, Germany, and France are moving toward a greater role for public input into executive or agency decisions, in some cases with EU support.

As Chapter 3 demonstrated, the legal status of public participation is more firmly established in the US than in the other countries. The notice-and-comment procedure embodied in the APA, however, gives no special status to cause-based groups, and it only requires rulemaking bodies to publish their draft rules, hold open-ended hearings, and provide reasons when they issue a rule. The administration need not ensure broad input through outreach or funding for intervenors. The law treats business interests and not-for-profit advocacy groups with formal equality. Such nominal equality favors wealthy organized interests, primarily in the business community, although in some regulatory areas, groups such as labor unions and advocacy groups provide an important counterweight. Both presidents and supporters of the unitary executive theory downplay and undermine the independent role of rulemaking in departments and agencies. The powerful Executive Office of the President can undermine agency-level notice-and-comment procedures that further public involvement and transparency.[113]

In the US, some justify the growth of presidential power over policymaking by arguing for the political legitimacy of the president as the directly elected representative of popular will. That argument has the same weakness as the claim that parliamentary sovereignty makes public participation in government rulemaking undemocratic. In both cases, votes for an individual or a party are only roughly related to the specific policy choices that the government or an agency must make in putting a statute into effect. Vote totals are unlikely to translate easily into particular policy choices for two reasons: first, many issues were not salient at election time, and second, even if they are part of the overall electoral program, they need to be debated in the context of concrete policy choices based on both facts and values. Too great a power grab by the president risks undermining public debate. Although the APA notice-and-comment process is imperfect, the response should be to improve the process and enhance the public accountability of government departments and agencies, not to undermine the values that it expresses.

Turning to the other cases, the UK, Germany, and France have no general statutory requirements that govern the procedures used to promulgate rules with the force of law (see Chapter 3). All of them recognize the distinction between such rules and others, called, for example, guidelines, internal ordinances, and memoranda, that have considerable practical effect but no legal authority. The general resistance to binding legal requirements for notice-and comment procedures arises from the political nature of rules with the force of law. Some describe them, like statutes, as falling outside of administrative law because they are in the realm of politics. This leaves them in a no-law zone. Although UK statutory instruments must usually be approved by Parliament, approval is generally pro forma, a result to be expected in a parliamentary system if the government has a governing majority. Even during the period of coalition government before the Tory electoral victory in December 2019, SIs related to Brexit were approved by Parliament with little debate. In Germany the Upper House does sometimes raise objections to government rules that apply to the German states, but the reasons usually relate to financial and bureaucratic burdens, not policy differences.[114] In France, the Conseil d'État reviews rules with the force of law as well as draft statutes proposed by the government. Although its reports are not generally public, the existing evidence suggests that review mainly focuses on general legal principles and drafting issues.

All three European countries mandate consultations in some cases, but the emphasis is on major infrastructure projects and local-government planning, not national-government rules. Nevertheless, these mandates recognize that consultation can increase the public acceptance of both projects and plans. Germany's planning approval procedures (*Planfeststellungsverfahren*) include a consultation process for major infrastructure projects. In spite of laws passed to speed up project approvals after German reunification, consultation remains an important aspect of infrastructure project approvals and local-government planning.[115] The UK has statutory requirements for consultation involving major projects, such as a third runway at Heathrow, a high-speed train, and a new highway. The planners consult the local residents affected by these projects, but broad civil-society groups also participate that voice public-policy objections, not based on their members' individualized harm. France has similar consultation requirements, ranging from the traditional inquest for local projects to consultations organized by the National Commission for Public Debate at the regional level for projects such as rail lines and regional water supply. Several national-level policy debates have focused on the regulation of contested issues, such as climate-change policy that can feed into both statutory drafts as well as decrees and ordinances.[116]

Germany and France are also subject to the procedural framework of the Treaty of Lisbon of the European Union. Applied to the EU's own procedures, Article 8b states:

> 1. The institutions shall, by appropriate means, give citizens and representative associations the opportunity to make known and publicly exchange their views in all areas of Union action. 2. The institutions shall maintain an open, transparent and regular dialogue with representative associations and civil society. 3. The European Commission shall carry out broad consultations with parties concerned in order to ensure that the Union's actions are coherent and transparent.[117]

The European Parliament and the Commission carry out "consultation and dialogue with civil society representatives, including ad hoc and online consultations, public hearings, and institutionalized consultations through advisory committees and business test panels."[118] The EU focuses on stakeholders and concerned interests, leading to "a form of inclusive corporatism" or "restrictive interest group pluralism."[119] The efforts are neither mini-publics nor US-style notice-and-comment procedures.

The results of the EU's efforts appear to be limited. An assessment in 2008–2009 by Harvard's Kennedy School of Government found that the EU's European Citizens' Consultations for Tomorrow's Europe had not enhanced the legitimacy of EU institutions.[120] A 2013 volume, *Is Europe Listening to Us?*, found that various EU participatory mechanisms had enhanced the "civic potential" of participants but had little impact on the political process.[121] An EU-funded project, "Public Engagement Innovations for Horizon 2020," supports innovative public-engagement strategies for research and innovation.[122] As the European Commission becomes more open to public input, its actions may influence member states. At least in the area of telecoms regulation, the EU has been ahead of the member states, and, according to Psygkas, it has induced them to include more public participation in the regulatory procedures for privatized public utilities.[123]

As discussed in Chapter 3, the environmental area is at the forefront of the push for public participation and consultation in Europe. Under the Aarhus Convention, the European Union has spurred this activity with directives that require member states to prepare environmental impact assessments (EIAs) for projects and strategic environmental assessments (SEAs) for plans and programs that include public consultations.[124] The procedures must be open to both individuals and environmental organizations. The convention and EU directives also give such groups access to the national courts to enforce these requirements. France added a Charter for the Environment to its Constitution when it ratified Aarhus, and its Constitutional Council has given its participation rights binding force. Germany has an environmental clause in its Basic Law (art. 20a). Although not in the list of fundamental rights, the clause states: "Mindful of its responsibility towards future generations, the state shall protect the natural foundations of life and animals by legislation and, in accordance with law and justice, by executive, and judicial actions, all within the framework of the constitutional order." In light of this provision, a statute gives recognized environmental groups access to the courts to enforce procedural requirements.

Conclusions: Guidelines for Democracies

Implementing workable participatory processes in executive policymaking is not an easy task. Nevertheless, I conclude with some guidelines for representative democracies that draw on the experiences outlined earlier in the chapter.

First, participatory processes ought to make genuine judgments on the merits of policies, not just propose alternative ways to distribute benefits and costs. This implies that public agencies need to help participants learn about the pros and cons of various options, and the participants themselves must come to the table willing to engage in debate. The government should not be a gatekeeper that decides who may contribute, but it has an obligation to prepare material for public distribution that is understandable by citizens. In the US, the required notices published in the Federal Register often do not satisfy that requirement. Some independent groups provide this service, but it ought to be a public responsibility.

Second, consultation techniques that are close to the corporatist or stakeholder model may not reflect broad public concerns. If only a fixed number of organized interests meet around a table to discuss a policy topic, there are several risks. As shown in Hungary and Poland after the transition from socialism,[125] membership may be frozen at a point in time with participants that do not reflect changing conditions. In addition, each group may view participation as a technique for getting a larger share of the benefits for its constituents, not as an opportunity to reflect more deeply on the social value of the policy.

An open-ended opportunity to express views, as under the US notice-and-comment process, avoids that second group of problems. However, it may produce an overwhelming number of comments from a biased sample. Hearings and web portals may not be sites of genuine debate and dialogue. Hence, *third*, the bureaucracy should review written comments, hold hearings, and incorporate public input without accepting it uncritically. The public administration needs to have the resources to manage public responses without simply adding up the number of comments pro and con.

Fourth, the limits of open-ended notice-and-comment procedures suggest the value of complementing these processes with civic forums or mini-publics, where a sample of informed citizens discusses particular policies, without having the legal authority to set policy. Such processes require a commitment of public funds and staff; hence, they will not be feasible in all polities or for all policy choices, but they should be an option. The ultimate responsibility for making policy under statutory delegations must remain with civil servants and political appointees, informed not only by deliberating citizens but also by experts and by those who report their own benefits or costs.

Fifth, to be consistent with democratic values, officials must give public reasons for their choices and submit to limited judicial review. In justifying its rules, the regulatory body needs to explain how it incorporated public input, although it need not accept all the advice it receives.

Public officials in the executive have delegated authority to make the policy choices under substantive statutes. In exercising their discretion, officials ought to take public input into account, not just in elections, but also as part of the policymaking process. Such procedures help further democratic values. Although criticisms of the notice-and-comment process in the US need to be addressed, the process does comply with two basic principles: first, an obligation to accept comments from anyone, not just from experts or selected stakeholders; and second, public justification of executive-branch policy decisions. Neither expert determinations nor surveys and focus groups are sufficient. Civic forums can help focus the policy debate by bringing in a cross-section of well-informed voices, but they should not replace more open-ended options. The goal of the administration should extend beyond what people want as "customers" or "consumers" of state services. Rather, policymakers ought to encourage individuals and groups to debate the merits of programs and proposed regulations as citizens, not just as economically self-interested individuals.

7. *The Varieties of Judicial Review*

Judicial review of policymaking procedures in the public administration has been the subject of ongoing controversy for generations. Scholars and judges, politicians and political activists have advocated and analyzed a broad variety of options—ranging from aggressive judicial activism to pervasive restraint. Within the legal community, a court-centered perspective has dominated the debate.

I reject that focus. Instead, my goal is to connect judicial review of executive policymaking with the underlying differences between political and legal regimes. Anchored in comparative politics, my approach asks how the judiciaries in the US, the UK, Germany, and France have confronted the problem of justifying executive-branch rulemaking and taken steps to fill the legitimacy gap. The United States provides the most notable example. Its Administrative Procedure Act requires rulemaking bureaucracies to provide public notice of proposed rules, hold open-ended hearings, and accompany final rules with a public and reasoned justification before they gain legal force. I have already argued that this system satisfies fundamental principles of political accountability, but the impact of these procedures arguably would have been much less pronounced without judicial checks on exercises of delegated authority.

Although the steps taken by executive decision-makers in my other case-study countries are modest by comparison, each has moved some way down the path of political accountability. Judicial review of these bureaucratic efforts has become part of the effort to reconcile executive rulemaking with democratic accountability.

In short, different democratic systems respond differently to the problem of political accountability, and these responses shape the judicial role in the legitimation process. Rather than a one-size-fits-all approach, the challenge is to develop a regime-based, comparative approach—not only in my four countries, but on a global basis.

As I shall suggest, a number of important developments in each of my cases have reshaped the role of the judiciary—for good and for ill—as a monitor of executive rulemaking. The aim of this chapter is to assess these developments—not only to provide an account of current practices, but also to encourage reflection on how each judicial system might reform its practices to confront present-day regulatory challenges.

Recall my two-by-two framework, introduced in Chapter 1. My cases include two countries with a common-law history (the US and the UK) and two with a civil-law background (Germany and France). The US is a separation-of-powers presidential system, and France has a strong president, in spite of also having a prime minister. Both Germany and the UK are parliamentary systems, with and without written constitutions. This political-economic framework, developed through the preceding chapters, helps to account for a number of judicial responses that court-centered approaches cannot well explain.

The United States: Common-Law Presidential

At first glance, US practice seems full of contradictions. Accountability to the public pervades the rulemaking sections of the Administrative Procedure Act, which provides for judicial review of both substance and process. In drafting the APA, the legislature delegated policymaking to the executive in many areas but recognized its own limited ability to monitor policy implementation. As a result, it gave the courts an important oversight role.[1] Judges, however, cannot decide cases unless they are willing to hear them, and the courts have restricted the ability of the concerned public to invoke judicial safeguards. Supreme Court case law grants standing only to those with concrete and particular interests in an agency's action. Once litigants access the federal courts, however, *FCC v. Sanders Brothers* holds that they can challenge the democratic legitimacy of the administrative process, as well as claimed violations of rights.[2]

Decisions by the new conservative majority on the Supreme Court seem to call into question the constitutionality of congressional efforts to limit the policymaking powers of the "unitary executive." It is important to recognize, however, that these procedural constraints are part of the quid pro quo that produced delegation in the first place. They strike a balance between the necessity of delegation and political accountability of policymaking in the executive.

Restricted Standing

The United States has perhaps the most inconsistent practice of my four cases. The Constitution states that the jurisdiction of the federal courts extends to cases and controversies, and the Supreme Court has struggled to articulate a law of standing based on these undefined terms.[3] The Supreme Court limits access for groups and individuals that have not suffered direct harm, for example, groups whose purpose is to further environmental values or to promote accountable procedures. In *Summers v. Earth Island Institute*, the Court found that advocacy groups cannot claim standing for an agency's failure to abide by required procedures in cases involving "deprivation of a procedural right without some concrete interest that is affected by the deprivation."[4]

At the same time, the Supreme Court has allowed standing for states to bring claims against agencies. In *Massachusetts v. E.P.A.*, the Court found that Massachusetts had a right to challenge the Environmental Protection Agency's failure to issue regulations regarding greenhouse-gas emissions, as "the rise in sea levels associated with global warming has already harmed and will continue to harm Massachusetts, [and] the risk of catastrophic harm, though remote, is real."[5] The Court's willingness to expand the standing of states, however, seems motivated less by a desire to recognize the value of states as routes to public accountability than by its reading of federalism.

Civil-society groups have responded to the requirement of direct harm by enlisting group members who claim individualized harm and bringing suits to defend their interests.[6] This effort often fails, but there are enough successful examples to encourage continuation of the practice.[7] For example, Our Children's Trust has organized groups of young people to participate in lawsuits to force government action to confront climate change, arguing that their lives will be affected by the warming climate.[8] In recent cases challenging the rescission of the Obama administration's policy of Deferred Action for Childhood Arrivals, standing was not an issue because the rescission immediately affected many students, a few of whom became plaintiffs. The cases were brought by a combination of institutions and individuals.[9] I discuss that case further below because it turned on the judiciary's role in reviewing the administrative process.

The narrowness of US standing law has kept certain administrative-law complaints out of the federal courts. The idea seems to be that those who have a personal interest in the outcome of the case will be better plaintiffs than a group whose public purpose is to advance the cause behind the case. This is questionable as an empirical matter, especially if the plaintiff claims a deficit in the democratic accountability of executive action. An advocacy group with a deep commitment to and knowledge of the issues at stake is likely to be an especially good plaintiff in such cases. These standing rules do help to limit the caseload of the federal courts, but in a way that arbitrarily filters access to judicial review, especially when policymaking accountability is at stake. As we will see, US courts are more restrictive than those in Germany, the UK, or France. Thus, the independence of the US courts and the vagueness of the constitutional text have combined to produce a standing doctrine that fits uncomfortably with other aspects of judicial review that are compatible with the dynamics of the US separation of powers.

Review of Rulemaking Processes

The APA frames executive rulemaking processes and provides for judicial review of agency compliance. Absent clear constitutional violations, the courts recognize the greater political accountability of the legislature compared to cabinet departments and independent agencies.[10] As a result, they provide active judicial oversight of executive rulemaking on both substantive and procedural grounds. As an appellate court stated in *Nova Scotia Food Products*, "agencies do not have quite the prerogative of obscurantism reserved to legislatures."[11]

Courts defer to legislative choices and, in particular, have upheld the constitutionality of open-ended statutory language that delegates policy-making to the executive and to independent agencies. A statement of purpose is not required and is often absent.[12] Even when it exists, the courts may give it little legal authority.[13] A non-delegation doctrine, expressed in two cases from the 1930s, has not been rigorously applied for decades. In the 1980 *Benzene* case, Justice William Rehnquist attempted to revive the doctrine to limit congressional efforts to pass on difficult decisions to the bureaucracy, but he could not attract the support of any other justices.[14] In 2001 and 2019 the Supreme Court rejected other efforts to revive the doctrine.[15]

Given frequently divided governments and weak party discipline, the legislative process requires compromises that often produce ambiguous statutory language. The Court's permissive approach to delegation is consistent with the reality of the American constitutional structure. Courts would intrude too much into the lawmaking process if they required statutes to comport with substantive claims of means-end rationality.[16] However, efforts to revive the non-delegation doctrine continue and are reflected in the bills introduced by congressional Republicans that I discussed in Chapter 3, and in lower-court opinions by recent appointees to the Supreme Court.[17]

Judicial review of administrative rulemaking processes is broad but limited. Because rulemaking is more open to public participation and more constrained by law than in the other systems that I study, it is more subject to judicial challenge. The APA permits review but frames and limits the challenges. A heavy layer of judicial interpretation has built up around the APA requirements for public notice, an open-ended hearing, and publication of the final rule along with a statement of reasons.[18] Because of the barebones character of these notice-and-comment provisions, taking up less than a page in the US Code, the courts have room to interpret the adequacy of procedures as well as to evaluate a rule's substance using a generally deferential "arbitrary and capricious" standard.[19]

In the 1970s, the federal Court of Appeals for the District of Columbia Circuit interpreted the APA to require additional procedures over and above the imprecise language of that statute. However, in *Vermont Yankee v. NRDC*, Justice Rehnquist, for the Supreme Court majority, reprimanded the lower court for its expansive view of the procedures subject to judicial review.[20] The rule in that case dealt with the award of government permits for nuclear power plants. Interested persons had submitted written comments and made oral comments before a government hearing panel. Environmental groups claimed that they should have had the right to cross-examine agency staff and to contest the factual basis of agency documents. The opinion by Chief Judge David L. Bazelon for the lower court found for the plaintiffs.[21] He argued that additional procedures could create "genuine dialogue." One judge favored a remand only to provide better documentation to the reviewing court.[22] In a separate statement, Judge Bazelon stressed the judges' inability to evaluate technical material, writing that "a focus on agency procedures will prove less intrusive, and more likely to improve the quality of decisionmaking, than judges 'steeping themselves' in technical matters."[23]

In spite of the reference to "genuine dialogue," the additional procedures were meant to aid the court, not necessarily to improve democratic accountability. The Supreme Court overturned the lower court's holding. An agency could introduce additional procedures on its own, but the federal courts should not require them, except in extreme situations. The opinion worried that interference by the courts would create uncertainty and overly judicialize proceedings. It stressed the role of Congress as the ultimate determinant of policymaking procedures in the executive.

Vermont Yankee limited creative judicial efforts to improve rulemaking procedures. Since that case, opinions that review rulemaking procedures have tended to be rather mechanical applications of the APA rulemaking requirements, without much concern for their link to public legitimacy. An agency's published statement of reasons, a mixture of substance and procedures, is subject to review.[24] However, review of technocratic choices ought to defer to standards of proof in science rather than those that prevail in civil and criminal law. Judicial deference to the policy expertise of government ministries and agencies reflects judges' relative lack of non-legal expertise.

Furthermore, courts do not always quash administrative actions that violate procedural rules. The doctrine of harmless error allows the courts to overlook a procedural error if they believe that it had little or no impact on the substantive outcome.[25] This avoids trivial and self-serving complaints, but if the procedure has a broader justification, failing to find a violation can undermine the democratic and technical justifications for required processes. Most troubling, the judges decide if following a procedure is an important value for the rule in question, but their holding may be applied to very different regulatory situations. For example, in *Little Sisters of the Poor v. Pennsylvania*, the majority of the Supreme Court held that labeling the document an interim final rule instead of a proposed rule was a harmless error, even though only the latter phrase is in the text of the APA.[26] Yet, the use of the words "interim final" could well discourage comments by suggesting a greater degree of agency commitment than "proposed."

The courts have explicitly recognized the value of open, transparent procedures. Yet, they sometimes blur the distinction between an agency's accountability to the public and its efforts to aid the courts' own review of executive action.[27] The cases that come closest to my own view support public input not only because it accords with APA requirements, but also because it is consistent with public accountability.

Because the APA requires agencies to provide an open-ended invitation for public comments, the courts do not need to insert their own justifications for such input in order to decide cases. Nevertheless, one occasionally sees explicit efforts to justify the use of notice-and-comment rulemaking. A particularly ingenious response came from Judge Richard Posner of the Seventh Circuit Court of Appeals in *Hoctor v. U.S. Department of Agriculture*. The government had issued an interpretive rule without notice and comment that set eight feet as the minimum height for containment fences for wild animals. Posner held that a notice-and-comment process was required *because* the height could not be set through a purely technocratic process. The agency needed input from those affected because its decision was essentially "legislative." As he writes: "Notice and comment is the procedure by which the persons affected by legislative rules are enabled to communicate their concerns in a comprehensive and systematic fashion to the legislating agency."[28]

Once an agency has issued a decision, it owes the public a reasoned explanation that is subject to judicial review. That principle then raises the question of how deeply a court should review an agency's reasoning. An iconic debate over so-called hard look review occurred in *Ethyl Corp. v. EPA*, from the DC Circuit Court of Appeals.[29] In a concurring opinion, Judge Bazelon argued that the courts should not "scrutinize the technical merits" of the decision but should, instead, review the process to be sure that it "can be held up to the scrutiny of the scientific community and the public." Judge Harold Leventhal in a second concurrence countered that judges need to acquire the necessary technical knowledge to judge administrative actions. That debate continues, with some confusion over whether the court is checking to be sure the agency took a hard look at the alternatives or whether the judges themselves are taking a hard look at the agency's reasoning and factual basis for a rule. Whatever the emphasis, the courts inevitably blend substance and process in assessing an agency's action.[30]

A 2018 decision from the Second Circuit Court of Appeals directly addressed the importance of public accountability in the notice-and-comment process. Criticizing the National Highway Traffic Safety Administration's suspension of such a process, the appellate court observed:

> Notice and comment are not mere formalities. They are basic to our system of administrative law. They serve the public interest by

> providing a forum for the robust debate of competing and frequently complicated policy considerations having far-reaching implications and, in so doing, foster reasoned decisionmaking.[31]

The Census and the "Dreamers"

In 2019 and 2020, the Supreme Court relied on administrative law to resolve two cases that dealt with the relationship between the United States government and the millions of residents who lack legal status. In each one, the Court rejected constitutional claims. Neither one involved notice-and-comment rulemaking or public participation; instead, both relied on principles of democratic legitimacy to review executive-branch actions. The decisions demand that public officials provide carefully balanced reasons for administrative actions, and they turn on the judiciary's ability to evaluate public officials' choices. Nevertheless, by requiring administrators to provide more clarity and to exercise balanced judgment, these holdings help give the public a better understanding of government policy choices.

The 2019 case, *U.S. Dept. of Commerce v. N.Y.*, reviews the inclusion of a citizenship question on the US Census. The Constitution requires a decennial count of all persons (not all citizens) to allocate seats in the House of Representatives.[32] The census is also the basis for the distribution of federal funds under many programs. Opposition to this question centered on the predicted undercount of immigrants, both legal and illegal. The Secretary of Commerce justified the question based on a statement by the Department of Justice that it would help in the enforcement of the Voting Rights Act. The Supreme Court majority held that this was an unconvincing pretext with no solid justification in the record. Chief Justice John Roberts, joined by four other justices, wrote: "The reasoned explanation requirement of administrative law . . . is meant to ensure that agencies offer genuine justifications for important decisions, reasons that can be scrutinized by courts and *the interested public*" (emphasis added).[33]

The 2020 case, *Dept. of Homeland Security v. Regents of the University of California*, concerned Deferred Action for Childhood Arrivals, an Obama-administration policy created in 2012 by a memorandum from the Department of Homeland Security (DHS). DACA assures a class of undocumented young people, labeled "Dreamers," that their status will not be challenged for two years (extended to three years in 2014), allowing them to study and hold jobs. Although their immigration status was not legalized, they could rely on the stated policy of non-enforcement. The Trump administration repealed DACA, also using a memorandum from the DHS. In responding to legal challenges, the administration argued that because the original memorandum was an illegal executive action, it could be rescinded through a similar memorandum without reasoned justification. The underlying statute gives the Attorney General the power to interpret the law, and he asserted the illegality of DACA, but that was not the end of the matter according to the Supreme Court. In a five-to-four decision, the majority found that the APA's requirement for reasoned explanation required the DHS to consider the reliance interests that the program created, even though the agency was not legally bound to continue the program. Those interests should have been explicitly taken into account in the justifications for winding down DACA.[34]

Furthermore, the DACA case limits the ability of an agency to rely on post hoc rationalizations to justify its actions because of the consequences for public accountability.[35] Reason-giving informs the public when an agency issues a rule, but post hoc explanations do not serve that purpose. They are designed only to aid the court, not to provide a public justification. As Chief Justice Roberts wrote for the majority in the DACA case:

> Requiring a new decision before considering new reasons promotes "agency accountability," by ensuring that parties and the public can respond fully in a timely manner to an agency's exercise of authority. Considering only contemporaneous explanations for agency action also instills confidence that reasons given are not simply "convenient litigating position[s]." Permitting agencies to invoke belated justifications . . . can upset "the orderly functioning of the process of review," forcing both litigants and courts to chase a moving target [internal citations omitted].[36]

As Chief Justice Roberts argued, procedures can improve accountability to the public and those affected by the policy, but they are not a substitute for substantive legislative action.

Remedies and Fee-Shifting

The APA does not cover suits for monetary damages, and such suits are seldom possible on other grounds. The Federal Tort Claims Act allows such suits, but mainly for actions that would be torts if committed by private actors.[37] An individual can bring an action against public officials for violating his or her constitutional rights, but such actions are uncommon in the rule-making context.[38]

If a court strikes down a rule, it is remanded to the agency to reformulate it in the light of the ruling. The court may vacate the rule, keep it in force provisionally, or require the agency to revert to an existing rule until an acceptable new one is in place. Some issues return several times to the courts before they are resolved.[39] If a rule is quashed and no reversion rule exists, the courts may set a time limit for agency actions, sometimes building on statutory provisions that mandate a fallback if the agency has failed to act. If the courts void a rule, they seldom craft a legally acceptable rule themselves, although they have sometimes dropped broad hints about what they would find acceptable.[40]

If the courts identify procedural failings, courts usually give the agency a chance to correct substantive violations, as in the 2019 case of *Smith v. Berryhill*:

> Fundamental principles of administrative law . . . teach that a federal court generally goes astray if it decides a question that has been delegated to an agency if that agency has not first had a chance to address the question . . . [I]n an ordinary case, a court should restrict its review to the procedural ground that was the basis for the Appeals Court decision and (if necessary) allow the agency to address any residual substantive question in the first instance.[41]

That holding, although superficially sensible, gives an agency an incentive to skimp on process in the hopes of avoiding a legal challenge. Even if the agency loses in court, the judiciary will not resolve the substantive issues itself; it will only require a new agency process. The courts lack remedies other than remand unless they engage in de novo review, an option reserved to "pure" questions of law.[42] A successful challenge may void the rule while a substitute is being considered by the agency. For example, in upholding challenges to the Obama administration rule covering the Waters of the United States Rule (WOTUS), the Court voided the rule, and until the agency issued a new rule, it left in place a rule dating from 1986.[43]

The incentive to bring a lawsuit depends not only on the hoped-for ruling but also on the cost of suits. Unlike European legal systems, in the US the losing party does not routinely pay the legal fees of both parties. US civil-society groups finance lawsuits from tax-deductible, private donations; corporations self-finance their efforts, often through industry-wide trade associations. Many suits dealing with administrative law have multiple private parties on both sides. These are expensive undertakings that can last for years and involve decisions at different levels of the federal courts, occurring long after the rulemaking process has concluded. In a break from usual US practice, most environmental statutes include one-sided fee-shifting where the private plaintiff that "substantially prevails" recovers its legal fees from the government, but the one that loses only pays its own lawyers and court costs. This provides a better incentive to challenge the government than two-sided fee-shifting. Of course, plaintiffs cannot simply announce their legal costs; to avoid overstatements, the courts must approve the award.[44]

Strengths and Weaknesses of US Judicial Review

Judicial review of rulemaking processes under the APA can support democratic accountability. Such review is more pervasive in the US than in my other cases, and, arguably, it arose from the separation of powers in the US presidential system. Because one or both houses of the Congress can be under the control of a party different from that of the president, statutes may include vague language as a way of forging a compromise. But this lack of clarity makes executive rulemaking necessary for policy implementation. Procedural constraints enforced by the courts can be part of the bargain that supports delegation in legislative texts. Congress delegates broadly and then requires procedures that make the process both open and publicly accountable to the public and subject to judicial review. Thus, the courts are central to the development of public law. They decide cases based on constitutional and statutory texts and draw on the common-law tradition of case-by-case legal development. With a tradition of dissents and concurrences in the Supreme Court and a common-law understanding of the fluidity of the law, the courts can accommodate a changing social/economic reality. It remains to be seen if they will do so. Although the APA's judicial-review provisions contribute to the public accountability of executive policymaking, notable weaknesses exist.

The standing doctrine limits those who can challenge administrative rules to those suffering a direct harm—a doctrine that is poorly crafted to further democratic values. The need to exhaust bureaucratic routes of appeal adds extra time between the issuance of the rule and a court's judgment.[45] Review often occurs after the rule has been promulgated, but before it takes effect. This timing is desirable for procedural challenges because evidence on process is likely to be more easily available soon after the process is complete. However, pre-enforcement review means that the concrete effect of the rule is untested.[46] The timing of review should be tailored to the nature of the legal challenge. If plaintiffs are challenging procedures, review should occur as soon as possible after the agency issues the rule. If the substance is in question, timing should depend upon the tradeoff between obtaining concrete evidence of the rule's effect and the value of promptly providing certainty to those affected.[47]

The ostensible policy-neutrality of review can be violated, even if judges do not explicitly take policy positions. In reviewing substance, a court may invoke one of the "canons" of legal interpretation. There are many canons, and judges may select those consistent with their own views of good policy. In the ongoing debate between the role of canons and legislative history, review of the administrative process may be pushed to one side.[48] The courts may decide a rulemaking challenge without considering the democratic legitimacy of agency procedures.

When executive rulemaking procedures are subject to review, the courts check the notice-and-comment process for transparency and openness to public comment. The agency's public statement of reasons must be persuasive and take account of the relevant comments, and the reasons must reflect the actual policy motivation of the agency.[49] Judicial review of rules gives agencies an incentive to compile thoroughgoing records to permit the courts to understand the agency's reasoning and to be sure that the hearing is open to outside input.[50]

However, there are limitations embedded in the nature of the APA and the subsequent case law. Draft rules must be published, but the process of producing drafts lacks legal constraints and, hence, judicial oversight. Public hearings may not produce broad-gauged public participation. Although the draft rule and notice of the hearing must be available to all, the government need not reach out to affected groups, and the agency decides for itself how to use the input. A statement of reasons may satisfy the judges but be difficult for ordinary people to understand. These limitations are baked into the informal rulemaking process and are not subject to remedy in court. In checking compliance with the underlying statutory authority, however, the courts could give less weight to rules that comply only minimally with procedural requirements.

Agencies and the chief executive may avoid notice-and-comment rulemaking by issuing memoranda and guidance documents. Although technically non-binding, they may pressure regulated entities to comply. The Executive Office of the President may instruct agencies how to manage enforcement and adjudication. Neither agency guidance documents nor EOP instructions are constrained by procedural requirements.[51] They cannot be inconsistent with statutes or the Constitution, but there is much room for unreviewable executive-branch action. However, if notice-and-comment rulemaking is not used, then the agency guidance does not have the force of law and cannot be invoked by the agency to cut off objections raised when the policy is put into effect. A clear statement of that doctrine is *McLouth Steel Products Corp. v. Lee M. Thomas,* where the EPA used a statistical model that set standards without going through the notice-and-comment process. The DC Circuit Court of Appeals held that, as a result, the model had to be open to challenge in a subsequent enforcement case.[52] In a different policy area, memoranda issued by cabinet secretaries first instituted and then repealed the DACA program. Even though the actions did not fall under the notice-and-comment process, the Supreme Court held that the Obama administration's original memorandum created reliance interests in the beneficiaries. Their reliance allowed for judicial review under the APA and required the agency to take those interests into account, thus preserving the program until President Biden took office.

The future of judicial review of the rulemaking process is unclear. Some judges and commentators do not accept the necessity of policymaking delegation. Rather than seeking to move executive policymaking in a democratically legitimate direction, they urge less delegation. A few critics challenge the constitutionality of the APA itself or seek debilitating amendments. Others would couple the APA with a draconian non-delegation doctrine. These radical proposals, discussed in Chapter 3, misunderstand the nature of modern policymaking. More cynically, they seek to force the state to disengage from dealing with pressing social and economic problems.

The United Kingdom: Common-Law Parliamentary

As we have seen, the UK, Germany, and France do not have general statutes covering the procedures for issuing rules with the force of law (secondary legislation). Their courts have few legal standards to apply beyond constitutional principles, European Union mandates, and the European Convention on Human Rights. A few substantive statutes in all three countries require consultation that can promote democratic accountability as well as protecting the rights of those directly affected.

In the UK's common-law parliamentary system, the same party or coalition controls both the legislature and the cabinet. Delegation does not allow the legislative majority to avoid blame for controversial choices. The governing majority has no incentive to support a statute giving the courts a role in overseeing its own rulemaking efforts, and none exists. Parliamentary sovereignty implies that the courts, including the Supreme Court, cannot review the constitutionality of statutes, although the judiciary can review statutory instruments with the force of law.[53]

The UK has a further source of legal authority derived from the common law that may limit the reach of statutory law. In practice, the application of the common law to the field of public law is contested, and its doctrines do not focus directly on the democratic legitimacy of administrative rulemaking processes. The common law emphasizes substantive law and its enforcement in particular cases. There is no common-law duty to consult persons who may be affected by a measure before it is adopted.[54] Nevertheless, although still a nascent development, several judicial opinions recognize the value of consultation in furthering democratic values.

A few statutes have specific consultation requirements. Some of these laws include a list of those whom the government must consult or else give discretion to officials to prepare the consultation list.[55] Infrastructure-planning laws emphasize consultations with individuals and communities that will be particularly affected, both positively and negatively. The Planning Act of 2008 covers both National Policy Statements (NPSs) for projects of national importance and more focused Nationally Significant Infrastructure Projects (NSIPs).[56] Both require some consultation, and NPSs also have to be approved by Parliament.

To understand the role of the UK courts in the review of executive policymaking processes, I first consider what the British call "permission" or "leave" to access the court, a more open-ended doctrine than the US law of standing. Second, I introduce traditional doctrines of judicial review of the administration and the legal status of consultation. The third section discusses a Supreme Court opinion by Lord Robert Reed that views consultation as furthering democratic values in a case where the common law also guided the Court. Fourth, I highlight several cases where the courts supported reason-giving and openness in public procedures. Although these cases deal with the protection of rights, they are consistent with the goal of furthering democratic accountability. Fifth, I show how civil-society groups use cases anchored in individual rights to bring broad policy issues before the courts. The border between legislative and executive action may be unclear in the UK parliamentary system, but, in the sixth section, I argue that it is an important line for courts to draw. Seventh, I discuss remedies, a topic related to the incentives to bring lawsuits and to raise generic issues relating to democratic functioning. Finally, I discuss the implications of the UK exit from the EU for rulemaking in UK administrative law. In particular, I highlight efforts by the government of Prime Minister Boris Johnson to limit the role of the courts, including the Supreme Court, in reviewing administrative actions and government policy choices.

"Permission (or Leave) to Address the Courts" and "Third-Party Intervenors"

Unlike US courts, those in the UK have a broad notion of standing or "permission to address the courts." It is quite easy for individuals and civil-society groups to bring cases, but the grounds of review are much narrower than in the US and less connected to the democratic legitimacy of state action.[57] Although there are dissenting jurists, a prominent line of cases argues for broad standing for organizations and individuals with "sufficient interest" to bring cases to court, especially in the areas of environmental law and human rights. The Human Rights Act of 1998 in S. 7(1) requires cases to be brought by individual victims. However, if a public policy produces a broad class of potential victims, they can seek judicial review based on the common law. Thus, in *R. (UNISON) v. Lord Chancellor*, the Supreme Court heard a challenge to employment-tribunal fees brought under both the common law and EU law.[58]

Two related cases illustrate the key point. The first, *Walton v. Scottish Ministers*, from 2012, is a challenge to a road scheme brought by environmentalists. Lord Reed stated:

> [T]here may also be cases in which any individual, simply as a citizen, will have sufficient interest to bring a public authority's violation of the law to the attention of the court, without having to demonstrate any greater impact upon himself than upon other

> members of the public. The rule of law would not be maintained if, because everyone was equally affected by an unlawful act, no-one was able to bring the proceedings to challenge it.[59]

He builds on Lord Kenneth Diplock's opinion in a 1981 case brought by a federation of self-employed individuals and small businesses:

> It would, in my view, be a grave *lacuna* in our system of public law if a pressure group, like the federation, or even a single public-spirited taxpayer, were prevented by outdated technical rules of locus standi from bringing the matter to the attention of the court to vindicate the rule of law and get the unlawful action stopped.[60]

The *Walton* case is of particular interest because the plaintiff was given leave to raise procedural objections to the government's approval of a road-building scheme. Nevertheless, the justices' statements only deal with access to the courts, not the outcome, and in both cases the plaintiffs were denied the remedies they sought.

Despite their willingness to hear cases from civil-society groups, the courts are unwilling to accommodate "mere busybodies," that is, people with no expertise or stake in the outcome. The term has an anti-democratic origin: a monarchist used it to denigrate those who sought to hold the king to account, that is, early democrats and liberals.[61] Given this history, many judges recognize the risks to democratic accountability of ruling out plaintiffs who aim to protect the public interest. Thus, in *Kides v. South Cambridgeshire District Council*, the judge objected to using the term "busybody" to deny standing to a committed advocate of a social cause or someone seeking more public accountability.[62] He quoted another judgment: "common sense should enable one to identify a sufficient interest when it presents itself. Like a horse which is difficult to define but not difficult to recognize when one sees it."[63] Although the judges' willingness to permit advocates of social causes to access the courts is a welcome development, the reliance on judicial "intuition" is quite vague.

To illustrate the tension in the judiciary, Lord David Hope in *Walton* eloquently supports standing for a person defending the interests of wildlife, but then goes on to rule out busybodies.

> An individual may be personally affected in his private interests by the environmental issues to which an application for planning

> permission may give rise. Noise and disturbance to the visual amenity of his property are some obvious examples. But some environmental issues that can properly be raised by an individual are not of that character. Take, for example, the risk that a route used by an osprey as it moves to and from a favourite fishing loch will be impeded by the proposed erection across it of a cluster of wind turbines. Does the fact that this proposal cannot reasonably be said to affect any individual's property rights or interests mean that it is not open to an individual to challenge the proposed development on this ground? That would seem to be contrary to the purpose of environmental law, which proceeds on the basis that the quality of the natural environment is of legitimate concern to everyone. The osprey has no means of taking that step on its own behalf, any more than any other wild creature. If its interests are to be protected, someone has to be allowed to speak up on its behalf.
>
> Of course, this must not be seen as an invitation to the busybody to question the validity of a scheme or order under the statute just because he objects to the scheme of the development. Individuals who wish to do this on environmental grounds will have to demonstrate that they have a genuine interest in the aspects of the environment that they seek to protect, and that they have sufficient knowledge of the subject to qualify them to act in the public interest in what is, in essence, a representative capacity . . . [T]here has to be some room for individuals who are sufficiently concerned, and sufficiently well-informed, to [have standing] . . . It will be for the court to judge in each case whether these requirements are satisfied.[64]

Lord Hope thus provides guidance to judges wishing to confront the problem of integrating democracy and expertise. The test would be the plaintiffs' ability to contribute to a more legitimate and democratically acceptable choice based on both their genuine concern for the policy outcome and sufficient knowledge to contribute to the government's balancing of pluses and minuses. His statement could also guide a government ministry or regulatory agency trying to design a process to make rules and draft statutory instruments that are both technically competent and incorporate the interests of the public and concerned stakeholders.

In addition to generous standing rules, the UK has become open to third-party intervenors in the public interest (amici curiae) since the 1990s.

In 1998, the House of Lords gave leave to Amnesty International and Human Rights Watch to intervene in the case involving Augusto Pinochet, the former president of Chile. The increase in interventions may be linked to the UK Human Rights Act and third-party interventions in the European Court of Human Rights.[65]

Rules regarding interventions, however, are uneven: the UK Supreme Court's rules make explicit reference to third-party intervenors, and the High Court's rules also indirectly refer to interventions, but the Court of Appeal has no clear mechanism for evaluating interventions. The Supreme Court will allow intervention by any official body or non-governmental organization (NGO) seeking to make submissions in the public interest; any person with an interest in the proceedings by way of judicial review; and any person who was an intervenor in the court below or whose submissions were taken into account. The "public interest" is understood in a broad common-law sense. In lower courts, there are no clear criteria for judging requests to intervene. Cases are decided one by one, but the court will ask whether the intervenor can provide a perspective not offered by the parties, and it will generally not grant the motion without consent of the parties. This consent requirement can become a barrier as certain parties, especially government agencies, can refuse to accept interventions. The Treasury, for instance, has refused consent for interventions by NGOs in certain high-profile cases. Another barrier is costs. For example, applications for permission to intervene in the UK Supreme Court cost £800.[66] Moreover, the risk of having to pay legal fees could dissuade would-be intervenors.[67]

Broad UK standing doctrine allows courts to enforce public rights, as well as private rights. Civil-society groups and individuals and third-party intervenors can work in tandem to facilitate judicial recognition of the value of democratically accountable procedures. If successful, these cases may encourage public rulemaking bodies to open their procedures to more input from citizens and civil-society groups as they make policy choices.[68]

The Common Law, Parliamentary Sovereignty, and Consultation

The government must follow the statutory laws enacted by Parliament. Hence, a plaintiff may claim that a government action is unreasonable, ultra vires, or outside the bounds of the governing statute or statutory instrument. The doctrine of ultra vires is a substantive standard. It does not refer to administrative procedures unless they are included in a statute. Linking ultra vires to parliamentary sovereignty, Paul Craig explains the historical concept:

> If authority had been delegated to a minister to perform certain tasks on certain conditions, the courts' function was to check that only those tasks were performed and only where the conditions were present . . . [The p]arliamentary monopoly [on sovereignty] thus demanded an institution to police the boundaries Parliament had stipulated. The ultra vires principle was the doctrinal tool used to achieve this end . . . [It] provided the justification for constraints on the way in which power was exercised.[69]

The courts cannot judge the constitutionality of parliamentary statutes, but some cases grapple with the legality of statutory instruments and other government actions.[70]

Critics of ultra vires as the main basis for review point to sources of law outside of statutory texts and to the difficulty of interpreting legislative intent from statutory language.[71] Unlike the US case law, judges do not often decide if the executive has followed the intent of the legislature. The unitary nature of parliamentary government makes that distinction untenable. A new government might repudiate the policies of a prior government, and it may amend statutes and replace old statutory instruments with new ones. There would be no need for a judicial challenge to make those changes, and those who favor the original position would gain little from a lawsuit because the incumbent government could use its majority in the Commons to enact its favored policies. Thus, even if the courts stood ready to make such judgments, they would seldom be asked to do so.

Traditionally, judicial review only considered whether the administrative process violated common-law standards of fairness or asked if the government's action was manifestly unreasonable in the sense of *Wednesbury*, a deferential standard close to the US standard in *Williamson v. Lee Optical*.[72] Most cases dealt with the treatment of individuals or businesses in their interaction with the state. Human rights cases added an extra layer to this individualized jurisprudence, and most of that law remains now that the UK has left the EU.[73] However, the cases that deal with fair procedure stress rights, not democratic accountability.

In the UK, there is no common-law right to consultation prior to government decisions. Much public consultation does takes place, but the aim is usually to acquire expertise or to hear the concerns of those affected—for example, in regulating privatized utilities or in making land-planning decisions at the local level.[74] In villages, those affected may include most residents, so the distinction between democratic accountability and fairness to affected households has little bite. At the national level, many policy decisions have an impact that cannot be divided into concrete individualized concerns. The developing law dealing with this second class of public actions is my concern here.

The Cabinet Office has issued internal guidelines for public bodies if they do consult, although the document has no formal legal force.[75] However, *Coughlan* held that if a consultation occurs, it must conform to certain "common law duties."[76] These duties mostly refer to the treatment of individuals or affected businesses, but they are consistent with assuring democratic legitimacy, over and above the fair treatment of individuals. Thus, according to *R. (Compton) v. Wiltshire Primary Care Trust*, "consultation must be undertaken at a time when proposals are still at a formative stage; it must include sufficient reasons for particular proposals to allow those consulted to give intelligent consideration and an intelligent response; adequate time must be given for this purpose; and the product of consultation must be conscientiously taken into account when the ultimate decision is taken."[77]

Moseley and Democratic Values

In 2014, the UK Supreme Court in *Moseley* interpreted a statute that required local authorities to consult "interested persons."[78] The five-justice panel signed on to the judgment of Lord Nicholas Wilson that emphasized the common-law duty of fairness in judging the borough's process of consultation. He held that the consultation was inadequate because it only mentioned the option preferred by the local authorities and gave no reasons for selecting it over other plausible responses to a change in government policy.[79] Going further, Lord Reed, joined by two other justices, accepted the common-law analysis but went on to view the consultation as a way to further democratic values. Although his holding is limited to the language of the statute, the underlying rationale invites a broader application to any statute that includes a consultation mandate:

> Such wide-ranging consultation, in respect of the exercise of a local authority's exercise of a general power in relation to finance, is far removed in context and scope from the situations in which the common law has recognised a duty of procedural fairness. The purpose of public consultation in that context is in my opinion not to ensure procedural fairness in the treatment of persons whose legally

> protected interests may be adversely affected, as the common law seeks to do. The purpose of this particular statutory duty to consult must, in my opinion, be to ensure public participation in the local authority's decision-making process.[80]

Lord Reed's opinion outlines "certain minimum requirements" that make meaningful public participation possible. It is not sufficient only to canvass individual harms and benefits. The public agency should give consultees basic information about the draft scheme, an outline of alternatives, and "an indication of the main reasons for the authority's adoption of the draft scheme."[81] Lord Reed quotes earlier cases that require the government "[to tell participants] enough . . . to enable them to make an intelligent response."[82] However, he puts that phrase in the context of a consultation that seeks to discover the public's view of a policy in their role as citizens.

Thus, there were essentially two majority opinions—one, from the entire panel, stressing fairness and the common law, and one, from three of the five justices, emphasizing that the statutory language sought to further democratic values. Lord Reed's opinion provides support for the claim that if Parliament places consultation requirements in a statute, the courts could articulate acceptable procedures that further the democratic legitimacy of executive and agency policymaking, not just the fairness of the process. Even Lord Wilson, with his emphasis on fairness and the common law, recognizes "the democratic principle at the heart of our society" and its connection to fair procedures.[83] We are left, then, with both the holding that the common law supports review of the administrative process and the assertion that consultation serves the purpose of involving the public in a governmental choice.

Reason-Giving and Openness

Consultation is not sufficient, however. Giving reasons is necessary, as under the notice-and-comment provisions of the US APA. Citizens should know not only what their government is doing but also why it has made particular choices.

For environmental policy, these principles have been given legal meaning under the Aarhus Convention ratified by the UK along with most European nations and the EU.[84] The treaty requires public participation before the approval of major projects with environmental effects, and it permits judicial review of the adequacy of participation. In 2017 a five-justice panel of the UK Supreme Court applied Aarhus in deciding *Dover District Council*.[85] A local planning authority granted permission for a large development in Dover against the advice of its professional advisors, who cited environmental harms. The case turned on whether the planners had given adequate reasons, and Lord Robert Carnwath, for the Court, complained that the UK rules on giving reasons were only contained in subordinate legislation and lacked coherence.[86] The EU's environmental impact assessments make reason-giving "an intrinsic part of the procedure essential to ensure effective public participation."[87] He went on to claim that although there is no general common-law duty to give reasons, "fairness may in some circumstances require it, even in a statutory context in which no express duty is imposed."[88] He was ready to extend the notion of fairness beyond the state's treatment of an individual to "a much wider range of parties, private and public," and to extend the principle of open justice or transparency to statutory inquiries and procedures, not just to the courts.[89] Thus, the justice applied a flexible, common-law approach outside its usual boundaries to extend the obligation to give reasons.

Statements of reasons require public bodies to share their background technical data and methods with outsiders. Such openness can help courts evaluate the body's decision, but it also informs the public. It permits citizens to understand and to challenge technical aspects of a decision.[90]

Recent cases demonstrate the courts' willingness to review policy-making processes. The cases arise for environmental issues that do not "directly and specifically" affect individuals,[91] and in the application of human rights norms. They relate to the future of nuclear energy, approval of a third runway at Heathrow and, outside the environmental area, a decision that links human rights concerns with administrative procedures.

Nuclear energy: The admissibility of procedural complaints linked to democratic legitimacy is especially important for environmental organizations with broad policy goals. Such groups play a key role in challenges to the procedures that implement general policies and apply to infrastructure projects with broad effects. For example, in *Greenpeace* that organization brought a procedural challenge to a policy process organized by the Secretary for Trade and Industry. The High Court in 2007 found that the consultation preceding the government's decision to expand nuclear power plant capacity was inadequate. Judge Jeremy Mirth Sullivan held that the government's consultation exercise was unlawful. In explaining his decision, he wrote that for a consultation process to be unlawful on the grounds of unfairness, the court must find "not only that something went wrong but that something went 'clearly and radically' wrong."[92] Fairness is the touchstone, not democratic legitimacy, but there seems to be little practical difference between the two criteria in this case.

Heathrow runway: Adding a third runway to Heathrow Airport would have both narrowly focused effects on nearby communities and broader environmental impacts. The Planning Act of 2008 requires extensive consultation for such projects. Greenpeace joined with local interests to challenge the consultation process behind the airport expansion. The government issued a National Policy Statement and carried out a mandated sixteen-week consultation on the initial plan and an eight-week consultation on the revised NPS. Passage of the NPS by the Commons in June 2018 triggered another round of consultations in 2019 under the same act. The act anticipated legal challenges, and five lawsuits were filed before the statutory deadline in August 2018 by local interests and environmental groups claiming, among other things, that the consultations were inadequate.[93] The law requires the government to consider the issues raised in the consultation and may also require a statement of reasons that applies to broad policy choices as well as to complaints from neighbors of the airport.[94]

In February 2020, the Court of Appeal ruled that the government had not adequately taken into account the Paris Agreement on Climate Change. That victory for the environmental groups was short-lived. In December 2020, the Supreme Court overruled the Court of Appeal and held that the Paris Agreement was not enforceable as domestic law. It also held that statements to that effect by cabinet ministers did not count as "Government policy." Nevertheless, the project still must surmount a number of administrative hurdles, as well as a lack of support from Prime Minister Boris Johnson.[95]

School dress codes: In *Denbigh High School*, the litigant claimed that a state-financed school's dress code violated the European Convention on Human Rights as applied to female Islamic students.[96] The 2006 case raised the especially sensitive issue of how far the state should go to accommodate cultural pluralism, and it turned, in part, on whether the school's procedures were sufficient. The Appellate Committee of the House of Lords (the predecessor to the UK Supreme Court) unanimously upheld the school's processes[97] and rejected the procedural steps proposed by the opinion in the lower court.[98] Lord Leonard Hubert Hoffmann described those procedures as "an examination paper," apparently a damming epithet.[99] He says that, although domestic judicial review is "usually concerned with whether the decision-maker reached his decision in the right way," the convention is "concerned with substance, not procedure."[100] The Lords praised the school administration for its care and thoughtfulness and supported a case-specific "pragmatic" approach, a statement that sounds very much like approval of the school's procedures. Aileen Kavanagh argues that the Lords "took account of the extent to which the primary decision-maker considered [Human Rights] Convention issues as part of its decision-making process."[101]

Judicial review of process can be a way of justifying or overturning substance. Similarly, judicial review of substance can depend upon the use of reasonable procedures. If courts assess the outcome of a balancing test, are they reviewing the substance of the resulting decision or the process that led to that outcome? The concept of proportionality used in these cases combines substance and process and provides a greater margin of appreciation to decisions taken with care.[102] *Denbigh* holds that schools should make such decisions "in a sound way, taking proper account of the affected interests"—that is, taking, as Lord Tom Bingham writes, a "pragmatic approach."[103]

Judicial Review of Cases with Implications for Policy

Judicial review of individual cases can sometimes have substantive and procedural implications for broad policies. If the courts quash or remand an executive action, officials may decide that, next time, they will consult representatives of the complainants. They may avoid subsequent legal challenges by hearing from groups with standing to sue. Decisions in individual cases may indirectly affect government policymaking procedures in a feedback loop.

For example, the Child Poverty Action Group (CPAG) states that "[t]hrough its strategic litigation work, CPAG brings or intervenes in cases where benefit claimants' rights are violated with a view to bringing about systemic change for others who find themselves in the same situation."[104] In cases that target named individuals, it challenges substantive policies that disadvantage children based on claimed violations of the UK Human Rights Act and the European Convention on Human Rights. It intervened in a Supreme Court case (*In the matter of Siobhan McLaughlin*) challenging a legal provision that denied the Widowed Parent's Allowance to a bereaved mother not married to her children's father.[105] CPAG's view prevailed in a four-to-one panel decision. The case involved the direct application of a statute, not a statutory instrument, so the Court could only rule on the individual case.[106] However, it held that the law would be incompatible with the Human Rights Act in "a legally significant number of cases," so it was "for the relevant legislature to decide whether or how it should be changed."[107] In *R. (DS and Others) v. Secretary of State for Work and Pensions*, CPAG acted on behalf of two single mothers to challenge the legality of a benefit cap.[108] The courts were willing to accept CPAG as an intervenor even though it suffered no direct harm. The Supreme Court found for the government in the latter case in a divided vote. The author of the primary opinion, however, noted that the Commons was considering an amendment to the statute, perhaps related to the evidence presented in the lawsuit.

Moving to the environment, a lower-court case in 2016 dealt with the UK's failure to implement the 2008 EU Air Quality Directive.[109] *ClientEarth (No 2) v. Secretary of State for the Environment, Food and Rural Affairs* (*ClientEarth2*)[110] challenged the government's ongoing breach of the directive. The government's December 2015 Air Quality Plan included a program to limit nitrogen dioxide to lawful levels. ClientEarth argued that because the modeling was flawed, the plan was unlawful.[111] The judge sided with ClientEarth and required the government to produce a new plan by April 2017. The revised plan exempted forty-five localities with nitrogen dioxide levels in excess of regulations. ClientEarth again challenged the government's policy, and the court found that, as applied to those forty-five localities, the plan did not ensure compliance with the relevant regulations.[112] It ordered the government to issue a supplemental plan to address the deficiencies in the previous plan. At the same time, in May 2018, the European Commission submitted a complaint to the Court of Justice of the EU challenging the UK's failure to control nitrogen dioxide emissions, consistent with relevant regulations.[113]

The *ClientEarth* litigation raises a fundamental question: Do the cases apply traditional grounds of review to a novel set of facts, or do they represent a reappraisal of the role of judges in checking the grounds of policy choice? Technical modeling exercises are not "procedural" on their face, but the fact that the court was willing to permit an environmental NGO to challenge a broad policy choice indicates a willingness to broaden its review. If the Supreme Court follows these lower-court decisions, the courts may decide cases where environmental groups challenge the implementation of

UK laws and statutory instruments, even with the UK's exit from the EU. If it does so, one predictable governmental response would be to include such groups in its consultation processes to be sure that the resulting regulation or other policy document has been well vetted. What appears to be a purely substantive challenge may produce more open and inclusive procedures inside government ministries and agencies as a pragmatic response by officials seeking to avoid future lawsuits.

Administrative Decisions and the Legislative Process

A massive high-speed rail project, HS2, confronts the distinction between legislative and executive powers. This distinction is blurred in a parliamentary system compared with the US. In a lawsuit that focused on environmental effects, litigants asked the courts to consider the adequacy of public consultations behind a proposed bill approving the first stage of the project. Such a bill, whose only goal is to approve a single project, is called a "hybrid-bill" in UK parlance.[114] The case is rooted in the Aarhus Convention. However, Aarhus does not apply to legislation. This raised a novel issue under UK law. To state the issue in its starkest form: Can a government with a majority in Parliament circumvent the Convention by recasting a cabinet decision as a special-purpose bill? If so, does the democratic legitimacy of Parliament moot legal complaints about inadequate consultation by the government with stakeholders or the general public? Brought when the UK was still a member of the EU, the lawsuit claimed that the parliamentary process would likely not comply with the deliberative and consultative processes required by the EU for projects with important environmental effects. In 2014 the Supreme Court held against those who challenged the process in *HS2 Action Alliance Ltd. v. Secretary of State for Transport*,[115] declining to review the adequacy of parliamentary procedures. It also did not review the government's own consultation because the final decision would be made by Parliament. However, the justices did reassure themselves and the public that they expected the future parliamentary deliberation to be well informed. The language of the opinion leaves some space for the courts to refuse to defer in an extreme case.

The justices raised and rejected the possibility of referring the case to the European Court of Justice (ECJ). If the ECJ had considered the case, it might have ruled for the Action Alliance because it had confronted the same issue a few years earlier, in *Marie-Noëlle Solvay & Others v. Région wallonne*.[116]

In that decision, invoking Aarhus, the ECJ held that pro forma legislative approval did not exempt a government's policy choice from EU consultation requirements.[117]

The first hybrid-bill on HS2 passed both houses with super-majorities and gained royal assent in early 2017. A pressure group, Stop HS2, remained opposed and pointed to cost overruns, environmental damage, and other costs that, to them, outweighed the benefits of the project.[118] Stop HS2 reports that the actual level of deliberation in both the Commons and the Lords was very short and not what the Supreme Court claimed to have expected.[119]

Hence, at least some UK jurists acknowledge the benefits of consultation and see it as a route to a more democratic and accountable government. They recognize the link between process and responsible policymaking. Nevertheless, the courts have not articulated clear public-law principles of procedure that apply to the decisions of governments and agencies, especially in the production of statutory instruments and other policy-relevant documents.

Remedies

Administrative-law remedies in the UK often consist of a statement by the court that the government has acted illegally. There are no monetary damages and no automatic right to a remedy even if the agency acted unlawfully.[120]

Unlike their US counterparts, the UK courts seldom remand a government regulation or, indeed, any administrative action, to correct procedural failings.[121] They may quash the government's action, but the courts have been reluctant to impose particular procedures on public bodies for fear that their choices will be overly judicialized and will interfere with the freedom of public officials to craft processes pragmatically to fit the particulars of individual programs. The level of parliamentary scrutiny can be subject to judicial review, but that seldom happens. In one case where a regulation was not laid before Parliament, as required by the parent act, Parliament simply passed a special act to correct the error.[122]

Even when a court finds that consultation was inadequate, the litigant may merely win a Pyrrhic victory in the form of a declaratory judgment without any direct benefit. For example, because of the passage of time, Ms. Moseley, in the case discussed above, won only a declaratory judgment that the process was inadequate. The court did not require a new consultation, noting that two years had passed.[123] In *Denbigh High School*, a victory for the plaintiff would have been merely symbolic because the student had transferred to another school. Carol Harlow and Richard Rawlings provide other examples. In one case, the court "conjured the shadow but denied the substance of judicial review" by holding for the plaintiff but refusing to apply its ruling to the case at hand in order to sustain orderly markets.[124] In *Edwards*, the Environment Agency granted a permit for new processes at a cement plant. The plaintiffs complained that the agency had commissioned a report on the impact of pollution but not released it until after the completion of the public consultation. The judges held that it was pointless to quash the permit in order to allow public consultation on what were now out-of-date data, especially given the extra time and resources needed.[125]

These "remedies" could discourage future litigants and embolden agencies to ignore procedural requirements. The refusal to enforce such requirements can make them irrelevant. In these cases, at least the government's actions received unfavorable publicity. However, if the court provides nothing except a declaration of illegality, certain challenges to the democratic legitimacy of government actions may never be subject to review.

The courts do occasionally require procedures to be redone. Thus, in *Greenpeace* the court quashed the initial government decision on procedural grounds. The statute required consultation, and the government decided not to appeal. It "immediately issued a statement confirming the Government's faith in both the consultation process and the case for new nuclear power stations."[126] It carried out a new consultation, and in 2008 decided once again to support expansion of the nuclear industry.[127] Harlow and Rawlings stress the difference between consultations required by statute, as in *Greenpeace*, and those organized voluntarily by the government. They worry that if the courts go further and evaluate the adequacy of consultations that are not required by statute, public bodies may be reluctant to engage in any consultations at all because of the possibility of court challenges.[128]

The *Aylesbury Mushrooms* case illustrates a different kind of problem with judicial remedies.[129] The court held that failure to consult the mushroom growers implied that they were not required to participate in a training program that would have assessed costs on the growers' association. The remedy was not to redo the consultation but, rather, to exempt the association from the program. Such a remedy could incentivize the government to consult all potential participants in future programs, but it might have little effect if the government body calculates that few such "squeaky wheels" would actually bring court challenges. More important, exempting those who complain about their exclusion from a consultation process is not feasible for many programs. For example, if those exposed to air or water pollution are not consulted, the government cannot insulate them from the harm they suffer. Only a new consultation process can satisfy the plaintiffs.

Brexit and Judicial Review

Parliamentary sovereignty and an unwritten constitution limit judicial review of the executive policymaking procedures. Nevertheless, common-law principles give the courts interpretive leeway within broad limits. However, those principles have little to say about executive policymaking. A few statutes require consultation, and the courts enforce these provisions to require good-faith efforts. Overall, the structure of the British legal and political system suggests a limited role for the courts as innovators in administrative policymaking processes. Nevertheless, there have been tentative judicial moves in support of enhanced public input. Perhaps some courts will go further, and one place to look is the judicial role in the process of exiting the European Union—Brexit.

The Supreme Court became involved in Brexit in reviewing claims that tested the relationship between the executive and Parliament. The *Miller I* case, discussed in Chapter 3, limited the government's use of prerogative powers that can be exercised without parliamentary involvement. *Miller II* constrained the prime minister's ability to prorogue Parliament to keep it from sitting. Prime Minister Boris Johnson, apparently, would like to rein in the Supreme Court to give the executive more freedom to act. The government is reported to be discussing plans to limit its jurisdiction and change the court's name to avoid analogizing it to the US Supreme Court with its power to judge the constitutionality of statutes.[130] One of the government's worries is that the Court will limit the use of statutory instruments to manage the Brexit process and will give restrictive interpretations of Henry VIII powers in transition statutes that will manage the UK's internal market. The Court could require publicly accountable processes for the review of statutory instruments and government guidance documents. Such processes could involve heightened public consultation. However, the *Miller I* decision is not an obvious guide because prerogative powers are generally reserved for foreign policy issues. The case did not concern domestic policymaking. If the sovereign Parliament does not police the extent of its policymaking delegation to the government, there is little that the British courts can do. They could read ambiguous statutory language to limit government policymaking discretion, but, so far, they have seldom done so.

The Supreme Court is not the only part of the judiciary experiencing government reform efforts. An Independent Review of Administrative Law is under way as I complete this manuscript. Its primary focus is on the case-by-case adjudication of individual complaints from households and businesses. However, the proposals open for discussion include possible limits on leave to sue (standing), especially with regard to public-interest groups with agendas that go beyond the parties to particular cases. The Terms of Reference mention ways to "streamline the process," suggesting less public accountability for decisions and greater difficulty in accessing the courts. The government worries that the courts are reviewing not just the scope of public power but also the way that power is exercised. If the process leads to legislative proposals, it could ultimately have a substantial impact on judicial review of questions of public law.[131]

These developments cast doubt on the ability of the courts to police the government and agency rulemaking processes associated with the UK's exit from the EU. Given the weakness of parliamentary oversight of statutory instruments, the courts could build on past cases that deal with rulemaking and infrastructure to emphasize the democratic value of participation. The courts could support public participation in rulemaking, not just to ensure fairness and factual accuracy, but also to increase the democratic legitimacy of the deals made necessary by Brexit. Publicly accountable procedures would allow individuals and groups with concerns about the new legal regime to participate in the transition. The UK's common-law history gives the courts space to innovate in order to deal with contemporary issues. Nevertheless, under siege, they, instead, may avoid taking steps that could lead to future clashes with the government. Future developments will depend not only on the staying power of the Johnson government but also on the willingness of Parliament to defend a constructive role for the courts in the review of administrative actions with policy consequences that extend beyond the rights and duties of the individual parties.

Germany: Written-Constitution Parliamentary

In Germany, constitutional and statutory law frame judicial review of administrative action. The post-war constitution, the Basic Law or Grundgesetz, establishes a parliamentary system and includes a long list of rights. The Constitutional Court reviews violations of rights under both statutes and national-executive rules. The legality of executive actions goes along with a guarantee of judicial remedy (*Rechtsschutzgarantie*) that protects individual rights.[132] The focus is on the protection of rights, not democratic participation.

At the same time, unlike the US Constitution, the Basic Law explicitly acknowledges the modern administrative state and permits delegation via statute so long as the text includes the "content, scope and purpose" of the delegation.[133] Except for requiring legislative approval of regulations (*Rechtsverordnungen*) by one or both houses, the Basic Law says nothing about the rulemaking process inside the executive. Furthermore, as in the UK parliamentary system, the governing coalition has little incentive to enact a general statute that would allow judicial review of rulemaking procedures. Executive rulemaking procedures are insulated from the constraints of written law. The legislature may provide direct input into a rulemaking process, but it would not benefit from judicial review of the openness of procedures or of the reasons given. The government has promulgated internal rules of procedure, but these cover prudential matters that are not subject to judicial review.

A key concept in German administrative law is the administrative act (*Verwaltungsakt*), an action that directly affects an individual, whether a human being or a legal entity such as a business firm. Germany has an Administrative Procedures Act, but it only mandates procedures for the enactment and adjudication of administrative acts and for planning and licensing decisions. It does not cover rulemaking.[134]

Formal legal texts are more important to judicial review in Germany than in the UK with its common-law tradition. The American APA places the US closer to Germany than to the UK, in spite of the United States' common-law heritage. Unlike the UK Supreme Court, both the US Supreme Court and the German Constitutional Court can hold that statutes violate the countries' written constitutions. All three can declare national rules or secondary norms unconstitutional, although distinctive features of German public law limit review of rulemaking processes.[135]

Most administrative-law cases are heard in specialized courts, including a three-tiered system of administrative courts (*Verwaltungsgerichte*) culminating in the Federal Administrative Court (*Bundesverwaltungsgericht*).[136] There are also specialized court systems for tax (*Finanzgerichte*), labor (*Arbeitsgerichte*), and social welfare (*Sozialgerichte*).[137] Most of their caseload consists of individual complaints of mistreatment or mal-administration. The Constitutional Court can decide administrative-law questions both through abstract review in cases brought by a closed list of political actors and through cases involving individual rights.[138] The multiplicity of court systems raises the question of which court should hear which cases, and sometimes the legislature makes surprising choices. For example, for the industries regulated by the Federal Network Agency (*Bundesnetzagentur*), telecommunication, post, and railway cases are heard in the administrative courts; electricity cases come before the ordinary courts. This difference arose from past ownership patterns and the present expertise of courts.[139]

The first section below discusses standing and the jurisdiction of the courts in the review of administrative actions. Next, I summarize the limited constitutional checks on rulemaking and their important impact on legislative drafting. Then I consider administrative-court review of rulemaking processes compared with review of procedures for projects and plans. As in the other European cases, there is more active review in the field of environmental law, based in part on the Aarhus Convention, although review of rulemaking remains limited even there. I end with remedies, a short section because few successful judicial challenges to executive rules occur on either substantive or procedural grounds.

Standing

Individuals can only access the Constitutional Court through a constitutional complaint claiming that the application of a rule, not the rule itself, violated their constitutional rights. Standing requires direct, individual harm to a subjective public right as the result of an administrative act.[140] General abstract review by the Constitutional Court is only available to designated political bodies, not to individuals or organized groups. Hence, private individuals or organizations that object to executive rules or policymaking procedures at the federal level generally cannot access the courts. Their only recourse is the ballot box or lobbying. If a consumer of a regulated service, such as telecoms, objects to an agency policy, he or she cannot generally bring a lawsuit. The interests of end users and businesses are meant to be protected by ordinary contract law and by the agency's efforts to promote competition.[141]

Some legal scholars advocate extending access to groups of plaintiffs with similar complaints, such as those who face a risk of harm from an unsafe bridge or a dangerous product. Others urge the courts to take cases brought by ideologically oriented groups whose members suffer no direct harm (*Verbandsklage*). Occasionally, such groups can become acceptable plaintiffs by purchasing land near the offending project and suing as property owners, but this is often not feasible. The highest administrative court ruled that if the plaintiff's property interest was created for the purpose of getting into court, then it should have less weight than that of other parties.[142]

The environment is an exception to the requirement of direct, individual harm. The Aarhus Convention, as applied by Germany and the EU, gives environmental groups access to the courts to challenge the procedures used to approve individual plans and projects.[143] The Convention does not cover substantive complaints. A German law implemented the EU directive and gives standing to "recognized" environmental groups. Recognition depends on several conditions. In particular, the group must operate in a quasi-democratic fashion, a standard that has excluded Greenpeace, the organization that has been especially active in the UK.[144] The Bund für Umwelt- und Naturschutz Deutschland (BUND) and Naturschutzbund Deutschland (NABU), two established umbrella groups, have brought most of the cases. The European Court of Justice upheld access of not-for-profit advocacy groups to the German courts in the *Trianel* case, which concerned the licensing of a German coal-fired power plant.[145] The holding, however, only applies to projects likely to have a significant effect on the environment; it does not give such groups standing to challenge general environmental ordinances.

In 2013 the Federal Administrative Court extended standing for not-for-profit groups to include clean-air plans with broad effects on citizens of a metropolitan area. It invoked both Aarhus and the case law of the European Court of Justice.[146] The Aarhus Convention only deals with the administrative process, but other German statutes concern substance.[147] The Federal Administrative Court in 2014 interpreted a statutory grant of standing broadly to allow a not-for-profit group to challenge the substance of a rule. A nature-protection organization, along with eight homeowners, opposed the rules governing the flight paths of airplanes at the Berlin Brandenburg Airport, a troubled project that finally opened in 2020 after many delays.[148] After granting standing, the court upheld the rule, and the rule itself was embedded in a particular project; it was not a general policy.

Some German legal scholars argue that standing doctrines should ensure that illegal government actions face court review. There is ongoing debate about whether that logic should extend to rulemaking and beyond the environmental area. For example, state obligations to protect public monuments and memorials are similar to obligations to protect the environment: many people value them, but the impact on any one person is small.[149] There are also calls for more public participation in city-planning decisions. For example, the Green Party/Social Democrat Coalition Agreement for Berlin called for more public participation in such decisions.[150] Other policy areas with similar characteristics are animal protection, aid to the disabled, and women in the workplace. Gender-based employment issues are mostly dealt with by placing individuals inside firms with access to their internal decision-making bodies, but the firms' responses have seldom been subject to court challenge.[151] Some state governments give "recognized" not-for-profit organizations access to courts, similar to their status in the environmental area, and they can bring cases that deal with both substance and procedure. For example, disabled individuals have standing, but they may face difficulties in bringing cases that challenge general policies. Cases dealing with access to buildings and other facilities are heard in the administrative courts, not the social court, but few cases have been brought.[152] Consumer law is enforced by individual lawsuits, not by general rules.[153] Similarly, occupational health and safety rules are topics for the labor courts, and self-governing bodies in health and social security operate quite independently of the ministries. Giving standing to concerned citizens could affect the implementation of police-law issues relating to data protection and surveillance. For example, individuals or groups might be given the right to challenge in court the pervasiveness of video cameras as an invasion of privacy.[154]

In all these cases, individualized harm may be hard to pin down, yet the social costs of neglect may be evident. As in the US, if cause-based groups cannot have standing on their own, no one may be able or willing to access the courts. Some legal commentators take a hard line against lawsuits by civil-society organizations that engage in advocacy. These opponents would not give such groups standing except to raise issues related to the organization and operation of the group itself. Others also seek to discourage such lawsuits by increasing their costs and disallowing settlements that benefit the plaintiff group. In 2019 a cabinet secretary proposed that if a group engages in cause-based lawsuits, it should lose its exemption from certain taxes unless the suit is closely linked to its other activities. A few days later, he withdrew the proposal in the face of widespread criticism.[155]

One way to support lawsuits with broad social effects is to allow intervenors or amici with no personal stake in the case. However, given the sharp distinction in Germany between law, on the one hand, and politics or policy (*Politik*), on the other, the admission of intervenors or amici is not widespread. Procedure law limits the participation of third parties, but does not exclude it. A recent study concluded that amici curiae should be a legitimate option, and they appear to be becoming more common in areas such as antidiscrimination law, consumer law, and gender-equality law.[156] The Constitutional Court can ask outside bodies to submit material relevant to particular cases, mostly in the form of expertise.[157] Unsolicited briefs are not allowed, but an organization that has not been asked to participate by the Court can ask to be added to the invitation list, and such requests are usually accepted. The administrative courts can also ask outside bodies to submit material, generally focused on factual, not policy, matters. However, the courts have very wide discretion to ask for or reject outside opinions, and submissions are not part of the case's official file. In the ordinary courts, the intervenor must have a legally protected right, a condition that excludes many civil-society and expert groups. Thus, if the courts accept a role in overseeing the democratic legitimacy of government policymaking, a more expansive role for amici would help further that goal.

Constitutional Court Decisions on Rulemaking

Although the constitutional text permits secondary norms, it says nothing about the procedures used for issuing such rules. The courts have done little to fill this gap. If an individual challenges a statute in a concrete case, the litigant must claim a violation of one of the fundamental rights guaranteed by the constitution. The iconic cases concern the consistency of general rules with the protection of rights. Occasionally, procedural issues arise in such cases, but they concern the protection of rights, not democratic accountability.[158]

During the heated national debate over nuclear power in the 1970s and 1980s, the Constitutional Court decided several foundational cases on the use of secondary norms (Rechtsverordnungen) connected with the licensing of nuclear power plants. In the *Kalkar* case from 1978, the Court found that it was constitutional for a statute to include undefined legal terms that require technical expertise to put into effect.[159] Rigid statutory language would not provide "flexible protection of life and property." However, the opinion did not deal with the procedures used by the government to "promote technical developments and adequate safeguards for life and property." The second case, *Mülheim-Kärlich* from 1979, concerned procedures in the context of granting an individual power plant license. It suggested that adequate procedures can justify substantive decisions. The decision "cautioned that certain kinds of formalities, such as public participation in nuclear power licensing procedures, may be necessary to protect basic rights and liberties."[160] The Court advocated public participation, not to enhance the democratic legitimacy of the project, but to protect rights. Nonetheless, it articulated procedural values that could also apply to general policymaking. The case arose in the midst of widespread public opposition to nuclear power. A third case, *Sasbach* from 1982, evaluated a rule that set time limits for public comments on plant-licensing proposals. The Court stated that review of process was less intrusive than review of substance and, therefore, was preferable.[161]

One strand of German legal thinking argues that the law ought to provide a stable framework for public and private life. The responsible administrator or judge follows the law and, hence, does not exercise discretion. This view creates a problem for judges if the statute itself gives discretion to public officials. How can something be "law" if the text itself explicitly gives officials unreviewable discretion? This was the puzzle that the Constitutional Court faced in reviewing the regulation of network industries by the Federal Network Agency.[162] In upholding a decision of the Federal Administrative Court, the Constitutional Court found that it was constitutionally acceptable for a statute to give the expert agency discretion to carry out its mandate without judicial interference. Some viewed the opinion as a striking departure. According to Jens-Peter Schneider, the case showed that both the high courts recognize the need for flexible judicial review in the regulation of telecoms. The reasoning in that case could extend to other areas, such as risk regulation in environmental law.[163] The relevant sentence in the Constitutional Court opinion is: "[The constitution] does not rule out the possibility that the legislator may grant the administration leeway in terms of design, discretion and assessment, which would limit the legal control of executive acts by the courts."[164]

To American readers it may seem odd that judicial deference to regulatory decisions would be a striking departure from past practice. However, recall that the German courts seldom rule on rulemaking discretion. So long as the statute expresses the content, purpose, and scope of the delegation, the government can issue rules with the force of law, and judicial review is limited. Thus, in the past, the courts were unlikely to face clear-cut opportunities to rule on executive-branch or agency policymaking procedures. The public administration only faced court challenges after it began to exercise discretion in particular enforcement actions.

A further indication of the changed role of the Constitutional Court vis-à-vis the rest of government concerned statutory drafting, not the production of administrative rules by government bodies. In 2010 the Court in *Hartz IV* imposed an obligation on the legislature to give reasons.[165] Americans will recognize that standard from notice-and-comment rulemaking, but in the US that standard does not apply to the review of statutory drafts. The holding rests on the "fundamental right to the guarantee of a subsistence minimum" for households, derived from the right to human dignity in article 1(1) of the Basic Law in conjunction with the principle of the social welfare state in article 20(1). Statutes must ensure a subsistence minimum to all individuals. In drafting a statute, the legislature has latitude to specify benefit levels that depend on the state of society and the prevailing conditions of life.[166] The Court reviewed the legislature's information-gathering processes when it enacted a law on social benefits that amended the Code of Social Law. Its opinion declared that the law's standard benefits were unconstitutional, primarily because the provisions were not based on data-driven statistical investigations. Instead of conducting empirical research, the legislature had relied on "random estimate[s]."[167] The Court ruled that the legislature must exercise its discretion consistently and transparently. The opinion concentrated on the procedure used to determine the subsistence minimum and found that it violated the Basic Law. Adequate procedures must compensate for the substantive latitude available to the legislature.[168] The opinion invoked transparency, stating: "In order to facilitate this constitutional review, there is an obligation for the legislature to disclose the methods and calculations used to determine the subsistence minimum in the legislative procedure."[169] Reason-giving is a mixture of process and substance, but the decision is unclear about how to strike a balance.

The procedural violations before the Constitutional Court arose from harm to individual rights-holders, not from problems facing the general public if it seeks to evaluate the policy impact of the law and hold politicians to account. The procedural requirements are not linked to the promotion of democratic values.[170] The Court demands transparency primarily to facilitate judicial review, not to improve democratic accountability. German law provides no review of statutes that affect the general public that cannot be pulled apart into a set of individualized harms—for instance, where legislative decisions concern the allocation of monetary resources or economic policy.

Even for programs that do have individualized effects, the Constitutional Court has not applied the procedural aspects of *Hartz IV* to the review of rulemaking. As a result, the legal system produces the same lacunae for regulations as for statutes and suggests the limits of rights review as an opening wedge to promote democratic accountability. The ministries and agencies that make rules and ordinances have less of a claim to democratic legitimacy than the directly elected legislature. For that reason, judicial review of the democratic legitimacy of administrative rulemaking could strengthen the legitimacy and transparency of policymaking. Indeed, as we have seen, that is a key motivation for judicial review of administrative rulemaking in the United States. In Germany, the delegation of lawmaking authority to the executive is constrained and checked by formal and informal inter-branch and internal executive control mechanisms. However, under the law, broad public participation is not a separate route to democratic legitimacy.

Judicial Review of Executive Rulemaking and Planning

At present, German law does not mandate public input into rulemaking processes subject to judicial review. No statute explicitly ties judicial review of executive regulations (Rechtsverordnungen) to democratic legitimacy or policymaking competence. Some statutes mandate procedures for individual projects, and some of these are large-scale, national undertakings, but they do not cover rules with legal force. The German government has issued internal guidelines for rulemaking, but these have no external legal effect and are not subject to judicial review. The legislature monitors and participates selectively in rulemakings, and the constitution requires the Upper House (Bundesrat) to approve rules that the states will implement.

A few statutes provide for consultation with outside groups, albeit limited to a closed list of participants, and the German courts provide little oversight. For example, the Nature Protection Act is a framework statute that requires the states to enact statutes to carry out its provisions. Several states require their own authorities and local governments to consult with "recognized" nature-protection organizations and also to give these groups access to the courts. In practice, the recognized organizations are established, middle-of-the-road membership groups. If civil-society groups ask for such oversight, the courts often do not provide it. They have been especially reluctant to decide cases involving policy choices rather than claimed violations of rights.

Recently, civil-society organizations have used the courts with some success to further their policy goals. Two leading groups, Umwelthilfe and ClientEarth, participated in court cases designed to uphold bans on diesel cars in urban areas with high concentrations of diesel pollution.[171] EU law requires such bans, but some German states and municipalities refused to implement them. Hence, German administrative courts used other instruments to counter the resistance of these governments. Because its earlier decision did not have the desired result, one court levied a fine of €25,000, which will be paid to a charity dealing with cancer in children.[172]

The Federal Immission Control Act (*Bundes-Immissionsschutzgesetz*, BImSchG) requires an open-comment period for the licensing of particular projects, but not for regulations. It states:

> Where an authorization for the issuance of ordinances and general administrative provisions requires a hearing of the parties concerned, an ad hoc group shall be heard that is to be constituted in each individual case from representatives of the parties directly affected, the scientific community and, where applicable, the business community and the transport sector, as well as of the supreme Länder authorities responsible for immission control.[173]

Thus, consultation is not open-ended. The public agency decides on the membership in the group using this guideline. Notice that environmental and civil-society groups are not mentioned, but only those "directly affected." For a general regulation setting ambient air standards or emission limits for industrial groups, civil-society groups may be unable to claim "direct" effects.

As noted in the discussion of standing, judicial review of the rule-making process has been somewhat expanded under the Aarhus Convention and German statutes related to that convention. Because the EU has ratified

Aarhus, the European Court of Justice can hear disputes over its application in member states. Because its provisions on regulations are much weaker than those for individual projects and plans, it is unlikely to help litigants achieve more public participation in the production of regulations. For example, in 2015 the European Court of Justice refused to review an environmental group's exclusion from a European Commission rulemaking process.[174]

Advocates often object to the lack of civil-society participation in planning processes. According to Miriam Dross: "The legislator has not explicitly regulated [participation by civil society], but it is recognized by the courts. However actions to enforce participation that are not combined with substantive objections are very rare."[175] Also, one cannot sue for failure to carry out an environmental impact assessment. The German statute governing the administrative courts gives short shrift to procedural faults. It states that an administrative act should not be voided if the error did not affect the ultimate outcome,[176] a doctrine that lets the courts decide that issue even if they have little expertise in the substantive area in question.

One overview of the cases brought to the administrative courts for 1996–2001 found 115 cases, with eighty-seven concluded at the lowest judicial level. The plaintiffs won nine (8.2 percent) and had a partial victory in twenty (17.4 percent). Only six dealt with rules ("subordinate legislation") (5.2 percent), and all were unsuccessful. Two constitutional challenges failed. Sixty-one (53 percent) dealt with plan-approval procedures that had local policy consequences. Overall, the cases were an infinitesimal share of administrative-law cases.[177] If this trend has continued, lawsuits of this kind are not an effective way to improve public involvement in policymaking.

Judicial review of executive rulemaking in the administrative courts apparently seldom takes place on either substantive or procedural grounds. Review of public participation in the planning process is uncommon and rarely successful. This could mean that existing procedures are adequate, but one cannot be confident of that conclusion. In any case, the courts do not provide a route for review of the democratic accountability of executive policymaking. Even the exception for environmental issues mainly applies to individual projects, although courts do sometimes acknowledge the broader policy implications of the projects they review. Decisions touch on the value of public input, but most cases are decided on substantive grounds.

Remedies and Fee-Shifting

The German courts infrequently deal with cases that seek to void a rule. Instead, the most prominent cases in public law deal with major infrastructure projects. In the past, these concerned the construction of nuclear power plants. Plaintiffs opposed nuclear power in general, but the cases, themselves, challenged the construction of individual plants.[178] They delayed construction and sometimes led to project cancelations. In one famous case, the shell of a proposed nuclear power plant was converted into an amusement park.[179] In the nuclear power cases, many plaintiffs brought identical suits against the licensing of a power plant. Plaintiffs seldom prevailed, but if they had succeeded, the resulting declaratory judgments would have required the public agency to correct its missteps. More recent lawsuits have focused on such projects as rebuilding the Stuttgart train station, long-distance power lines, and wind farms.[180] Energy companies have brought suits for compensation for nuclear power plant closures, leading to a costly settlement with the German government.[181]

There is little case law dealing with remedies in the rulemaking context. If a court decision favors the plaintiff, it results in a declaratory judgment of illegality. If a statute requires certain procedures, the courts will require them. However, the courts seldom quash a rule even if it has been unlawfully adopted. If a rule is unlawfully applied to the litigant, the holding only covers that plaintiff. The rule itself remains in place for everyone else.

Occasionally, a civil-society group obtains standing to represent the interests of large group, say, the residents of a particular metropolitan area. Once again, environmental cases provide examples. Thus, in the *Darmstadt* case, litigants challenged a metropolitan area's failure to reduce nitrogen oxide pollution. The remedy was a remand to the local government to redo its air pollution plan as soon as possible. The city might need to mandate traffic limitations, but the court did not insist on any particular solution. It held that the government could implement the new plan in steps, and in the meantime, the existing plan would remain in place.[182] This decision, although giving standing rights to environmental groups, said nothing about the democratic legitimacy of the subsequent administrative process. The emphasis was on the pollution level, which violated EU legal standards.

One Constitutional Court case does concern a remedy to correct a procedural violation in rulemaking. In the *Legehennenverordnung* (regulation for laying hens) case, the Court found the hearing process inadequate but gave the government over two years to correct the mistake. The opinion claimed that voiding the rule without a substitute would have been too harmful.[183] It gives independent value to procedural norms, but its remedies have little impact on ongoing public programs.

A final issue is the cost of bringing a lawsuit. As in the other European cases, the general rule is that the loser pays the legal fees and court costs of both sides, a rule that disadvantages civil-society groups without the resources to absorb the risk of loss. Thus, test cases may never be brought to court because no one has a sufficient stake in the case. Legal fees in the civil courts are tied to the amount at stake, but this may be impossible to calculate for administrative-law disputes. Hence, the administrative courts have responded with a list of legal fees based on a purported "value" in conflict. Litigants can pay their own lawyer much more, but can only recover the set amount if they win. According to Miriam Dross, the courts usually recommend €10,000 for public-interest actions, but even that may be too high a bar for low-budget non-governmental organizations. "Together with their own lawyers' fees, the NGOs are frequently obligated to meet the costs for the lawyers for the opposite side (when actions are lost), cost for additional legal opinions and expert opinions, own personnel costs, as well as further costs (for example, public relations)."[184]

Review of Rulemaking Procedures: An Almost Empty Box

The administrative process can further the democratic legitimacy of government executive actions, but this possibility is not central to debates in German public law. Nothing in the Basic Law forbids statutory law from requiring rulemaking procedures or prevents the administrative courts from interpreting existing laws to support participation. Up to now, however, the German courts have had little impact on rulemaking procedures in the executive. The Federal Administrative Court has decided a few procedural cases in the environmental area that draw on the Aarhus Convention and EU law. A few statutes include procedural requirements that the courts will enforce, but the emphasis is on substance and violations of constitutional rights. Occasionally, a case that concerns rights may raise procedural issues, but these relate to the underlying dispute over rights. In the Constitutional Court, abstract review, in cases brought by political institutions, could challenge administrative procedures on democratic grounds, but this has not been done. Individuals can access the Constitutional Court only to claim violations of their rights. Thus, the democratic accountability of the administration takes a back seat to a jurisprudence of rights. As in the UK parliamentary system, the Bundestag, whose coalition controls the government, has little incentive to impose procedural requirements on the cabinet when it makes general rules under delegated authority. The Basic Law does acknowledge the role of the bureaucracy and the cabinet in policymaking, but it does not give the courts an obvious route to intervene to enhance public participation and transparency.

Nevertheless, there are countervailing tendencies. In the 1990s, after the nuclear power cases were decided, two prominent German professors of public law interpreted the Basic Law to require transparent and accountable procedures for setting the government's environmental and technical norms. Erhard Denninger argued that consultation ought to include environmental and public-interest groups, not just directly affected neighbors. Rudolf Steinberg made a similar argument, particularly for atomic power.[185] More recently, Hermann Pünder has argued that courts should not impose judicialized procedures on the administration. Rather, based on comparisons with America and Britain, he supports rulemaking procedures that enhance democratic legitimacy as well providing legal protection for individual rights.[186] He quotes a 1977 decision of the Federal Administrative Court dealing with the construction of the Hamburg metro. The court stated that "[t]he necessity for a dialogue between the administration and the citizen, corresponds to the constitutional appreciation of the position of the citizens within the state."[187] The case dealt with a public construction project, not a rule, but the language could have broader application. Perhaps courts could apply the reasoning in the Hamburg metro case to other areas where the arguments for public participation are similar. However, lacking the external support of a treaty or of EU law, the judiciary may not reach beyond major infrastructure projects or specific statutory texts. The courts recognize the necessity of delegation for the effective functioning of modern government and understand that procedures can be a route to legitimate executive action, but they have not gone further to accept a role in policing the public accountability of rulemaking procedures.

France: Strong Presidential

France has a strong presidential system in spite of the existence of both a president and a prime minister. The president usually has firm control of the National

Assembly and has no incentive to seek passage of a law that would limit executive rulemaking powers by giving the courts an oversight role. At the same time, the very strength of the president makes judicial review of the administration especially salient for the preservation of democratic values, including public consultations over executive policy choices. However, although access to the courts is quite easy, they have not played a central role. Two recent cases dealing with climate change, *Commune de Grande-Synthe,* decided by the Conseil d'État, and *Croix de Seguey-Tivoli*, a judgment of the Administrative Court of Paris, may nevertheless signal heightened judicial activism.[188]

France has a three-tiered system of administrative courts culminating in the Conseil d'État. Its case law concentrates on official abuses of power that violate individual rights. Secondary legislation is seldom challenged on procedural grounds. The administrative courts can review rules, and, unlike the narrower German concept, an administrative act (*acte administratif*) refers to both rules and adjudications. However, there is little case law dealing with the policy process, and the few cases that exist apply the concept of rights to these procedures. The administrative courts seldom interfere with governmental interpretations of their statutory or constitutional mandates. However, since a 2008 constitutional reform, questions concerning constitutional rights can be referred by the Conseil d'État to the Conseil Constitutionnel.These are called *questions prioritaire de constitutionnalité* (QPCs), and they allow for constitutional review of laws after they have been enacted. Under its recently expanded jurisdiction, the Conseil Constitutionnel has acted to enhance public accountability in a few instances, especially for environmental policymaking. Nevertheless, as a general matter, public law lacks a vocabulary and a conceptual framework for monitoring the democratic and technical legitimacy of policymaking inside the administration.

Standing and Amici Briefs

Judicial review of administrative acts is open to organizations as well as individuals who bring claims of unlawfulness against government actions. The courts' jurisdiction is broad, and those who have "an interest in the annulment of the administrative decision" can bring cases. The administrative courts interpret the interest-based standard generously. For example, those filing the challenge do not have to demonstrate a "specific" or "exclusive" interest. Thus, a user of a public service was able to challenge the organization of the agency charged with its delivery.[189] The liberal standing rules remain unscathed even after reforms that aimed to mitigate the overload of administrative cases. Furthermore, cost-shifting rules and other cost reductions are widespread,[190] and in some cases plaintiffs do not need lawyers.[191] Individuals can challenge most administrative decisions in court without first having to exhaust administrative routes.

As in Germany, the admission of briefs from amici is a relatively recent development, but they are now widely permitted.[192] Intervenors from the Ministère Public assist the court as a representative of the public interest, mediating between society and the courts.[193] The Cour de Cassation, the highest civil court, first accepted an amicus brief in 1991, and the Conseil d'État amended its rules in 2010 to allow for their submission. The material submitted is only available to the courts and the parties, not to the general public. This has led to debate in France about the practice of keeping amici confidential. That secrecy forces the justices to articulate public reasons that only depend on the law as applied to the case at hand, not arguments of amici that go beyond purely factual or technical legal matters. However, their acceptance suggests that the courts recognize that their work needs to be responsive to broad public concerns beyond the particular case that are not well reflected in the arguments of the parties. The permissive standing rules also make it possible for civil-society groups to challenge executive policymaking directly, not just intervene as amici in cases brought by individuals suffering harm.

Recent litigation dealing with climate change illustrates both France's broad standing doctrine and the acceptance of intervenors. In a 2020 case, the Conseil d'État (CE) granted standing to a commune threatened with rising sea levels, but denied standing to the mayor of the commune both as a resident and as a citizen. The CE then allowed interventions from two cities and several environmental organizations. In a second case, the Administrative Court of Paris allowed environmental groups to have standing to sue for material compensation. However, that case will likely be appealed to the CE and perhaps to the Conseil Constitutionnel, so the impact of that decision remains uncertain.[194]

Nature of Review

The expanded jurisdiction of the Conseil Constitutionnel since 2011 makes increased judicial review of policymaking processes possible, but only if the issues are cast in the language of rights. The French administrative courts generally provide intensive review if they accept jurisdiction. Both structural and substantive factors contribute to this "judicialization of the administration." The administrative courts accept appeals over excesses of power (*recours pour excès de pouvoir*) by public officials, and over time the Conseil d'État has widened the grounds for such review.[195] Courts also review the strength of factual claims (*contrôle de l'exactitude matériel des faits*). The public-interest goal behind such review explains the courts' openness to citizen complaints.[196] They seek not just to right individual wrongs but also to ensure a well-functioning public sector.[197]

Judicial review has become progressively less deferential under the standard of regular review (*contrôle normal*), and some authors talk about the decline (or the death) of the deferential standard of review (*contrôle restreint*).[198] Occasionally, the courts carry out a stringent review in which they balance the pros and cons of a given decision in order to assess its legality (the so-called *contrôle du bilan*, which some call "maximum review").[199] In some cases, such as the review of administrative sanctions, the European Court of Human Rights imposes a non-deferential standard, but the Conseil d'État has extended this approach even in the absence of legislation.[200] Thus, France's standards of review appear to be developing toward more stringent oversight.

The French courts have not created any new concepts to aid their review of technically complex decisions taken by regulatory agencies and ministries. They apply the concepts developed for the review of non-specialized administrative actions.[201] Theoretically, French administrative courts apply a deferential standard of review to highly technical[202] or politically sensitive cases.[203] In practice, they are less prone to defer than their American counterparts.

Consider the case law on mergers.[204] The Conseil d'État applies regular review to decisions taken by the French minister or by the antitrust agency. It reviews technical assessments and fact-finding, leaving no "margin of appreciation" or discretion to administrative authorities. The Conseil d'État has reviewed market definition and anti-competitive effects for "correctness," assessed the very existence of a merger, and established the criteria under which the "exception of the failing firm" could be accepted. In the opinion that inaugurated this approach, the public reporter (*rapporteur public*) argued that the relevant market is an "objective notion that is imposed upon economic actors and the antitrust authority, which has no leeway to choose one market over another."[205] In practice, the definition of the relevant market for a given merger operation is often a highly technical and debatable issue in which courts have no special expertise. Economists have long debated the concept of market definition.[206]

The courts do not recognize the political component of many regulatory decisions. This is particularly clear in the domain of statutory construction. French courts usually claim legitimacy to interpret ambiguous terms.[207] They view such concepts as "legal" because they are in the statutory text and, therefore, open to judicial interpretation. French courts define the realm of law broadly, allowing for far-reaching review. In cases where American courts have usually acknowledged that agencies are engaged in policymaking and should be left alone,[208] French courts tend to view agencies as making legal decisions that are, therefore, reviewable.

In general, French jurists are less open than courts elsewhere to claims that administrative authorities have a comparative advantage in dealing with technical issues. Although such claims do appear in the opinions of the public reporters who advise the judges,[209] they are quite rare. As a consequence, both democratic legitimacy and deference to expertise play a comparatively less pronounced role in French judicial review of administrative action. Under the influence of the EU and European Court of Human Rights, rights have risen in importance,[210] but there is little straightforward confrontation with democratic values or technical competence as grounds for either review or deference.

There is a relative paucity of cases that judge the validity of rules as opposed to adjudications in individual cases. Nevertheless, such cases do exist. For example, in *Compagnie Alitalia* the Conseil d'État required the state to act under an EU directive. It held that silence or inaction by a minister could be an abuse of power just as much as action.[211] A second case involved a quite aggressive review of a substantive rule that set doctors' fees.[212] The case turned on an interpretation of the principle of equality and took on the substantive merit of a policy in a fairly functional way, even if the ground was the familiar one of abuse of power.[213]

In 2011 the Grand Chamber of the Conseil d'État signaled a willingness to review participatory processes, outside areas involving experts or established commissions. A decree, issued by the Minister of Higher Education and Research, would have merged two high schools in Lyon. The

Dantony decision upheld a procedural challenge to the decree on excess-of-power grounds and found that the procedural violations were serious enough to have possibly affected the final decision.[214] The first flaw was a failure to consult the joint committees of employees at each school who were not part of the teaching staff. The second was the inadequacy of a meeting to discuss the proposal. The opinion holds that the meeting was not truly deliberative and suggests that the head of one of the schools dominated the discussion and limited debate. It voided the merger but allowed a delay, with the holding only taking effect in June 2012.

The decision is particularly important because the Conseil d'État acted under the Warsmann Law II, article 70, which states that procedural violations should not lead the courts to void an administrative act unless they are serious enough to have possibly affected the outcome.[215] The ruling further suggests that the Conseil d'État will evaluate the efficacy of participatory processes if opponents claim to have been sidelined. It sends a signal to those who issue decrees that they should organize consultations up front to avoid being frustrated ex post.[216]

The merger of two schools is an essentially political decision, with both cost savings and losses of institutional identity and jobs. However, the focus of the administrative action was relatively narrow. It did not implicate the national public interest, as would be the case for decisions about, for example, the use of genetically modified organisms (GMOs) in agriculture or the levels of power plant pollutants. In the *AGPM* case from 2013, the Conseil d'État decided a case dealing with GMOs, but it rested on the quality of the scientific evidence; it did not address the issue of public consultation.[217]

The Conseil Constitutionnel has not been much involved in reviewing the process of making rules. However, as in my other cases, environmental law is an exception. The Charter for the Environment, appended to the Constitution, includes article 7 stating: "Everyone has the right, in the conditions and to the extent permitted by law, . . . to participate in the public decision-making processes likely to affect the environment." The right is not conditioned by a requirement for individual harm; it applies to everyone. The central case, *Association France Nature Environnement* (AFNE) (2011),[218] involved the list of facilities subject to various licensing criteria under the environmental laws (*régime des installations classées*).[219] The classification of facilities matters both to the owners of installations and to members of the public concerned with environmental harms. The AFNE argued that the process of promulgating the list violated article 7 because there was insufficient consultation, particularly with environmental organizations. The Conseil Constitutionnel confirmed, first, that article 7 created a constitutional right to consultation, the key to exercising its jurisdiction. It then held that the statutory text violated this right, and it set a deadline of two years for amendment of the statute.[220] The decision implies that whenever parliament takes measures that affect the environment, it must incorporate public participation into executive regulatory procedures. The Conseil Constitutionnel provided no precise guidance concerning acceptable responses. The subsequent amendments to the air pollution statute established a bare-bones notice-and-comment procedure that the Conseil subsequently approved.

The pollution statute was unconstitutional under the doctrine of "negative ultra vires." Parliament cannot leave constitutional rights and liberties unprotected; it has to give statutory protection to these rights and not leave the executive free to decide their content. Under that broad rubric, the Conseil Constitutionnel decided several closely related cases in favor of the plaintiffs.[221] These decisions raise challenges to administrative procedures that go beyond the treatment of aggrieved individuals and extend to broad-based policies affecting the rights of many citizens.

In July 2019, the Conseil d'État stepped in to enforce the amended statute's specific requirements. It voided an order by the Minister for Ecological and Inclusive Development (*Ministre de la Transition Écologique et Solidaire*), who heads the ministry that enforces the environmental laws. In 2018, the ministry suspended hunting of two endangered shorebirds in certain regions of France. An association of hunters complained that the ministry issued its order one day after the close of the comment period without waiting for the minimum of the four days that the statute required. The Conseil d'État held in favor of the association, suspended the order, and awarded the association €3,000 to cover some of its legal fees. The ministry had no extraordinary reason to evade the requirement, and it did not synthesize or respond to the comments received.[222]

Several advocacy groups have challenged French policy on climate change by bringing a joint action for failure to act (*un recours en carence fautive*) against the French government.[223] They are basing their action on the same Charter for the Environment invoked in the *AFNE* case along with French statutes and international law. The case is analogous to the US legal challenges by Our Children's Trust. The groups notified the prime minister and other members of the government in late 2018 of their demands for government action. The French government rejected the groups' request, and the groups then brought a case in the Administrative Court of Paris that issued a decision in February 2021 designed to force the government to act but without giving specifics.[224] The government will surely appeal the decision, but whatever the ultimate result in the courts, it will raise public awareness.

Elsewhere in Europe, groups are making similar rights-based claims to protect the climate. Thus, in *Urgenda v. Netherlands*, the Supreme Court of the Netherlands in December 2019 found that the state had a duty to reduce greenhouse gases grounded on the duty to protect the right to life and the right to respect for private and family life in articles 2 and 8 of the European Convention on Human Rights. In Norway, the Supreme Court has heard a case arguing that the Norwegian Constitution's right to a healthy environment ought to prevent the government from proceeding with licenses to permit exploration for oil and gas in the Arctic off the country's coast.[225]

Although such litigation in France and elsewhere can affect public opinion, in France, at least, the impact of the French courts on government and agency policymaking is muted. There are several reasons for this. First, court decisions have traditionally been quite concise, with conclusions left unexplained beyond references to legal texts. Courts make crucial decisions concerning the regulation of important areas like telecommunications or energy in a few short paragraphs.[226] However, that critique may be obsolete. A 2012 duo of Conseil d'État decisions dealing with telecom firms' failure to comply with the terms of a merger ran to sixty pages.[227]

Second, in most cases the decisions do not explain why the Conseil Constitutionnel's rulings are superior to alternative possible holdings. The lack of dissent compounds this tendency along with the secrecy of deliberations.

Third, if courts characterize the issues as purely legal questions, this may hide the fact that there may have been room for choice. If there are ambiguities in the text, the courts choose an interpretation and claim that it is the only legally possible one. The opinion presents political or policy choices as legal impositions. Open-ended "legal" concepts like "proportionality" and "general interest" empower courts to balance interests when they decide cases that are essentially political in nature.

Fourth, the Conseil d'État seldom assesses the reasons given by the administration. Absent specific statutory provisions, the only decisions that require reasons are those that derogate a law or a regulation and several types of unfavorable decisions.[228] General rules, favorable decisions, and decisions falling outside the statutory list are free from the duty to give reasons unless a particular statutory provision applies.[229] For example, if a government agency assigns a license for the use of radio frequencies to an applicant, it does not have to provide a statement of reasons because the decision is beneficial to the firm, even though other companies could have been harmed by the choice, and radio listeners are affected as well.[230] Even if there is an obligation to give reasons, they are meant to protect rights and facilitate judicial challenges. Reason-giving is not connected to more general ideas of transparency and political legitimacy.[231] The Conseil Constitutionnel has also ruled that there is no general constitutional duty to give reasons.[232] It has not recognized executive reason-giving as an essential feature of republican government. French scholars have critiqued the lack of a general duty to give reasons as "a hardly justifiable archaism"[233] or as posing a threat of "anachronistic authoritarianism."[234]

Fifth, even if the law requires reasons, the doctrines of the "substitution of reasons" and "overabundant reasons" limit the transparency of administrative actions. The reasons that agencies give when they issue decisions do not bind them before the reviewing court. They can ask for the "substitution of reasons" *(substitution des motifs)* while the suit is still pending.[235] The judge can correct the legal ground of a decision, instead of annulling it.[236] In most cases, the administration requests the substitution.[237] Judges can also make the switch on their own.[238] The judge can substitute either the legal grounds (*base légale*) or the legal reasoning (*motifs*) of the challenged decision. Although the substitution of reasons avoids useless annulments, it also discourages agencies from putting much effort into articulating the reasons because those reasons can be amended or reformed before the courts. If the Conseil d'État did review the reasoning behind secondary norms, these doctrines would limit government accountability to the public because the government can modify its original reasons to suit the court. Notice the difference from the US Supreme Court's ruling in *Department of Homeland Security v. Regents of the University of California*, dealing with the "Dreamers" (DACA). As I noted earlier, the Supreme Court was explicit about the illegality of providing new reasons for a policy when the policy comes before a court.

A French judge can also apply the so-called *théorie des motifs surabondants*. If the administration presents a multiplicity of reasons and only some are illegal, *Ministre Économie et Finances c. Perrot* held that the judge can disregard the illegal reasons and uphold the decision so long as the remaining reasons are sufficient.[239] The illegal reasons are either "decisive" or "overabundant" (*surabondants*).[240] This doctrine would undermine public accountability if applied to government decrees and ordinances. It gives agencies an incentive to supply many reasons to increase the chances of avoiding annulments. Multiple, inaccurate reasons can be as detrimental to accountability as no reasons at all. This problem appears not to arise in the review of rules in the US, perhaps because agencies worry that the courts will remand a rule if any of the justifications is faulty.[241]

Essentially, in spite of the courts' permissive standing rules and broad jurisdiction, government policymaking made through decrees and ordinances is seldom subject to judicial review, and even if review does occur, existing doctrines are not well suited to the task. The Conseil d'État has virtually ignored the difficulties of reviewing regulatory policy decisions and has done little to accommodate public-law doctrines to the realities of the modern regulatory state. This does not mean that the French approach to judicial review is problematic overall. Nevertheless, it privileges the protection of legality—to the detriment of other goals, such as administrative efficiency, technical competence, and political accountability.

However, the Conseil d'État does evaluate decrees and ordinances ex ante, in its capacity as government advisor. It reviews draft secondary legislation before it is issued. Although the review, in principle, could be wide-ranging, in practice, it appears to focus on the rule's legal basis. Its reports, unlike the litigations (*contentieux*) decided by the Conseil d'État, are not public unless the government wants to release them; hence, one can only examine a biased sample. Still, the available examples indicate that they are similar to its judicial opinions. Subsequently, decrees and ordinances sometimes come to court in a lawsuit, but most of them are not reviewed for policymaking accountability. As Thomas Perroud and I argue, this practice eliminates the possibility of examining the policymaking process.[242] If the Conseil d'État did engage in judicial review of policy instruments, it would need the institutional capability to address technically complex and politically sensitive issues.

Remedies

The remedy for a procedural failure is to quash the resulting decision and require the administration to redo the process in line with the court's decision. Sometimes the courts set a time limit either for redoing the process or for amending the statute. The former was the Conseil d'État's response for the case of the merging high schools in Lyon and for the hunting ban mentioned earlier. The latter was the Conseil Constitutionnel's response to the lack of consultation under the air pollution statute because the act itself did not include a consultation requirement. Taking a somewhat different tack, the CE in *Commune de Grande-Synthe* refused to order the government to take immediate action to remedy its *refus implicite* (implicit failure) to take the measures required to combat climate change. Instead, it gave the commune three months to submit supplementary material to the court on the measures that should be taken. Three months is a very short window of time, and the CE did not give any guidance on procedure.[243]

In other cases, the courts may hold that a procedural failure had no impact on the ultimate decision and so should have no legal consequences. Alternatively, the court may find in favor of the plaintiff, but if the disputed project was completed in the meantime, it will not be dismantled and no damages will be paid. Reforms in 2000, nevertheless, allow the administrative courts to issue injunctions that suspend the effects of administrative decisions in a wide range of cases.[244]

The 2021 case decided by the Administrative Court of Paris is noteworthy for the judges' willingness to consider claims for compensation raised by civil society plaintiffs. The groups only requested nominal monetary damages but also asked the court to require the government to provide material compensation in the form of mitigating measures to deal with climate change.[245] Obviously, if that claim survives judicial review in the CE and Conseil Constitutionnel, it would represent an unexpectedly aggressive use of judicial power.

Case Law, Codes, and Presidential Power

France's strong presidency has not been constrained by judicial review of government policymaking processes. The judiciary has not taken the initiative; the executive is unlikely to propose such a statute, and the legislature cannot act alone. The Constitution only imposes procedural constraints on rulemaking in the field of environmental policy. Referenda are also a possible way to enact a statute or to amend the Constitution. There are two ways of holding referenda on bills relating to a broad range of topics. One route depends on a presidential initiative, but a second route does not. If initiated by one-fifth of the legislature and subsequently supported by one-tenth of the electors, a referendum on a proposed law can take place.[246] In 2019–2020, opponents of President Macron's plan to privatize the Parisian airports attempted to use that process. However, although the petition obtained over 1 million signatures, the number was far below the requirement of 10 percent of eligible voters.[247] This process, operating independently of the president, could, in principle, produce a statute specifying publicly accountable procedures for the issuance of decrees and ordinances.

However, referenda have the problems illustrated by the UK's Brexit vote. That vote suffered from considerable misinformation and illustrated the weaknesses of making policy through direct democracy. In France, the Citizens' Assembly on Climate is a more positive example of citizen input and debate. The organizers provided background information on the topic to a small, diverse group of citizens that met over several weekends. However, the assembly was a presidential initiative that merely provided recommendations. The government's response to the recommendations will go through the same type of review as any other legislative or regulatory action. The proposed constitutional amendment placing environmental protection into article 1 must be approved not only by the legislature but also through a referendum open to all voters.

France had a chance to move in the notice-and-comment direction with the passage of the Code of Administrative Procedure in 2015.[248] Until that time, in a nation famous for codifying private law, the case law of the Conseil d'État comprised French administrative law. The Conseil largely drafted the new code itself, and it mostly codifies existing doctrine.

Both the Conseil d'État and the Conseil Constitutionnel occasionally review government policymaking procedures. For example, a 2017 Conseil d'État decision upheld a straw poll designed to assist a public body in selecting the name for a region of southwest France. Although no consultation was required, the Conseil d'État held that if carried out, the process must ensure that citizens are properly informed of the options and of the possibility of participation. Although only 200,000 participated out of the 6.1 million eligible to cast a ballot, the decision accepted the process as an input into the final government decision.[249] Thus, as in the UK, even if the law does not require a consultation, if one occurs, the public body must act in good faith.

Conclusions

Judicial review of administrative policymaking processes depends on a country's constitutional structure and its civil- or common-law background.

Furthermore, statutory law framing administrative procedures arises from the relationship between the legislature and the executive. If courts seek to further procedural values in executive rulemaking procedures, they must operate inside existing constitutional and statutory frameworks. Misalignments between judicial orders and political reality can backfire. The challenge for courts is to harmonize their rulings with the reality of their position in the structure of government and with the interests and values of political actors in the legislature and the executive.

Constitutional courts have a mandate to uphold the rights articulated in their nations' constitutions, and that role allows them to overturn the choices made by the executive branch that violate those rights. In the US, France, and Germany, that mandate extends to statutory law as well. In this volume, I go further to argue that courts ought to play a second role in upholding the basic principles of democratic government. Assuring the integrity of elections and of legislative behavior is one aspect of this oversight, but I argue for a second role—review of policymaking processes in executive ministries and independent agencies.[250] Those policy choices are subject to weak checks flowing from the electorate through their elected representatives to the executive. Judicial review can further democratic accountability by supporting public engagement with executive-branch rulemaking and with policymaking in independent regulatory agencies.

In fulfilling that oversight role, the courts can support both public input into executive policy choices and transparency about the reasons behind these choices. Unfortunately, with the partial exception of the environment, public law has done little to further public participation in my European cases. Lacking clear mandates in the constitutional text, constitutional courts have been reluctant to go further. Jurists invoke the chain of legitimacy as a reason for them to stand aside. In the US, the APA covers rulemaking and mandates notice, public consultation, and reason-giving. However, the lack of a clear constitutional connection opens the way to simplistic unitary-executive theories and makes the administrative process vulnerable to short-term political whims.

Even when courts invoke the values of transparency and reason-giving, they often do so only to help the judges themselves understand the actions of the executive. Their motivation is not to improve public accountability but, instead, to enhance judicial competence. Judicial review should also examine the executive's accountability to ordinary citizens, not just its relationship to reviewing courts. Some courts ask the executive to provide them with reasons in ongoing lawsuits, a request that may help the courts but does not increase policymaking transparency or public engagement with the work of the bureaucracy.

Similarly, some courts have accepted agency practices that share policy-relevant information only with a designated list of stakeholders and experts, perhaps through their appointment to advisory committees. The aim is to ensure that the policy reflects both state-of-the-art expertise and the interests of specific constituencies. Agency officials with particular policy goals can bias the choice of appointees. Some committees include members of the legislature, providing a link to political actors. However, if the general public is poorly represented, such consultations are not a substitute for more open-ended methods.

Constitutional courts, as well as administrative tribunals and general courts, can have an oversight role that goes beyond the protection of rights. Unfortunately, absent a clear constitutional text, political actors may not have an incentive to draft statutes that further democratic values inside the administration. For example, legislative majorities in parliamentary systems have little interest in limiting the rulemaking freedom of their own governments, and they cannot bind future governments with different political goals. In France, the powerful president has little reason to tie his hands procedurally. Hence, efforts by the judiciary to innovate may meet with opposition from politicians, who charge them with overstepping their role. Even in the US, where judicial review of the rulemaking process is entrenched in the APA, there has been a drumbeat of criticism claiming that the judiciary has exceeded its monitoring role. These criticisms threaten to obscure the key role of the APA in furthering democratic legitimacy. Conversely, if the UK Supreme Court or the constitutional tribunals in France and Germany required notice-and-comment procedures for major executive rules, such holdings would fit uncomfortably with current practices and conventional constitutional interpretations.

What, then, ought reformers to do if they wish to push both the legislature and the courts in the direction of reform? Judicial review can take many forms. At one extreme, the courts limit their jurisdiction, defining many issues as political questions beyond their ken and refusing to consider challenges linked to policymaking in the executive or independent agencies. One way to do this is to impose stringent standing rules that limit review of policy choices or that confine review to narrow issues of ultra vires. Somewhat more extensive review can focus on the conformity of substantive rules with statutes or the constitution, but with considerable deference to government or agency interpretations. Whatever route it takes, substantive review must confront the limited technical competence of judges trained in the law rather than in science or social science. Even if they routinely consult experts, the ultimate balancing act is in their hands. As a result, a procedural turn in judicial review would be consistent with both democratic accountability and with the inherent difficulty of judicial review of substance.

Courts can police the procedures that government bodies use as they promulgate rules with the force of law. They can check if the executive and the agencies provide public reasons and consult not only with experts but also with the citizenry. This procedural approach reverses the prevailing doctrine in some polities where procedural failures are legally relevant only if they affect the substance of the government action. In those cases, the courts focus on substance, where they may have little expertise, and review process only if it affects substance. They may judge a procedural failure to be a "harmless error," but such rulings place the courts in the position of evaluating substance under the guise of procedural review.

Review of process places the courts in their proper relationship with the rest of the modern state. Judges' legal training, nevertheless, may make review of executive policymaking procedures difficult or ineffective if they give priority to court-like procedures. Judges may be unable or unwilling to take account of the technical and democratic nature of executive policymaking. In evaluating the adequacy of public participation, the trial is not an appropriate model to impose on public administration. There are no "parties" in the sense of a lawsuit or an individualized adjudication, but there are stakeholders, interest groups, and citizens. Courts need to be familiar with alternative routes to public involvement that are consistent with the democratic character of the state. Judges must also have some ability to evaluate substance to decide if the process is well matched to the underlying policy issues.

Review of procedures should stress the government's willingness to listen to voices from outside the closed circle of the bureaucracy, elected officials, and those with narrow personal or financial interests. The incentives of sitting politicians in both the legislature and the executive are not always consistent with outside consultation and participation. Cabinet officials and top bureaucrats may wish to avoid the bother of publicly accountable processes and may favor organized groups with large economic stakes. Cautious or unsympathetic officials may fail to carry out statutory mandates when they issue rules. The goodwill of official policymakers is an insufficient check. Hence, policymaking accountability needs legal entrenchment, subject to judicial review.

But can citizens trust the courts to uphold democratic values? Judges may seek to further their own interests at the expense of the rule of law. On the one hand, corrupt judges may take payoffs from the parties and decide in favor of the highest briber. Apart from a few "bad apples," such outright self-seeking does not seem a major problem in my case-study countries, at least in high-level courts dealing with public law.[251] On the other hand, judges' policy preferences and political leanings may affect their decisions, along with their commitments to constitutional and legal principles.[252] Although judges are likely to temper their decisions in the light of political reality and their own beliefs, most do not flout clear legal mandates. They may interpret open-ended texts to comport with their preferred policies, but their commitment to "the rule of law" can lead them to rule against their own policy preferences. Even the common law, with its reliance on the unfolding case law, constrains judges to justify departures from long-standing principles in both the US and the UK. Judiciaries in representative democracies are wary of becoming overtly involved in politics. Their decisions may fall on one or another side of the political spectrum, but most seek to maintain a reputation for the impartial application of the law.

Responsible judges are sensitive to their status as unelected officials who should not interfere aggressively with political choices. This sense of their role helps to constrain them from imposing doctrines that are deeply at odds with the practical operation of the political system. Such behavior is both principled and strategic. It derives from a normative commitment to their judicial role, but it also acknowledges that the judiciary cannot enforce its decisions without political and popular support. Although their policy views influence their judgments, responsible judges act with restraint based both on their role in the political system and on a realistic view of their power relative to other actors.[253]

If the courts are to help further the democratic accountability of policymaking, they must be willing to hear from those who feel aggrieved, both individuals and groups. Those who claim rights violations or unfairness are conventional plaintiffs. At the same time, groups that represent particular interests and policy areas or have specialized expertise can help judges review claimed public-law violations. Admitting external actors is in tension with the traditional role of courts in resolving individual cases on the basis of law. Legal systems, such as those of Germany and France, with specialized administrative-court systems more easily accept the judiciary's role in maintaining the public-service aspect of the state, beyond individual complaints about state overreaching. Nevertheless, the use of non-legal expertise to decide cases is often controversial because it is in tension with the judges' own training and view of their role.

Judges on constitutional and administrative tribunals in the UK, Germany, and France are beginning to accept a role for courts in maintaining the democratic and popular legitimacy of participatory procedures in rulemaking. This is by no means a uniform or clear-cut development; it depends on the language of individual statutes and most often arises in the environmental area. Nonetheless, some judicial opinions defend broad concepts of citizen participation. Science and data quality frequently interact with claims based on either democratic legitimacy or the protection of rights, and they push the courts to judge mixed questions of fact and law. Even if particular cases have a narrow focus—for instance, pollution standards, an airport runway, or welfare benefits—the language of justification is sometimes consistent with a more general defense of public involvement through hearings, public comments, and reason-giving. These opinions do not challenge the ultimate authority of the executive to make policy within the framework of the law; rather, they support government and agency choices that further policymaking accountability.

Without summarizing the vast scholarship on constitutional rights, one can still see how the language of rights intersects with the administrative process. Do constitutional or supreme courts recognize procedural rights that further democratic values, or do they only consider the process that is due to individuals seeking to protect themselves against state overreaching? In my European cases, does the jurisprudence of rights substitute, in part, for the lack of statutes that specify administrative policymaking processes? If so, how do these constraints differ from those in the US presidential system?

In spite of the awkward fit between legal training on the one hand and executive policymaking on the other, courts can check that those making rules have not ignored major bodies of knowledge and opinion, while recognizing that no policy choice can satisfy everyone.[254] Preserving democratic legitimacy and checking competence are appropriate judicial roles, but ones that need to be exercised with restraint. Judges are neither politicians nor technocrats, but they can help prevent abuses and encourage positive developments.

8. *Policymaking Accountability as a Democratic Value*

In this concluding chapter, I put my four case studies into a broader international context. The book's coverage is highly selective, but I hope to convince my readers that its perspective is relevant elsewhere, especially to countries making a transition to democracy and to middle-income countries whose governments are seeking a stronger system of public law. Here, I draw on my past work on Hungary and Poland, but my aim is to encourage others to carry out more thorough investigations—not only in Europe but also in Africa, Asia, Latin America, and the Middle East. The need to balance technocratic knowledge with public accountability is a fundamental requirement for any nation struggling to sustain a credible democracy, regardless of its geographic location.

Comparative scholarship is particularly valuable in this regard. It can enable reformers to look beyond a country's inherited legal traditions and consider a richer array of options. This is especially important in the many cases where existing frameworks were inherited from a colonial or authoritarian past. Although each country confronts special problems, the successes and failures of other national efforts are an essential resource for self-conscious choice.

My approach differs from two excessively deterministic strands that currently dominate the literature. One stresses the role of inherited legal traditions in determining present conditions. The second, in contrast, sees a worldwide convergence on a common package of accountability methods.

Some work in law and economics falls into the first category. This cross-country empirical work asks whether common-law or civil-law systems are better at promoting economic growth. Some data-driven studies seek to vindicate the claims of the common law.[1] Others dispute these results and conclude that legal traditions are not very significant once one takes other factors into account.[2] The debate continues, but each side focuses its attention on macroeconomic aggregates related to economic growth.[3] In contrast, my interest is in the democratic pedigree of public regulatory law under alternative historical traditions and constitutional structures, not just the links between law and economic performance. I agree that law has real effects on the world, but I focus on the ways that administrative-law procedures can enhance the democratic legitimacy of the state. The impact of law on economic development is only one part of the story.

My approach also differs from a second important trend that challenges the very idea that different legal forms have a significant causal impact on the resolution of real-world problems. These scholars contend that global social, economic, and political forces are pushing legal systems toward convergence. In the economic sphere, they point to the way in which institutions like the World Bank, the World Trade Organization, and international arbitration tribunals are creating norms and legal rules on a global or regional basis.[4] They also point to similar developments in the fields of human rights and anti-corruption advocacy, supported by such organizations as Amnesty International and Transparency International.[5]

These writers overstate the degree and type of convergence—often because they have a clear idea of the end-state to which countries should converge. But the trend toward universalization is hardly inexorable—even in places like the European Union.

There is a conceptual problem with the current debate. It does not unpack different legal systems to take into account the way the structure of government (presidential or parliamentary) interacts with its legal tradition (common law or civil law). What is more, the literature highlights commercial law and private economic law, with occasional bows to other areas of law, such as ownership of the media and judicial independence.[6] It does not consider the benefits of public regulations in providing environmental protection, occupational health and safety, and protections for consumers, debtors, or workers.[7] Nor does it consider the systemic difficulties involved in implementing such regulations effectively. Both scholarly trends, in short, operate at much too high a level of generality.

This book, in contrast, asks reformers in different legal traditions to challenge their own preconceptions of the role of public law in representative democracy—that is, to unpack "the law" and distinguish between substantive and procedural aspects. The serious pursuit of political accountability will challenge the status quo and the political-economic interests that are advantaged by it. Successful reform requires the mobilization of political will, not reliance on the inexorable effects of pre-existing legal traditions or worldwide forces.

Reform also requires a clear focus on a number of key decision points. I highlight six in particular. The chapter begins with issues involving the internal structure of the executive: (1) its rulemaking procedures and their relation to the decree power of the executive and (2) the autonomy permitted to quasi-independent public regulatory agencies and quasi-private bodies. I turn next to policymaking techniques: (3) cost-benefit analysis and impact assessment and (4) public participation and consultation. Once the importance of these background conditions is recognized, I place (5) judicial review within the overall regime. Finally, I bring in (6) the exploitation of public regulatory power for private gain—both through blatantly illegal forms of corruption, as well as more subtle, but no less important, forms of private influence on public policymaking.

Executive Policymaking via Regulations and Decrees

Many administrative procedure statutes cover decisions in individual cases but do not constrain the production of either rules with the force of law or executive decrees and guidance documents. Constitutional principles may view procedural restrictions as inapplicable to executive policymaking because it is a political not a legal activity. For example, the German Basic Law or Grundgesetz requires statutory delegations to list their "content, purpose, and scope," but it does not govern rulemaking procedures. The chain of legitimacy is the only other constraint on executive policymaking. German administrative-procedure law only deals with "administrative acts," a term that omits regulations, that is, secondary norms, and guidelines. The recently enacted French administrative procedure code is mostly a restatement of existing case law and does not include a general right of public participation in rulemaking. The UK rulemaking process inside the government is similarly unconstrained. In all three countries, however, the legislature must approve some secondary norms, and some substantive statutes require the government to hold public hearings and organize other forms of participation.

The lack of general procedural constraints not only results from each country's legal tradition; it also depends upon the distribution of power. The powerful US Congress supported a statute placing procedural checks on executive rulemaking, and the president accepted this check on his power, at least in part for political reasons. Many democracies, especially outside Europe and the British Commonwealth, have strong presidents with weak legislatures, whose members are not strong or well organized enough either to resist policy delegation or to demand policymaking accountability from the executive. France comes the closest to this model in my study, but outside Europe there are more extreme examples of strong elected presidents—for example, in Argentina and the Philippines.[8] Furthermore, to the extent that presidents use patronage and other individualized benefits to control legislators, neither branch will want accountable and transparent policymaking. This combination of a strong chief executive, a weak legislature, and political alliances built on personal ties or even outright payoffs produces executive policymaking that is unaccountable to the electorate.[9] The executive may find it politically expedient to consult with key stakeholders or even with the general public. In the absence of a legal mandate, officials will do so only in their own interest.

Cutting across these differences, environmental policymaking stands out as an area where many polities accept public participation in executive policymaking. In my European cases, a specialized treaty supports civil-society input and has constitutional status in France. However, public input has a functional justification in the environmental area beyond the formal law. In this technically complex area, delegation to the executive is inevitable, but such delegation implies a public responsibility to hear from concerned groups and citizens over and above votes in periodic elections. Many environmental harms and benefits are spread broadly across society, so the government cannot rely on aggrieved individuals to hold it to account. Civil-society advocacy groups can help to move executive policymaking in a more democratically accountable direction that complements the statutory law. The role of such groups goes beyond the protection of individual rights. The chain of legitimacy back to the voters is a key anchor for any representative democracy, but it is an insufficient check, especially for environmental policy. Public law needs to incorporate public input and to require executive policymakers to give public reasons for their choices.

In any policy area, organized advocacy is important both to educate the public and to provide clear and useful input to the executive. The law ought to make it easy to register as a not-for-profit advocacy organization, subject to disclosure rules to limit the creation of for-profits in disguise. Banging on pots and pans in Argentina (*cacerolazos*) or wearing yellow vests (*gilets jaunes*) in France can help raise awareness of particular issues both among the citizens and inside government.[10] Lasting impact requires hard work both to master technical details and to mobilize people to testify at hearings and monitor the actions of the executive, including bringing court challenges. Institutional survival requires resources, but non-governmental organizations (NGOs) should not be beholden to incumbent governments or opposition parties. Tax exemptions for both donors and organization provide incentives for donations. Other options include earmarking certain public funds to support NGOs, but with the allocation made by a body that operates independently of the government.[11]

As outlined in earlier chapters, one model for executive and agency policymaking procedures is the notice-and-comment procedure of the US APA.[12] The APA requires agencies to post draft rules publicly and mandates a hearing open to anyone with an interest in the subject at hand. Final rules must include a public statement that explains the statutory basis of the rule and justifies the outcome. Rules are subject to judicial review for conformity with the underlying statute, the Constitution, and APA procedures. The US system is imperfect, and even its strong points have been undermined by executive and agency efforts that limit its impact. The rise of what Peter Shane calls "presidentialism" is undermining the policy role of cabinet departments.[13] Furthermore, the US model may be difficult to transfer to other political systems. In using US practice as a guide to reform, I both recognize its practical limitations and acknowledge that differences in political structure and in the organization of society can undermine its applicability. Nevertheless, it expresses an important goal: public participation in executive policymaking needs to be taken seriously in all polities. The goal is to complement, not override, the role of political parties.

Assuring the democratic legitimacy of executive-branch policymaking is especially important in democracies where the legislature is weak, divided, and poorly institutionalized. A legislature may have few staff resources and many inexperienced members. As a result, chief executives may face few effective checks and may issue decrees with minimal legal constraints. Even if decrees require eventual parliamentary approval, that process is pro forma in some presidential systems and is unlikely to matter much in parliamentary ones. Decrees give the chief executive and the cabinet a first-mover advantage. The head of government, whether a president or a prime minister, is unlikely to propose constraints on his or her power. Conversely, if there are no binding procedures for public input or for government transparency and reason-giving, legislative backbenchers and opposition party leaders may push for legislative vetoes over executive rules—in the form of either an up-or-down vote or a report-and-wait requirement, as in the UK. In a presidential system, where different parties may control different institutions, such oversight may seem especially attractive given the difficulty of covering all the relevant issues in statutes. In this second case, legislative oversight is an alternative to the lack of public input into regulatory drafting. In practice, the legislature often provides little effective check on the executive. In the worst case, a fractious, divided legislature engages in patronage appointments, private payoffs, and illegal political party financing to follow the lead of the president.[14]

Nevertheless, even weak legislative oversight may help in the absence of strong administrative capacity. Requiring the executive and the agencies to place rules before the legislature or a relevant committee would ensure some level of transparency with the accompanying media attention. In the UK, for example, some statutory instruments must survive an up-or-down vote in both houses. Under another version, the legislature would not have the power to rescind or amend the rule, but could demand that cabinet ministers appear in Parliament and could issue a critical report. Recall, however, my earlier criticism that legislative vetoes undermine the purpose of delegation in the first place. That critique holds true here as well, but it is balanced by the need to interject public oversight into executive policymaking.[15]

If a country is making a transition to democracy from an authoritarian past, assuring the policymaking accountability of the executive is especially important. For example, consider the cases of Hungary and Poland during their transition after 1989.[16] Although each has its own particular history, they faced common challenges. One legacy of the authoritarian system in both countries was the perceived illegitimacy of executive rulemaking. Their socialist governments used executive decrees and guidance documents to manage the economy and society with little or no public input. After the transition, rather than seek effective public involvement in executive rulemaking, the drafters of the new legal order in Poland strictly limited the use of executive rules.[17] Thus, some statutes are difficult to implement effectively because the executive cannnot issue binding rules; the government may administer others non-transparently through informal acts and case-by-case adjudications. The Hungarian Constitution authorizes the issuance of decrees but has no provisions covering procedures.[18] Hence, consultation is mainly under the control of the government and can change dramatically when the political coalition shifts. Hungary's 1992 freedom of information act had an exception stating: "Unless otherwise provided by law, working documents and other data prepared for the authority's own use, or for the purpose of decisionmaking are not public within 30 years of their creation."[19] After amendments in 2011 and 2018, the time period fell to ten years,[20] but even the reduced time limit constrains effective outside review of draft laws or regulations. In fact, that seemed to be one of its goals. Although in both Hungary and Poland ministries must publish their final rules, neither country has institutionalized public input into rulemaking. My 2005 study of the transition in those countries concluded that the failure to institutionalize the procedures for executive rulemaking left a loophole for unaccountable executive policymaking. Current governments are arguably using that loophole aggressively.

The lack of consultation may reflect the worry that strong voluntary organizations could inhibit the creation of strong political parties. The German focus on the chain of legitimacy expresses that same concern. The suspicion of interest-based representation in eastern Europe surfaces in debates over the role of non-party groups in political life.[21] One sees it in the fate of Hungary's Law on Normative Acts, passed at the end of the socialist period. The act specifies consultation procedures for ministerial decrees. It provides that "citizens—directly or through their representative bodies—participate in the preparation and creation of legal regulations [i.e., normative acts] affecting their daily life."[22] Prior to promulgating a decree, "jurisdictional bodies, social organizations and interest representative organs have to be involved in the preparation of draft legal regulations which either affect the interests represented and protected by them or their social relations."[23] However, the government decides who is to receive the draft and how much time to allocate for comments. This looks like a good start toward a notice-and-comment process, but these provisions were repealed in 1990 by the first democratic government on the ground that they were window dressing enacted by the last socialist government to enhance its democratic credentials.[24] Instead, the new government could have given the act real meaning. No sharp contradiction need exist between political-party strength and a vibrant civil society focused on particular policy arenas. The chain of legitimacy through elections is inadequate. The general language of statutes enacted by political parties in the legislature can be made concrete through regulations whose legitimacy is enhanced by civil-society input.[25]

As in my west European cases, environmental regulation is a partial exception. Under pressure from the European Union accession requirements, Polish law requires the preparation of strategic environmental impact assessments and public consultation. The EIA process mandates "social consultation with all interested subjects, not only with those who can prove their legal interest."[26] This broadening of consultation makes it possible for civil-society groups to participate. The Freedom of Information Act may also facilitate the involvement of NGOs. However, the act is vague about how the participation process should be structured.[27] A 2008 act focuses on access to information and public participation in environmental protection and EIA. However, the European Commission argues that the Polish government has not made efforts to inform the public and encourage participation.[28] Other commentators cite the limited sucess of public-participation efforts.[29] In Hungary, the Environmental Protection Act includes participation requirements, mostly in the form of advisory committees.[30] The European Commission's Environmental Implementation Review for Hungary for 2019 critiques two factors that may limit public participation: "(i) a tendency to exclude participation by multiple individuals or groups; and (ii) the fact that administration procedures are streamlined and accelerated."[31]

The Polish and Hungarian governments have not developed generally accountable policymaking procedures inside the executive. Both lack ways to ensure public knowledge, open processes, government justifications, and effective judicial review. Their governments do not routinely publicize draft regulations and statutes. Even when plans and drafts are made public, few laws require open-ended access to hearings or information-gathering from the public. Instead, consultation is limited to pre-set advisory groups or a select group of insiders. Consultation through these routes is sometimes quite broad, but the nature of consultation is limited by the advisory committees' composition and by the level of government interest in hearing from those outside the national government. Neither country requires written justifications for normative acts (regulations), and such justifications are seldom prepared.

Both cases complement my case studies by highlighting the need for representative democracies to go beyond elections, representative legislatures, and the establishment of political parties. Executive policymaking should have a legal basis that accepts its necessity and gives it democratic legitimacy through structures of policymaking accountability—that is, transparency, public input, and reason-giving, with judicial review of process. These procedures ought to be a priority for reformers not only in countries making a transition from an authoritarian past, but also for any country that is rethinking the connection between its adminstrative-law system and constitutional structures that entrench democratic institutions.

Independent Public Agencies and Delegation to Private or Quasi-private Bodies

Many transitional democracies arose in political-economic systems with extensive state ownership. For example, most of the economy was state-owned in eastern Europe, and public utilities, natural resources, and network industries were in state hands elsewhere. Democratic governments have sometimes privatized parastatals or, at least, overseen their incorporation as private-law entities with substantial residual state ownership. Some formerly public firms now operate as ordinary private firms, subject only to antitrust, environmental, labor, and health and safety rules. Many privatized or quasi-private firms are natural monopolies or operate in markets with serious imperfections. Then, states usually create industry-specific regulatory agencies with a degree of independence from both the firms and the state. Unfortunately, in polities worldwide, firms subject to regulation may capture the agency. Capture can occur either because of or in spite of the aims of the country's politicians. Even when independence is a way to resist capture by corrupt officials and their cronies, such bodies may seem illegitimate and undemocratic because of their weak connection to the political branches.

Chapter 4 outlined the options and their strengths and weaknesses in my cases. Other examples can help illustrate the difficulties. Argentina and the Philippines are both presidential systems that carried out extensive privatizations of public utilities. Following US and European models, they created specialized regulatory agencies that are independent of the rest of government and embody considerable industry-specific expertise. At the same time, both countries gave their presidents emergency powers that permitted them to take over nominally independent agencies. Presidents used these for their own political purposes.[32] These cases illustrate the difficulty, especially in presidential systems, of entrenching agency independence.

One answer is a constitution that does not give presidents unchecked emergency powers.[33] Nevertheless, even if a president does not interfere in an agency's day-to-day operation, he or she may choose a pliable official as its head or stack its board with allies. My case studies provide important guides: multi-member commissions with rotating membership, fixed terms that are not coterminous with that of the government or president, independent funding, and appointment processes that ensure political balance and/or require relevant expertise. However, some regulatory agencies are unable to issue rules with the force of law, a limitation that reduces their independence. Other agencies, as in the US, may require partisan balance, and the appointment of commissioners may require both the executive and the legislature to play a role. These provisions help avoid too close a link to the politicians in control of the core executive, but they may open up the body to the excessive influence of the regulated industry. To limit that result, the procedural constraints of administrative law, such as a transparent notice-and-comment process, can help, so long as the agency's activities are of interest to public-interest groups and members of the business community distinct from the regulated firms. These might include, for example, the users of electricity and gas for the public-utility regulator, the users of the internet for the communications commission, and freight suppliers for railroads and trucking.

In general, either the core executive or the regulated industry or both can undermine the supposed benefits of independence. There are ways to limit those risks through the design of the agency itself, but if the risk of political capture is very high, there is an alternative. Rather than trying to limit the influence of the regulated industry, the government could outsource that responsibility to private or quasi-public bodies explicitly controlled by the industry or profession. These bodies are not captured; instead, they are set up to serve the interests of a particular industry or profession. At first, this seems a paradoxical solution to the problem of capture, but it can be the least-bad option. The government may lack the needed specialists in, say, engineering, law, accountancy, or medicine and be unable to attract elite practitioners to sit on a commission. Then, professional self-regulation can seem viable. The risks are obvious, but the dangers of assigning regulatory tasks to poorly trained and motivated government officials may outweigh the risks of relying on self-interested private firms. The implementing statutes should impose strong procedural constraints on these bodies, similar to the requirements of US notice-and-comment rulemaking, to ensure that the public, customers, and suppliers have a voice. These bodies essentially create customary law; those who challenge the rules have a high burden of proof. The risk for any polity is that they act only in the interest of regulated entities, upholding monopoly power and becoming so entrenched that the state lacks regulatory control over the industry or profession.

Another alternative is what Mariana Prado and Michael Trebilcock call "institutional bypasses." The government permits the creation of new regulated financial or other markets without closing down an existing regulatory structure that the established elites have captured. Individuals and firms can choose their preferred market. A good example here is the Novo Mercado, a Brazilian alternative to the existing stock market with rules that provide better protection to minority stockholders. The two markets operate in parallel, but, over time, investors and firms may shift to the new option. This is not a general solution for problems such as environmental pollution, where it would produce a race to the bottom, but for financial markets with well-informed participants, it could be a way to work around otherwise entrenched interests.[34]

The puzzle of how to combine expertise with political accountability is particularly acute for regulatory agencies where the regulated industry is politically powerful. The industry may lobby for a body that is not dependent on the cabinet, believing that it will be better off dealing with a regulator that is not beholden to politicians. In other situations, firms may prefer a politically dependent agency that will bow to the wishes of politicians who benefit from industry payoffs—bribes, future employment, or campaign contributions.

Cost-Benefit Analysis and Impact Assessment

In Chapter 5, I outlined the limitation of the analogy between CBA and democracy and highlighted the limits of CBA as a general normative principle for government action. Nevertheless, governments should measure and weigh the costs and benefits to individuals when making policy. The problem is not the individualistic basis of CBA, but, instead, the way benefits and costs are quantified and aggregated. Most of the steps in the process require input from technical experts, but governments ought not to leave the final policy choices to technocrats with no special claims either to make value choices or to represent the voting public. Policy choices are not purely technical exercises.

Technocratic choices that fail to take account of public sentiment can result in a public backlash that public officials cannot neutralize with the claim that the government's decision was backed up by solid analysis. Here are some recent examples. Riots erupted in 2019 when the Chilean government raised transit fares by a small amount based on the recommendation of an expert committee that pointed to the increase in the price of diesel fuel and the fall in the exchange rate against the US dollar. The facts were not in doubt, but the government believed that the imprimatur of experts was sufficient.[35] In Germany, the planned rebuilding of the train station in Stuttgart triggered protests that the police put down in an excessively aggressive fashion. The railroad claimed that it had complied with all the needed procedures, but the public was not satisfied.[36] In France, an increased gasoline tax, meant to combat climate change, sparked the yellow vests (*gilets jaunes*) protests. These examples are lessons for those in emerging democracies who think that technocratic solutions are sufficient. At the same time, it is important to make realistic estimates of the costs of public programs, and responsible politicians need to make difficult choices. However, they need to take the time to explain these choices and, if possible, to involve the public early in the debate. This process can be especially difficult in new or poorly institutionalized polities, but that is all the more reason to be sure that the citizenry has bought into policy conclusions built on expert analysis.

Public Participation and Consultation

How can the executive and the agencies balance expertise with accountability to citizens? As outlined in Chapter 3, transparent procedures combined with public reasons are a necessary part of the answer; they allow citizens to know what the government is doing and how it justifies its actions. As a result, individuals, watchdogs, and the media can critique government actions, and both incumbents and political opponents can use that information at election time. However, after-the-fact review may come too late to affect contemporary policy choices. If expertise is essential, the ballot box is an imperfect instrument for connecting citizens to policy outcomes.

The limitations of transparency and reason-giving suggest that rulemaking procedures ought to engage the public directly when policies are still under discussion inside the executive. Chapter 6 explored a variety of techniques and argued that most are poorly suited to large polities facing technically complex problems. Public participation should involve not just the application of the law in individual cases and local communities but also consultation by the executive branch when it promulgates general rules. My interest is in public participation as an input into rulemaking processes that government bodies organize. For technically complex and society-wide issues, grassroots participatory systems can have only a limited effect, even under ideal circumstances. Rulemaking should ensure adequate participation and transparency, but it cannot mimic village-level engagement. Central-government policymaking is necessary and cannot be made in a decentralized manner.

In recent decades, active public engagement has spearheaded national social and legal transformations. Social movements have generated fundamental shifts in public attitudes toward women, racial and religious minorities, and sexual orientation. These transformations typically take many years and include many different individuals and institutions. For example, a study of US public attitudes toward sexual orientation describes a twenty-eight-year process.[37] The author shows how cultural attitudes can change over time, but the time line of this study is not a realistic model for the time-limited procedures that accompany ordinary policymaking exercises. True, the promulgation of a rule can be part of a deeper process of social change that occurs over decades, but my interest is in the organization of inclusive processes by government agencies making rules under time pressure. The chain of legitimacy operates, but it is insufficient. In a democracy whose citizens have diverse views, unanimous consent is not the goal. Generally, there will be both losers and winners, but the state can institute processes that citizens accept as legitimate even if they do not always get the outcome that they want.

If CBA sets the stage within which public participation occurs, the process must overcome its limits. That implies that participation must be open to those at the bottom of the income ladder, and officials need to address fears of intimidation in an open and straightforward fashion. Long-standing patron-client relationships between politicians and local elites, on the one hand, and ordinary citizens, on the other, may make open-ended citizen participation difficult to institutionalize. The public administration should create a space for independent, issue-oriented citizen involvement.

A transition to democracy from authoritarianism may occur with the assistance of even a weak civil society. Organized citizen groups frequently have been crucial to such transitions. For example, Solidarity in Poland and environmental activists in Hungary catalyzed broader discontent and helped to achieve regime change.[38] After the transition, conversely, Hungarian civil-society groups struggled to survive and to become institutionally relevant. The initial success of Solidarity in Poland did not produce broader civil-society activism. The voluntary nonprofit sector remains thin, private philanthropy is limited, and the government is not open to input from the groups that do exist.[39] Hence, even if the law did require consultation, those provisions might not have had much impact.

Nevertheless, some of the most interesting experiments in public participation come from middle-income countries, some emerging from non-democratic pasts. The most prominent examples are participatory budgeting in Brazil and deliberative polls organized by James Fishkin and his associates throughout the world. I discuss both in Chapter 6. Here, I wish only to suggest the importance of understanding and replicating these and other exercises in citizen involvement under different conditions.

Judicial Review

Rulemaking processes do not always further democratic accountability, even if the law on the books is adequate. Strategic actors can hijack the process; hence, the losers need avenues of appeal to argue that the government has not followed its own procedures or has acted lawlessly.

Judicial review can make corruption and other types of self-dealing harder to hide by forcing review both of the process and of the substantive outcome. Courts should check that agencies have correctly followed procedures and that the result complies with legislative purposes or constitutional principles.[40] However, courts are constrained by the laws on the books. Requiring notice and an ability to comment may have little effect if agencies are not required to give reasons and are not subject to judicial oversight.

For example, the Hungarian Law on Normative Acts includes no provisions for judicial review, so its consultation requirements are not enforceable. Its provisions are essentially internal orders to the bureaucracy and the ministers. The only possibility would be to claim a violation of individual constitutional rights. Under rules on legal standing for civic associations implemented in 2017, environmental groups can serve as litigants, but the Constitutional Court has not been sympathetic to reading consultation requirements into the constitution.[41] In Poland as well, individuals can only access the Constitutional Tribunal if they believe that a final decision of a public body violates their individual rights. Review can only deal with substance, and litigants cannot defend the democratic values of participation and consultation.[42] Non-governmental organizations do not have standing to challenge local laws that contradict national regulations, unless the organization itself has suffered an injury.[43]

As in my cases, the NGOs have leveraged individual rights to seek judicial review of policy, sometimes successfully. To enhance the democratic legitimacy of executive policymaking processes, more straightforward statutory or constitutional assurances of policymaking accountability would give the courts a justification to review procedures without overstepping into explicitly political matters.

Judicial review of executive policymaking procedures only makes sense, however, if the judiciary itself is competent and has an adequate budget; review can be counterproductive in states with weak, underfunded, or corrupt courts. Judicial independence is necessary but not sufficient. Taken alone, it risks impunity. A corrupt judiciary can undermine reforms and override legal norms. When dealing with such courts, the wealthy and the corrupt are confident that a well-placed payoff will resolve any legal challenges they face. An honest government administration will be difficult to establish if the judiciary is venal. In practice, no country has an entirely independent judiciary. Some accountability to the government and the citizens is consistent with a well-functioning judiciary, and it acts as a check on judicial corruption and other forms of self-dealing.

A case in point is Latin America, where surveys indicate widespread dissatisfaction with the courts, and long delays and corruption are a problem in some countries.[44] An International Bar Association report in 2016 pointed to difficulties with reform related both to the appointment of judges and disciplinary processes. It argued for stronger efforts to promote judicial independence, while also establishing clear and transparent processes for disciplining judges who are corrupt or incompetent.[45] Similarly, the

Inter-American Development Bank claims: "Historically, in much of the region the judicial branch has been characterized by dependence on the executive and a lack of activism in interpreting the law, in challenging the legality of executive actions, or in reviewing the constitutionality of laws."[46] A report from 2002 argues that, in Latin America, "[j]udiciaries are never the leaders in adopting modern management techniques or new technologies, and it is not uncommon for them to be decades behind the rest of the public sector in this regard. Arcane personnel practices, procedural requirements, and even equipment are the norm not the exception."[47]

On top of criticisms of poor management and weak competence, others argue that political considerations can be relevant in the selection of justices on constitutional courts and other high courts with a role in the oversight of the government. Even with nominal independence and terms that overlap those of the president, chief executives have frequently determined Supreme Court composition upon taking office. As in the US, prosecutors are presidential appointees in some countries, although in others they are independent and appointed on merit.[48] Furthermore, the picture is not entirely bleak.[49] The selection of judges for Latin American supreme courts, as in the US, often has been a political act, but, as in France and Germany and in contrast to the US, lower-court judges are mostly civil servants with lifetime career paths. The problems for them are often low budgets and few staff to handle caseloads effectively.

One response to the problems with Latin American courts has been the creation of judicial councils (*consejos de la magistratura*) charged with selecting judges on merit, but this has had mixed results.[50] One commentator suggests that councils might work better if they were required to operate transparently and to develop participatory processes that consult with concerned citizens.[51] Some of the same issues relating to accountability and public legitimacy arise with the courts as with the executive rulemaking procedures themselves.

Even in the best of cases, judges may need additional training in the social sciences, policy analysis, and public administration to decide public-law disputes. If traditional legal training is formalized and legalistic, lawyers may lack the tools to carry out reviews of executive policymaking procedures at the intersection of the technical and political spheres. Outside of some US law schools, lawyers receive little training in fields relevant to the review of public-law cases, even for judges on administrative courts. Judges may need to call on outside advisors (*Sachverständige* in German) to complement their legal training, or (as in the US) hire as clerks recent law graduates with the relevant expertise. For example, if called upon to resolve a legal challenge to an environmental rule or standard, judges need at least a rudimentary understanding of the social and technical issues at stake.[52] The courts' goal is not to judge the science directly but to be sure that the agency has acted consistent with democratic mandates. An intermediate case is the French Conseil d'État, which includes many members trained at the French Higher School of National Administration (ENA). Only within the last decade ENA introduced classes in policy analysis along with its traditional focus on public administration. In 2021, President Macron announced that ENA would be replaced with a new public management school.[53]

A judiciary that is competent and not captured by the executive, nevertheless, may be unable to act because restrictive rules of standing and jurisdiction limit its docket, especially cases that challenge rulemaking processes.[54] In addition, lawyers who bring public-interest cases without wealthy named plaintiffs may be unable to earn a living. There may be relatively few public-interest law firms, and these may be poorly funded and unable to reach financial settlements that could finance future suits. Most challenges may come from business firms and trade associations—biasing the caseload of the courts. In Europe and elsewhere, the courts require the loser to pay both sides' legal and court fees. This discourages frivolous lawsuits, but it also discourages risky suits that test the limits and meaning of vague statutory and regulatory language. A lawsuit brought to improve the clarity of the law usually has social benefits to many not directly involved in the lawsuit. Hence, there is a public interest in encouraging such suits. Two-sided fee-shifting can discourage such risky suits, as can rules where each side pays its own fees. One response, embodied in some US environmental laws, is one-sided fee shifting, where the public-interest plaintiff does not have to pay the government's legal fees if it loses, but the government pays the plaintiff's legal fees if it wins.[55] These provisions provide an incentive to test the law's interpretation without opening up the plaintiffs to large liabilities if they lose.

Establishing an effective system of judicial review of executive policymaking is a complex undertaking where the basic competence and honesty of the judiciary interact with the nature of judicial review. Review is, however, necessary to further the policymaking accountability of the executive ministries and regulatory agencies.

Corruption and the Revolving Door

Some critics of public participation in executive policymaking highlight the risks of corruption and self-dealing. The rulemaking process may tempt officials to offer quid pro quos in return for outright bribes or implied jobs with the relevant industry once they leave government. Because many government decisions affect the wealth and income of powerful groups and industries, the top management and board members of private firms have an incentive not just to present cogent arguments but also to influence decisions through illicit payoffs and other benefits. They can spend resources on hiring talented lawyers and persuasive lobbyists or on providing personal benefits to public officials.

The risk of corruption and conflicts of interest is present in legislative deliberations as well, especially if campaign finance rules permit implicit quid pro quos.[56] However, campaign contributions are public knowledge in many democracies, and even when the actual volume of payments is unknown, some of the benefits show up in published legislative texts that can be traced to donors. The exception is "casework" where legislators favor donors or constituents with individualized favors, including privileged access to key executive-branch decision-makers.[57] These are important problems, but my focus here is on executive-branch policymaking, given the content of legislation.[58]

Self-dealing can undermine executive rulemaking processes in any polity, but the risk is especially high during transitional periods where few established rules exist and unreviewable official discretion is high. During a change of regime, statutes may delegate the "details" of public programs to the administration because the legislature enacted many new laws rapidly. Those with financial resources may take advantage of the institutional vacuum. The press of time also applies to executive rulemaking; oversight is likely to be weak from both the courts and the media, and private watchdog groups may be weak or nonexistent. Interests with financial clout but little public sympathy may prefer broad, general statutes that give public officials leeway to dispense favors as they put statutes into effect. Furthermore, even stable states with weak oversight and a dense regulatory structure can be subject to corrupt interactions between officials and the private sector. Stability may simply indicate that payoffs are holding a corrupt system together at public expense.

Public officials seeking financial payoffs might influence a program's design by building in complexity, discretion, and red tape to encourage payoffs. If eventual employment in the regulated sector is the main motivation for public officials, they may want to ensure that their expertise as bureaucrats will be useful to the regulated firms. They may support programs that require their scarce technical expertise in the private sector. There is a difference between monetary payoffs and employment. If officials seek bribes, they want programs that create a smokescreen for their malfeasance through vague and perhaps inconsistent provisions. If, instead, they seek future employment, they will want to signal their technical competence. The latter incentive seems more benign than the former, but if officials support overly technical and complex rules, the result may be harmful as well.

For firms, both bribes and complex rules are costly. Vague and opaque laws help bribe-payers hide payoffs and can discourage competitors. The design of a policy can favor both high-level officials and private-sector elites who share the rents of the program. If lower-level officials obtain private benefits, they may be co-opted into a corrupt system that mainly benefits higher-up officials and business leaders. In that case, collusive corruption distorts the content of the secondary norms and rules produced by the executive branch and regulatory agencies.

Corruption and an active revolving door implicate powerful public and private interests. If a regulatory agency or cabinet department is under the control of the political allies of major business interests, no explicit bribes need to be paid. The quid pro quo, instead, is part of the political deal that keeps the incumbents in power.

The collective benefit from a lax rule can lead to free-riding by those who hope to benefit from corruption without having to pay the bribes themselves. Unless there is one dominant firm or a cartel of industry leaders, no individual firm may be willing to bribe. They have to collude to make corruption worthwhile.[59] Those willing to be corrupt may not be able to overcome their collective-action problems without help from the bribe-takers themselves. Conversely, a cartel that permits firms to monopolize the market can organize the corruption of public officials. The firms are in a self-reinforcing spiral where the cartel permits bribes that produce favorable policies, which in turn increase profits through lax regulation and barrier to entry.

Over the last forty-five years, I have written on the general problem of corruption and self-dealing.[60] Here, I consider only its role in the promulgation of general regulations or secondary norms inside the executive and the agencies. Even if a statute seems designed to further public-interest goals, self-seeking actors can undermine the rulemaking process. No payoffs may occur, but special interests may get what they want because they have more time and money and a greater interest in the content of the rules than anyone else. They may also be able to command expertise that intimidates their opponents and even honest public officials. Payoffs add further vulnerability that can buy favorable legal rules, whatever the mix of public comments.

The risks of self-dealing are particularly high in polities where rule-making procedures are not transparent and are not constrained by law. Even if the legislature can overturn rules, as in Germany and the UK, the parliamentary system makes that unlikely, except under a weak party coalition. A presidential system, such as France, without a robust set of mandated rule-making procedures will be similarly at risk of corrupt policymaking or of quid pro quo arrangements involving employment, contracts, and so on. The US has a more transparent and procedurally constrained system of rule-making, but the complexity of policy problems and the level of profits at stake produce strong incentives for business to try to influence the content of rules. Firms may seek to keep their efforts secret through preliminary meetings before draft rules are published or by seeking favorable treatment outside the notice-and-comment process. The main problems in the US appear to be biases in the level of lobbying expenses and in access to officials. The revolving door between the public and the private sectors contributes to the tilt toward wealthy economic interests.

The risk of corruption and self-dealing provides an additional reason for procedural constraints that produce a transparent record, a well-reasoned public statement of reasons, and judicial review of process. These procedures both deter corruption and make it more difficult for private wealth to determine policy outcomes. Even if a polity has no law governing rule-making procedures, all established democracies require the publication of rules. Public opinion and the media can then critique them. Freedom of information acts (FOIAs) in a growing number of countries provide a check, but individuals can make such requests only once the process is complete.[61]

Research in Indonesia and Pakistan found that political connections had measurable economic worth that reflected the concentration of power.[62] In the US, in contrast, the links were not so easy to untangle given the size and diversity of the economy and the wide range of relationships between firms and government bodies.[63] At least one reason for the US results could be the more transparent process for making regulatory policy. Private wealth is a very powerful influence on government, but it does not always win, and the courts have pushed back against especially obvious examples of bias in favor of regulated firms.[64] The strength of institutions providing oversight and permitting public participation is likely weaker in consolidating democracies than in those with a longer history. Under the Trump administration, however, clear conflicts of interest arose between policy choices and private financial interests.[65] In state and local governments, corrupted rulemaking processes can increase the profitability of infrastructure by, for example, setting lax building codes; undermining rules for hiring, pay, and working conditions; and influencing zoning maps to permit more development. Developers corruptly get the rules they want and then operate "honestly" with rules that are skewed in their favor.

In Germany, the automobile industry undermined the integrity of tests for the level of pollutants emitted by diesel automobiles. Stringent rules were in place, linked to EU requirements, so the violations were illegal efforts to avoid the regulations, not efforts to rewrite the regulations themselves.[66] In other cases, the automobile industry's political clout produces favorable laws and rules, with no need for direct payoffs. For example, the Energiewende was concerned with the generation of electric power, not with emissions from vehicles. In the UK, major scandals involved the foreign business dealings of UK multinationals,[67] but the 2017 Grenfell Tower fire, in which an apartment house in London burned rapidly, killing seventy-two people and injuring seventy, was a domestic example of lax enforcement of fire safety standards.[68] Criticism of Boeing and the Federal Aviation Administration in the US after two fatal crashes of the 737-MAX has concentrated on the overly close relationship between the firm and its regulators.[69] In other words, the rules themselves were not corrupted, but their application was lax. In France, scandals have implicated major overseas investors, such as the private water companies and the Total and ELF oil companies.[70] Some argue that the economic and political elite wields disproportionate power, a circumstance made easier by the lack of transparency in the production of secondary norms.[71] In short, bribery and self-dealing occur in all four countries, and sometimes undermine the enforcement of regulatory standards in areas such as building codes and occupational health and safety. Yet, national-government rulemaking does not seem to be a major locus for outright payoffs. The sources of influence are more veiled and subtle, but, nonetheless, they can skew regulations in favor of powerful interests. More transparent and open processes can counteract those tendencies, but cannot stop them in the face of entrenched and economically powerful interests.

The possibility of corrupted rulemaking procedures suggests the importance of adding procedural and transparency checks that mirror US notice-and-comment procedures. These procedures, however, can introduce their own incentives for corruption and self-dealing. Those who will bear the costs of the rules may seek to delay their promulgation and stymie their enforcement. They may do so through legal, but costly, delaying tactics or by paying officials to set the agenda and skew decisions in their favor. In the extreme, the judiciary can be corrupted to aid the interests of those subject to regulation. The procedural practices that I espouse here are not a panacea and cannot substitute for norms of honesty and competence, but they can help push the administrative process toward more politically legitimate and less corrupt outcomes. The corruption risks are especially salient during transitions to democracy and the market because the rules are likely to be unclear and in flux and because many officials in the executive, the legislature, and the courts are likely to be inexperienced and tempted to resolve difficulties through payoffs.

Self-dealing and favoritism are always concerns when the executive implements public policies. Future employment in the regulated industry creates obvious conflicts of interest. The downside is that preventing such career moves would limit the pool of available talent. The usual response is to limit direct involvement with issues that former bureaucrats worked on while in government. This is not a perfect response, but it does reward expertise while reducing the possibility of self-dealing.

Outright corruption in the form of bribes and kickbacks raises the stakes. Corruption can undermine otherwise good-faith efforts to improve the policymaking process. Those who hope to delay a rule may pay officials to slow down the process or abandon it altogether. Others may try to write the rule so that it favors them and their allies, giving them privileged status relative to competitors and rivals. They may lobby aggressively and trade political support or campaign funds for a favorable rule. Officials might seek personal enrichment in return for their cooperation. Of course, the corrupt value of a rule depends upon how likely it is to be enforced or reversed by a new administration. Reversal depends both on the chance of a political turnover that would bring opponents of the rule to power and on whether supporters of the rule can protect their gains against changes in political control. Can beneficiaries sign contracts and take actions based on the new rule that a subsequent administration cannot void without paying compensation? Because corrupt and ineffective governments lack political legitimacy, however, benefits that result from corrupt payoffs may be particularly difficult to entrench if the malfeasance is publicized and punished.[72]

The Reform Agenda

All democracies face the same basic challenges if they seek to institutionalize accountable executive policymaking processes. Constitutional and administrative law must confront the difficulties of balancing competence, public participation, and government accountability. Every country needs its own diagnosis, but several pervasive problems reoccur that suggest directions for reform. Seven types of reform relate to the issuance of executive rules with the force of law. They involve:

(1) procedures for issuing rules that balance competence and democratic values;
(2) better civil-service training and integrity;
(3) laws that facilitate the establishment and accountability of civil-society groups;
(4) balanced oversight of independent agencies and quasi-private regulatory bodies;
(5) experimentation with alternative routes to public participation in rulemaking;
(6) judicial review of the democratic efficacy of the administrative process, supported by standing for non-governmental advocacy groups; and
(7) improved legislative capacity to evaluate delegated authority.

First, administrative-law reform may need to limit executive decree powers, especially as the drafting capacity of the legislature improves. As the US example demonstrates, placing procedural constraints on the issuance of rules with the force of law may lead to circumvention of these procedures through case-by-case implementation and the use of instruments, not subject to notice and comment. Presidents, ministers, and regulatory commissions may issue executive orders, guidance documents, policy statements, or memoranda. These are familiar workarounds in the US, and they could spread to other governments newly subject to notice-and-comment procedures. Thus, administrative-procedure acts should set explicit limits on efforts at circumvention. They should provide for their use in clearly defined areas and forbid them in others.

At the same time, the law of administrative procedures ought to reflect the time and trouble of using these procedures. There is no value in red tape for its own sake. Some reforms can succeed through internet portals; others require face-to-face interactions. We need more and better research on alternatives that combine modern technology and human interaction. Sometimes simply streamlining and clarifying procedures is sufficient to improve government functioning. If citizens and businesses know what they need to do to comply with the rules, streamlining can increase both the competence and the public acceptability of public policies. However, administrative reforms of that sort cannot solve underlying policy problems. The state can make compliance with rules easy and quick, but if the policies that they reflect do not incorporate public concerns or even acknowledge public discontent, the population may resist them, sometimes violently. Simplicity of implementation is only one value.

Second, the quality and honesty of the bureaucracy set the background conditions for executive policymaking. The civil service needs officials trained in policy analysis based on economics, social science, and the technocratic knowledge at the heart of their offices' mandates (for example, meteorology for the weather bureau, statistics for the census bureau, the effects of toxic chemicals for the regulation of pesticides and food additives). Some officials may have few technical qualifications beyond party loyalty and patronage links; others may be competent technocrats who lack an understanding of the operation of government and its interactions with the public. These contrasting concerns have been central to the field of public administration.[73] Bureaucracies operate in a political context, and career officials need to be aware of the connections between their professional expertise and the shifting political imperatives of periodic elections. Most officials will need to balance their specialized training with deference to political appointees at the top of their agencies. In extreme cases, they will face sharp tensions between professional and technocratic norms and political pressures.

The fundamental background conditions for an effective civil service are limits on conflicts of interest and the prevention of corrupt inducements. These conditions also ought to apply to political appointees and to private contractors. Tension exists between the government's ability to tap into private-sector expertise and the worry that experts have political biases that will compromise their impartiality. There is no easy way to resolve this tension, but the public sector can mitigate it in several ways. Thus, those who leave government for the private sector may be restricted from private-sector work related to their previous government service. Furthermore, rulemaking procedures that promote democratic accountability also help make bureaucratic actions more transparent and act as a check on official self-dealing. Policies that limit conflicts of interest can also limit corruption, but more direct anti-corruption policies are necessary both to reduce the economic rents in public programs and to discipline and suspend the corrupt.

Third, the law should make it inexpensive and easy to establish civil-society advocacy groups, at the same time as it requires transparency about their finances and backers. NGOs that are "for-profits in disguise" are a risk if reporting requirements are lax and taxes on for-profit firms are high. In turn, public authorities must not deny licenses to NGOs for political reasons.

A related issue is the tax-deductibility of financial donations to NGOs, an important issue in countries with substantial income taxes. The US, for example, distinguishes between charitable or educational institutions that can accept tax-deductible donations and political-advocacy organizations that cannot. The law serves as a major incentive for households who wish to support policy reforms in such areas as social welfare and environmental protection. Those that engage in direct political advocacy form two distinct organizations—one for tax-deductible charitable and educational work and a second for political advocacy. In practice, the line between lobbying and educating politicians can be unclear, and both types flourish in the American system.[74] Germany is engaged in a debate over the nonprofit status of organizations that take policy positions.[75] Independent institutions with policy agendas are important in my cases and some participate in executive consultations, especially for major infrastructure projects and as watchdogs over administrative policymaking. Middle-income countries, such as those in eastern Europe and Latin America, generally have less well-established civil-society institutions. They may need to reform the laws governing NGOs and clarify the rules governing advocacy and charitable groups and their overlapping goals. In all countries, the diversity of views and expertise these bodies can bring to policymaking provides valuable inputs. Although no government agency should accept such input at face value, a diversity of voices can limit what some call "tunnel vision" inside the bureaucracy.[76] Narrow ideologues, as well as well as profit-seeking businesses, can capture regulators.

Fourth, the policymaking roles of independent government agencies raise distinctive issues. Are these agencies too independent of central political control or not independent enough? Their constitutional status may be in question. In the US, the judiciary has upheld the constitutionality of independent agencies and allowed them to make rules with the force of law in the same way as cabinet departments. The parliamentary systems of the UK and Germany limit the policymaking role of agencies, although many have de facto rulemaking power. In France, such agencies adjudicate individual cases. They do not make rules, although the relevant ministries consult them. The tripartite separation of powers into legislative, executive, and judicial does not accord well with the functional requirements of modern government. Independence from both the core executive and the legislature, constrained by judicial oversight, is a pragmatic response to certain kinds of regulatory challenges in the modern state. Both wealthy countries and middle-income democracies have implemented such institutional reforms, especially in Latin America in connection with the privatization of public utilities. The key point is not so much the need for independent expertise, which government can obtain through consulting contracts. Rather, the primary justifications are the value of insulating regulators from day-to-day political imperatives and from the ministry that makes economic decisions as part owner of the firm, even after privatization. Politicians may seek to favor their constituents and donors. The relevant ministries may resist regulatory policies that increase competition but lower the profits of regulated firms. The arguments against independence focus on the possibility of a rogue agency captured by some portion of the regulated industry or by an interest group. These risks imply that the participation of nonpartisan, civil society and of affected groups is especially important when independent or quasi-independent agencies issue rules with the force of law. Independence may promise impartial, expert agency actions, but it needs to include input from ordinary citizens.

Fifth, both government ministries and civil-society groups should be encouraged to experiment with alternative ways of encouraging public participation in policymaking, and funds should be available to test alternative routes to public involvement. Analysts should measure effectiveness not by asking the participants if they are "satisfied" with the process but rather by looking at the impact of the process on the administration's policy choices. Within my framework, the goal is not to have "the public" make rules and regulations by itself. Rather, rulemaking ought to be the responsibility of cabinet departments and independent agencies operating under delegated authority. But these bodies ought to seek input, not just from regulated entities and technical experts but also from citizens and organized advocacy groups. Furthermore, once this input has been provided, the public body ought to issue a public statement of reasons that tells the electorate what policy it has chosen and why. The judiciary can review this decision if someone brings a case, but only to check the procedures used and the rule's consistency with the statute and the constitution. It should not second-guess policy choices but rather focus on the democratic legitimacy of the outcome and the process.

One model that seems worth developing merges some aspects of American-style notice-and-comment rulemaking with lessons from participatory experiments elsewhere. The key features would include the following steps:

- a preliminary technocratic exercise by a public agency that produces a set of feasible options;
- an open-ended public website for the provision of input on these options, with comments posted on-line;
- a sifting process that consolidates the agency's options with the public comments to isolate the key points of contention;
- selection of a limited-sized group that represents a cross-section of those with an interest in the policy;
- a moderated discussion among the group members either to reach a consensus recommendation or to produce a report laying out areas of disagreement.

With that information in hand, the agency then decides on its course of action and issues a rule along with a statement of reasons. This process does not include ex post review, such as US review by OIRA, inside the government to test the rule's compliance with CBA principles. To the extent that analysts use CBA or impact assessment, these studies would enter the process up front when the agency drafts the options, but before public consultation occurs. This proposal is just a sketch, not a blueprint. It combines elements of existing systems to bring together expertise and public input. If the political will exists, it could operate in both wealthy and middle-income countries.

Sixth, laws that require public participation may mean little in practice unless those excluded from the administrative process have access to the courts. The courts can review not just the administration's acceptance of outside input but also the extent to which government agencies actually take it into account. Such oversight risks converting the courts into policymakers, but it is possible to craft doctrines of review that stress, first, the proper use of procedures, and second, the consistency of executive rules with statutory mandates. The argument for the judicial review of procedures is precisely that it distances the courts from substantive policymaking and stresses the connection between the government and bureaucracy, on the one hand, and the citizenry, on the other.

Seventh, legislative capacity to review statutory delegation needs strengthening in many countries. This could involve better staff support for members, parties, and committees, as well as non-partisan training programs for new members at the start of each session. Such training is especially important in a separation-of-powers polity, such as the US, where bills are both drafted and modified inside the legislature, rather than presented to it by the cabinet as an almost finished product. Better legislative capacity could also help members of parliament to push back against unilateral efforts by the cabinet to impose statutory drafts on the legislature without providing for adequate evaluation and discussion of their consequences. Controversial efforts to achieve open-ended delegations to the government would then be subject to more intelligent debate both inside and outside the legislature. One thinks of the consequences of the rapid passage of the German law that shifted the country toward renewable power with little debate over the controversial tradeoffs now engaging the public. Laws can still pass in the heat of a political moment, but, at least, the legislature would have the capacity to raise informed questions about government initiates.

Some may challenge a rule as a violation of individual rights, and such review is an important part of the judiciary's responsibility. Nevertheless, rights review should not prevent the courts from acting as a backstop to help promote the democratic accountability of government policymaking. Because policymaking delegation is the only realistic course for the legislature in a modern democratic policy, the law should empower the courts to check on the responsible use of such delegated power. This may be a difficult task for legally trained judges with little in-depth knowledge of substantive policy, and that weakness suggests caution. It explains why judges may review procedures and defer to well-justified policy choices. If a policy choice is reflected in rules, however, the judiciary should be careful not to impose procedures that mimic those used in the courts themselves—procedures that do not acknowledge the mixture of technical knowledge and democratic responsiveness necessary in a representative democracy seeking to respond competently to the challenges of governing a regulatory/welfare state.

Administrative law and constitutional law interact whenever statutes delegate policymaking outside the legislature. Law, here, is not independent of political and policy concerns. It constrains the exercise of both pure political expediency and technocratic expertise. Law regulates the democratic structure of government with enforcement by the courts, but the political incentives for policymaking accountability differ across constitutional structures. The US is a separation-of-powers presidential system. Germany and the UK are parliamentary systems with and without written constitutions, respectively. The common law underpins the UK's unwritten constitution. France has a strong president with a relatively weak parliament. All four countries have professional bureaucracies and competent courts, but their constitutional structures have had a strong influence on the democratic accountability of policymaking within the government in each country. I have outlined those differences, but all four face similar challenges when it comes to executive-branch rulemaking. Other wealthy and middle-income countries seeking technically competent and democratically acceptable delegated policymaking face similar challenges. The variety of constitutional frameworks helps explain the differences in administrative rulemaking practices and the role of the courts. It does not excuse them. I have argued that even if the political incentives embedded in certain constitutional structures suggest that sitting politicians will have little interest in reform, the need for reform remains. I have presented some general options for more democratically responsible executive policymaking, and I hope that they will generate debate both in countries with few procedural constraints on rulemaking and in the US, where rulemaking procedures need reform. The US notice-and-comment process may be losing some of its standing as a protector of democratic legitimacy in an atmosphere of distrust of government. The process itself can leave out important voices, and public officials, elected presidents included, are finding routes to policymaking that lack even the imperfect protections of the APA. Those concerned about the future of representative democracy should include rulemaking reform in their list of priorities. Structural issues linked to the openness and accountability of regulatory bodies should not be ignored in the heat of day-to-day crises that soak up the headlines.

Notes

Introduction

1. I use the term "agency" in the American sense as a synonym for any public body, whether or not it is part of the cabinet structure of government. Thus, in the US the term includes the Department of Commerce, whose head is a member of the cabinet; the Environmental Protection Agency, also in the core executive, but lacking cabinet status; the Food and Drug Administration, inside the Department of Health and Human Services; and the Federal Communications Commission, a regulatory authority with a multi-member board not under direct presidential control. If distinctions between these bodies are relevant for my argument, I will make that clear in the text.
2. Stewart (1975), pp. 1675–77, introduces the term and argues that it is unrealistic to expect it to apply in practice.
3. See, for example, Lawson (1994).
4. Böckenförde (1992); Weber (1946 [1916]).
5. The terms in the German legal definition are: *Regelung*, *Einzelfall*, *hoheitlich*, *Außenwirkung*, and *behördlich*. § 35 sentence 1 VwVfG, https://www.gesetze-im-internet.de/vwvfg/__35.html (accessed April 5, 2020).
6. Wendel (2019), p. 91ff, argues that the executive should follow procedures that further democratic legitimacy as well as protecting rights.
7. It includes both administrative acts directed at particular individuals and general regulatory acts (*actes administratifs réglementaires*).
8. A referendum in 2000 reduced the president's term from seven to five years. A 2008 amendment limited the president to two consecutive terms. French Constitution, art. 6, includes these provisions.
9. Shortening the president's term to five years means that the presidential election occurs shortly before the election of the National Assembly, increasing the likelihood that the president's party will control the Assembly.

10. The House of Lords can vote down an SI, but it seldom exercises that power. See Chapter 2.
11. According to its website: "We are a specialist court within the Queen's Bench Division of the High Court of Justice." https://www.gov.uk/courts-tribunals/administrative-court (accessed April 5, 2020).

Chapter 1. Policymaking Accountability and Public Law

1. Davis and Trebilcock (2009); Rose-Ackerman (2004).
2. Kagan (2007).
3. Accountability is often translated into French as *responsabilité*, but that term includes three concepts: political accountability (*responsabilité politique*), criminal liability *(responsabilité pénale)*, and civil liability (*responsabilité civile*). To capture the broader implications of the English term, French sometimes uses the plural, *responsabilités*, or *reddition de comptes*. The German terms for accountability are *Verantwortlichkeit* and *Rechenschaftspflicht*. Psygkas (2020) provides an overview, focusing on the US, the UK, and France. Harlow's (2002) definition (pp. 6–24) is consistent with my own. On France, see Ziller (2008), pp. 84–85.
4. On corruption in the civil service, see Rose-Ackerman and Palifka (2016), pp. 51–204.
5. Magnetter (2003).
6. Schneider (2007), p. 311.
7. Ibid., p. 312.
8. Nicholas (1970).
9. European Convention on Human Rights, https://www.echr.coe.int/Documents/Convention_ENG.pdf; European Union Charter of Fundamental Rights, https://www.europarl.europa.eu/charter/pdf/text_en.pdf (both accessed April 5, 2020). The EU Charter applies to EU institutions and to member states only when implementing EU law.
10. The right to education is contained in article 34 of Charter of Fundamental Rights and in article 2, protocol n° 1 to the European Convention on Human Rights. The right to health is stipulated in art. 35 of the Charter of Fundamental Rights.
11. See the case studies in Rose-Ackerman, Egidy, and Fowkes (2015).
12. German Basic Law (Grundgesetz), art. 2(1).
13. The distinction is not hard and fast. For example, the German administrative courts and the Constitutional Court sometimes deal with disputes between

individuals that raise both public and private law issues. Consider, for example, the right to be forgotten (*Recht auf Vergessen*). 1 BvR 276/17—Recht auf Vergessen, 27/11/2019.

14. Carey and Shugart (1998).
15. Even here politics can intervene if scientific labs are located in various political constituencies, if the research will eventually benefit certain economic interests, or if the research raises ethical issues of concern to citizens.
16. See the discussion in Chapter 5.
17. Rose-Ackerman (1992), pp. 33–42. A second argument for requiring cost-benefit analysis is that legislators have less incentive to hide special-interest efforts in seemingly neutral language. Congress would have to be explicit about its special-interest aims in the statutory language. If voters oppose such giveaways, they may punish the incumbents at the next election, thus deterring legislators from passing such bills.
18. Stigler (1971); Carpenter and Moss (2014).
19. *Seila Law, LLC v. Consumer Financial Protection Bureau*, 140 S. Ct. 2183 (2020). The decision found that it was unconstitutional for an agency to have a single head who is removable only for cause. The remedy was to make the head removable by the president at will. Some of the justices seemed ready to review the constitutionality of multi-member bodies with for-cause removal. See Chapter 4.
20. For example, ombudsmen in Hungary must be confirmed by a two-thirds vote in the parliament. When the political system was competitive, this led to either compromise or deadlock (Rose-Ackerman [2005], pp. 80–83).
21. Rose-Ackerman and Perroud (2013).
22. See § 5(1) BEGTPG, https://www.bundesnetzagentur.de/EN/General/Bundesnetzagentur/AdvisoryCouncil/AdvisoryCouncil_node.html (accessed April 5, 2020).
23. The filibuster rule in the Senate, requiring sixty affirmative votes, gave the minority party considerable impact on appointments, but in 2013, the Senate changed its rules to eliminate the filibuster for all executive-branch and judicial appointments, except for the Supreme Court. In 2017, a Senate rule added Supreme Court nominees. Jeremy W. Peters, "In Landmark Vote, Senate Limits Use of the Filibuster," November 21, 2013, https://www.nytimes.com/2013/11/22/us/politics/reid-sets-in-motion-steps-to-limit-use-of-filibuster.html. Allan Smith, "Senate Goes Nuclear," *Business Insider*, Nov. 21, 2013, https://www.businessinsider.com/nuclear-option-gorsuch-filibuster-senate-2017-4 (accessed Oct. 23, 2020).

24. For example, the Federal Trade Commissioner has five commissioners appointed for seven years. No more than three can be from a single party. https://www.ftc.gov/about-ftc/commissioners (accessed April 5, 2020). If a commissioner leaves office before the end of his or her term, the new appointee serves out that person's term. The president appoints the chairperson.
25. Shapiro (2010).
26. In the UK, these commissions are part of the large body of organizations called quangos (quasi-autonomous non-governmental organizations) (Barker [1982]).
27. See Chapter 4.
28. This critique applies to other occupations, such as barbers and interior decorators, that have gained similar authority (Stigler [1971]).
29. Lijphart (1977, 2012).
30. Silvia (2013); Wallerath (1997).
31. An example is Volkswagen's cheating on automobile emission tests. Its behavior was revealed by US regulators, not by the company's "stakeholders." Roger Parloff, "How VW Paid $25 Billion for 'Dieselgate' and Got Off Easy," *Fortune*, Feb. 6, 2018, https://fortune.com/2018/02/06/volkswagen-vw-emissions-scandal-penalties/. Subsequently, Germany brought legal actions against executives and corporations. Sören Amelang and Benjamin Wehrmann, "'Dieselgate'—A Timeline of the Car Emissions Fraud Scandal in Germany," *Clean Energy Wire*, Sept. 5, 2019 (accessed Oct. 23, 2020).
32. Radin (2013).
33. See Chapter 6.
34. "The Environment and People Power: Revolutions Coloured Green," *The Economist*, Nov. 22, 2008, p. 71.

Chapter 2. Constitutional Paradoxes

1. The electoral systems differ between the UK and Germany: candidates elected from single-member districts under a first-past-the-post rule in the UK, and a mixture of proportional representation and single-member districts in Germany. I ignore some special features of the German case discussed in Rose-Ackerman, Egidy, and Fowkes (2015), and I leave aside complications introduced by minority or coalition governments.
2. An example of such a misjudgment was the Tory Party's disastrous showing in the snap election of 2017. "May Hung in June: British Voters Defy the Polls in a Dreadful Night for the Tories," *The Economist*, June 10, 2017.

3. Evans (2020).
4. Human Rights Act 1998, http://www.legislation.gov.uk/ukpga/1998/42/section/3 (accessed April 5, 2020). Even after exit from the EU, the UK will remain in the Council of Europe and subject to the rulings of its Court of Human Rights.
5. The German Basic Law, arts. 1–19, lists the basic rights, including human dignity in article 1. Article 1(3) binds the legislative, the executive and the judiciary to respect these rights, and article 19(4) makes them enforceable in the courts. Art. 93 lists the jurisdiction of the Federal Constitutional Court, with art. 93(1), s. 4a permitting individuals to bring a constitutional complaint if a public authority has violated their rights.
6. German Basic Law, art. 80(1), s. 2.
7. An early Constitutional Court decision ruled that the Basic Law permitted general regulations with the force of law (*Rechtsverordnungen*), *Kalkar Case*, BVerfGE 49, 89 (1978).
8. §§ 62–68 Joint Rules of Procedure of the Federal Ministries (*Gemeinsame Geschäftsordnung der Bundesministerien*—GGO) provide guidelines for the preparation, drafting, and promulgation of Rechtsverordnungen. https://www.bmi.bund.de/SharedDocs/downloads/EN/themen/moderne-verwaltung/ggo_en.pdf?__blob=publicationFile&v=1 (accessed Nov. 17, 2020).
9. Administrative Procedure Law (V*erwaltungsverfahrensgesetz*, VwVfG) of May 23, 1976, as amended Jan. 23, 2003, BGBl I 102, most recently amended by art. 5(25) of the act on June 21, 2019, BGBl I 846. Administrative acts are regulated by § 35 VwVfG.
10. Eifert (2014).
11. The United Kingdom also has increased the independence of the parliaments in Scotland, Wales, and Northern Ireland, but this is not reflected in the upper house.
12. German Basic Law, arts. 80(2) and 83.
13. French Constitution, art. 12.
14. Under "co-habitation," when the president's party does not control the National Assembly, the prime minister needs to satisfy the opposition. The less-powerful Senate is selected indirectly and can have a majority opposed to the president, but it plays no role in the selection of the prime minister.
15. French Constitution, arts. 9, 13. Reitz (2006), p. 605. The president's independent powers are mostly limited to foreign policy, national security, and emergencies (art. 16).

16. On the development of French law, see Bermann and Picard (2012). Ackerman (2019) provides a history of the Constitution of the Fifth Republic.
17. Some move into more lucrative positions in the private sector, often near the end of their career at the Conseil d'État. Throughout French society, France and Vauchez (2017) discuss the blurring of the private-public divide.
18. Conseil d'État, *Avis sur un Projet de Loi Constitutionnelle, Complétant l'Article 1er de la Constitution et Relatif à la Préservation de la Environnement*, January 21, 2021, https://www.conseil-etat.fr/ressources/avis-aux-pouvoirs-publics/derniers-avis- publies/avis-sur-un-projet-de-loi-constitutionnelle-completant-l-article-1er-de-la- constitution-et-relatif-a-la-preservation-de-l-environnement (accessed February 2, 2021).
19. In addition, the Court of Auditors (*Cour des Comptes*), an elite body, reviews the fiscal integrity of government programs. It is called a *cour*, or court, but it audits government finances on its own initiative.
20. Code des Relations entre le Public et l'Administration (2015). See Chapter 3 and Custos (2017).
21. See Chapters 3 and 7.
22. US Constitution, art. II, sect. 3.
23. Rose-Ackerman, Egidy, and Fowkes (2015), pp. 31–102. See also Rose-Ackerman (1995).
24. Tsebelis (2002).
25. See McCubbins, Noll, and Weingast (1987, 1989). Rose-Ackerman, Egidy, and Fowkes (2015), pp. 31–102, build on their work and that of other scholars to discuss the US case in comparison with Germany, South Africa, and the EU.
26. US Code, Ch. 5, II (1946)—Administrative Procedure Act (APA).
27. Landes and Posner (1975). See *Food and Drug Administration v. Brown & Williamson Tobacco Corp.*, 529 U.S. 120 (2000) (disallowing FDA efforts to regulate tobacco).
28. APA § 551(4).
29. If a statute requires a formal, more court-like process, other sections of the APA apply, but agencies seldom use those procedures for rulemaking.
30. APA § 706(2)(D).
31. *Sierra Club v. Costle*, 657 F. 2d 298, 395–410 (D.C. Cir. 1981) (Holding that the Clean Air Act and various pragmatic considerations imply that information submitted after the close of the comment period is acceptable so long as it is docketed. If it does not add materially to information already available, the agency need not reopen the comment period.)

32. Stigler (1971); R. Posner (1974).
33. Mayhew (1974).
34. Justice William Rehnquist's partial concurrence in *Industrial Union Dept., AFL-CIO v. American Petroleum Inst.* (the *Benzene* Case), 448 U.S. 607, 671–688 (1980). Further efforts at revival failed in *Whitman v. American Trucking Ass'ns*, 531 U.S. 457 (2001) and in *Gundy v. U.S.*, 139 S. Ct. 2116 (2019). However, in *Gundy* a strong dissent by Justice Neil Gorsuch may signal a willingness to revisit the issue in the future.
35. Strauss (2007).
36. Grisinger (2012) claims that the APA's procedural provisions were in widespread use before the law's passage.
37. Hilliard (2017).
38. Chapter 4 discusses recent cases that may limit the organizational options for independent agencies and considers these agencies in comparison with the other cases.
39. Shane (2009); E. A. Posner and Vermeule (2010).
40. Michaels (2017), pp. 59–77, defends an "administrative separation of powers" involving presidential appointees, civil servants, and civil society.

Chapter 3. Policymaking inside the Executive

1. I leave to one side unelected presidents and monarchs without executive responsibilities, such as the federal president of Germany and the queen of the UK.
2. President's Commission on Administrative Management (1937); Fesler (1987); Brand (2008).
3. For a summary and critique of Margaret Thatcher's NPM in the UK, see Psygkas (2017), pp. 193–99.
4. I omit foreign policy, national security, and emergencies, policy areas where the head of government typically has heightened levels of independent authority. Particular problems arise from the "war on terror" and its use as an umbrella term to justify executive power. See Koh (1990); Ackerman (2004).
5. Lewis (2019).
6. In 2018, the Rt. Hon. David Lidington, MP, then leader of the House of Commons, identified six circumstances in which the government believes it may use delegated legislation:

   (1) to fill in a level of detail not thought appropriate for primary legislation, possibly as it needs to be updated on a frequent basis;

> (2) to enable consultation to take place on the detailed implementation of a policy . . . ; (3) to deal with things which it is anticipated may change in future (e.g. updating for inflation); (4) to provide an acceptable level of flexibility to accommodate small policy changes . . . ; (5) to deal with matters, concerning the technical implementation of a policy, which cannot be known at the point when the primary legislation is being passed; and (6) to accommodate the fact that the detailed policy has to work differently for different groups of people, different areas, etc.

House of Lords Select Committee on the Constitution, *The Legislative Process: The Delegation of Powers*, HL Paper 225 (2018), ¶9.

7. Craig (2016), pp. 577–631. Alleged human rights violations are seldom a route to judicial review of broad policies; they must be tied to an individual victim [section 7(1)]. However, Craig notes (p. 608) that a public interest group with a sufficient interest in a matter might obtain standing in the UK by claiming that the "challenged action was ultra vires in accord with the common law protections of fundamental rights."
8. The supremacy principle of EU law was recognized in s. 2 of the European Communities Act 1972 (ECA). Although s. 1 of the European Union (Withdrawal) Act of 2018 repealed the ECA, s. 1 of the European Union (Withdrawal Agreement) Act 2020 saves the effects of the ECA during the implementation period.
9. According to the Supreme Court: "Subordinate legislation will be held by a court to be invalid if it has an effect, or is made for a purpose, which is *ultra vires*, that is, outside the scope of the statutory power pursuant to which it was purportedly made. In declaring subordinate legislation to be invalid in such a case, the court is upholding the supremacy of Parliament over the Executive." *R. (The Public Law Project) v. Lord Chancellor* [2016], UKSC 39, ¶23.
10. Tomkins (2006).
11. The decision held that the prime minister could not invoke the royal prerogative to notify the EU of the UK's intention to withdraw. The House of Commons had to approve that action as a statute. *R. (Miller and another) v. Sec'y of State for Exiting the European Union* [2017], UKSC 5 (appeal taken from Eng., Wales, and N. Ir.) [Miller I].
12. European Union (Notification of Withdrawal) Act 2017, C. 9 (Eng.).
13. "Prorogue" means to discontinue a legislative session without dissolving it, in other words, without triggering an election.

14. *R. (Miller) (Appellant) v. The Prime Minister (Respondent)*; *Cherry and Others (Respondents) v. Advocate General for Scotland* [2019], UKSC 41 [*Miller II*].
15. Backbenchers and the opposition sometimes defeat government bills (Russell and Cowley [2016]). The Commons voted several times to reject the deal with the EU negotiated by Theresa May's government.
16. Fox and Blackwell (2014), p. 89. Box 4 lists other forms of delegated legislation with the force of law, some of which do not require parliamentary affirmation.
17. A Henry VIII clause in the Climate Change Act, for instance, authorizes the secretary of state to amend by order the 2050 carbon-reduction targets in several circumstances. Climate Change Act of 2008, C.27, § 2(1)–(2) (Eng.). An SI has amended the target carbon account for 2050 stipulated in the act from "at least 80% lower than the 1990 baseline" to "100% lower." The Climate Change Act of 2008 (2050 Target Amendment) Order 2019, 2019 No. 1056, § 2 (Eng.).
18. The relevant act of Parliament determines whether an SI must obtain parliamentary approval. A statute can establish that an SI is not subject to parliamentary procedure. Otherwise, an act can require negative resolution—whereby the SI becomes law unless the House of Commons objects; or affirmative resolution—whereby the SI cannot become law without approval by both houses. Statutory Instruments Act 1946, 1946 c. 36, §§ 4–6 (Eng.).
19. The quote is from House of Lords, Select Committee on the Constitution, *United Kingdom Internal Market Bill*, 17th Report of Session 2019–2021, Oct. 16, 2020, HL paper 151, paragraph 125. See also Jeff King and Stephen Tierney, "The House of Lords Constitution Committee Reports on the United Kingdom Internal Market Bill," *UK Constitution Law Association*, Oct. 16, 2020, https://ukconstitutionallaw.org/2020/10/16/jeff-king-and-stephen-tierney-the-house-of-lords-constitution-committee-reports-on-the-united-kingdom-internal-market-bill/ (accessed Nov. 16, 2020).
20. Its members are a mixture of hereditary peers and those appointed for life, many with no party affiliation (cross-bench peers) or affiliated with the opposition. As of April 5, 2020, the breakdown was: Conservative, 244; cross-bench, 184; Labour, 179; Liberal Democrat, 91; Lord Speaker, 1; non-affiliated, 49; other, 16; and bishops, 26. "Lords by party, type of peerage, and gender." UK Parliament, https://www.parliament.uk/mps-lords-and-offices/lords/composition-of-the-lords/ (accessed April 5, 2020).

21. The Parliament Act of 1911 established the primacy of the Commons for the passage of statutes. However, the act retained the Lords' power to veto SIs. Russell (2013), pp. 32, 84.
22. Ibid., p. 84.
23. House of Lords (2016–2017).
24. Southern Rhodesia (United Nations Sanctions) Order 1968.
25. Greater London Authority Elections (Expenses) Order 2000.
26. Russell (2013), pp. 140–41. Figure 6.1 (p. 138) shows all government defeats, including on bills.
27. Ibid., pp. 140-41; Tax Credits (Income Thresholds and Determination of Rates) (Amendment) Regulations 2015.
28. Patrick Wintour, "How George Osbourne Got Himself into a Fix over Tax Credits," *The Guardian*, Oct. 27, 2015, https://www.theguardian.com/politics/2015/oct/27/how-george-osborne-got-himself-into-a-fix-over-tax-credits?CMP=share_btn_link.
29. Since the 1980s the Lords has had a particular interest in what Meg Russell calls "constitutional propriety." She argues that government bills allocate too much discretionary authority to the executive (Russell [2013], pp. 187–89).
30. Fox and Blackwell (2014); Tucker (2018).
31. Consultations may include informal discussions or more structured exchanges around "green papers" (documents prepared by the government to allow for input from inside and outside Parliament). Since 2008, the government has circulated, and periodically updated, a set of non-binding consultation principles. *Consultation Principles 2016*, https://assets.publishing.service.gov.uk/government/uploads/system/uploads/attachment_data/file/492132/20160111_Consultation_principles_final.pdf (accessed April 5, 2020). In 2017, the House of Lords organized a review of existing consultation practices: House of Lords Select Committee on the Constitution, *The Legislative Process: Preparing Legislation for Parliament*, HL Paper 27 (2017), https://publications.parliament.uk/pa/ld201719/ldselect/ldconst/27/27.pdf (accessed April 5, 2020).
32. Chapter 7 reviews the case law.
33. Constitutional Reform and Governance Act 2010, s. 7(4).
34. Constitutional Reform and Governance Act 2010, s. 15 defines "special advisors." S. 7(5) stated that they need only operate "with integrity and honesty." The Ministerial Code discusses special advisors in sections 3.2–3.4.
35. Tomkins (2006).

36. Psygkas (2017), p. 194.
37. As an example, in 2007 the Attorney General quashed a corruption investigation concerning BAE that was being carried out by the Serious Fraud Office (SFO) (Rose-Ackerman and Billa [2008]).
38. The convention, signed on June 25, 1998, in Aarhus, Denmark, is at http://www.unece.org/env/pp/treatytext.html (accessed April 5, 2020).
39. See European Commission-Directorate-General on the Environment, *Case-law on Access to Justice in Environmental Matters: Judgments Delivered by the EU Court of Justice Since the Adoption of Commission Notice, update n. 2* (March 10, 2019), http://ec.europa.eu/environment/aarhus/pdf/3-%20UPDATE%20OF%20THE%20NOTICE%20-%20FINAL%20-%2008%2003%2019.pdf (accessed April 5, 2020).
40. "A Minister of the Crown may by regulations make such provision as the Minister considers appropriate to prevent, remedy, or mitigate—(a) any failure of retained EU law to operate effectively, or (b) any other deficiency in retained EU law, arising from withdrawal of the UK from the EU." European Union (Withdrawal) Act 2018, 2018 c. 16, § 8(1) (Eng.). The time limit was one year in s. 8(8) of the 2018 Act, but was extended to two years under s. 27(5) of the EU (Withdrawal Agreement) Act of 2020. For a summary of the 2018 act, see Elliot and Tierney (2018); Mark Elliott, "1,000 Words/The European Union (Withdrawal) Act 2018," *Public Law for Everyone*, June 28, 2018, https://publiclawforeveryone.com/2018/06/28/1000-words-the-european-union-withdrawal-act-2018/ (accessed Nov. 17, 2020).
41. For an overview of SIs enacted, withdrawn, or before Parliament under the European Union (Withdrawal) Act 2018, see https://www.gov.uk/eu-withdrawal-act-2018-statutory-instruments (accessed April 5, 2020).
42. Chloe Anthony, Ffion Thomas, and Emily Lydgate, "Not Just a Technical Exercise: A Look at New UK Pesticides Regulation," *UK Trade Policy Observatory*, May 15, 2019.
43. House of Lords, Select Committee on the Constitution, "European Union (Withdrawal Agreement) Bill," HL Paper 5 (2020); Institute for Government, Withdrawal Agreement Act (Feb. 4, 2020), https://www.instituteforgovernment.org.uk/explainers/withdrawal-agreement-act (accessed April 5, 2020).
44. FoE argued: "Given the highly unusual situation we are in and the very broad and far-reaching powers in the Bill that are not ordinarily given to the executive, there should be enhanced scrutiny and effective public participation." *Friends of the Earth Statement: Public Participation in the UK's*

Withdrawal from the EU, Aug. 11, 2017, https://www.unece.org/fileadmin/DAM/env/pp/mop6/Statements_and_Comments/MOP6_6b_Friends_of_the_Earth_statement.pdf (accessed April 5, 2020). The Aarhus Compliance Committee holding is at ACC/C/2017/150, "United Kingdom: Preliminary Determination of Admissibility of Communication to the Aarhus Compliance Committee Concerning Compliance by the United Kingdom Regarding Public Participation in the Context of the 'Great Repeal Bill,'" 15 December 2017, https://www.unece.org/fileadmin/DAM/env/pp/compliance/C2017–150/Preliminary_determination_of_admissibility_C150.pdf (accessed April 5, 2020).

45. The European Communities approved the Aarhus Convention in Council Decision 2005/370/EC of Feb. 17, 2005. The convention applies to the EU itself and to member states. Directive 2003/35/EC, May 26, 2003, requires member states to provide for public participation in the drawing up of certain plans and programs relating to the environment and to enhance access to justice. Directive 2003/4/EC, Jan. 28, 2003, requires member states to provide public access to environmental information. The role of environmental groups is illustrated by the work of Naturschutzbund Deutschland (NABU) and Deutsche Umwelthilfe (DUH). NABU pushed for more public participation in the last elections to the federal parliament, and the DUH has been very active in lobbying. https://www.nabu.de/imperia/md/content/nabude/umweltpolitik/170301_hintergrundpapier_bt-wahlen_2017_endfassung.pdf; https://www.duh.de/projekte/umweltgesetzbuch/oeffentlichkeitsbeteiligung/ (both sites accessed April 5, 2020).

46. Baugesetzbuch, § 3.

47. The term originated in the Systems Theory of Renate Mayntz and Helmut Willke (Willke [2007]).

48. Ruffert (2007); Schmidt-Aßmann and Hoffmann-Reim (2004); Eifert (2014); Voßkuhle and Wischmeyer (2017).

49. Voßkuhle (2007); Voßkuhle and Wischmeyer (2017).

50. Ruffert (2007), p. 10.

51. See Chapter 7.

52. For telecoms, Psygkas (2017) documents the role of the EU.

53. German Basic Law, art. 80(1): "The Federal Government, a Federal Minister or the Länder [state] governments may be authorized by statute to issue regulations with the force of law [Rechtsverordnungen]. The content, purpose and scope of the authorization so conferred shall be laid down in the statute concerned." Art. 80(2) states the situations in which the Bundesrat, the upper

house that represents the Länder, must consent to regulations, especially those that will be administered by the states.

54. Schmidt-Aßmann and Möllers (2006).
55. *Kalkar Case I* (1978), BVerfGE 49, 89. The BVerfG acknowledged the Kalkar I decision in a case involving the German phase-out of nuclear power: BVerfGE 143, 246 (2016).
56. Derlien (2005), pp. 110–11.
57. Schmidt-Aßmann and Möllers (2006), p. 268.
58. I follow US usage and use the word "federal" to refer to the national government, i.e., the *Bund* in German.
59. Wallerath (1997); Silvia (2013); Schulz-Nieswandt (2011). See Chapter 4.
60. For the party composition of the Bundesrat in 2020, see https://www.bundesrat.de/DE/bundesrat/verteilung/verteilung-node.html (accessed April 5, 2020).
61. Furthermore, the states retain the authority to legislate in all areas not explicitly assigned to the federal government. Basic Law, art. 70(1).
62. Of the 400 rules with the force of law sent to the Upper House between 2013 and 2017, only one was voted down by that body. Between 1994 and 2017, seventeen were voted down out of 2,981. *Die Arbeit des Bundesrates im Spiegel der Zahlen*, Nov. 17, 2017, https://www.bundesrat.de/SharedDocs/downloads/DE/statistik/gesamtstatistik.html?_= (accessed April 6, 2020).
63. The practice has provoked controversy because the option is not mentioned in the Basic Law, art. 80, dealing with the delegation of rulemaking powers. Kotulla and Rolfsen (2010); Saurer (2003).
64. VwVfG, Jan. 23, 2003, BGBl I 102, amended by art. 3 of the act of July 25, 2013, BGBl I 2749. Administrative acts are regulated by § 35 of the VwVfG.
65. Public input may include hearings of affected interests (*Anhörung beteiligter Kreise*).
66. The situation in the mid-1990s is outlined in Rose-Ackerman (1995). Recent developments are outlined below, but the basic framework remains unchanged. See the chapter on Germany, researched by Stefanie Egidy, in Rose-Ackerman, Egidy, and Fowkes (2015), pp. 189–215.
67. The Act on the Assessment of Environmental Impacts requires public input for many infrastructure projects. *Gesetz über die Umweltverträglichkeitsprüfung, Anlage 1: Liste "UVP-pflichtige Vorhaben."* The same act requires strategic environmental assessments (SEAs), with public input, for strategic planning around air traffic routes, urban development, waste management, etc. *Anlage 5: Liste "SUP-pflichtige Pläne und Programme."* Similarly, the Public

Participation Act (*Öffentlichkeitsbeteiligungsgesetz*) largely incorporates EU directives on public information and consultation derived from the Aarhus Convention. The Network Expansion Acceleration Act likewise mandates public consultations on expansion of the electricity network. *Netzausbau-beschleunigungsgesetz*, § 9: Behörden-und Öffentlichkeitsbeteiligung. See Rose-Ackerman and Riemer (May 6, 2019).

68. "Each party shall strive to promote effective public participation at an appropriate stage, and while options are still open, during the preparation by public authorities of executive regulations and other generally applicable legally binding rules that may have a significant effect on the environment." Aarhus Convention, art. 8.
69. See Chapter 7.
70. Pünder (2014), p. 244.
71. The transition is central to the work of the Federal Network Agency (*Bundesnetzagentur*), discussed in Chapter 4. The factual matter here draws on Groebel (2013) and Durner (2014).
72. Renn, Webler, and Wiedemann (1995a), pp. 27–28.
73. The legislation, the *Netzausbaubeschleunigungsgesetz Übertragungsnetz* (NABEG) and amendments to the *Energiewirtschaftsgesetz* (EnWG), §§ 12a ff., and the Renewable Energy Sources Act (*Erneuerbare-Energien-Gesetz*, EEG) aim to speed up grid expansion and thus enable the phase-out of nuclear power. The EEG was amended in 2014. The amended Atomic Energy Act changed the deadlines for plant closures to 2022. In addition, legislative provisions seek to increase the efficiency of energy use and conservation.
74. Earlier controversies over nuclear power in Germany are summarized in Rose-Ackerman (1995), pp. 73–75, 84–87.
75. The goal refers to electric power only, not to heating or transportation. Craig Morris, "Germany Nearly Reached 100 Percent Renewable Power on Sunday," *Energy Transition: The Germany Energiewende*, May 1, 2016, https://energytransition.org/2016/05/germany-nearly-reached-100-percent-renewable-power-on-sunday/ (accessed Nov. 2, 2020).
76. Julian Wettengel, "Renewables Cover Almost Half of German Electricity Use in First 9 Months 2020—Preliminary Data," *Clean Energy Wire*, Sept. 25, 2020, https://www.cleanenergywire.org/news/renewables-cover-almost-half-german-electricity-use-first-9-months-2020-preliminary-data (accessed Nov. 20, 2020).
77. German prices moved from parity with California prices in 2006 to almost one and a half times higher in 2015 in spite of California's own shift to renew-

ables with the goal of 50 percent by 2030. Leslie Hook and Ed Crooks, "California's Cleaner Dream," *Financial Times*, October 19, 2016.

78. Sören Amelang,"Germany agrees to pay energy companies over 2 billion euros in nuclear exit compensation," *Clean Energy Wire*, March 5, 2021, https://www.cleanenergywire.org/news/germany-agrees-pay-energy-companies-over-2-billion-euros-nuclear-exit compensation (accessed April 25, 2021). That agreement followed a 2016 decision, BVerfGE 143, 246, holding that the utility firms must obtain compensation for losses based on their legitimate expectations. In addition BVerfG, order of April 13, 2017, 2BvL 6/13, struck down a tax on nuclear energy companies, requiring refunds.

79. Ralph Diermann, "Energiewende: Missionarisches Predigen Hilft Nicht" (interview with Professor Armin Grunwald), *Spiegel*, Jan. 20, 2019, https://www.spiegel.de/wissenschaft/natur/energiewende-es-wird-auch-verlierer-geben-a-1248615.html.

80. Bundesbedarfsplangesetz, July 23, 2013. In 2015, the FNA reaffirmed the importance of building new long-distance transmission lines from the North to the South. Kerstine Appunn, "German Grid Agency Stresses Need for New Power Lines," *Clean Energy Wire*, Feb. 27, 2015, http://www.cleanenergywire.org/news/german-grid-agency-stresses-need-new-power-lines (accessed Oct. 23, 2020).

81. Kropp (2015); Spieker (2018).

82. Andreas Mihm, "Energie Wende: Behörde gibt grünes Licht für Stromautobahn," *Frankfurter Allgemeine Zeitung*, Aug. 6, 2019, https://www.faz.net/aktuell/wirtschaft/energiewende-behoerde-gibt-gruenes-licht-fuer-strom autobahn-16320568.html.

83. "Germany's Underground Cable Law: New Rule Aims to Accelerate Grid Expansion," *Global Transmission Report*, April 6, 2016, https://www.globaltransmission.info/archive.php?id=25738 (accessed Oct. 23, 2020).

84. In 2019 almost no new wind farms were built due to public protests and court cases. Klaus Stratmann, "Die Abstandsregelung für Windräder ist vom Tisch Zumindest Vorerst," *Handelsblatt*, Nov. 28, 2019, https://www.handelsblatt.com/unternehmen/energie/windenergie-die-abstandsregelung-fuer-windraeder-ist-vom-tisch-zumindest-vorerst/25279036.html.

85. See, for example, a debate in the Bundestag in March 2019: https://www.bundestag.de/dokumente/textarchiv/2019/kw11-de-fukushima-595194. Some scientists are arguing that nuclear power is climate-friendly; see Axel Bojanowsi, "Der Atomausstieg ist ein großer Fehler," *Spiegel-Wissenschaft*, Nov. 15, 2017, https://www.spiegel.de/wissenschaft/natur/klimawandel-der-atomausstieg-ist-ein-grosser-fehler-interview-a-1178009.html (both accessed Nov. 17, 2020).

86. The main sponsors are Deutsche Umwelthilfe, the Hirschen Group, and the IKU_DIE DIALOGGESTALTER (a private business-management consultant company that organizes public-participation initiatives: http://www.dialoggestalter.de/startseite/ (accessed Nov. 2, 2020). The Federal Ministry for Economic Affairs and Energy co-sponsors the initiative. I am grateful to Lena Riemer for informing me about this effort.
87. https://www.buergerdialog-stromnetz.de/im-dialog/frage-stellen/ (accessed Oct. 23, 2020).
88. See Chapter 6 for other experiments in public participation.
89. This section draws on and updates Rose-Ackerman and Perroud (2013). I am also grateful to Joachim-Nicolas Herrera and Estelle Cambas, who assisted with aspects of French public law. I am responsible for any errors.
90. Lasser (2009).
91. Conseil d'État, *Rapport Public: Consulter Autrement, Participer Effectivement* (2011).
92. *Code des Relations entre le Public et l'Administration* (2015). The National Assembly modified the code in 2016 and 2018. Art. L131–1 outlines principles for public participation in the elaboration of an administrative project or act. The Conseil d'État (CE) elaborated these requirements, including "principles of equity and impartiality," in CE, 19 juillet 2017, *Association Citoyenne pour Occitanie et Pays Catalan et Autres, n° 403928.*
93. Dominique Custos (2017) argues that in one respect the code is more expansive than US law because it applies to non-legislative rules.
94. Baranger (2006), p. 241.
95. French Constitution, art. 13.
96. The French Constitution, art. 38, stipulates that "[i]n order to implement its program, the government may ask Parliament for authorization, for a limited period, to take measures by ordinance that are normally the preserve of statue law," after consultation with the Conseil d'État.
97. French Constitution, art. 34.
98. French Constitution, art. 37.1: "Matters other than those coming under the scope of statute law shall be matters for regulation."
99. French Constitution, art. 49.3. President Macron enacted a contested pension reform by invoking that article in February 2020. David Keohane, "France Bypasses Parliament to Enact Pension Reform," *Financial Times*, Feb. 29, 2020. The action must relate to finances or to social security and is subject to censure by the National Assembly within twenty-four hours. In this case, the censure motion did not pass.

100. Reitz (2006), p. 605; Massot (2001).
101. Rose-Ackerman and Perroud (2013), pp. 236–45.
102. French Constitution, art. 61.1.
103. Conseil Constitutionnel Décision n° 2011–183/184 QPC, 14 octobre 2011. See Chapter 7.
104. The law on public inquests dates from March 8, 1810 and allowed landowners to comment on proposed projects that involved the taking of land (Dupré de Boulois [2011]; Blatrix [2009]). *Code de l'environnement*, art. L123–1. The expanded coverage was introduced by Loi n° 2010–788 du 12 juillet 2010.
105. Jégouzo (2007), pp. 577–78.
106. Loi n° 76–629 du 10 juillet 1976 relative à la protection de la nature; Loi n° 83–630 du 12 juillet 1983 relative à la democratisation de l'enquête publique; Loi n° 2010–788 du 12 juillet 2010 portant engagement national pour l'environnement.
107. Décret n° 2011–2018 du 29 décembre 2011 portant réforme de l'enquête publique relative aux opérations susceptibles d'affecter l'environnement; and Décret n° 2011–2021 du 29 décembre 2011 déterminant la liste des projets, plans et programmes devant faire l'objet d'une communication au public par voie électronique dans le cadre de l'expérimentation prévue au II de l'article L. 123–10 du code de l'environnement.
108. Bétaille (2010).
109. Prieur (2011), p. 91; Loi n° 76–629 du 10 juillet 1976 relative à la protection de la nature.
110. Blatrix (2009). After an inquest has approved a project, environmental associations can appeal to the administrative courts to prevent the commencement of the project. After domestic procedures are exhausted, a disappointed property owner may be able to bring a case before the European Court of Human Rights, but with the remedy limited to compensation for lost property rights.
111. Loi n° 83–630 du 12 juillet 1983 relative à la democratisation de l'enquête publique.
112. Prieur (2011), p. 110, contends that the provisions for publicity in the law are "disappointing."
113. Conseil d'État (2011), p. 19.
114. *Programme Concertation, Décision, Environnement*, http://concertation-environnement.fr /; see also http://www.concertation-environnement.fr/documents/regards_croises/seance_12.pdf (study of 30 years of research on concertation) (both accessed April 7, 2020).

115. *Programme Concertation, Décision, Environnement*, p. 21.
116. Loi n° 95–101 du 2 février 1995 relative au renforcement de la protection de l'environnement. Blatrix et al. (2011) compare French and British perspectives on the issue and the history of the development of concertation.
117. Delaunay (2011).
118. It began to operate in 1997, headed by a member of the Conseil d'État, and in 2002 it was given the status of an "independent administrative authority."
119. Loi n° 2002–276 du 27 février 2002 relative à la démocratie de proximité; Commission Nationale du Débat Public, http://www.debatpublic.fr (accessed April 12, 2020). See Blatrix (2009), pp. 106–07; Blatrix (2007), p. 56.
120. René Dosière and Christian Vanneste, *Comité d'Évaluation et de Contrôle des Politiques Publiques*, Assemblée Nationale (Dec. 1, 2011). Three cases involved nanotechnologies, nuclear waste disposal, and a national highway in the Rhone Valley. The nuclear waste debate operated in a satisfactory way. The nanotechnology debate was disrupted by strong opponents; it became a series of media events where the organizations that participated took refuge in a sort of bunker ("*se réfugier dans une sorte de bunker*"). See also Blatrix (2009), p. 113.
121. Commission Nationale du Débat Public (2011), p. 96, reports that the cost of the public debate for developers in 2008–2009 totaled €550,000 to €3 million; see also Delaunay (2011) analyzing the shortcomings. See also Commission Nationale du Débat Public (2019).
122. Delaunay (2004).
123. Lascoumes (2011).
124. *Le Grenelle de l'environnement: Quels Engagements*, https://www.vie-publique.fr/eclairage/268585-le-grenelle-de-lenvironnement-quels-engagements (reporting ongoing activities).
125. Durance (2010); Chevallier (2011b).
126. Hamdan (2011); Lascoumes (2011), p. 2.
127. For example, the Brigitte Bardot Foundation's group Animal Concern was not allowed to participate on that ground.
128. Lascoumes (2011), p. 285.
129. Lascoumes (2011). See also Whiteside et al. (2010).
130. The French government organized a similar exercise in 2020 to debate climate change policy. See p. 69 and Chapter 6.
131. Loi n° 2010–788 du 12 juillet 2010. See Boy et al., 2012.

132. Loi n° 2009–967 du 3 août 2009 de programmation relative à la mise en œuvre du Grenelle de l'environnement; Loi n° 2010–788 du 12 juillet 2010 portant engagement national pour l'environnement.
133. Pierrette Crosemarie, *Bilan du Grenelle de l'Environnement*, CESE, Paris, février 2012, https://www.lecese.fr/sites/default/files/pdf/Avis/2012/2012_04_grenelle_environnement.pdf (accessed April 10, 2020).
134. Art. L 1412–1-1, Code of Public Health; Loi n° 2011–814 du 7 juillet 2011 relative à la bioéthique.
135. Chevallier (2007). Under the ancient tradition of états généraux, public participation is linked with the idea of revolution. The états généraux met during the ancien régime and were appointed by the king. At present, the government uses the term to show that it aims to gather everyone together to debate and solve a specific problem.
136. Loi n° 2016–1321 du 7 octobre 2016 pour une République numérique.
137. The website, republique-numerique.fr, lists those making suggestions, reactions by other participants, voluntary votes, and the government's responses.
138. Ministère de l'Économie, de l'Industrie et du Numérique, Secrétariat d'État au Numérique, *Projet de loi pour une République numérique: 21,330 citoyens ont co-écrit le projet de loi*, https://www.republique-numerique.fr/media/default/0001/02/da09b380f543bfab2d13da7424cec264dca669c6.pdf (accessed April 6, 2020).
139. Peter S. Goodman, "Inequality Fuels Rage of 'Yellow Vests' in Equality-Obsessed France," *New York Times*, April 15, 2019, https://www.nytimes.com/2019/04/15/business/yellow-vests-movement-inequality.html; Arthur Goldhammer, "The Yellow Vest Protests and the Tragedy of Emmanuel Macron," *Foreign Affairs*, Dec. 12, 2018, https://www.foreignaffairs.com/articles/france/2018-12-12/yellow-vest-protests-and-tragedy-emmanuel-macron.
140. Buge and Morio (2019).
141. The Aarhus Convention, discussed in the sections on the UK and Germany, frames environmental policymaking processes. France has added a Charter for the Environment at the end of the constitutional text. Article 34 of the Constitution lists the environment as an area that must be covered by statutes that lay down basic principles. See Custos (2010b), p. 279; Bourg and Whiteside (2007). The Conseil Constitutionnel affirmed the charter's status as enforceable constitutional law in Décision n° 2008–564DC 19, 19 juin 2008, Rec. [313].
142. French Constitution, Charter for the Environment, art. 7.

143. The Conseil Supérieur de la Prévention des Risques Technologiques was formerly the Conseil Supérieur des Installations Classées.
144. *Association France Nature Environnement (AFNE)*, CC Décision n° 2011–183/184QPC, 14 octobre 2011. The plaintiffs challenged two provisions of the Environmental Code, art. L 511–2 and paragraph II of art. L 512–7, which set out the procedures for classifying certain facilities based on the risks they posed to the environment. For an overview of the first two QPC's challenging government action on the basis of the Charter of the Environment, see Marrani (2014).
145. Loi n° 2012–1460 du 27 décembre 2012 relative à la mise en oeuvre du principe de participation du public defini à l'article 7 de la Charte de l'environnement.
146. *Ministère de l'Écologie, du Développement durable et d'Énergie, Consultations publiques*, http://www.consultations-publiques.developpement-durable.gouv.fr/projet-de-loi-relatif-a-la-mise-en-oeuvre-du-principe-de-participation-du-public. The list of the administrative decisions subject to public consultation is available at http://www.consultations-publiques.developpement-durable.gouv.fr/ (accessed April 6, 2020).
147. Loi n° 2012–1460, art. 3. The proposal for a neutral referee or "guardian" is an innovative aspect of the experimental process.
148. The Conseil Constitutionnel did not receive a request for review, so it is unclear whether the statute meets constitutional standards.
149. Conseil d'État, 12 juillet 2019, Décision n° 424600. The relevant part of the statute is L. 123–19–1.
150. Art. L 132–1, CRPA.
151. Conseil d'État, 19 juillet 2017, *Association Citoyenne pour Occitanie et Pays Catalan et Autres*, Décision n° 403928, 403948. I discuss the case further in Chapter 7.
152. Jauvert (2017).
153. US Constitution, art. II, sect. 3.
154. *National Petroleum Refiners Ass'n. v. FTC*, 482 F. 2d 672 (D.C. Cir. 1973).
155. The Supreme Court has only twice struck down statutes on the basis of non-delegation, both in 1935. In the first, the Court found that Congress had impermissibly delegated regulatory powers over petroleum transportation to the executive without sufficiently clear standards. *Panama Refining Co. v. A. D. Ryan*, 293 U.S. 388 (1935). In the second, the Court rejected a statutory provision delegating regulatory authority to an industry group. *A.L.A. Schechter Poultry Corp. v. U.S.*, 295 U.S. 495 (1935).

156. Farber, Heinzerling, and Shane (2018).
157. *Preserving and Fortifying Deferred Action for Childhood Arrivls (DACA)* is at: https://www.whitehouse.gov/briefing-room/presidential-actions/2021/01/20/preserving-and-fortifying-deferred-action-for-childhood-arrivals-daca/ (accessed January 28, 2021). For a comparison of immigration policy-making under President Obama and in the early years of the Trump administration, see Mashaw and Berke (2018).
158. The exception is an emergency, such as the bills passed rapidly in response to the coronavirus outbreak in 2020.
159. Rose-Ackerman, Egidy and Fowkes (2015), pp. 31–55.
160. A change in administration may prompt an agency to reverse course or halt rulemakings that are inconsistent with a new president's agenda (O'Connell [2011]).
161. The FDA lost its attempt to (lightly) regulate cigarettes in *FDA v. Brown & Williamson Tobacco Co.*, 529 U.S. 120 (2000). *Motor Vehicles Mfrs. Ass'n. v. State Farm Mut. Auto. Ins. Co.*, 463 U.S. 29 (1983) struck down some of the Reagan administration's efforts to reduce regulation of the automobile industry.
162. *INS v. Chadha*, 462 U.S. 919 (1983), held that legislative vetoes are unconstitutional. In response, Congress passed the Congressional Review Act (CRA), 5 U.S.C. §§ 801–808, under which a statute can repeal a rule under an expedited process within certain time limits. However, statutes must be signed by the president or passed by a super-majority in each house. The CRA was used during the early months of the Trump administration to void rules issued both by cabinet departments and by independent agencies. The Biden administration is considering its use because Congress is under Democratic control. However, that route risks returning to a weak status quo. See: Coral Davenport, "Restoring Environmental Rules Rolled Back by Trump Could Take Years," *New York Times*, January 22, 2021, https://www.nytimes.com/2021/01/22/climate/biden-environment.html.
163. Shane (2009); Strauss (2007, 1997).
164. Shane (2009), pp. 143–74.
165. Farber et al. (2018). Based on a report by the Administrative Conference of the United States, the authors recommend improved agency procedures and outreach to community groups and engaged citizens.
166. 5 U.S.C. §§ 551–559, 701–706.
167. 5 U.S.C. § 706(2)(A); some rules must pass an apparently stricter "substantial evidence" test, § 706(2)(E).

168. The APA exempts matters related to "a military or foreign affairs function of the U.S.," or "a matter related to agency management or personnel to public property, loans, grants, benefits or contracts." 5 U.S.C. § 553(a). Rulemaking procedures are not applied to "interpretive rules, general statements of policy, or rules of agency organization, procedure, or practice," or "when an agency finds for good cause that notice and public procedure is impracticable, unnecessary, or contrary to public interest." 5 U.S.C. § 553(b).
169. 5 U.S.C. §§ 701–706.
170. Strauss (1996); Walker (2017).
171. *Vermont Yankee Nuclear Power Corp. v. Natural Resources Defense Council*, 435 U.S. 519 (1978); see also *Perez v. Mortgage Bankers Ass'n*, 575 U.S. 92, 135 S. Ct. 1199 (2015).
172. Ackerman (2007); Eskridge and Ferejohn (2010).
173. Elliott (1992); McGarity (1992).
174. A study of rules issued between 1983 and 2006 showed that many were issued quite quickly (Yackee and Yackee [2009]). A study of Department of the Interior rules from 1950 to 1990 by the same authors found the evidence for ossification mixed and weak overall (Yackee and Yackee [2012]).
175. They studied over thirty low-salience rules (fewer than 200 comments) issued between 1994 and 2001 by four agencies (Yackee and Yackee [2006]).
176. See *Little Sisters of the Poor Saints Peter and Paul Home v. Pennsylvania*, 140 S. Ct. 2367, 2385–2386 (2020), arguing that courts do not apply an "open-mindedness test" in evaluating the rulemaking process. Those who apply that test ask if the text of the rule changed in response to public comments.
177. Heinzerling (2014).
178. OIRA has a role in enforcing several oversight statutes, https://www.whitehouse.gov/omb/information-regulatory-affairs/ (accessed April 6, 2020). EO 12866: Regulatory Planning and Review, Sept. 30, 1993, Sect. 6(a)(3)(C) sets out the cost-benefit requirement for significant regulatory actions as defined in sect. 3(f)(1). The definition also includes regulatory actions that "adversely affect in a material way the economy, a sector of the economy, productivity, competition, jobs, the environment, public health or safety, or State, local, or tribal governments or communities." The term "material" is not defined. Chapter 5 discusses the conceptual underpinnings of cost-benefit analysis. EO 12866, sect. 4 (c). The regulatory plan must include "significant regulatory actions that the agency reasonably expects to

issue in proposed or final form in that fiscal year or thereafter." The original Reagan administration order is EO 12291: Federal Regulation, Feb. 17, 1981. On the history of centralized regulatory review, see Tozzi (2011); Shane (2009), pp. 143–58.

179. EO 12866, sect. 9.
180. The White House, *Memorandum: Modernizing Regulatory Review*, January 20, 2021. https://www.whitehouse.gov/briefing-room/presidential-actions/2021/01/20/modernizing-regulatory-review/ (accessed January 29, 2021).
181. Shapiro and Murphy (2015); Strauss (2007).
182. Bressman and Vandenbergh (2006); Ketcham-Colwill (2014). Sally Katzen (2007), a former OIRA head, critiques the empirical work of Bressman and Vandenbergh. Cass Sunstein (2013), another former head of OIRA, also defends its work.
183. Breyer (1993), pp. 59–61; B. Ackerman (2000b), pp. 688–714. Rose-Ackerman (2011) recommends that OIRA be reconstituted as an independent body.
184. Brand (2008).
185. APA § 553 (e). Farber et al. (2018), p. 8.
186. Kagan (2001). Shane (2009), pp. 153–58, argues that Clinton's assertions of presidential power were less intrusive than those of George W. Bush.
187. Farber (2019) provides an overview of OIRA and CBA in limiting regulations under the Trump administration.
188. Strauss (2007).
189. For example, Congress mandated the EPA to update its regulations on renewable fuels by 2008. After missing its deadline, the EPA issued regulations in 2010, which were subject to subsequent litigation. *Nat'l Petrochemical & Refiners Ass'n v. EPA* (*Nat'l Refiners Ass'n I*), 630 F.3d 145, 147–62 (D.C. Cir. 2010). See Schmitter (2012–2013); Yeatman (2013–2014). The Nutrition Labeling and Education Act included a "hammer" provision, requiring the FDA to issue regulations requiring nutritional labeling within twelve months of the statute's enactment, or else the proposed regulations would become final regulations. See Magill (1995); Gerson and O'Connell (2008).
190. Nou (2013).
191. Mashaw and Berke (2018) compare Presidents Obama and Trump with respect to immigration policy, climate change, and executive-branch structure.

192. EO 13771, 82 Fed. Reg. 9339 (Feb. 3, 2017) ("Reducing Regulation and Controlling Regulatory Costs"), https://www.whitehouse.gov/presidential-actions/presidential-executive-order-reducing-regulation-controlling-regulatory-costs/. See https://www.reginfo.gov/public/do/eAgendaEO13771. A guidance document was issued on Feb. 22, 2018: https://www.whitehouse.gov/wp-content/uploads/2017/12/Final-3c-EO-13771-guidance.pdf (all accessed April 6, 2020). President Biden revoked EO 13771 along with several others. See *The White House; Revocation of Certain Executive Orders Concerning Federal Regulation*, January 20, 2021, https://www.whitehouse.gov/briefing-room/presidential-actions/2021/01/20/executive-order-revocation-of-certain-executive-orders-concerning-federal-regulation/ (accessed January 29, 2021.
193. Dooling (2018).
194. Coral Davenport, "Trump Administration Plans a Major Weakening of Mercury Emissions Rules," *New York Times*, Sept. 30, 2018, https://www.nytimes.com/2018/09/30/climate/epa-trump-mercury-rule.html. The industry/union letter in opposition is at: https://www.eenews.net/assets/2018/07/11/document_gw_04.pdf (accessed April 6, 2020). See also Sayid (2018).
195. Stephanie Kirchgaessner. "Billion-dollar US Energy Firm Opposes Trump Plan to Roll Back Mercury Rules," *The Guardian*, Nov. 16, 2018, https://www.theguardian.com/us-news/2018/nov/15/energy-company-takes-stance-against-trump-effort-to-rollback-mercury-rule. Similarly, in mid-2020, the EPA weakened a regulation covering methane leaks, a major contributor to greenhouse gases. Major energy companies opposed the rollback because of past investments to promote natural gas. Coral Davenport, "E.P.A. Weakens a Rule Regulating Methane, Even as Leaks Are Worsening," *New York Times*, Aug. 14, 2020.
196. Nadja Popovich, Livia Albeck-Ripka, and Kendra Pierre-Louise, "The Trump Administration Is Reversing Nearly 100 Environmental Rules: Here's the List," *New York Times*, Oct. 15, 2020, https://www.nytimes.com/interactive/2020/climate/trump-environment-rollbacks-list.html.
197. Nou (2019). The annual survey of the Office of Personal Management shows an overall decline in morale for the last two years, but with considerable cross-agency variation. Michael Stratford, "Trump's Been President for 3 Years: Government Morale Has Dropped for Two of Them," *Politico*, Dec. 17, 2019, https://www.politico.com/news/agenda/2019/12/17/government-morale-trump-federal-administration-084835.

198. Data from the US Office of Personnel Management for 2016–2018 shows that "almost 8% of Senior Executive Service positions were vacated or remained empty due to a higher-than-usual level of voluntary departures and lower-than-usual number of accessions." However, attrition in rank and file was not unusual during 2017–2019 and was not unusual compared to 2005–2016. Daniel Lim, "Federal Workforce Attrition Rate under the Trump Administration," *Government Executive*, December 28, 2020. For an in-depth overview of the civil service see Light (2008).
199. Richardson (2019), based on a survey of 3,500 federal civil servants, showed that if they were not supportive of the policy agendas of political appointees, they were more likely to leave government and, if they remained, to spend less time improving their level of expertise.
200. Verkuil (2017); data on employees paid through contracts and grants is included in Paul C. Light, "The True Size of Government Is Nearing a Record High," *Fixgov: The Case for Major Government Reform*, The Brookings Institution, October 7, 2020, https://www.brookings.edu/blog/fixgov/2020/10/07/the-true-size-of-government-is-nearing-a-record-high/ (accessed January 30, 2021).
201. For a range of views see the essays published in the Regulatory Review of the Penn Program on Regulation, https://www.theregreview.org/2017/12/04/valuing-professional-government/ (accessed April 6, 2020). Michaels (2017) warns of excessive contracting out.
202. *Motor Vehicle Manufacturers' Ass'n v. State Farm Mutual Automobile Insurance Co.*, 463 U.S. 29 (1983).
203. Buzbee (2019).
204. Executive Order 13778, February 2017.
205. Michael Gerrard, quoted in Coral Davenport, "Restoring Environmental Rules Rolled Back by Trump Could Take Years," *New York Times*, January 22, 2021, https://www.nytimes.com/2021/01/22/climate/biden-environment.html. The rule issued by the Trump administration is at: RIN 2040-AF75: Revised Definition of "Waters of the United States," Fed. Reg., Vol. 84, No. 31, pp. 4,154–4,220 (April 21, 2020). See Adler (2019). On the lawsuits accompanying the repeal of the 2015 rule see Pamela King, "Clean Water Act: WOTUS Lawsuits Start Long, Muddy Legal Battle," *E & E News*, October 24, 2019, https://www.eenews.net/stories/1061365079 (accessed November 17, 2020). After the issuance of the Navigable Waters Protection Rule lawsuits were filed in numerous district courts seeking to enjoin the rule. One problem for opponents was

that, with the 2015 rule rescinded, an injunction would revert to the 1986 regulatory definition. The National Conference of State Legislatures produced a "Legal & Regulatory Timeline of 'Waters of the United States'" through April 2020: https://www.ncsl.org/Documents/standcomm/scnri/wotus_timeline.pdf (accessed Nov. 17, 2020).

206. 5 U.S.C. § 553(b)(3)(A).
207. *Sierra Club v. Costle*, 657 F. 2d. 298, 395–410 (D.C. Cir., 1981) (meetings with Sen. Robert Byrd and his staff after the end of the formal comment period were acceptable).
208. See note 162 above on the CRA.
209. 5 U.S.C. §§ 551–559, 701–706. Judicial review is discussed in Chapter 7.
210. The texts of REINS are at S. 21 https://www.congress.gov/bill/115th-congress/senate-bill/21/text, and H.R. 26, 115th Cong. (2017) https://www.congress.gov/bill/115th-congress/house-bill/26/text (both accessed April 6, 2020).
211. H.R. 26—Regulations from the Executive in Need of Scrutiny Act of 2017, § 2.
212. The Senate Committee Minority Report states: "The REINS Act would replace the current system's reliance on science, expertise and public process in developing rules with Congress' partisan considerations and the potential influence of industry lobbyists . . . Members of Congress simply do not have the technical and scientific expertise that agencies possess . . ." Senate Committee on Homeland Security and Governmental Affairs, Regulations in Need of Scrutiny Act of 2017, Report together with Minority Views, Oct. 16, 2017, VII. Minority Views, p. 12. The full report is at https://www.congress.gov/congressional-report/115th-congress/senate-report/169/1?overview=closed (accessed April 6, 2020).
213. The Minority Report, pp. 11–12, states: "One practical effect of REINS would be to discourage agencies from taking on major rulemakings in the first place and could grind the entire rulemaking process to a halt if they choose to pursue rulemaking."
214. RAA is at H.R. 5, 115th Cong. (2017), https://www.congress.gov/bill/115th-congress/house-bill/5. The amended Senate bill retains some of the most restrictive aspects of the House bill. It is at https://www.congress.gov/bill/115th-congress/senate-bill/951/text?r=18 (both accessed April 6, 2020). Levin (2019).
215. Formal rulemaking imitates a judicial proceeding with cross examination and a rule made "on the record" of the hearing (5 U.S.C. § 556). Barnett (2017) and Nielson (2014) criticize the trend away from formal rulemaking.

216. *Chevron, U.S.A. v. Natural Resources Defense Council*, 467 U.S. 837, 104 S. Ct. 2778 (1984).
217. Farina and Newhart (2013).
218. Wagner (2010).
219. Coglianese (2006).
220. Noveck (2004).

Chapter 4. Why Independent Agencies Should Be Independent

1. B. Ackerman (2000b).
2. In America, many state and local governments directly elect officials with executive or law enforcement responsibilities such as school boards, prosecutors, and even judges.
3. Verhoest, Van Thiel, Bouckaert, and Laegreid (2012).
4. § 706(2)(A). The general standards of judicial review in APA § 706 apply to both cabinet departments and independent agencies. See Chapters 3 and 7.
5. Shugerman (2016); Mashaw (2012); Rabin (1986).
6. Thatcher (2005), pp. 50–52; C. Scott (2005), pp. 67–87.
7. Kuztenov (2015); Szabados (2015).
8. On EU telecoms regulation, see Psygkas (2017).
9. Thatcher (2003), pp. 129–34.
10. Majone (1996, 2001).
11. Maggetti and Verhoest (2014); Verhoest et al. (2012).
12. The FCC can issue regulations "as public convenience, interest, or necessity requires." 47 U.S.C. § 303. The US Supreme Court has held that "an administrative agency's power to regulate in the public interest must always be grounded in a valid grant of authority from Congress." *Food and Drug Admin. v. Brown & Williamson Tobacco Corp.*, 529 U.S. 120, 161 (2000).
13. Everson (2005), pp. 141–63. On the EU see Curtin (2005).
14. Nesti (2016); Lodge and Stirtin (2012).
15. Verhey, Broeksteeg, and Van den Driessche (2008).
16. Breger and Edles (2015) provide a history and overview of the development and diversity of agencies' forms and responsibilities.
17. Their websites are https://cpsc.gov/ and https://www.fec.gov/about/leadership-and-structure/ (both accessed April 6, 2020). On the FEC see Scott and Bowman (2000).
18. The ICC followed the model of many state-level railroad regulators (Merrill [2011]). See also *Wiener v. U.S.*, 357 U.S. 349, 355 (1958), referring to the judicial character of the War Claims Commission.

19. *Nat'l Broadcasting Co. v. U.S.*, 319 U.S. 506 (1943); *American Trucking Ass'n. v. U.S.*, 319 U.S. 190 (1943). See Merrill and Watts (2002).
20. *Nat'l Petroleum Refiners Assoc. v. FTC*, 482 F. 2d 672 (D.C. Cir. 1973). See Custos (2006).
21. Now-Justice Brett Kavanaugh, when a judge on the District of Columbia Court of Appeals, used that phrase in dissent in *PHH Corp. v. Consumer Financial Protection Bureau*, 881 F. 3d 75,165 (D.C. Cir. 2018, en banc, Jan. 31, 2018).
22. *Lucia v. S.E.C.*, 138 S. Ct. 2044 (2018) (administrative law judges are "Officers of the United States," covered by the Appointments Clause of the Constitution, and subject to appointment by the president with the advice and consent of the U.S. Senate). Mascott (2018) explores different historical definitions of "officer of the US."
23. See Breger and Edles (2015).
24. Examples include the Federal Communications Commission, the Federal Trade Commission, and the National Labor Relations Board. Breger and Edlas (2015); Krotoszynski, Jr., Hodge, and Wintermyer (2015).
25. Here, too, there are exceptions in practice; see Breger and Edlas (2015).
26. In the past, even if the president's party held a majority, the filibuster rule permitted a minority of 40 senators to block confirmation of a nominee. In 2013 and 2017 the Senate changed its rules, and now only a bare majority is needed for confirmation to executive offices and the federal courts. https://www.nytimes.com/2013/11/22/us/politics/reid-sets-in-motion-steps-to-limit-use-of-filibuster.html. https://www.businessinsider.com/nuclear-option-gorsuch-filibuster-senate-2017-4.
27. After the National Labor Relations Board lost a quorum, it no longer had the authority to make legally binding decisions. *New Process Steel, L.P. v. N.L.R.B.*, 560 U.S. 674 (2010).
28. Feinstein (2017, 2018). However, a few, such as the Federal Reserve Bank, have their own sources of funds.
29. Weingast and Moran (1982); Moe (1985); Yackee and Yackee (2016); DeShazo and Freeman (2003).
30. Zhang (2015); McGarity (2012).
31. Stigler (1971); Posner (1974). Recent literature is more nuanced, e.g., Walters (2019).
32. Balleisen and Jacoby (2019); Dempsey (1979, 2011–2012).
33. Melnick (1983), pp. 1–23.
34. *FCC v. Fox Television*, 556 U.S. 502, 539 (2009) (Stevens, J., dissenting).

35. For example, the Supreme Court upheld the legality of the Sentencing Commission and the Independent Counsel Act against claimed violations of the separation of powers. *Mistretta v. United States*, 488 U.S. 361 (1988); *Morrison v. Olson*, 487 U.S. 654 (1988).
36. In a May 2019 memorandum, the director of the Office of Management and Budget told independent agencies that they must inform OIRA of upcoming rules to determine whether they are "major rules" subject to the CRA's notification-and-review requirements: M-19–14 "Guidance on Compliance with the Congressional Review Act": https://www.whitehouse.gov/wp-content/uploads/2019/04/M-19–14.pdf (accessed April 6, 2020). If the same party controls the presidency and both houses of Congress, the Congressional Review Act can be used to overturn independent agency rules. See, for example: Mark Kantor, "Congress Disapproves CFPB Rule Prohibiting Arbitration," *ABA*, November 3, 2017, https://www.americanbar.org/groups/litigation/committees/alternative-dispute-resolution/practice/2017/congress-disapproves-cfpb-rule-prohibiting-arbitration/ (accessed Nov. 5, 2020).
37. *Free Enterprise Fund v. Public Co. Accounting Oversight Board*, 561 U.S. 477 (2010).
38. The members of the PCAOB are not classed as government officials or employees. They are recruited from the private sector and paid private-sector salaries. *Free Enterprise Fund v. PCAOB*, 561 U.S. 477 (2010), opinion of the Court at 484–85.
39. Ibid. at 486
40. As the dissent points out, however, it is not obvious that the holding increases the president's power of oversight. The SEC can now dismiss a member of the PCAOB because of a policy disagreement, but the president cannot dismiss members of the SEC if he or she disagrees with that action. See *Free Enterprise Fund*, 561 U.S. 477 (2010), Breyer, J., dissenting, at 524–30.
41. Ibid., at 523.
42. Ibid., Appendix A at 524–30. Justice Stephen Breyer located four additional bodies inside other bodies with two layers of for-cause removal.
43. *Seila Law LLC v. Consumer Financial Protection Bureau (CFPB)*, 140 S. Ct. 2183 (2020).
44. 12 U.S.C. § 5491(c). The original proposal from the Obama administration and then-Professor Elizabeth Warren recommended a conventional multi-member agency.
45. Other single-headed bodies with for-cause removal would seem to suffer from the same deficiency—for example, the Federal Housing Finance

Agency. See *Collins v. Mnuchin*, 938 F. 3d 553 (5th Cir., 2019) (en banc) *cert. granted*, 2020 WL 3865249 (Mem.) (July 9, 2020).

46. *Seila*, opinion of the Court and Thomas, J., concurring in part and dissenting in part. Calabresi and Yoo (2008) defend the unitary executive theory. Shane (2009) provides a strong critique.
47. *Humphrey's Executor v. United States*, 295 U.S. 602 (1935). The case upheld for-cause removal in the case of a member of the Federal Trade Commission. The Supreme Court held that giving the president the power of removal would have a "coercive influence [that would] threaten the independence of a commission . . . [that was] created by Congress . . ." (p. 629).
48. *Seila*, Kagan, J., dissenting.
49. *Seila*, opinion of the Court. See also Harvey (2019), calling for the CFPB to be changed into a multi-member board in order to shield it from likely future constitutional challenge.
50. Thatcher (2003), p. 137.
51. Prosser (1997).
52. Thatcher (2003). There are also many non-ministerial bodies with a range of advisory and regulatory responsibilities, and the devolved governments of Scotland, Wales, and Northern Ireland have their own agencies in some areas. Other bodies enforce the law in particular cases, but do not make rules. House of Commons, Public Administration Select Committee (2014). A list of departments, agencies, and public bodies in the UK is at https://www.gov.uk/government/organisations (accessed April 6, 2020). The Bank of England is a special case; see Tucker (2018).

    I do not discuss the Next Steps reform, begun in 1988, because its main focus was on service delivery, not policymaking, and it declined in importance after 1999. Collin Talbot and Carole Talbot, "One Step Forward, Two Steps Back? The Rise and Fall of Government's Next Steps Agencies," *Civil Service World*, September 23, 2019, https://www.civilserviceworld.com/news/article/one-step-forward-two-steps-back-the-rise-and-fall-of-governments-next-steps-agencies (accessed Nov. 5, 2020).
53. Thatcher and Stone Sweet (2003), p. 29; Thatcher (2003), p. 139.
54. Examples are the Competition and Markets Authority (CMA) and the Equality and Human Rights Commission. The Water Services Regulation Authority (Ofwat), the Office of Rail and Road (ORR), the Food Standards Agency (FSA), and the Office of Communication (Ofcom) are governed by boards that engage in overall strategic planning. National Audit Office, "A Short Guide to Regulation" (September 2017), https://www.nao.org

.uk/wp-content/uploads/2017/09/A-Short-Guide-to-Regulation.pdf (accessed April 6, 2020).

55. Thatcher (2003), p. 126.
56. Tomkins (2008), pp. 265–66. See Hansard Society (2001), chapter 8, and House of Lords (2004).
57. A report by the House of Commons, Public Administration Select Committee (2014) noted, for instance, that although "Parliament has made some public bodies accountable to Parliament rather than the government . . . [t]hese arrangements are variable and inconsistent," and "not enough up-to-date information is available."
58. Psygkas (2017), pp. 177–291.
59. Ofgem, *Consumer First Panel Report: Understanding Consumers' Views on Network Access and Forward-Looking Charging Frameworks*, December 2019, https://www.ofgem.gov.uk/system/files/docs/2019/12/consumer_first_panel_report_0.pdf (accessed Nov. 5, 2020).
60. German Basic Law, art. 20(2). This section draws from Rose-Ackerman, Egidy, and Fowkes (2015). Stefanie Egidy was the first author of the German chapter. Lena Riemer provided helpful comments on current developments.
61. Dohler (2003), p. 111.
62. Schneider (2007), p. 309.
63. Basic Law, art. 87(3), first sentence, permits the creation of "selbstständige Bundesoberbehörde" by statute. BVerfGE 14, 197 upholds a federal supervisory authority for the banking sector. Burgsmüller (1967), pp. 27–28. The German term *Bund* refers to the central government, that is, the federal or national government in the US.
64. The EU norms requiring and specifying the level of independence are: art. 3, para. 3a, Dir. 2002/21/EC, as amended by Directive 2009/140/EC; art. 35, para. 4, sent. 2, Dir. 2009/72/EC; art. 39, para. 4, sent. 2, Dir. 2009/73/EC. The German statute places the FNA under the supervision of two ministries and requires Germany to comply with EU and international law. https://www.gesetze-im-internet.de/bkorgerl_2013/iv_.html (accessed April 6, 2020).
65. Bundeskartellamt, Organisation, https://www.bundeskartellamt.de/EN/AboutUs/Bundeskartellamt/Organisation/organisation_node.html (accessed April 6, 2020). Könen (2013).
66. Mehde (2008), p. 108.
67. Dohler (2003).
68. Dohler (2003), p. 108; Schneider (2007), p. 311.

69. Steinbach (2017).
70. Bundesbeauftragte für den Datenschutz und Informationsfreiheit, https://www.bfdi.bund.de/EN/Home/home_node.html (accessed April 6, 2020).
71. EU directive 95/46/EG.
72. *European Commission v. Germany*, March 9, 2010, C-518/07, at http://curia.europa.eu/juris/document/document.jsf;jsessionid=A26E39C2CA82B5644E301BAD778D7BBD?text=anddocid=79752andpageIndex=oanddoclang=ENandmode=lstanddir=&occ=first&part=1andcid=7748019 (accessed April 6, 2020).
73. Dohler (2003), p. 102.
74. The agency website is http://www.bundesnetzagentur.de/ (accessed April 6, 2020).
75. Supervision by the Federal Ministry for Transport and Digital Infrastructure dates from Dec. 17, 2013. A 2017 report by the Scientific Research Service of the Bundestag discusses three issues: (1) the legal status of the agency; (2) supervisory authority over the agency; and (3) parliamentary control. As to (1) and (2), the agency is described as relatively independent and protected from political and economic influence. The report concluded: "§ 117 Telecommunications Act does not exclude instructions from the Ministry of Economic Affairs and the Ministry of Transport to the Federal Network Agency." However, they must be published in the Federal Gazette. Such instructions have never been given. In contrast to antitrust merger control, regulatory law does not recognize a ministerial permit (*Ministerialerlaubnis*). As to (3): the report refers to the Advisory Council, referenced in the text, without going into detail. https://www.bundestag.de/resource/blob/529464/17d91d69577a4b1697c7c012218ed18b/wd-3–158–17-pdf-data.pdf (accessed April 6, 2020).
76. Wendel (2019), pp. 265ff. (Franziska Bantlin translated and summarized Wendel's arguments).
77. In addition to the Advisory Council (*Beirat*), there is the Railroad Infrastructure Body (*Eisenbahninfrastrukturbeirat*) and the Federal Planning Body (*Bundesfachplanungsbeirat*). The Network Agency also has the duty of disclosure in certain areas if the Advisory Council requests information.
78. The members of the Advisory Council are appointed by the federal government upon the proposal of the Bundestag and the Bundesrat. A list of the members can be found here: https://www.bundesnetzagentur.de/SharedDocs/Downloads/EN/BNetzA/FederalAgency/AdvisoryCouncil/201405809MembersAdvisoryCouncil.pdf?__blob=publicationFile&v=87.

The Council's duties and legal basis are here: https://www.bundesnetzagentur.de/EN/General/Bundesnetzagentur/AdvisoryCouncil/AdvisoryCouncil_node.html (both accessed April 6, 2020).

79. For the laying of new cables, citizens can make suggestions that the Network Agency should consider. For the final section of one cable, for example, public participation extended for a month in 2019. "Bundesnetzagentur startet Öffentlichkeitsbeteiligung für letzten Abschnitt des SuedOstLink" (Bundesnetzagentur Launches Public Participation for Last Section of SuedOstLink), June 19, 2019, https://www.bundesnetzagentur.de/SharedDocs/Pressemitteilungen/DE/2019/20190619_SOL.html (accessed April 6, 2020).
80. See Chapter 7.
81. The Federal Constitutional Court (*Bundeverfassungsgericht*) in 1 BvL 6/14, 1 BvL 6/15, 1 BvL 4/15, 1 BvL 3/15 (Nov. 22, 2016) held that restrictions in the Telecommunication Act, which give the FNA certain leeway, are not in accordance with the right to access to justice. The level of acceptable independence must be adjusted as market conditions change.
82. On the relationship between FNA and the ministries, see Ruthig and Storr (2015), pp. 105–09.
83. Schneider (2007), p. 311.
84. The 2017 Network Enforcement Law (*Gesetz zur Vorbesserung der Rechtsdurchsetzung in sozialen Netzwerken*), also called the Facebook Law, outlines social networks' responsibilities for monitoring unlawful content, responding to reports of unlawful content, and submitting periodic reports on these complaints. https://www.gesetze-im-internet.de/netzdg/ (accessed April 6, 2020).
85. The overall project is called Ultranet. BNA, "Bundesnetzagentur startet weitere Öffentlichkeitsbeteiligung zu Ultranet," https://www.bundesnetzagentur.de/SharedDocs/Pressemitteilungen/DE/2017/25102017_Ultranet.html (accessed April 6, 2020).
86. Bundesnetzagnetur, Öffentlichkeits beteiligung zum Rahmenpapier Bodenschutz, https://www.netzausbau.de/SharedDocs/Termine/DE/Konsultationen/181219_Bodenpapier.html (accessed April 6, 2020).
87. D'Alberti (1992), p. 91.
88. Thatcher (2003), p. 137.
89. D'Alberti (1992), p. 91.
90. The material on France draws on and updates portions of Rose-Ackerman and Perroud (2013).

91. D'Alberti (1992), p. 40.
92. D'Alberti (1992) (trans. 1995), p. 40.
93. Ibid., p. 26.
94. Ibid., pp. 40, 91–92.
95. Psygkas (2017).
96. Brown and Bell (1998), pp. 26–27; Ziller (2008), pp. 91–92; Thatcher (2003), pp. 128, 132.
97. The only exception is a 2008 constitutional amendment that created a new independent agency, the Défenseur des Droits, an ombudsman. French Constitution, art. 71–1.
98. The Conseil Constitutionnel has, however, tried to limit the regulatory power of agencies and to protect citizens and businesses when parliament grants sanctioning powers to these bodies. See Conseil supérieur de l'audiovisuel, 17 janvier 1989, n° 88–248 DC, Recueil p. 18; Commission des opérations de bourse, 28 juillet 1989, n° 89–260 DC, Recueil p. 71.
99. Postal & Electronic Communications Code, art. L-45 (Fr.).
100. Its French name is l'Association Française pour le Nommage Internet en Coopération (AFNIC). It appears analogous to an independent agency, but, perhaps because of its quasi-public status, it is not listed in http://www.vie-publique.fr. Its site is http://www.afnic.fr/. The Conseil Constitutionnel decision is Décision n° 2010–45 QPC du 6 octobre 2010 (Mr. Mathieu P.).
101. *Panama Refining Co. v. Ryan*, 293 U. S. 388 (1935); *A.L.A. Schechter Poultry Corp. v. United States*, 295 U.S. 495 (1935).
102. See, for example, *Whitman v. American Trucking Ass'ns., Inc.*, 531 U.S. 457 (2001).
103. The new law correcting the unconstitutional provision is Loi n° 2011–302, art. 19.
104. The Conseil d'État ruled in 1944 that the administration cannot restrict liberties through normative acts; only statutes passed by parliament can restrict liberties. See, e.g., Conseil d'État, 5 mai 1944, Rec. Lebon [133] [Dame veuve Trompier-Gravier].
105. French Constitution, arts. 13, 37, 38.
106. French Constitution, art. 24.4, and https://www.senat.fr/lng/en/index.html (accessed Nov. 17, 2020).
107. Sénat, *Un État dans l'État: Canaliser la Prolifération des Autorités Administratives Indépendantes pour Mieux les Contrôler* (A State within the State: Limiting the Proliferation of Independent Agencies), No. 126 (201502016),

28 octobre 2015, https://www.senat.fr/notice-rapport/2015/r15–126–1-notice.html (accessed April 6, 2020).

108. The Senate relied on a 2008 constitutional amendment that added a sentence to article 24 stating that the parliament "evaluates public policies" (*évalue les politiques publiques*).

109. Rose-Ackerman and Perroud (2013). For background consult Rapport Annuel 2018, Conseil Supérieur de l'Audiovisuel (hereinafter CSA Rapport Annuel) at https://www.csa.fr/Informer/Informations-publiques-et-ressources-humaines/Les-rapports-annuels-et-bilans-du-CSA/Le-rapport-annuel-2018-du-CSA (accessed April 6, 2020).

110. A second agency, the Autorité de Régulation des Communications Électroniques et des Postes (ARCEP), regulates telecommunications' physical infrastructure and economic conditions. For an in-depth treatment of ARCEP, see Psygkas (2017).

111. This is a common method of appointment in France. For example, this is how the Conseil Constitutionnel is appointed. A National Assembly report recommends, instead, that chairs be appointed by a vote of three-fifths of the members of the relevant committees in the two houses. The government opposed this proposal, stating that the committee might in the future seek the commission's advice on some legislative matter. The proposal was also opposed by an Assembly committee on the law. The agencies have "gone to the mat" (*montées au créneau*) to defend their independent existence. René Dosière, Reporter, MP, Statement to the Comité d'Évaluation et de Contrôle des Politiques Publiques (Dec. 1, 2011).

112. Loi n° 86–1067 du 30 septembre 1986 relative à la liberté de communication (hereinafter CSA Act), art. 5. In contrast, service on some advisory boards and commissions is a part-time responsibility.

113. The Conseil Constitutionnel, in *Conseil Supérieur de l'Audiovisuel*, n° 88–248 DC of 17 janvier 1989, upheld the creation of the CSA but restricted the permissible level of delegation. The delegation must cover only measures of limited scope in terms of both application and content.

114. CSA Act, art. 31.

115. CSA Act, arts. 29, 30–1, 30–5, 30–6.

116. These consultations are not legally required and create no legally enforceable rights. The agency sets time limits for comments, and it either poses particular questions or puts a draft decision on the web and awaits comments. The CSA writes a synthesis of the comments and is free to decide whether or not to take them into account before issuing its decision.

E-mail from Elisabeth Mauboussin, legal director, Conseil Supérieur de l'Audiovisuel, to Rose-Ackerman and Perroud (June 15, 2012).

117. In 2018 twenty-three cases were referred to the Conseil d'État, and it overturned the CSA in two cases involving individual licensing decisions. It declined to refer two questions to the Conseil Constitutionnel in a case that seems to implicate the way the CSA enforces the obligation of stations to further the "broadcast of songs in French" (*diffusion de chansons d'expression française*). CSA Rapport Annuel 2018.

118. The CSA has frequently given advice to the government on draft decrees, but this practice has only been formally required by statute since Loi n° 2009–258 du 5 mars 2009 on Audiovisual Communication and New Public Television.

119. Limited decree authority is a general feature of French independent agencies (Custos [2010a], pp. 281–82).

120. For a defense of this relationship between agencies and governments in France and Germany, see Marcou and Masing (2011). This shared competence is a common feature of European regulatory agencies.

121. Some international private bodies, such as the International Electrotechnical Commission (IEC) and the International Organization for Standardization (ISO), set standards across national boundaries. The UK, Germany, and France have bodies responsible for issuing industrial standards. They are recognized as official representatives of national interests in international standardization bodies. The US does not have a national standardization body, but instead relies on private organizations in specific industries, such as Underwriters Laboratories for certain electrical equipment (https://www.ul.com/) or the American Welding Society (https://www.aws.org/)(both accessed April 6, 2020).

122. Examples include the American Bar Association; the Legal Services Board and the Solicitors Regulation Authority in the UK; the Conseil National des Barreaux in France; and the Bundesrechtsanwaltskammer in Germany. In the UK, Germany, and France, these professional bodies are granted specific regulatory functions by law.

123. DVD standards, for instance, are developed by DVD Forum and DVD+RW Alliance, two associations of manufacturers.

124. In the US, the National Institute of Standards and Technology, an entity within the Department of Commerce, manages a Standards Incorporated by Reference (SIBR) Database, identifying privately developed standards incorporated by reference into federal regulations. https://www.nist.gov

/standardsgov/what-we-do/federal-policy-standards/sibr (accessed April 6, 2020).

125. For example, in the UK, the Legal Services Act of 2007 grants the Legal Services Board regulatory functions. German law does not explicitly recognize the Bundesrechtsanwaltskammer as a regulatory authority, but it operates as a public corporation with de facto federal regulatory powers over the legal profession. No law specifically gives the American Bar Association (ABA) regulatory powers, but legislatures of all but one US state have adopted the ABA's Model Rules of Professional Conduct as state law. De Bellis (2011).

126. Some assessments of self-regulation recommend the voluntary adoption of such practices. For example, a report on the food industry urges the adoption of 'best practices' including transparency, involvement of non-industry experts and NGOs, and "procedures for outside parties to register objections to self-regulatory standards and their enforcement." Sharma, Teret, and Brownell (2010).

127. The ABA, for example, takes decisions by a majority of its House of Delegates, elected by its general membership, but does not require consultation with the broader public.

128. A related issue concerns the role of the courts. Should quasi-public bodies be treated as public-law entities, hence permitting judicial review? In the UK, the Court of Appeal in the *Datafin* case held that the Panel on Takeovers and Mergers, an "unincorporated association without legal personality," was subject to judicial review, although the judges sided with the panel's decision and articulated very limited grounds for overturning panel decisions. *R. v. Panel on Takeovers and Mergers, ex parte Datafin Plc* [1987] Q.B. 815; [1987] 2 W.L.R. 699 CA; Cr, 27–029, 27–030, pp. 843–45.

129. Cafaggi (2012: 702) in an article that is supportive of transnational, private regulatory bodies, discusses the importance of consultation with stakeholders. A standard "can be considered a public good when its production has given access to the relevant constituencies . . ." As an example, he mentions that the production of ISO 26000, dealing with socially responsible business practices, "was preceded by MoUs [Memoranda of Understanding] that regulated the involvement of international organizations (. . . as well as other public and private organizations) in the drafting process" (ibid., p. 714).

130. Akerlof (1970).

131. For an overview of the tradeoffs, see Daniel Castro, "Benefits and Limitations of Industry Self-Regulation for Online Behavioral Advertising," *The*

Information Technology & Innovation Foundation, December 2011, https://itif.org/files/2011-self-regulation-online-behavioral-advertising.pdf (accessed Oct. 26, 2020).

132. Salop and Scheffman (1983).
133. Lena Riemer provided background research on the German case.
134. Dohler (2003), p. 106.
135. https://www.din.de/en/about-standards/a-brief-introduction-to-standards; https://www.din.de/en/about-standards/standards-and-the-law/legal-significance-of-standards (both accessed April 6, 2020); Rose-Ackerman (1995), pp. 63–65.
136. https://www.din.de/en/about-standards/standards-and-the-law/legal-significance-of-standards (accessed April 6, 2020).
137. https://www.din.de/en/about-standards/benefits-for-the-public-sector/an-instrument-of-deregulation-62670 (accessed April 6, 2020).
138. https://www.din.de/en/din-and-our-partners/din-in-europe (accessed April 6, 2020). At any given time, a particular industry may be subject to national standards issued by the German Standards Institute, European standards issued by the EU, and international standards developed by International Standards Organization. On the legal incorporation of German standards into French product-safety law, see Brüggemeier et al. (2011).
139. Its website is https://www.vde.com.
140. Kilimnik (1988).
141. See http://drafts.bsigroup.com/) (accessed April 6, 2020).
142. Brissy (2016): "Self-regulation by professional bodies leads to the establishment of a professional legal order, but a legal order that is integrated within the state legal order . . . The regulation of professional life falls within [state] action. This restricts the scope of professional, self-regulation bodies in the standards they can adopt and implement. This restriction of the normative power of professional associations is a sign of a conception of state action that is not exclusively limited to governing functions such as security and justice. As the state became the organizer of public services and a welfare state, it had to organize professional life" (L'autorégulation par les professions conduit certes à mettre en place un ordre juridique professionnel mais un ordre juridique intégré à l'ordre étatique . . . L'organisation de la vie professionnelle entre dans [le] champ d'action [de l'État] et conduit à limiter l'autorégulation par les professions à la fois dans leur capacité à créer des normes et dans celle de les faire appliquer. Cette restriction du pouvoir normatif des organisations professionnelles est le signe d'une

conception du rôle de l'État qui ne se limite pas à des fonctions régaliennes telles que la sécurité et la justice. L'État étant organisateur des services publics et devenant un État providence se devait d'intervenir dans l'organisation de la vie professionnelle). Translation by Marie Cirotteau.

143. CENELEC, "About CENELEC: Who We Are," https:// www.cenelec.eu /aboutcenelec/whoweare/europeanpartners/europeancommissionsandefta .html (accessed Nov. 17, 2020).

144. CEN/CENELEC, "Making Standards for Europe," https://www.cencenelec .eu/aboutus/governance/Pages/default.aspx (accessed Nov. 17, 2020).

145. *Dep't of Transp. v. Ass'n of Am. R.R.*, 575 U.S. 43, 135 S. Ct. 1225 (2015) (holding that Amtrak is a governmental entity, rather than an autonomous private entity).

146. Passenger Rail Investment and Improvement Act of 2008, P.L. No. 110.432, Div. B, October 16, 2008, Amtrak/High Speed Rail.

147. *Ass'n of Am. R.R. v. U.S. Dept. of Transp.*, 821 F. 3d 19 (D.C. Cir. 2016) (en banc denied 9/9/16).

148. Strauss (2013–2014). For a lawsuit lost by a private building-code body, see *Veeck v. Southern Building Code Congress International*, 293 F 3d 791 (5th Cir. 2002).

149. O'Donnell (1998).

150. The Supreme Court held that the GAO was essentially accountable to Congress. See *Bowsher v. Synar*, 478 U.S. 714 (1986).

151. The office, established by statute in 1921, was originally called the General Accounting Office, 31 U.S.C. § 702(a) (2006). The 2004 name change reflects its dual role as accountant and policy analyst. For background see Cross and Gluck (2020); O'Connell (2014).

152. O'Connell (2007) reports that congressional requests as a share of the GAO's work went from close to zero in 1978 to over 80 percent by 1998.

153. https://www.nao.org.uk/about-us/ (accessed April 6, 2020).

154. Sossin (2017); Meinel (2018).

155. https://www.nao.org.uk/about-us/our-work/value-for-money-programme/ (accessed April 6, 2020).

156. Basic Law, art. 114(2). The constitutional provision is implemented through a statute that makes the Bundesrechnungshof "subject only to law." The material in the text is available at its website: https://www.bundesrechnungshof .de/de (accessed April 6, 2020).

157. See, for example, media reports from 2018–2019: *Spiegel*: https://www .spiegel.de/thema/bundesrechnungshof/ (Spiegel ONLINE has a special

section on reports of the Bundesrechnungshof, presenting it as a guardian of the taxpayers' money and a monitor of the government); *Tagesspiegel*: https://www.tagesspiegel.de/politik/bundesrechnungshof-gorch-fock-war-nicht-uneingeschraenkt-seetuechtig/24055558.html. Here, the BRH publicly contradicts statements made by the Ministry of Defense with regard to the safety of the personnel on a training sailing ship of the German Navy (both websites accessed April 7, 2020).

158. Consult the website of the Cour des Comptes: https://www.ccomptes.fr/en (accessed April 6, 2020).

159. See https://www.fec.gov/about/leadership-and-structure/ (accessed April 6, 2020); Potter (2017).

160. https://www.electoralcommission.org.uk/ (accessed April 6, 2020).

161. https://www.electoralcommission.org.uk/our-work/roles-and-responsibilities (accessed April 6, 2020).

162. Political Parties, Elections and Referendums Act 2000, 2000 c. 41, Part I; Electoral Administration Act 2006, 2006 c. 22, Part 1.4; Political Parties and Elections Act 2009, 2009 c. 12, Part 1; Local Electoral Administration (Scotland) Act 2006, 2001 asp. 10, Part 2.

163. Clark (2015); Toby (2013). On campaign finance in the UK, see Torres-Spelliscy and Fogel (2011). For a comparative perspective, see Skahan (2018).

164. https://www.bundeswahlleiter.de/en/ueber-uns/aufgaben.html (accessed April 6, 2020).

165. Basic Law, art. 93(4c) permits associations that have not been recognized as parties by the federal election committee to challenge those decisions before the Constitutional Court; art. 41(2), (3) also permits Constitutional Court challenges to Bundestag scrutiny of elections; https://www.bundeswahlleiter.de/en/service/glossar/b/beschwerde-bundesverfassungsgericht.html; https://www.bundeswahlleiter.de/en/service/glossar/b/bundeswahlausschuss.html (both accessed April 6, 2020).

166. https://www.bundeswahlleiter.de/en/service/glossar/w/wahlorgane.html (accessed April 6, 2020).

167. The German system of campaign finance in 2015 is briefly summarized in Rose-Ackerman and Palifka (2016), pp. 369–71.

168. French Electoral Code, as amended 2018, art. L85–1.

169. The CNCCFP's annual report for 2018 is at http://www.cnccfp.fr/docs/commission/cnccfp_rapport_activite_2018.pdf (accessed April 6, 2020).

170. French Constitution, arts. 58, 59, 60.

171. Décision n° 2019–28 ELEC du 21 février 2019, https://www.conseil-constitutionnel.fr/sites/default/files/as/root/bank_mm/decisions/201928elec/201928elec.pdf (accessed April 6, 2020).
172. The role of ombudsmen in federal agencies is discussed in Houk et al. (2016).
173. The Défenseur des Droits is a constitutionally mandated office. French Constitution, art. 71–1. Chevallier (2011a, 2013).
174. 1958 French Constitution, art. 71–1.
175. If a petition is signed by 50,000 citizens or more, it must be considered by the Petition Committee in an open hearing. Pünder (2015), p. 733.
176. The Parliamentary and Health Service Ombudsman combines the role of Parliamentary Commissioner for Administration and that of Health Service Commissioner for England. The devolved regional governments have their own ombudsmen.
177. Private citizens may complete complaint forms and ask an MP to sign them and to refer them to the ombudsman. https://www.ombudsman.org.uk/making-complaint/before-you-come-to-us (accessed April 6, 2020).
178. For example, see Katherine McIntire Peters, "Trump Fires Intel IG, Taps White House Confidant for Pandemic Oversight Role," *Government Executive*, April 4, 2020, https://www.govexec.com/oversight/2020/04/trump-fires-intel-ig-taps-white-house-confidant-pandemic-oversight-role/164370/ (accessed Nov. 17, 2020).
179. The Polish ombudsman was in such a situation when I interviewed him in 2001. He worried about his inability to investigate social problems that did not produce many individual complaints because those affected were old, sick, or poor. Rose-Ackerman (2005), pp. 76–80.
180. Scott (2005), pp. 79–80.

Chapter 5. Policymaking Norms

1. This chapter draws on some material in Rose-Ackerman (2016).
2. For the European Commission see *Impact Assessments*, https://ec.europa.eu/info/law/law-making-process/planning-and-proposing-law/impact-assessments_en. For the OECD see *What Is Impact Assessment?* (2014), https://www.oecd.org/sti/inno/What-is-impact-assessment-OECDImpact.pdf (both accessed April 6, 2020).
3. OECD, *Better Regulation Practices across the European Union*, March 19, 2019, https://www.oecd.org/gov/regulatory-policy/better-regulation-practices-

across-the-european-union-9789264311732-en.htm (accessed April 6, 2020). The report contains summaries of the situation in EU member states. On policy analysis in general, see OECD (2020). The OECD document reports on a survey of OECD member states plus a few others. It is mostly a report of positive developments, but it acknowledges the weak implementation by many governments.

4. National Environmental Policy Act, P.L. 91–190 (1970).
5. See *Calvert Cliffs' Coordinating Committee v. Atomic Energy Commission*, 449 F.2d 1109 (D.C. Cir. 1971), cert. denied, 404 U.S. 942 (1972).
6. Lazarus (2012), p. 1507.
7. On the Trump administration's NEPA rulemaking see: Ellen M. Gilmer, "Trump's Environmental Permitting Update Could Spark Legal Frenzy," *Bloomberg Law*, July 15, 2020, https://news.bloomberglaw.com/environment-and-energy/trumps-environmental-permitting-update-to-spark-legal-frenzy (accessed Nov. 14, 2020). The Biden administration will seek to rescind the 2020 NEPA rule, but that will take time because the EPA must go through the notice-and-comment process. Ellen M. Gilmer, "Biden Officials Rethinking Trump Environmental Review Rule (1)," *Bloomberg Law*, March 17, 2021, https://news.blomberglaw.com/environmental-and energy/biden-officials-rethinking-trump-environmental-review-rule (accessed April 25, 2021).
8. The directives are 2014/52/EU (for Environmental Impact Assessment, revising an earlier directive) and 2001/42/EC (for SEA), https://ec.europa.eu/environment/eia/index_en.htm (accessed April 6, 2020). The Aarhus Convention is discussed in Chapter 3.
9. Consult the European Commission website referenced in note 2 above.
10. Arrow et al. (1996); Adler and Posner (2006). See a basic text, such as Boardman, Greenberg, Vining, and Weimer (2018).
11. Many other voting rules aggregate individual preferences into a public choice and incorporate more than two options, e.g., runoffs and rank-order voting. Mueller (2003), pp. 128–81.
12. Willingness-to-accept is less tied to individual budget constraints. Hicks (1943).
13. Bentham (1789, 1988); Ryan (1987). Von Neumann and Morgenstern (1953) produced a cardinal utility scale for individuals based on revealed preferences over lotteries, but it does not permit interpersonal comparisons. See Binmore (2009), pp. 58–59.
14. Samuelson (1947).

15. Kaldor (1939); Hicks (1940).
16. Little (1958).
17. *Michigan v. EPA*, 576 U.S. 743; 135 S. Ct. 2699 (2015).
18. Heal (2007).
19. For different perspectives see Heal (2007); Kaplow (2007); Kysar (2007).
20. Nordhaus (2013), p. 192.
21. Ibid., p. 193.
22. Page (1997), p. 584.
23. The government can diversify over risks; individuals cannot adequately diversify (Arrow and Lind, 1970).
24. See the debate in the US over the regulation of arsenic in drinking water. Wilson (2001); Burnett and Hahn (2001); F. Ackerman and Heinzerling (2004); Heinzerling (2002); Sunstein (2002a).
25. Kunreuther and Slovic (1996).
26. Batie and Shugart (1989), p. 125.
27. Herz-Roiphe (2014).
28. J. Wiener (2006), pp. 483–89.
29. Arrow et al. (1996).
30. Rose-Ackerman (1992), pp. 33–42.
31. Vining and Weimer (1992).
32. Mathews (2017). Schwarze (2006), pp. 685–92, provides a concise introduction. For a discussion in the context of UK and EU law, see Craig (2016), chap. 21, pp. 633–68.
33. Coen-Eliya and Porat (2010), p. 284.
34. J. B. Wiener, Rogers, Hammitt, and Sand (2011). For a skeptical view see Sunstein (2011).
35. Craig (2012), chap. 21.
36. J. B. Wiener et al. (2011).
37. Sunstein (2002c).
38. For example, Phelps (1961).
39. Samidas and Weisbach (2007).
40. Gollier (2013).
41. Newell and Pizer (2003).
42. Gollier (2013), p. 32.
43. Cai, Judd, Lenton, Lontzek, and Narita (2015); Gollier (2013), pp. 149–67.
44. Cai et al. (2015).
45. Arrow and Fisher (1974). See also Traeger (2014).
46. Cai et al. (2015); Nordhaus (2013), p. 2013.

47. Gollier (2013), p. 223.
48. Page (1997).
49. For example, Little (1958).
50. Haveman and Margolis (1970). The formal title of the Evidence Act is: The Foundations for Evidence-Based Policymaking Act of 2018, Pub. L. No. 115-4351. Its text highlights both the need for solid evidence and competent evaluation in policymaking. It applies to most Cabinet agencies and a few other bodies. The Office of Management and Budget issued two memoranda, M-19-23 and M-20-12; the second deals with evaluation. However, the act and the memoranda are hortatory, lacking in specifics, and do not provide additional funding for evaluation. The OECD (2020) highlights the act at Box 2.3 p. 42, but, so far, it appears to have had little concrete impact. There has not been any litigation under the act, probably because it does not appear to provide for any direct causes of action.
51. The White House, *Memorandum for the Heads of Executive Departments and Agencies: Modernizing Regulatory Review*, January 20, 2021, https://www.whitehouse.gov/briefing-room/presidential-actions/2021/01/20/modernizing-regulatory-review/ (accessed February 4, 2021). For background on OIRA see: Pildes and Sunstein (1995); Croley (2003).
52. Congressional Budget Office, *How CBO Prepares Cost Estimates*, February 2018, https://www.cbo.gov/system/files/115th-congress-2017–2018/reports/53519-costestimates.pdf (accessed Nov. 6, 2020).
53. The text simplifies a somewhat more complex reality discussed in Rose-Ackerman, Egidy, and Fowkes (2015), pp. 37–55.
54. OECD *Sustainability in Impact Assessments*. doc SG/SD(2011)6/FINAL (2011). https://www.oecd.org/gov/regulatory-policy/Sustainability%20in%20impact%20assessment%20SG-SD(2011)6-final.pdf (accessed Nov. 17, 2020).
55. Department for Business Innovation and Skill, S (2011). *Impact Assessment Toolkit. A Guide to Undertaking an IA and Completing the IA Template*. https://s25924.pcdn.co/wp-content/uploads/2017/11/UK_Govt-Impact-Assessment-Toolkit_2011.pdf (accessed Nov. 17, 2020). Atkinson et al. (2018).
56. The National Audit Office evaluates IAs according to a number of quality criteria. See https://www.nao.org.uk/search/Impact+Assessment/ (accessed Oct. 16, 2020). Echoing findings elsewhere, e.g., Hahn and Dudley (2007) for the US, these documents indicate that it cannot be taken for granted that use of CBA is always synonymous with "good quality."
57. The picture is complicated by the fact that some private-law corporations are majority-owned by the state. Électricité de France is owned almost 85 percent

by the French state. *The EDF Share: Capital Structure*, https://www.edf.fr/en/the-edf-group/dedicated-sections/investors-shareholders/the-edf-share/capital-structure (accessed April 6, 2020).

58. The paper from 1956 was published in an American journal as Boiteux (1971).
59. For arguments that cost-benefit analysis ought to be routinely used for policymaking, see Revesz and Livermore (2008); Sunstein (2002b). For contrary views see Ackerman and Heinzerling (2004); Shapiro and Glickman (2003). See also OECD, *Improving Governance* (cited in note 2 above).
60. OECD, Regulatory Policy Outlook, 2015, https://www.oecd.org/governance/oecd-regulatory-policy-outlook-2015–9789264238770-en.htm (including figures documenting the material in the text).
61. Information on the RSB is at: https://ec.europa.eu/info/law/law-making-process/regulatory-scrutiny-board_en (accessed Nov. 15, 2020). To avoid confusion, note that EU statutes take the form of "regulations" or "directives." What I have been calling executive rules or secondary legislation are called "tertiary legislation" in the lexicon of the EU.
62. Wiener and Alemanno (2017) compare OIRA in the US with the EU's RSB.
63. Vogel (2010).
64. Hahn and Renda (2017).
65. *Regulatory Policy Outlook, Germany* (2015), https://www.oecd.org/gov/regulatory-policy/Germany-web.pdf (accessed Nov. 6, 2020). The *Nationaler Normenkontrollrat*, NNKR, was established in 2016 by federal law. Its website is https://www.normenkontrollrat.bund.de/nkr-en (accessed Nov. 6, 2020). See Karpen (2015).
66. Karpen (2015).
67. Ibid.
68. Ibid.
69. Wiener (2013).
70. As a 2011 OECD report observed: "The team did not pick up any clear evidence of [IAs'] influence . . . The approach is comprehensive on paper, but practice appears to fall some way short of the conceptual objective . . . Assessments tend to come at a relatively late stage of the law making process." OECD, *Better Regulation in Europe: Germany* (2010), https://www.oecd.org/gov/regulatory-policy/45079989.pdf. A more recent report found substantial improvement: OECD: https://www.oecd.org/gov/regulatory-policy/Germany-web.pdf (both accessed Nov. 6, 2020).
71. OECD, *Better Regulation in Europe: France* (2010). https://www.oecd.org/gov/regulatory-policy/45706677.pdf (accessed Nov. 6, 2020).

72. Ibid. (citing French and EU reports).
73. The Constitutional Act of July 23, 2008 amended article 39 of the Constitution to require a Framework Act that set the conditions under which draft legislation is submitted to the legislature. The act does not cover parliament-initiated draft legislation, and certain categories of legislation are exempt, including draft constitutional legislation, finance scheduling legislation, and draft bills extending states of emergency. The obligation does not apply to draft decrees. See also OECD, *Regulatory Policy Outlook 2015*. The relevant constitutional text is: "Le présentation des projets de loi déposés devant l'Assemblée nationale ou le Sénat répond aux conditions fixées par une loi organique" (When the government puts a proposed law before the National Assembly or the Senate it must comply with the conditions determined by a framework law [implementing the amendment]).
74. OECD, *Better Regulation in Europe: France* (2010). https://www.oecd.org/gov/regulatory-policy/45706677.pdf (accessed Nov. 6, 2020).
75. Ibid.
76. Ibid.
77. Ibid.
78. For example, German efforts to enact an Environmental Law Code (*Umweltgesetzbuch*), prepared with "considerable scientific input," failed at the political level. In reflecting on the code's failure, Ruffert (2007), p. 52, concludes, "politics may be quite immune to generally accepted proposals of administrative reform, e.g., in evaluating the importance of procedural rules." He worries that lawmakers too often fail to recognize the importance of procedures.
79. Hahn and Dudley (2007); Weiner (2013). OECD, *Improving Governance* (2020).
80. Hahn and Litan (2005), p. 495, n. 74.
81. Brennan and Buchanan (1980). Reviewed by Rose-Ackerman (1982).
82. Hahn and Litan (2005).
83. On the mix of analysis and politics in the United States, see Radin (2013).

Chapter 6. Public Participation

1. Renn, Webler, and Wiedemann (1995b), p. 2.
2. Habermas (1981); Renn, Webler, and Wiedemann (1995b), p. 3.
3. Renn, Webler, and Wiedermann (1995b), p. 4.

4. Liebenberg (2017); Ray (2016).
5. For a discussion of public involvement in the legislative processes in two of my four cases, see Rose-Ackerman, Egidy, and Fowkes (2015).
6. On the courts see Chapter 7.
7. For example, a 2014 German consultation process on climate change policy combined a meeting of experts and stakeholders (*betroffene Zielgruppen*) with a survey based on anonymous comments posted on-line. Beteiligungsportal Baden-Württemberg, *Anpassungsstrategie an den Klimawandel: Öffentlichkeitsbeteiligung und Umfrage* (2014), https://beteiligungsportal.baden-wuerttemberg.de/de/mitmachen/lp-15/arbeitsauftrag-klimawandel-schutz-und-anpassung/oeffentlichkeitsbeteiligung-online-umfrage/ (accessed April 6, 2020; Lena Riemer provided this example).
8. Della Cananea (2016), p. 111, claims that "participation" is justified as promoting human dignity, but he acknowledges that it "performs a democratic role, in the sense of allowing citizens to express their views within decision-making processes." See also Mashaw (1985a).
9. Farhang (2010).
10. Surowiecki (2004).
11. Surowiecki (2004), p. 128.
12. The theorem was articulated by the Marquis de Condorcet in 1785. Mueller (2003), pp. 128–33.
13. Noveck (2015); Surowiecki (2004).
14. Noveck (2015).
15. Hammerschmid et al. (2016) reviews European public administration reforms contrasting Weberian reforms with New Public Management and mixed systems.
16. Coglianese (2003).
17. Rose-Ackerman (1994). In the US, regulatory negotiation is permitted under the Negotiated Rulemaking Act, 5 U.S.C. §§ 561–570, but it must be followed by the notice-and-comment process under the APA.
18. This ideal is espoused by Buchanan and Tullock (1962). However, they recognize that it is an impractical decision rule. Epstein (1985) argues that the US government should compensate the losers from policies that affect the value of property rights.
19. The German government favored "locally rooted" citizen energy cooperatives of at least ten citizens, so long as a majority lived in the region of the project. The goal was to turn potential opponents into financial "stakeholders." Boris Gotchev, "Federal States Introduce Schemes for Citizen

Participation in Wind Energy Projects—Part 1," *Blog-IASS-Potsdam*, April 28, 2016, https://www.iass-potsdam.de/en/blog/2016/28/federal-states-introduce-schemes-citizen-participation-wind-energy-projects-part-1 (accessed April 6, 2020). However, a change in the auction laws makes it more difficult for local groups to participate. Julien Wettengel, Citizens' Participation in the Energiewende," *Clean Energy Wire*, October 25, 2018, https://www.cleanenergywire.org/factsheets/citizens-participation-energiewende.

20. For example, consider the demand-revealing procedure described in Mueller (2003), pp. 160–68.
21. Rae (1975).
22. A few national-level efforts also promoted deliberation over constitutional reforms, but they involved small countries such as Denmark, Iceland, Ireland, and Finland, and the procedures often faced pushback from both professional politicians and voters (Reuchamps and Suiter [2016]).
23. Kaliarnta, Hage, and Sabine (2014), p. 242.
24. Rousseau (1762 [1997]) Book 2, Section 3:

> If the populace held its deliberations (on the basis of adequate information) without the citizens communicating with one another, what emerged from all the little particular wills would always be the general will, and the decision would always be good. But when plots and deals lead to the formation of partial associations at the expense of the big association, the will of each of these associations, the general will of its members, is still a particular will so far as the state is concerned; so that it can then be said that as many votes as there are men is replaced by as many votes as there are associations . . . If the general will is to emerge clearly it's important that there should be no partial society within the state, and that each citizen should think only his own thoughts . . . And if there are partial societies, it's best to have as many as possible and to prevent them from becoming unequal . . . These precautions are the only ones that can ensure that the general will is always enlightened and that the populace is never in error.

I am grateful to Blake Emerson for this reference.

25. Even Rousseau recognized that the state cannot prevent organizations from forming; rather, it should encourage large numbers of groups to organize and seek to mitigate inequalities of resources and power. See the last two sentences in the quote from Rousseau above.

26. Thus, I omit participatory budgeting exercises that have the legal authority to decide on the allocation of portions of a government budget. The most well-known example is Porto Alegre, Brazil. The process was supported by strong mayors facing opponents in their city councils and seeking an alternative route to connect to voters. These procedures highlight the tensions between representative democracy and direct citizen participation. See Stolzenberg and Wampler (2018). On Brazil see Avitzer and Wampler (2005); Wampler (2007).
27. A group of scholars actively promote "deliberative democracy." Mansbridge et al. (2012).
28. Karpowitz and Raphael (2014). For a particular version of this model, see the Deliberative Polls organized by James S. Fishkin (2009) and his collaborators. See also Luskin, Fishkin, and Jowell (2002). Mini-publics have a similar composition. Goodin and Dryzek (2006); Elstub (2014).
29. Goodin and Dryzek (2006); Elstub (2014); S. Niemeyer (2011); French and Laver (2009); Robert C. Luskin, Fishkin, and Jowell (2002).
30. Grönlund, Setälä, and Herne (2010).
31. Karpowitz and Raphael (2014).
32. Goodin and Dryzek (2006).
33. Compare Fishkin (2009) with Sunstein (2000a). See also Mansbridge (1983).
34. Fung (2007). Compare Chambers (2009).
35. Curato et al. (2017); S. J. Niemeyer (2014).
36. Pogrebinschi (2013).
37. Lafont (2015).
38. Dryzek (2010); Pourtois (2013).
39. Curato and Böker (2016).
40. The deliberations are Agenda 21 processes that follow a similar overall pattern: http://www.agenda21-treffpunkt.de/ (accessed April 6, 2020). The state of Thüringen has surveyed its lower-level governments to assess the effectiveness of participatory process in connection with the German shift to renewable power discussed in Chapter 3. Deutsches Institut für Urbanistik, *Difu-Umfrage: 'Öffentlichkeitsbeteiligung bei Infrastrukturvorhaben und im Netzausbau'* (2019), https://difu.de/node/12495 (accessed April 6, 2020).
41. Rask, Maciukaite-Zviniene, and Petrauskiene (2012).
42. Fung (2003).
43. Beetham (2012).
44. Geissel (2012).
45. Mansbridge (1983).
46. Geissel (2012), p. 178.

47. Dryzek and Tucker (2008), pp. 868–69.
48. Ibid., p. 870.
49. Ibid.
50. The Stanford Center for Deliberative Democracy collects the result of these polls, https://cdd.stanford.edu/results/ (accessed April 6, 2020). In the US, a deliberative poll on renewable energy in Texas showed that the informed participants supported more emphasis on renewable energy and programs to aid the poor; see https://cdd.stanford.edu/1998/deliberative-polling-texas-electric-utilities/ (accessed April 6, 2020).
51. The organization G1000, associated with the Belgian Foundation for Future Generations, developed a model for citizen participation that relies on mini-publics. See http://www.g1000.org/en/ and https://www.foundationfuturegenerations.org/en/contact.
52. Anna Stuers, "Permanent Citizens' Dialogue in East Belgium," European Committee of the Regions, *From Local to European; Putting Citizens at the Centre of the EU Agenda*, Brussels, 2019, pp. 17–20, https://www.cor.europa.eu/en/engage/brochures/Documents/From%20local%20to%20European/4082_Citizens%20Consult_brochure_N_FINAL.pdf. G1000; "German-speaking Community of Belgium Becomes World's First Region with Permanent Citizen Participation Drafted by Lot," https://www.foundationfuturegenerations.org/files/documents/news/20190226_dgpermanentcitizensassembly_pressrelease.pdf (both accessed April 6, 2020).
53. European Committee of the Regions, From Local to European; Putting Citizens at the Centre of the EU Agenda, Brussels, 2019, https://www.cor.europa.eu/en/engage/brochures/Documents/From%20local%20to%20European/4082_Citizens%20Consult_brochure_N_FINAL.pdf (accessed April 6, 2020). Many of these activities occurred before elections for the EU Parliament in 2019 and aimed to motivate citizens to participate by stressing the EU's impact on their lives.
54. For example, the German state of Baden-Württemberg has experimented with organized citizen deliberation. In that state the Green Party led a coalition with the Christian Democrats in 2019.
55. Richard Youngs, "Can Citizen Participation Really Revive European Democracy?," European Committee of the Regions, *From Local to European; Putting Citizens at the Centre of the EU Agenda*, Brussels, 2019, pp. 90–96, https://www.cor.europa.eu/en/engage/brochures/Documents/From%20local%20to%20European/4082_Citizens%20Consult_brochure_N_FINAL.pdf (accessed April 6, 2020).

56. The deliberative process took place under the auspices of the Economic, Social and Environmental Council, a third chamber with only an advisory role. French Constitution, arts. 69-71. https://www.lecese.fr/en (accessed April 6, 2020).
57. President Macron plans to propose an amendment to article 1 using the procedure in article 89. Identical amending language must be passed by a majority of each house, followed by a referendum. His draft echoed language in the report of the Citizens' Convention: "[La France] garantit la préservation de la biodiversité et de l'environnement et lutte contre le dérèglement climatique" ("France guarantees the preservation of biodiversity and the environment and fights against climate change."). As noted in Chapter 3, the Conseil d'État objected to the word "garantit," so the proposed language may change before presentation to the legislature.
58. Audrey Garric and Rémi Barroux, Les Citoyens de la Convention pour le Climat à Matignon pour Défendre Leur Propositions," *La Matinale du Monde*, October 1, 2020. Louise Guillot, "French Citizens Bring Their Climate Case to Brussels," *Politico*, July 22, 2020. Angelique Chrisafis, "Citizens' Panels Ready to Help Macron Set French Climate Policies," *The Guardian*, January 10, 2020, https://www.theguardian.com/world/2020/jan/10/citizens-panels-ready-help-macron-french-climate-policies. The French experiment is summarized at mid-point for a UK audience in Claire Mellier-Wilson, "Convention Citoyenne pour le Climat: What Can We Learn from French Citizens?" *Involve*, January 15, 2020, https://www.involve.org.uk/resources/blog/opinion/convention-citoyenne-pour-le-climat-what-can-we-learn-french-citizens (accessed April 6, 2020).

    In a similar vein, a UK deliberation, involving 110 citizens, was mandated by the House of Commons in 2019. The deliberation produced a set of policy proposals that could be enacted into statutory law or put in place through executive decrees. Fiona Harvey, "Thousands of Britons Invited to Climate Crisis Citizens' Assembly," *The Guardian*, November 2, 2019, https://www.theguardian.com/environment/2019/nov/02/thousands-britons-invited-take-part-climate-crisis-citizens-assembly.
59. Buge (2020); Owen and Smith (2015), p. 232.
60. Rose-Ackerman (1995), pp. 103–06; Rose-Ackerman (2005).
61. The Dutch Environmental Assessment Agency found that the agency's motives for stakeholder participation were to win support for their work and to gather information, not to engage in dialogue. Hage, Pieter Leroy, and Petersen (2019), p. 258.

62. Summarized in Rose-Ackerman (1995), p. 105.
63. Reed (2008).
64. The stakeholder processes assessed by Reed (ibid.) differ from situations where decision-makers seek input from stakeholders without deliberation. For example, in setting a policy to deal with coastal erosion risks to a particular area in France, one study relied on technical material and interviews with stakeholders, but involved no deliberation. Roca, Gamboa, and Tàbara (2008).
65. Rose-Ackerman and Perroud (2013); Lascoumes (2011); Whiteside et al. (2010).
66. On the organization of the Grenelle de l'environnement of 2007, see https://web.archive.org/web/20080528013550/http://www.legrenelle-environnement.fr/grenelle-environnement/ (accessed April 6, 2020).
67. Chevallier (2007).
68. Rose-Ackerman and Perroud (2013).
69. The plan is only a framework for policy and a statement of intent. Philip Oltermann, "German Coalition Agrees to Cut Carbon Emissions Up to 95% by 2050," *The Guardian*, November 11, 2016, https://www.theguardian.com/environment/2016/nov/11/german-coalition-agrees-to-cut-carbon-emissions-up-to-95-by-2050.
70. The process is described in Kerstine Appunn, "Climate Action Plan 2050: Negotiating a Path to Decarbonisation Page 2," *Clean Energy Wire*, May 6, 2016, https://www.cleanenergywire.org/factsheets/climate-action-plan-2050-negotiating-path-decarbonisation. The quotes in the text are from that document. Bundesministerium für Umwelt, Naturschutz, Bau und Reaktorsicherheit, *Climate Action Plan 2050*, June 9, 2015, https://www.bmu.de/fileadmin/Daten_BMU/Download_PDF/Klimaschutz/klimaschutzplan_2050_impulspapier_en_bf.pdf (both accessed April 7, 2020).
71. Responsibility for energy policy was shifted in 2013 from the Environmental Ministry to the Economics Ministry. In compensation the Environmental Ministry obtained jurisdiction over building regulation. Their formal titles are: Federal Ministry of Environment, Nature Protection, Building, and Nuclear Safety, and the Federal Ministry for Economics and Energy.
72. See Philip Oltermann, "German Coalition Agrees to Cut Carbon Emissions Up to 95% by 2050," *The Guardian*, November 11, 2016, https://www.theguardian.com/environment/2016/nov/11/german-coalition-agrees-to-cut-carbon-emissions-up-to-95-by-2050. Comments from various interests are at Sven Egenter, Susanne Götze, and Julian Wettengel, "Reactions to Germany's Climate Action Plan 2050," *Clean Energy Wire*, Nov. 12, 2016,

https://www.cleanenergywire.org/news/reactions-germanys-climate-action-plan-2050 (accessed Nov. 7, 2020).

73. *U.S. v. Nova Scotia Food Prods. Corp.*, 568 F. 2d 240 (2d Cir. 1977).
74. Furlong and Kerwin (2005); Wagner (2016).
75. Coglianese (1997), pp. 1283–84.
76. Barry Meier and Danielle Ivory, "Business under Trump: Worker Protections Are Viewed with New Skepticism," *The New York Times*, June 5, 2017, https://www.nytimes.com/2017/06/05/business/under-trump-worker-protections-are-viewed-with-new-skepticism.html?_r=0. Julia Hart and Peter Eisler, "The Dismantling of a U.S. Workplace Safety Rule, and the Political Battles behind It," *Reuters*, Jan. 22, 2019, https://www.reuters.com/investigates/special-report/usa-beryllium-rule/.
77. Mendelson (2003), p. 623.
78. See Wu (2003), p. 144 (discussing the "normative principle of network neutrality").
79. For example, "FCC Chair Ajit Pai Explains Why He Wants to Scrap Net Neutrality," PBS *Newshour*, https://www.pbs.org/newshour/show/fcc-chair-ajit-pai-explains-wants-scrap-net-neutrality (accessed Nov. 17, 2020).
80. April Glaser, "A Broken System Helped the FCC to Kill Net Neutrality," *Slate*, Oct. 3, 2019, https://slate.com/technology/2019/10/net-neutrality-fcc-comments-system-broken.html. Kevin Collier and Jeremy Singer-Vine, "Millions of Comments about the FCC's Net Neutrality Rules Were Fakes. Now the Feds Are Investigating," *BuzzFeed News*, Dec. 8, 2018, https://www.buzzfeednews.com/article/kevincollier/feds-investigation-net-neutrality-comments?mod=article_inline (accessed Nov. 7, 2020); James V. Grimaldi and Paul Overberg, "Millions of People Post Comments on Federal Regulations—Many Are Fake," *The Wall Street Journal*, Dec. 12, 2017, https://www.wsj.com/articles/millions-of-people-post-comments-on-federal-regulations-many-are-fake-1513099188.
81. "New York Times Granted Judgment in FOIA Suit Over 'Net Neutrality' Rule Comment Logs," *Law.com*, May 15, 2020, https://www.law.com/newyorklawjournal/almID/1589289680NY18Civ86/?slreturn=20200613123941 (accessed Nov. 20, 2020).
82. Kerwin and Furlong (1992).
83. Mendelson (2003). In the first half of 2020 the Trump administration rushed to rescind and replace rules, especially in environmental areas, to beat the deadline of the Congressional Review Act, discussed in Chapter 3. The Biden administration may use the CRA to void Trump's end-of-term rules.

84. Golden (1998).
85. West (2004).
86. S. W. Yackee (2015).
87. Yackee and Yackee (2009, 2012).
88. Schuck (1977).
89. Furlong and Kerwin (2005).
90. Golden (1998).
91. Kerwin (2003); Schlozman and Tierney (1986).
92. Yackee and Yackee (2006).
93. Psygkas (2017), pp. 108, 152–53, 247.
94. Ibid., p. 136.
95. Golden (1998); S. W. Yackee (2015).
96. Magat, Krupnick, and Harrington (1986).
97. Ibid., pp. 145–46.
98. Ibid., p. 147; Yackee and Yackee (2006).
99. Mendelson (2003), p. 628.
100. Beierle and Cayford (2002).
101. Ibid., p. 74.
102. Ibid., pp. 29, 60–61. See also Reed (2008), pp. 2417–31.
103. Golden (1998); Kerwin (2003).
104. Wagner, Barnes and Peters (2011) study 90 air toxics' rules. The EPA issued Advanced Notices of Proposed Rulemaking (ANPR) that invited public comments before the required APA notice-and-comment process began. Nelson and S. W. Yackee (2012) evaluated coalition lobbying during the ANPR stage for DOT rules. Krawiec (2013) studied early-stage input for rulemaking to implement section 619 of the 2010 Dodd-Frank Act (Pub. L. No. 111-203, 124 Stat. 1376 [2010]), which regulates financial institutions. The act requires agencies to docket all early-stage contacts, both meetings and written submissions. I am grateful to Roberta Romano for these references. On the general issue, see Strauss (1974); Wagner (2016).
105. Raso (2015); Nou (2013).
106. Haeme (1999).
107. The Frank R. Lautenberg Chemical Safety for the 21st Century Act, enacted on June 22, 2016. See https://www.epa.gov/assessing-and-managing-chemicals-under-tsca/frank-r-lautenberg-chemical-safety-21st-century-act (accessed April 6, 2020).
108. West (2004).

109. The APA anticipates that the comment period will influence the drafting of the final rule. However, the courts will require a second round if the revised rule is not a "logical outgrowth" of the original draft. That term has no precise definition, but the aim is to permit interested parties to have a say on major shifts in an agency's approach. Kannan (1996).
110. Dewey (1927).
111. Palermo (2015) argues that the complexity of modern policy problems makes democratic control more complex and difficult. He argues for new tools that are both participatory and deliberative, and that complement but do not replace elected assemblies.
112. Owen and Smith (2015).
113. For critiques see Strauss (2007); Metzger (2017).
114. For example, consider the 2017 disagreement between the Upper and the Lower Houses over the introduction of highway tolls for cars and the exception for areas close to national borders. Markus Balser, "Der Streit um die Pkw-Maut eskaliert," *Süddeutsche Zeitung*, March 21, 2017, https://www.sueddeutsche.de/politik/grenzregionen-der-streit-um-die-pkw-maut-eskaliert-1.3429922.
115. Rose-Ackerman (1995).
116. See Chapter 3.
117. Treaty of Lisbon, art. 8b.
118. Lindgren and Persson (2018).
119. Ibid., p. 238.
120. Geissel (2012).
121. Kies and Nanz (2013).
122. The Horizon 2020 project is described at https://ec.europa.eu/programmes/horizon2020/en (accessed April 6, 2020).
123. Psygkas (2017).
124. UN Economic Commission for Europe, Convention on Access to Information, Public Participation in Decision-making and Access to Justice in Environmental Matters (Aarhus Convention), 25 June 1998, http://www.unece.org/env/pp/treatytext.html (accessed April 6, 2020). The most recent versions of the EU directives are 2014/52/EU and 2001/42/EC, for EIAs and SEAs, respectively.
125. Rose-Ackerman (2005).

Chapter 7. The Varieties of Judicial Review

1. Landes and Posner (1975), McCubbins, Noll, and Weingast (1987, 1989).
2. *FCC v. Sanders Brothers Radio Station*, 309 U.S. 470 (1940).

3. US Constitution, art. III, sect. 2. The Supreme Court has read "cases and controversies" restrictively to require: (a) an injury in fact that is concrete and particularized and actual or imminent; (b) a causal connection between the injury and the conduct complained of; and (c) a finding that it is likely that the injury will be redressed by a favorable decision. *Lujan v. Defenders of Wildlife*, 504 U.S. 555 (1992). In addition, the party must be within the zone of interests Congress intended to protect under the given statute. *Data Processing Service Organizations v. Camp*, 397 U.S. 150 (1970). See Scalia (1981). In contrast, Caleb (2019) proposes that standing should extend to anyone arguably within the zone of interests of a statute.
4. *Summers v. Earth Island Institute*, 555 U.S. 488, 496 (2009).
5. *Massachusetts v. E.P.A.*, 549 U.S. 497, 526 (2007). On state standing see the symposium introduced by Grove (2018).
6. Collins (1974).
7. *Lujan v. Defenders of Wildlife*, 504 U.S. 555 (1992). Sunstein (1992); *Monsanto Co. v. Geerston Seed Farms*, 561 U.S. 139 (2010) (increased risk may also constitute an injury that creates standing); *Cetacean Community v. Bush*, 386 F. 3d 1169 (9th Cir. 2004) (no standing to bring suit on behalf of the world's whales, but Congress could grant animals standing through statute).
8. Our Children's Trust, https://www.ourchildrenstrust.org/juliana-v-us (accessed October 27, 2020). These cases rely on the public-trust doctrine and claimed violations of constitutional rights to life, liberty, and property. They do not concern the administrative process.
9. In the resulting Supreme Court case, *Department of Homeland Security v. Regents of the University of California*, 140 S. Ct. 1891 (2020), standing was not an issue, but reviewability was.
10. On limited judicial review of the US legislative process, see Rose-Ackerman, Egidy, and Fowkes (2015), pp. 37–55.
11. *United States v. Nova Scotia Food Prods. Corp.*, 568 F. 2d 240, 252 (2d Cir. 1977).
12. Stack (2012), p. 392, n. 197 (calculating that fewer than 13 percent of public laws in the 107th–111th Congresses included statements of purpose).
13. See *Pennhurst State School v. Halderman*, 451 U.S. 1 (1981). The statute includes a Bill of Rights for the Developmentally Disabled. Justice Rehnquist, writing for the majority, held that the section did not create substantive rights that required the appropriation of funds. Hence, Congress can include vague and hortatory language in statutes, and it can then fail to

provide adequate funds to carry out their stated goals (Rose-Ackerman [1992], pp. 70–79).

14. *Industrial Union Department, AFL-CIO v. American Petroleum Institute* (the *Benzene* case), 448 U.S. 607 (1980), Justice Rehnquist, concurring at 672. The earlier cases are *Panama Refining Co. v. Ryan*, 293 U. S. 388 (1935); *A.L.A. Schechter Poultry Corp. v. United States*, 295 U.S. 495 (1935).
15. *Whitman v. American Trucking Ass'ns. Inc.*, 531 U.S. 457 (2001). However, given the courts' acceptance of delegation, they do review agencies' interpretation of statutory terms. See Sunstein (2000b).
16. But see Justice Ginsburg's dissent in *Gonzales v. Carhart*, 127 S. Ct. 1610 (2007) (Carhart II).
17. In the Tenth Circuit, and in at least one recent case before the Supreme Court, Justice Gorsuch has voiced a belief that the "intelligible principle" standard should be revisited, and the non-delegation doctrine reframed in terms of separation of powers. *Gundy v. U.S.*, 139 S. Ct. 2116, 2133–2143 (2019) (Gorsuch, J., dissenting); *U.S. v. Nichols*, 784 F. 3d 666, 671–674 (10th Cir. 2008) (Gorsuch, J., dissenting); *U.S. v. Hinckley*, 550 F. 3d 926 (10th Cir. 2008).
18. 5 U.S.C. § 533. Merrill (2011).
19. 5 U.S.C. § 706(2)(D) instructs the courts to "hold unlawful and set aside agency action, findings, and conclusions found to be without observance of the procedure required by law."
20. *Vermont Yankee Nuclear Power Corp. v. Natural Resources Defense Council*, 435 U.S. 519 (1978).
21. *Nat. Res. Def. Council, Inc. v. U.S. Nuclear Regulatory Comm'n*, 547 F. 2d 633 (D.C. Cir. 1976).
22. Ibid. at 658 (Judge Tamm, concurring).
23. Ibid. at 657 (Chief Judge Bazelon, separate statement).
24. Stack (2007), pp. 993–98, argues that agencies are constitutionally required to give reasons.
25. For example: *Zero Zone, Inc. v. U.S. Dept. of Energy*, 832 F. 3d 654 (7th Cir. 2016); *Ozark Auto. Distributors, Inc. v. NLRB*, 779 F. 3d 576, 582 (D.C. Cir. 2015).
26. *Little Sisters of the Poor Saints Peter and Paul Home v. Pennsylvania*, 140 S. Ct. 2367, 2385 (2020).
27. For an example of the latter see: "The orderly functioning of the process of review requires that the grounds upon which the administrative agency acted be clearly disclosed and adequately sustained," *SEC v. Chenery Corp.*, 318

U.S. 80, 94 (1943); see also *Department of Commerce v. New York*, 588 U.S.—, 139 S. Ct. 2551 (2019).

28. 82 F. 3d 165, 171 (7th Cir. 1996).
29. 541 F. 2d 1 (D.C. Cir. 1976) (en banc), *cert. denied*, 426 U.S. 941 (1976).
30. Discussion of hard-look review has focused on reasoned explanation and the public's access to information (Wagner [2010]); Stephenson (2006) proposes that hard-look review can help reviewing courts overcome their comparative informational disadvantage or verify the substantive content of justifications provided by government.
31. *Natural Resources Defense Council v. National Highway Traffic Safety Administration*, 894 F. 3d 95, 115 (2d Cir. 2018).
32. US Constitution, art. I, § 2, cl. 3, amend. art. 14 § 2.
33. *U.S. Dept. of Commerce v. New York*, 139 S. Ct. 2551, 2575–2576 (2019). The case dealt with a memo from the Secretary of Commerce adding a citizenship question to the 2020 US census. The memo was not a rule and did not go through notice and comment, but the majority, nevertheless, held that the secretary's stated reason was reviewable and was a mere pretext that was "incongruent" with the record and was not a "reasoned" outcome.
34. *Department of Homeland Security v. Regents of the University of California*, 140 S. Ct. 1891 (2020).
35. S. A. Shapiro and Murphy (2016) propose that agencies should be allowed to offer post hoc rationalizations for their actions.
36. *Department of Homelan Security v. Regents of the University of California*, 140 S. Ct. 1891,1901 (2020).
37. The Federal Tort Claims Act (FTCA; 28 U.S.C. §§ 1346(b), 2671–80) allows plaintiffs to seek damages for injuries caused by the US government or its employees by waiving the federal government's sovereign immunity for certain tort law claims. However, the United States retains sovereign immunity against various injuries, including those caused by employees acting in the exercise of regulatory discretion. Damages are also limited. Lewis (2019).
38. See *Bivens v. Six Unknown Named Agents of Fed. Bureau of Narcotics*, 403 U.S. 388 (1971) (recognizing a private right of action against federal law enforcement officials for violations of Fourth Amendment protections against unlawful search or seizure). Since *Bivens*, courts have allowed suits based on violations of citizens' constitutional rights. Liability attaches to individual agents of the US government, and punitive damages may be awarded. Judges, prosecutors, legislators, and the president, when acting within the

scope of their duties, enjoy absolute immunity from *Bivens'* claims. *Nixon v. Fitzgerald*, 457 U.S. 731 (1982); *Butz v. Economou*, 438 U.S. 478 (1978). Qualified immunity further applies to officials for the reasonable exercise of discretionary authority. *Harlow v. Fitzgerald*, 457 U.S. 800 (1982). In recent years the Supreme Court has narrowed the scope of liability. See, e.g., *Jesus C. Hernandez v. Jesus Mesa, Jr.*, 140 S. Ct. 735 (2020).

39. For example, litigation over the Department of Labor's decision to reclassify certain workers at automobile dealerships to make them "employees" under the Fair Labor Standards Act went twice to the Supreme Court. First, the Court found that the regulation was arbitrary and capricious because the agency failed to consider all the relevant factors. *Encino Motorcars, LLC v. Navarro*, 136 S. Ct. 2117 (2016). Subsequently, the Court reviewed the merits, finding the agency was wrong to reclassify the workers in question. *Encino Motorcars, LLC v. Navarro*, 138 S. Ct. 1134 (2018).
40. *S.E.C. v. Chenery Corp. (Chenery I)*, 318 U.S. 80, 92–94 (1943). Sometimes statutes include "hammer" provisions that go into effect if the agency has not acted or if a rule is voided by the courts (Hickey [2018]). For example, the Nutrition Labeling and Education Act includes a provision requiring the Food and Drug Administration to issue regulations requiring nutritional labeling within twelve months of the statute's enactment or else proposed regulations would become final regulations (Magill [1995]).
41. *Smith v. Berryhill*, 587 U.S.—, 139 S. Ct. 1765 (2019). See also *Harrison v. PPG Industries, Inc.*, 446 U.S. 578 (1980) (Remand is the appropriate remedy when a reviewing court "finds itself unable to exercise informed judicial review because of an inadequate administrative record").
42. De novo review occurs when the issues are purely "legal" and hence suitable for the court to decide. *U.S. v. Reynolds*, 710 F. 3d 498 (3rd Cir. 2013).
43. See Chapter 3.
44. Environmental statutes authorizing fee-shifting include the Clean Air Act, 42 U.S.C. § 7607(f); Toxic Substances Control Act, 15 U.S.C. § 2618–2622; Endangered Species Act, 16 U.S.C. § 1540(g)(4); Alaska National Interest Lands Conservation Act, 16 U.S.C. § 3117(a); Federal Cave Resources Protection Act of 1988, 16 U.S.C. § 4307(c); and Surface Mining Control and Reclamation Act, 30 U.S.C. § 1270–1293. Cohen (2008) reviews fee-shifting as authorized by federal statutes.
45. The APA, § 704, provides judicial review of "agency action made reviewable by statute and final agency action for which there is no other adequate

remedy in court." Although subject to various exceptions, courts will not hear claims until the case is "ripe" and administrative options are exhausted. *Myers v. Bethlehem Shipbuilding Corp.*, 303 U.S. 41 (1938).

46. Mashaw (1994) proposes that judicial review of agency regulations should take place later rather than sooner; Seidenfeld (1997) argues that delaying judicial review of rules until the agency has enforced them would be best determined by Congress, and only in limited circumstances.
47. The leading cases are *Abbott Laboratories v. Gardner*, 387 U.S. 136 (1967) and *Toilet Goods Ass'n. v. Gardner*, 387 158 (1967) (federal agency actions ripe for judicial review where the issue is appropriate for judicial resolution, and the denial of immediate judicial relief will cause sufficient hardship).
48. Gluck and Bressman (2013, 2014).
49. *Dep't of Commerce v. N.Y.*, 139 S. Ct. 2551 (2019). See also Jennifer Nou, "Census Symposium: A Place for Pretext in Administrative Law?," SCOTUS Blog, June 28, 2019, https://www.scotusblog.com/2019/06/census-symposium-a-place-for-pretext-in-administrative-law/ (accessed Oct. 27, 2020).
50. See, e.g., *Sec. & Exch. Comm'n v. Chenery Corp.*, 318 U.S. 80, 87 (1943) (holding that "[t]he grounds upon which an administrative order must be judged are those upon which the record discloses that its action was based"); *Camp v. Pitts*, 411 U.S. 138, 142 (1973) (clarifying that "the focal point for judicial review should be the administrative record already in existence, not some new record made initially in the reviewing court").
51. Parrillo (2019b) claims that the benefits of public participation and consultation when agencies issue guidelines may be uncertain, and Parrillo (2019a) finds that many regulated parties are bound by agency guidelines; Mantel (2009) calls for notice-and-comment-like procedures for some agency guidelines.
52. *McLouth Steel Products Corp. v. Lee M. Thomas*, 838 F. 2d 1317 (D.C. Cir. 1988). The standard from *McLouth* was reiterated in subsequent cases. See, e.g., *Chamber of Commerce of U.S. v. S.E.C.*, 443 F. 3d 890, 904 (D.C. Cir. 2006).
53. The sovereignty of Parliament is asserted in the English Bill of Rights of 1689. An ingrained principle of British constitutional law is that courts cannot strike down parliamentary legislation as unconstitutional. Harlow and Rawlings (2009, pp. 143-149), however, provide some nuance. For example, if the meaning of statutory terms is unclear, the courts have referred to legislative proceeding for guidance, although some commentators and jurists find

this inappropriate. Furthermore, UK accession to the European Convention on Human Rights has placed the Parliament and the Supreme Court in tension over that court's decisions that refer to that Convention.

54. Craig (2016), sects. 12–032, 12–033, 15–018 to 15–024, at pp. 362–65, 449–54. Lord Reed in a 2014 case cites Judge Stephen Sedley from *BAPIO Action Limited*, stating that there is no general common-law duty to consult persons who may be affected by a measure before it is adopted. However, there may be a statutory duty to consult; or an obligation to consult may arise because of the common-law duty of fairness. See *R. (Moseley) v. London Borough of Haringey* [2014] UKSC 56 [2014] 1 WLR 3947 (appeal taken from Eng. and Wales) (quoting *R. (BAPIO Action Limited) v. Sec'y of State for the Home Dept.* [2007], EWCA Civ 1139; [2008] ACD 20 at [43]-[47]). Lord Reed stressed that the duty to consult is highly fact-specific, i.e., it depends on the circumstances. See [41].

55. Craig (2016), sects. 12–032, at 362–64. To take an extreme example, one statute requires the decision-maker only to consult the Treasury. Local Democracy, Economic Development and Construction Act 2009, c. 20, at Schedule 1, § 11.

56. Planning Act 2008, c. 29 (Eng.).

57. For an overview see Craig (2016), sects. 25–013–25–049.

58. *R. (UNISON) v. Lord Chancellor* [2017] UKSC 51. The panel unanimously found that the fee schedules interfered unjustifiably with the constitutional right of access to justice that is "inherent in the rule of law" (para. 66) because they deterred many claims, especially by low-income individuals. The fees were set by an SI subject to parliamentary approval. The Supreme Court noted that "[t]hese proceedings are not based on the Human Rights Act 1998, since the appellant is not a 'victim' within the meaning of section 7(1) of that Act. Nevertheless, the case law of the Strasbourg court [i.e., the European Court of Human Rights] concerning the right of access to justice is relevant to the development of the common law" and it was "considered in the context of the case based on EU law" (para. 89). Hence, the fee schedule was subject to judicial review, and parliamentary approval of the SI did not limit the intensity of review. The Court ordered the government to amend the SI.

59. *Walton v. Scottish Ministers* [2012] UKSC 44 (at [94]).

60. *R. v. Inland Revenue Commissioners, ex p. National Federation of Self Employed and Small Businesses Ltd.* [1981] UKHL 2.

61. An opponent of publishing legal material for all to read argued: "The people must not be busy-bodies to pry into the prince's duty" (Ross [1998], p. 452,

quoting Robert Sibthorpe, *Apostolic Obediences* 33 [1627])). Ross refers to Joseph Hall, the bishop of Exeter, who included "the busybody" as one of his vices, second only to the hypocrite. Hall (1998 [1608]).

62. *R. (Kides) v. South Cambridgeshire DC* [2001] EWHC Admin 839, [109]; Craig (2016) at p. 773.
63. *R. v. Legal Aid Board, ex parte Bateman* [1992] W.L.R. 711, [720].
64. *Walton v. Scottish Ministers* [2012] UKSC 44, [152]–[153].
65. JUSTICE (2016). Neudorf (2013) reviews recent trends in intervention in the UK Supreme Court.
66. The Supreme Court Fees Order 2009, 2009 No. 2131 (L. 25), Schedule 1.
67. However, the Supreme Court Rule 46(3) stipulates that costs will generally not be entered for or against intervenors (2009 No. 1603 [L. 17]). In contrast, the Criminal Justice and Courts Act 2015 provides that—except under "exceptional circumstances"—a cost order must be made where (a) an intervener has behaved unreasonably, or (b) has in effect taken on a role as one of the main parties to the dispute; or (c) an intervention is not of significant assistance to the court, or (d) relates in significant part to matters which are not necessary for the court to consider. See JUSTICE (2016), p. 28.
68. Cane (1995) distinguishes between "associational standing" for a group or corporation to represent the interests of its members and "public interest standing." He argues for both types and defends the latter, as an important aspect of democratic accountability.
69. Craig (2016), sect. 1–003, p. 4. Sects. 1–004 to 1–014, pp. 5–15, discuss its pros and cons.
70. Craig (2016), sects. 15–025 to 15–033, pp. 454–59, summarize the case law as of 2016.
71. Craig (2016), sect. 1–011, pp. 10–11. See the varying views in Forsyth (2000).
72. Compare *Associated Provincial Picture Houses Ltd. v. Wednesbury Corporation* [1948] 1 KB 223 (EWCA Civ 1) with *Williamson v. Lee Optical Co.*, 348 U.S. 483 (1955). Craig (2016), pp. 633–45.
73. The UK Human Rights Act of 1998 remains in force, and the UK will remain a member of the Council of Europe, whose European Court of Human Rights interprets the European Convention on Human Rights. After leaving the EU, the UK will not be subject to the EU's similar Charter of Fundamental Rights.
74. Craig (2016), sects. 15–018 to 15–024.
75. Cabinet Office, *Consultation Principles*, 17 June 2012 (last revised March 19, 2018), https://www.gov.uk/government/publications/consultation

-principles-guidance (accessed April 8, 2020). The document states that consultations should be clear and concise, have a purpose, be informative, take "a proportionate" amount of time, be targeted, etc.

76. *R. v. North and East Devon Health Authority, ex parte Coughlan* [2001] QB 213.
77. *R. (Compton) v. Wiltshire Primary Care Trust* [2009] EWHC 1824 (Admin), [104] (citing *R v. Brent London Borough Council, ex parte Gunning* (1985) 84 LGR 168). See also *R v. North and East Devon Health Authority, ex parte Coughlan* [2001] QB 213, [108].
78. See *R. (Moseley) v. London Borough of Haringey* [2014] UKSC 56 (appeal taken from Eng. and Wales).
79. Ibid. at [19].
80. Ibid. at [38].
81. Ibid. at [39].
82. Ibid. (quoting *R. v. N. & E. Devon Health Auth., ex parte Coughlan* [2001] QB 213 [112]).
83. Ibid. at [24].
84. See Chapter 3. The text is at https://www.unece.org/env/pp/treatytext.html (accessed April 8, 2020).
85. *Dover District Council v. CPRE Kent* and *CPRE Kent v. China Gateway International Ltd.* [2017] UKSC 79.
86. Ibid. at [23].
87. Ibid. at [48].
88. Ibid. at [51].
89. Ibid. at [55].
90. For example, a case concerned government failure to approve an expensive drug for coverage by the National Health Service. The Court of Appeal held that the National Institute for Health and Clinical Excellence must make available a "fully executable" version of its economic model, instead of a read-only version. *R. (Eisai Ltd.) v. National Institute for Health and Clinical Excellence* [2008] EWCA Civ 438.
91. House of Commons, High Speed Rail (London-West Midlands) Bill: Promoter's Note on Locus Standi Challenges Relating to Petitions against Additional Provisions ("Aps"), 2015–16.
92. *R. (Greenpeace Ltd.) v. Sec'y of State for Trade and Ind.* [2007] EWHC 311 [63] (Admin). For an overview of the nature of consultation in that case, see Psygkas (2017), pp. 213–16. See also *Devon CC v. Sec'y of State for Communities and Local Gov't* [2010] EWHC 1456 (Admin); *R. v. Boundary Committee* [2008] EWHC 2929 (Admin).

93. "Judicial Review Launched against Heathrow Expansion," *Newsletter of Hillingdon, London* (June 18, 2018), https://perma.cc/J3DB-Y56V?type=image (accessed Nov. 17, 2020).
94. The Heathrow Third Runway Litigation [2019] EWHC (Admin), 1 May 2019; https://www.judiciary.uk/wp-content/uploads/2019/05/Heathrow-third-runway-litigation-judgment-press-summary.pdf.
95. See Roger Harrabin, "Heathrow Wins Court Battle to Build Third Runway," *BBC News*, December 16, 2020, https://www.bbc.com/news/business-55322340. The Court of Appeal case is: *R. (Plan B Earth) v. Secretary of State for Transport* [2020] EWCA Civ 214, 27 February 2020, https://www.judiciary.uk/wp-content/uploads/2020/02/Heathrow-judgment-on-planning-issues-27-February-2020.pdf. (The opinion also resolves in favor of the government the other cases brought by Friends of the Earth and by Greenpeace and several locally affected communities.) The Supreme Court overturned the lower court's opinion and found in favor of Heathrow Airports in *R. (Friends of the Earth Ltd. and others (Respondents)) v. Heathrow Airports Ltd. (Appellants)* [2020] UKSC 2020/0042, 16 December 2020, https://www.supremecourt.uk/cases/uksc-2020-0042.html (all accessed February 2, 2021).
96. *R. (Begum) v. Headteacher and Governors of Denbigh High School* [2006] UKHL 15, 1 AC 100 (HL) (appeal taken from Eng. and Wales).
97. Some justices found that the student's rights had not been violated, and others found a violation but one "directed to a legitimate purpose" and "proportionate in scope and effect" under the European Convention on Human Rights. *R. (Begum) v. Headteacher and Governors of Denbigh High School* [2006] UKHL 15, [49], [93] (appeal taken from Eng. and Wales).
98. *R. (SB) v. Denbigh High School* [2005] EWCA Civ 199.
99. *R. (Begum) v. Headteacher and Governors of Denbigh High School* [2006] UKHL 15, [66] (appeal taken from Eng. and Wales).
100. Ibid. at [68].
101. Kavanagh (2014).
102. The exact nature of that concept is much discussed; for an overview in the UK context, see Craig (2016), pp. 645–68. Proportionality is commonly applied in cases where a right is violated and the court must decide if the violation is permissible as a proportionate response to a legitimate objective.
103. *Denbigh High School* [30]. Kavanagh (2014).

104. Consult the website of the CPAG at https://cpag.org.uk/ (accessed April 8, 2020).
105. *In the matter of Siobhan McLaughlin* [2018] UKSC 48 (appeal taken from N. Ir.).
106. Ibid. at [34].
107. Ibid. at [43].
108. [2019] UKSC 21, 15 May 2019. CPAG also intervened in an earlier case, which lost in a divided Supreme Court panel, *R. (SG) v. Sec'y of State for Work and Pensions* [2015] UKSC 16 (appeal taken from Eng. and Wales).
109. 2008 O.J. (L 152).
110. *ClientEarth (No. 2) v. Sec'y of State for the Environment, Food and Rural Affairs* [2016] EWHC 2740 (Admin). The ClientEarth matter has not been heard by the Supreme Court since its original ruling in 2015. However, in *R. (on the application of ClientEarth (No. 3)) v. Secretary of State for the Environment, Food and Rural Affairs and Others* [2018] EWHC 315, the High Court again found the clean-air plan unlawful (based on failure to develop a comprehensive strategy for Wales and local areas). For additional information see https://www.documents.clientearth.org/wp-content/uploads/library/2019-03-15-what-do-clientearths-legal-cases-mean-for-local-authority-plans-to-deliver-nitrogen-dioxide-compliance-in-england-and-wales-ce-en.pdf (accessed Oct. 26, 2020).
111. The discussion in the text draws on Bell (2017).
112. *ClientEarth (No. 3) v. Sec'y of State for Env't, Food and Rural Affairs* [2018] EWHC 315 (Admin).
113. The progress of the litigation is reviewed in https://www.documents.clientearth.org/wp-content/uploads/library/2019-03-15-what-do-clientearths-legal-cases-mean-for-local-authority-plans-to-deliver-nitrogen-dioxide-compliance-in-england-and-wales-ce-en.pdf (accessed April 8, 2020).
114. *R. (HS2 Action Alliance Ltd.) v. Sec'y of State for Transp.* [2014] UKSC 3 [57] (appeal taken from Eng. and Wales).
115. Ibid. at [108]–[113].
116. 2012 E.C.R.C-182/10.
117. In *HS2 Action Alliance*, the ECJ *Solvay* decision is cited along with other cases.
118. Stop HS2's platform is available at http://stophs2.org (accessed April 8, 2020). See also Eleni Courea, "Northern MPs Tell Labour: Change Your

Mind on HS2," *The Guardian* (Oct. 27, 2018), https://www.theguardian.com/uk-news/2018/oct/27/northern-mps-tell-labour-change-your-mind-on-hs2 [http://perma.cc/7F8Y-QGKX].

119. The HS2 bill was rushed through with just thirty-seven minutes of debate, http://stophs2.org/news/15313-hs2-rushed-37-minutes-debate-56bn-spend (accessed April 8, 2020). Since then, the cost estimates have increased, and the completion dates have been pushed back. Boris Johnson appointed a committee in August 2019 to review the project. It operated out of the public eye, with no additional public consultation. The report issued in February 2020 supports the project with some caveats, arguing that net benefits remain positive, even under new estimates of increased costs and reduced benefits (Gwyn Topham, "Oakervee Report Gives Boris Johnson Cover for HS2 Decision," *The Guardian*, Feb. 11, 2020, https://www.theguardian.com/uk-news/2020/feb/11/oakervee-report-gives-boris-johnson-cover-for-hs2-decision).

120. "In judicial review an otherwise successful claimant has no automatic right to a remedy: even if the agency is held to have acted unlawfully, it is the court's prerogative to deny or fashion any relief" (Harlow and Rawlings [2009], p. 723).

121. Craig (2016), sect. 15–033 and chap. 26.

122. Craig (2016), sect. 15–025. The act was the National Fire Service Regulation (Indemnity) Act.

123. See *R. (Moseley) v. London Borough of Haringey* [2014] UKSC 56 (appeal taken from Eng. and Wales) at [33].

124. Harlow and Rawlings (2009), pp. 317–18, 723; *R. v. Panel of Take-overs and Mergers, ex p Datafin plc* [1987] QB 815.

125. Harlow and Rawlings (2009), pp. 651–52, 723; *R. (Edwards) v. Environment Agency* [2008] UKHL 22.

126. Harlow and Rawlings (2009), p. 178.

127. In May 2007, the government issued a new consultation document to comply with the High Court ruling. Dep't of Trade & Indus., *The Future of Nuclear Power* (May 2007), https://perma.cc/2JJ7-G7BX (accessed April 8, 2020). A 2008 document further sets out the decision taken after the new consultation: Dep't for Bus., Enter. & Regulatory Reform, *Meeting the Energy Challenge: A White Paper on Nuclear Power* (January 2008), https://perma.cc/QKW8-SWUZ (citing *Greenpeace* [2007] EWHC 311; accessed April 8, 2020). I am grateful to Athanasios Psygkas for this information.

128. Harlow and Rawlings (2009), p. 178.

129. *Agricultural, Horticultural and Forestry Industry Training Board v. Aylesbury Mushrooms* [1972] 1 All ER 280.
130. Edward Malnick, "Supreme Court to Be Overhauled to Curtail Its Constitutional Powers," *The Telegraph*, Nov. 14, 2020, https://www.telegraph.co.uk/politics/2020/11/14/britains-supreme-court-faces-overhaul-concerns-us-style-election/ (accessed November 16, 2020). This discussion is linked to the Independent Review of Administrative Law mentioned in the next note. The cases are: *R. (Miller and another) v. Sec'y of State for Exiting the European Union* [2007] UKSC 5 (appeal taken from Eng., Wales, and N. Ir.), and *R. (on the Application of Miller (Appellant)) v. The Prime Minister (Respondent), Cherry and Others (Respondents) v. Advocate General for Scotland* [2019] UKSC 41.
131. *Terms of Reference—Independent Review of Administrative Law*. https://assets.publishing.service.gov.uk/government/uploads/system/uploads/attachment_data/file/915624/independent-review-admin-law-terms-of-reference.pdf. See the statement of the UK Administrative Justice Institute: Lee Marson, Maurice Sunkin, and Theodore Konstadinides, "UK Administrative Justice Institute Response to the Independent Review of Administrative Law," *UK Administrative Justice Institute* (Oct. 26, 2020). https://administrativejusticeblog.files.wordpress.com/2020/10/ukaji-response-to-iral-october-2020.pdf.UKALi has also collected all the comments submitted at: https://ukaji.org/2020/11/04/collection-of-responses-to-the-independent-review-of-administrative-law-iral/ (all websites accessed Nov. 16, 2020).
132. Thanks to my co-author Stefanie Egidy and to Lena Riemer and Franziska Bantlin for research help on issues of judicial review. See generally Rose-Ackerman, Egidy, and Fowkes (2015); Schneider (2007); Ruffert (2007).
133. Basic Law (Grundgesetz), art. 80(1).
134. Administrative Procedures Act (Verwaltungsverfahrensgesetz—VwVfG). The plan approval procedures (*Planfeststellungsverfahren*) are in §§ 72–78. Questions of EU law or of individual rights under German constitutional law can be referred to the ECJ and the Constitutional Court by judges hearing individual cases (art. 267 AEUV; Basic Law, art. 100). Individual rights claimed can also be brought to the European Court of Human Rights.
135. In Germany this review power applies only to federal rules or norms.
136. §§ 2, 40, 49 Verwaltungsgerichtsordnung (VwGO).
137. § 40 VwGO lays out the jurisdiction of the Verwaltungsgerichte compared to the other specialized courts. See also §§ 1, 2 FGO, § 1 ArbGG, §§ 1, 2 SGG.

138. The Basic Law, art. 93, outlines the jurisdiction of the Constitutional Court.
139. Energy law review of Federal Network Agency (*Bundesnetzagentur*) actions is provided by the Oberlandesgericht Düsseldorf, the appeal court in civil law matters. The first-instance court for telecoms law is the administrative court in Cologne (§ 137 Telekommunikationsgesetz vom 22.06.2004). Those cities house the headquarters of legacy firms in those industries. Deutsche Telekom, founded in 1996 as private company from a former state firm, is headquartered near Cologne; EON, a large energy holding company, is located in Düsseldorf. Courts in these jurisdictions have expertise in those industries. The use of ordinary courts for electricity stems from the highly decentralized nature of the electricity sector in Germany, with many generators operating as private-law companies but often with local government ownership.
140. Basic Law, art. 93. Abstract review of the constitutionality of federal or state law can be brought to the court by the federal government, a Land government, or one-third of the Bundestag. Basic Law, art. 93(1), no. 2. Individuals can bring complaints to the Constitutional Court, but only on the basis of a violation of their rights. Basic Law, art. 93(1), no. 4a. Under the abstract review provision, the Constitutional Court can be asked to rule on the constitutionality of a proposed statute before its passage.
141. Interview with Annegret Groebel, Federal Network Agency, April 27, 2015, Berlin.
142. Rose-Ackerman (1995), pp. 89, 165. BVerfGE 82, 15–18 (1985); BVerwGE 92, 262 (1993).
143. Aarhus Convention, arts. 6, 9. EU Directive 2003/35/EC. See also Chapter 3.
144. The Environmental Legal Remedies Act (*Umwelt-Rechtsbehelfsgesetz-*UmwRG []), § 3. See Dross (2005).
145. The ECJ has ruled that a nongovernment organization may challenge the issuance of an infrastructure permit under the Aarhus Convention's Article 9, even if it would not have standing to sue under German environmental law. *Trianel Kohlekraftwerk Lünen* (Case C-115/09 [2011]). See also *Slovak Brown Bear*, C-240/09 (2011).
146. *Darmstadt*, BVerwG 7 C 21/12 (2013).
147. For example, the UmwRG and the Nature Protection Act (*Bundesnaturschutzgesetz*, BNatSchG).
148. 4 C 35/13, Dec. 18, 2014.
149. Mast (2019) argues that the UmwRG should apply to groups concerned with the protection of monuments and that the legislature should enact a new law explicitly to permit *Verbandsklagen*.

150. The agreement between the Green Party and the Social Democrats mentions this goal: https://www.berlin.de/rbmskzl/regierender-buergermeister/senat/koalitionsvereinbarung/ (accessed April 8, 2020).
151. The list is from an interview with Sabine Schlacke, professor, University of Münster Law School, April 21, 2015. See also Schlacke, Schrader, and Bunge (2019).
152. The example comes from my interview with Schlacke.
153. However, the European Union has proposed a directive permitting representative actions for the collective interests of consumers, but it has not yet been enacted. A draft is here: https://eur-lex.europa.eu/legal-content/EN/TXT/?uri=CELEX%3A52018PC0184 (accessed April 8, 2020).
154. Interview with Eberhard Schmidt-Aßmann, Berlin, April 25, 2015.
155. "Gemeinützigkeit: Bundesfinanzminister Stoppt umstrittene Steuerpläne für Vereine," *Die Zeit Online*, Nov. 29, 2019, https://www.zeit.de/politik/deutschland/2019-11/gemeinnuetzigkeit-olaf-scholz-vereine-reform-stopp (accessed Nov. 17, 2020).
156. Kühne (2015).
157. Ibid., pp. 310, 321. See § 27a BVerfGG.
158. Rose-Ackerman, Egidy, and Fowkes (2015), pp. 207–12; Rose-Ackerman (1995), pp. 72–93.
159. BVerfGE 49, 89 (1978).
160. BVerfGE 53, 30 (1979).
161. BVerfGE 61, 82, 115 (1982). See also BVerfGE 83, 130, 149–54 (1990) (a statute setting up a committee to review the promotion and marketing of books to youth was unconstitutional because the process of selecting members lacked democratic legitimacy).
162. For more on the FNA, see Chapter 4.
163. Schneider (2013), pp. 59–60.
164. 1 BvR 1932/08; BVerfGK 19, 229. Translation by Franziska Bantlin.
165. BVerfGE 125, 175 (2010), available in English at http://www.bverfg.de/entscheidungen/ls20100209_1bvl000109en.html (accessed April 8, 2020). The discussion of *Hartz IV* relies heavily on Stefanie Egidy's work, reflected in Rose-Ackerman, Egidy, and Fowkes (2015), pp. 207–12. A later case affirmed *Hartz IV*, BVerfGE 132, 134 (2014).
166. *Hartz IV*, para. 138.
167. *Hartz IV*, paras. 171, 175.
168. Brenner (2011); Nolte (2013), p. 250; Dann (2010); Petersen (2013), p. 114.
169. *Hartz IV*, para. 144.

170. *Hartz IV*, para. 133 ff.

171. 10 S 1977/18, 2019 VGH Baden-Württemberg. See Mac Ranner, "Umweltschutz: Akte Weltrettung," *Die Zeit Online* April 3, 2019, https://www.zeit.de/zeit-wissen/2019/02/umweltschutz-client-earth-ngo-klimawandel-rechtsanwaelte/komplettansicht (accessed Nov. 23, 2020).

172. VG Stuttgart, 17 K 5255/19, Jan. 21, 2020. See "Streit um Stuttgarter Fahrverbote: Zwangsgeldzahlen an gemeinnützige Organisationen?", *Legal Times Online*, Feb. 2, 2020, https://www.lto.de//recht/justiz/j/vg-stuttgart-17k525519-luftreinhalteplan-fahrverbot-deutsche-umwelthilfe-zwangsgeld-gemeinnuetzige-private-organisation-kinder-krebsstiftung/ (accessed Nov. 23, 2020). Other courts have threatened to detain officials who resist enforcing EU law. The European Court of Justice recognized the need for an effective remedy, but set the standard high for detention of an official compared with repeated fines: C-752/18, decision from Dec. 19, 2019.

173. BImSchG, § 51: Hearing of the Parties Concerned.

174. ECJ, joined cases C 401/12 P to C 403/12 P, 2015.

175. Dross (2005), pp. 78–79.

176. § 46 VwVfG: "Consequences of procedural and formal errors: The annulment of an administrative act which is not void under paragraph 44 cannot be claimed solely on the ground that it was adopted in breach of rules of procedure, form or local jurisdiction if it is obvious that the breach did not affect the decision on the substance." See Fisahn (2002), pp. 340–78.

177. Dross (2005), pp. 72–73.

178. Rose-Ackerman (1995), pp. 72–75.

179. The amusement park is called *Wunderland Kalkar* and is advertised here: https://www.wunderlandkalkar.eu/en (accessed April 8, 2020).

180. Several criminal-law judgments related to Stuttgart 21 concerned police violence. On Nov. 18, 2015, the Stuttgart Administrative Court found that the dissolution of the protests violated the right to peaceful assembly as guaranteed in art. 8, GG. On wind farms, NABU went to court against the licensing authority in Detmold, claiming that potential dangers to protected species (birds) were not sufficiently considered before the establishment of wind farms. The case is at the OVG Münster for a reassessment: BVerwGE 7 C 5.18, 2019.

181. Sören Amelang, "Germany agrees to pay energy companies over 2 billion euros in nuclear exit compensation," *Clean Energy Wire*, March 5, 2021, https://www.cleanenergywire.org/news/germany-agrees-pay-energy

-companies-over-2-billion-euros-nuclear-exit-compensation (accessed April 25, 2021).

182. BVerwG 7 C 21/12 at paras. 59–63. The government had not obtained input from the Animal Protection Commission.
183. BVerfGE 127, 293 10/12/2010. The case was brought by the state of Hesse, which sought abstract review in the Constitutional Court.
184. Dross (2005), pp. 80–81.
185. Denninger (1990), pp. 178–80; Steinberg (1994), pp. 94–98.
186. Pünder (2009, 2014, 2015). In his 2009 article he criticizes the lack of congressional oversight in the US, but goes on to argue that both the UK and Germany should consider public participation in rulemaking to increase democratic legitimacy. See also Della Cananea (2016).
187. BVerfGE 45, 297, 335 (1977 [translation by Pünder]). The quote appears in Pünder (2014), p. 243.
188. Much material in this section benefited from my joint work with Thomas Perroud and Edgardo Jordão. See Rose-Ackerman and Perroud (2013); Jordão (2016). The recent cases are discussed later in this section, and my reports on them also benefitted from correspondence with Perroud. They are: Conseil d'État, 19 novembre 2020, *Commune de Grande-Synthe*, n° 427301; Tribunal Administratif de Paris, 3 février 2021, *Asso. Oxfam et al.* n° 1904967. n° 1904968, n° 1904976/4-1 (called: *L'Affaire du Siècle* by that court's own press office), https://www.dalloz-actualite.fr/sites/dalloz-actualite.fr/files/resources/2021/02/ta_paris-3_fevr._2021.pdf. The press release is at: http://paris.tribunal-administratif.fr/Actualites-du-Tribunal/Communiques-de-presse/L-affaire-du-siecle. (All accessed February 4, 2021.) These cases are hereinafter cited as *Commune du Grande-Synthe* and *Asso. Oxfam et al.*
189. Conseil d'État, 21 décembre 1906, *Syndicat des propriétaires et contribuables du quartier Croix de Seguey-Tivoli*, GAJA, n° 16. A taxpayer could challenge a town's expenses (Conseil d'État, 29 mars 1901, *Casanova*). Someone who might want to camp in the future could challenge a town's regulation on camping (CE, 14 février 1958, *Abisset*, p. 98).
190. In general, proceedings before an administrative court are less expensive than proceedings before a civil court. A law of Dec. 30, 1977, exempted applicants from most of the costs in both jurisdictions. Before the administrative courts, besides a minimal *droit de timbre*, the only costs that parties face are lawyers' fees and fees for expertise and inquiries required by the courts. Those costs are usually borne by the party that loses the case, unless

particular circumstances recommend otherwise. Judicial aid for poor citizens can reduce or eliminate even those costs (art. 441–1 of the Code of Administrative Justice and CE, 22 juillet 1992, *Marcuccini*). According to article 761–1 of the Code of Administrative Justice, the judge can condemn the losing party to pay any other costs that the winning party has faced (*frais irrépétibles*), but the judge should take into consideration the economic situation of the parties.

191. Parties must usually hire a lawyer when they challenge administrative actions (art. 431–2 CAJ). However, there are exceptions (art. 431–3 CAJ).

192. Groups that would not have standing are almost always able to intervene as third parties. If the Conseil d'État reviews regulatory agencies' decisions, third-party interventions are also generally accepted. See, for example, Conseil d'État, 27 avril 2009, *Société Bouygues Télécom* and Conseil d'État, 24 juillet 2009, *Société Orange France et Société Française de Radiotéléphonie*. The company Free was allowed to intervene, even though it was not yet an operator. Noguellou (2010), p. 825.

193. Kühne (2015). "Ministère Public," *Britannica* on-line, Aug. 20, 1998, https://www.britannica.com/topic/ministere-public (accessed Nov. 1, 2020). The Ministère Public also acts as prosecutor in criminal cases, acting for the state. For civil cases, including those involving public bodies, its interventions are meant to express the "general will," not the partisan interests of the government in power.

194. In *Commune de Grande-Synthe*, the CE allowed for the participation of the cities of Paris and Grenoble along with Oxfam, Greenpeace, la Foundation pour la Nature et l'Homme.

195. The right to challenge an administrative action in court is a fundamental liberty (Conseil d'État, 13 mars 2006, *Bayrou et Assoc. de Défense des Usagers des Autoroutes Publiques de France*) and a constitutional right by both the Constitutional Council (Cons. Const., décision 96–373 DC, 9 avril 1996) and the Conseil d'État, 29 juillet 1998, *Syndicat des Avocats de France*. This right is also part of the European Convention on Human Rights—articles 13 and 15 (CEDH 26 octobre 2000, *Kudla c. Pologne*, Rec. CEDH § 157; CEDH 27 juin 2000, *Ihlan c. Turquie*, Rec. CEDH § 97).

196. Administrative actions can be subjected to two kinds of challenges (*recours*): those based on a claim of objective illegality (*recours objectifs*) and those based on a claimed violation of individual or collective right (*recours subjectifs*). The recours objectifs promote the general interest in legality and are subject to very lenient rules of standing.

197. Review of the decisions of independent administrative agencies generally rests with the administrative tribunals, but the rule may be derogated by law "in the interest of good administration of justice" (Cons. const. n° 86–224 DC du 23 janvier 1987, Loi transférant à la juridiction judiciaire le contentieux des décisions du Conseil de la Concurrence). Thus, the legislature has denied jurisdiction to the administrative courts over some matters involving antitrust and financial regulation and given first-instance jurisdiction to the Court of Appeal of Paris. However, review of secondary legislation remains with the administrative courts.
198. Truchet (2017).
199. Conseil d'État, 28 mai 1971, *Ville Nouvelle Est*, Requête n° 78825. There is a controversy in French legal literature over the number of standards of review. Most find two standards: restricted review (*contrôle restreint*) and regular review (*contrôle normal*). Some claim that in some cases the administrative judges apply a third, more intrusive standard that they call maximum review (*contrôle maximum*). Restricted review applies when the administration has discretionary powers. The judge will only annul the decision where there is a "manifest error of appraisal" (*erreur manifeste d'appréciation*) (Conseil d'État, 15 février 1961, *Lagrange*).
200. The Conseil d'État ruled that if the administration imposes fines, judicial review is unlimited, even in the absence of a specific legislative provision (Conseil d'État, 16 février 2009, *Société Atom*). This holding might be the result of pressure from the European Court of Human Rights, which decided that administrative sanctions can only be accepted when unlimited judicial review is available (Cour EDH, 27 octobre 1987, *Boden et Pudas*). The courts do not hesitate to assess the proportionality of sanctions and to reform them (Conseil d'État, 22 juin 2007, *Arfi*).
201. French law does not have the concept of "complex economic assessments" that leads to deferential review under European law. Théophile and Parmentier (2006), pp. 39–46.
202. For example, some telecom regulation cases have received restricted review due to their complexity. See, for example, Conseil d'État, 10 juillet 2006, *Société Cégétel*, Requête n° 274455 (on the distribution of the costs of the universalization of the service); and Conseil d'État, 5 décembre 2005, *Fédération Nationale UFC Que Choisir*, Requête n° 277441–277443–277445 (on the establishment of a price-floor regulation to dominant companies).
203. Examples are the review of the so-called *mesure de haute police* (Conseil d'État, 25 juillet 1985, *Mme Dagosstini*, and Conseil d'État, 3 février 1975,

Min. intérieur c. Pardov, on measures against foreigners on French soil) and of refusals to apply an administrative sanction, due to the principle of the *opportunité des poursuites* (Conseil d'État, 28 juillet 2000, *Société Copper Communication*; Conseil d'État, 30 décembre 2002, *Rimonteil de Lombares*).

204. The relevant case law is cited and analyzed in Jordão (2016).

205. Jacques-Henri Stahl conclusions to Conseil d'État, 9 avril 1999, *Société The Coca-Cola Company*, Requête n° 201853.

206. Rubinfeld (2000); Huettner (2002).

207. See, in the domain of the broadcasting authority, Conseil d'État, 30 juillet 1997, *Société d'Exploitation Radio-Chic (SERC)*; Conseil d'État, 18 mai 1998, *Société World Satellite Guadeloupe*, Requête n° 182244; and Conseil d'État, 07 juin 1999, *Société M6*.

208. See *Chevron v. Natural Resources Defense Council*, 467 U.S. 837 (1984), which defers to the Environmental Protection Agency's interpretation of a statutory term, finding that Congress had not spoken directly to its meaning and that the EPA's interpretation produced a reasonable policy choice that the courts should not overrule.

209. See, for example, the conclusions of the *rapporteur public* Prada-Bordenave in Conseil d'État, 25 février 2005, *France Télécom*; or those of Fédéric Lenica in Conseil d'État, 27 avril 2009, *Bouygues Télécom*.

210. On the situation in France, see Lasser (2009).

211. Conseil d'État, 3 février 1989, *Compagnie Alitalia*.

212. Conseil d'État, 16 juillet 2007, *Syndicat National de Défense de l'Exercise Libéral de la Médecine à l'Hôpital*.

213. French judges work with "general principles of the law" to resolve cases. Besides equality, others are: liberty (freedom of trade), security (right to judicial review, right to administrative appeal, natural justice, bias, non-retroactivity, the obligation to revoke an illegal act, the right to live a normal life), respect for the dead (for doctor's ethical obligations), and the continuity of public services, etc. See Lasser (2005).

214. Conseil d'État, 23 décembre 2011, *Danthony*, Recueil Lebon, p. 649.

215. Loi n° 2011–515 du 17 mai 2011 de simplification et d'amélioration de la qualité du droit (Law on Simplifying and Improving the Quality of Law).

216. This jurisprudence draws on old case law about "substantive irregularities." If the consultation is compulsory by law, the decree will be quashed. By contrast, if a procedural omission did not breach a right protected by the rule, the decree will not be quashed (Frier [2012]).

217. The Conseil d'État ruled that a government decree banning the genetically modified corn MON 810 was unlawful because the government did not establish that it constituted a "serious risk to human health, animal health, or the environment." CE 1 août 2013, *Association générale des producteurs de maïs (AGPM) et autres.*
218. Conseil Constitutionnel, Décision n° 2011–183/184 QPC, 14 octobre 2011. The legal and factual background is summarized in the *Commentaire aux cahiers*, available along with the decision. See also Conseil d'État (2011).
219. For a German-French comparison of this aspect of environmental law, see generally Marcou and Masing (2010, 2011).
220. Under the doctrine of negative ultra vires, or incompetence, parliament cannot leave constitutional rights and liberties unprotected. In this case, consultations with the Conseil d'État and the Conseil Supérieur des Installations Classées (now the Conseil Supérieur des Risques Technologiques) were not sufficient to protect rights.
221. CC Décision n° 2012–262 QPC, 13 juillet 2012; CC Décision n° 2012–269 QPC, 27 juillet 2012; CC Décision n° 2012–270 QPC, 27 juillet 2012; CC Décision n° 2012–283 QPC, 23 novembre 2012; CC Décision n° 2012–282 QPC, 23 novembre 2012. All of these decisions found Code Civil art. L. 120–1 unconstitutional. The provision struck down by the CC required neither a general consultation nor a special consultation with stakeholders.
222. Décision n° 424600 du 12 juillet 2019 du Conseil d'État. See also CE, 29 janvier 2018, *Société Marineland, Société Safari Africain de Port St Père et autre*, n° 412210, 412256, p. 14, *s'agissant du critère tiré de ce que la participation a été privée d'effet utile*; CE, 17 avril 2013, *Commune de Ramatuelle*, no 348311, T. 874–875.
223. This type of action has been used in other cases of a government failure to regulate involving asbestos and coastal pollution from seaweeds. See CE 3 mars 2004, *Min. de l'emploi et de la solidarité c/ Cts Bourdigon*; CAA Nantes 1er déc. 2009, *MEDD c/ Assoc. Halte aux marées vertes.*
224. A summary of the groups' activities in this case is at *Notre Affaire à Tous v. France*, http://climatecasechart.com/non-us-case/notre-affaire-a-tous-and-others-v-france/. Their brief is at https://notreaffaireatous.org/wp-content/uploads/2019/05/Brief-juridique-ADS-EN-1.pdf (both accessed April 8, 2020).
225. *Netherlands v. Stichting Urgenda*, Supreme Court of Netherlands, No. 19/00135, Dec. 20, 2019. The Supreme Court of Norway is hearing a similar case based on the right to a healthy environment added to the Norwegian

Constitution in 2014. It seeks to void licenses to explore for oil and gas in the Arctic off the coast of Norway. Henrik Pryser Libell and Isabella Kwai, "Norway's Supreme Court Hears Rights Challenge to Arctic Oil Drilling," *New York Times*, Nov. 5, 2020.

226. This problem is partially mitigated by the reasons given by the rapporteur public, a member of the Conseil d'État who proposes a solution to the case. His or her reasons are often longer and more developed than the ones in the actual decisions of the courts. However, those reasons are not necessarily the reasons of the Conseil d'État itself.
227. CE, 21 décembre 2012, *Société Groupe Canal plus Société Vivendi Universel*, n° 353856; and CE, 21 décembre 2012, *Société Groupe Canal plus et autres*, nos. 362347, 363542, 363703.
228. Loi n° 79–587, du 11 juin 1979. See also CE 30 juillet 1997, *Sté d'Exploitation Radio-Chic*, n° 153402, and art. 1 of the Loi n° 79–587, du 11 juin, 1979.
229. CE, 7 juillet 2000, *Synd. intercommunal pour la collecte et le traitement des ordures ménagères de la région d'Issoudun*, Lebon 304, and CE, 9 décembre 1983, Vladescu, Lebon 497 *L'Actualité Juridique Droit Administrative* (AJDA) 1984.
230. CE, 30 avril 2007, *Assoc. Magnum Radio*, n° 286348. The same problem is pointed out by Autin (2011a).
231. The Conseil d'État stated that if reason-giving is required, the agency should include all elements of fact and law "to enable *the affected person* to challenge their legality" (italics added). CE, 18 mai 1998, *Sté World Satellite Guadeloupe*, Req. n° 182244.
232. Décis. Cons. Const. n° 2004–497 DC du 1 juillet 2004, *Loi relative aux communications électroniques*, considérant no. 14.
233. Autin (2011a).
234. Morand-Deviller (2009), p. 403.
235. Contrast this with the *Chenery* Doctrine in American law, whereby a court will not substitute its judgment for that of the agency.
236. CE, 3 décembre 2003, *Préfet Seine-maritime c. El Bahi*, Lebon, p. 479, concl. Stahl.
237. CE, 19 décembre 2008, *Ministre Économie, Finances et Industrie c. Darmon.*
238. CE, 27 septembre 2006, *Sté Janfin*, Rec. 401.
239. CE, 12 janvier 1968, *Ministre Économie et Finances c. Perrot*, n° 70951 Lebon.
240. Ibid. and CE, 22 avril 2005, *Cne de Barcarès*, AJDA (2005), p. 16321.

241. If US agencies present several reasons for their decisions, the reviewing courts tend to find all of them either acceptable or unacceptable (e.g., *Ranchers Cattlemen Action Legal Fund United Stock-Growers of America v. Dept. of Agriculture*, 415 F. 3d 1078 [9th Cir. 2005]). In a case involving an Interstate Commerce Commission (ICC) grant of a certificate to a carrier, the Supreme Court accepted one of two ICC responses to a study, rejected the other, and upheld the ICC's action: *Bowman Transp. Inc. v. Arkansas Best Freight Systems, Inc.* 419 U. S. 281, 287 (1974). I am grateful to Blake Emerson for help in locating the case law.
242. For a fuller discussion see Rose-Ackerman and Perroud (2014).
243. *Commune de Grande-Synthe*, article 6. In *Oxfam et al.*, the court, similarly, gave the plaintiffs two months to provide supplementary material to the court to help it decide on the remedy.
244. A law of June 30, 2000, created the *référé-suspension* and the *référé-liberté* and reformed the system of *mesures d'urgence* (art. L-521–1, Code de Justice Administrative).
245. *Oxfam et al.* Four environmental groups were each awarded one euro in "moral damages" (article 3). The opinion refuses to state exactly what the parties must do until the case has concluded, but it leaves open the possibility that it may order the government to take specific actions.
246. French Constitution, article 11 as amended in 2008. Article 11 also permits the president to submit to a referendum any bill on a list of covered topics, now including economic, social, or environmental policy. Article 89 permits the Constitution to be amended by a government or a private member's bill that is approved by referendum. (The government can avoid a referendum if it can obtain the approval of a supermajority of the legislature sitting as a whole.) Thus, it is conceptually possible to enact an amendment through a referendum based on a private member's bill that is opposed by the president.
247. Nicole Trian, "Opponents Work for Referendum on Macron's Plan to Privatise the Paris Airports," *France 24*, Nov. 30, 2019, https://www.france24.com/en/20191130-opponents-work-referendum-macron-plan-privatise-paris-airports-french-economy (accessed Nov. 17, 2020).
248. Code des Relations entre le Public et l'Administration: Statutory provisions: Ordinance 2015–1341, Oct. 23, 2015; Regulatory Provisions: Decree 2015–1342, 23 octobre 2015. See Custos (2017).
249. Conseil d'État, 19 juillet 2017, *Association Citoyenne pour Occitanie et Pays Catalan et Autres*, n° 403928. Those who challenged the process, first, asserted that it should have included the entire French population. Second,

they objected to using the Condorcet method to pick the winner out of five options. Voters ranked the five options, and the process asks if one option obtains a majority in all the pairwise comparisons. Only one option satisfied that criterion, even though it only gained 44 percent of the first-place votes. The case is discussed in Buge and Morio (2019).

250. Rose-Ackerman, Egidy, and Fowkes (2015) discusses the limited role of the courts in the review of the legislative process in the US and Germany. The same is true of France, and parliamentary sovereignty prevents judicial review of the UK Parliament's procedures. In contrast, the South African Constitutional Court emphasizes openness and inclusion and is a promoter of participatory democracy (Fowkes, 2016).
251. But for corruption involving US judges, see Pahis (2009).
252. Eskridge and Ferejohn (2010), pp. 22–28.
253. One study found that judicial decisions of US courts of appeals are more centrist if judges sit in panels whose members were nominated by presidents of different parties. They argue for substituting the current practice of random assignment with one that requires more balance. Judge Wald critiques the proposal arguing that judges decide cases under the law, although in close cases their judgments are inevitably affected by their personal philosophies and experiences. Cross and Tiller (1998); Tiller and Cross (1999); Wald (1999).
254. M. Shapiro (1988); Stewart (1975).

Chapter 8. *Policymaking Accountability as a Democratic Value*

1. La Porta, Lopez-de-Silanes, Shleifer, and Vishny (1997, 1998, 1999, 2002).
2. Some suggest reverse causality whereby countries improve their laws protecting investors as their financial markets develop. Others argue that the legal-origins thesis omits alternative variables—for instance, legal origins may influence contract enforcement and subsequent financial development. See, e.g., Symposium on Legal Origins (2009); Siems (2007); Roe (2006).
3. La Porta, Silanes, and Shleifer (2008) argue that legal origins represent a broad system of social control, wherein "the common law stands for the strategy of social control that seeks to support private market outcomes, whereas civil law seeks to replace such outcomes with state-desired allocation"). Thus, the "common law" has become a metaphor.
4. Elkins, Ginsburg, and Simmons (2013); Jackson (2005). La Porta, Silanes, and Shleifer (2008), p. 327, acknowledge convergence through international

trade and investment and speculate that in quiet times market-friendly legal approaches will dominate.

5. Crettez, Deffains, and Musy (2013, 2016).
6. La Porta Silanes, and Shleifer (2008).
7. For example, the World Bank's *Doing Business* report only deals with the business environment and does not consider whether costly rules and red tape have social benefits. It ignores the value of regulations in providing benefits such as environmental protection, occupational health and safety, and protections for consumers, debtors, or workers. See Rose-Ackerman (2009). The 2020 report is at http://documents.worldbank.org/curated/en/688761571934946384/pdf/Doing-Business-2020-Comparing-Business-Regulation-in-190-Economies.pdf (accessed April 9, 2020).
8. Rose-Ackerman, Desierto, and Volosin (2011).
9. Brazil illustrates that situation (Cheibub, Figueiredo, and Limongi, 2000; Prado, 2017).
10. "Argentines Bang Pots and Pans to Protest Government," *Reuters*, June 7, 2012, https://www.reuters.com/article/us-argentina-protest/argentines-bang-pots-and-pans-to-protest-government-idUSBRE85704920120608. Peter S. Goodman, "Inequality Fuels Rage of 'Yellow Vests' in Equality-Obsessed France," *The New York Times*, April 15, 2019, https://www.nytimes.com/2019/04/15/business/yellow-vests-movement-inequality.html.
11. In countries such as France with a weak philanthropic tradition, some have sought ways to tap public funds while retaining civil-society independence. Thomas Perroud has proposed that the damage awards and monetary sanctions imposed by government agencies should flow into a fund earmarked for civil-society groups. Hungary had a program called Green Source that awarded about $1 million in small grants to environmental groups that averaged about $11,500. A 15-member committee allocated the funds. The seven members from environmental groups reviewed the applications and made recommendations to the entire committee that were usually accepted. The civil-society members, chosen by a national committee of NGOs, served one- to two-year terms. Rose-Ackerman (2005), pp. 177–78.
12. 5 U.S.C. §§ 551–559, 701–706.
13. Shane (2009) contrasts presidentialism with pluralism, a system that gives a stronger role to the Congress and to public input.
14. Rose-Ackerman and Pimenta (2020).

15. Some Latin American countries permit the president to issue decrees with the force of law. In those cases ex post review is especially important, e.g., in Argentina and Brazil. Bowen and Rose-Ackerman (2003).
16. See Rose-Ackerman (2005). Maciej Kisilowski translated and evaluated the Polish-language material used there.
17. The Constitution of 1997 specifies a closed list of sources of "universally binding" law that included "regulations" (Konst. Pol. [1997], art. 87). See Biernat (1998).
18. Sólyom and Brunner (2000).
19. Act on Protection of Personal Data and Disclosures of Data of Public Interest (Act LXIII/1992). Rose-Ackerman (2005), pp. 149–53.
20. Act CXEE of 2011 as amended, available in English at https://njt.hu/translated/doc/J2011T0112P_20190426_FIN.pdf (accessed April 9, 2020). Section 27.5 states: "any data compiled or recorded by an organ performing public duties as part and in support of its decision-making process within the limits of its powers and duties shall not be disclosed for ten years from the date it was compiled or recorded. After considering the weight of public interest with respect to granting or denying access, the head of the organ that processes the data in question may permit access." Section 27.6 states that "[a] request to access data underlying a decision may be dismissed after the decision is adopted but within the time limit referred to in paragraph (5), if the data underlies future decisions, or access to it would jeopardize the performance of its duties without any undue external influence, such as, in particular the free expression of the standpoint of the organ which generated the data during the preliminary stages of the its decisionmaking process."
21. In Germany, as well, some claim that non-partisan, civil-society groups have too great an impact on policymaking. Especially subject to criticism is the German Environmental Aid Association (Deutsche Umwelthilfe); see, for example Marcus Rohwetter, "Gemeinnützigkeit und Transparent?," *Die Zeit*, March 6, 2019, https://www.zeit.de/2019/11/deutsche-umwelthilfe-gemeinnuetzigkeit-tranzparenz-ngo-vereine-attac.
22. Law on Normative Acts, XI/1987, art. 19 (translations by Katalin Füzér and Csilla Kaloscai). The act attempted to put some order into the chaotic state of legal rules and decrees that characterized the late Socialist period. See Galligan and Smilov (1999), p. 117.
23. XI/1987, art. 20. Jurisdictional bodies are local and regional governments and other ministries involved in implementing a regulation; social organizations include groups such as environmental and women's groups with policy

agendas; and interest representative organizations are trade unions and business and professional associations.

24. Act XXXI/1990.
25. In practice, the problems go beyond the weaknesses of rulemaking procedures. Bozóki and Hegedüs (2018); Pech and Scheppele (2017).
26. Environmental Protection Act of April 27, 2001 (Dz. U. 2001, No. 62, Item 627 with amends.), arts. 31–39. Hańderek (2002), p. 53.
27. Hańderek (2002), pp. 55–56.
28. European Commission, "The Environmental Implementation Review 2019: Country Report: Poland" (2019), https://ec.europa.eu/environment/eir/pdf/report_pl_en.pdf (accessed April 9, 2020).
29. For example, Cent, Grozinska-Jurczak, and Pietrzyk-Kaszynska (2014).
30. See Environmental Protection Act LIII/1995, M.K. No. 52, 2780–2799.
31. European Commission, "The Environmental Implementation Review 2019: Country Report: Hungary" (2019), pp. 32–33, https://ec.europa.eu/environment/eir/pdf/report_hu_en.pdf.
32. Rose-Ackerman, Desierto, and Volosin (2011).
33. For example, the president of France can declare a state of emergency, but article 16 of the French Constitution, in paragraph 6, added in 2008, permits specified members of the legislature to request an opinion of the Constitutional Council after 30 days of such a declaration. If the Council finds that the emergency continues to be justified, it must revisit the issue every 60 days thereafter.
34. Prado and Trebilcock (2019). The Brazilian experiment is described in Gilson, Hansmann, and Pargendler (2011); Pargendler is responsible for the material on Brazil.
35. John Bartlett. "Chile Students' Mass Fare-dodging Expands into City-wide Protest," *The Guardian*, Oct. 18, 2019, https://www.theguardian.com/world/2019/oct/18/chile-students-mass-fare-dodging-expands-into-city-wide-protest; Amanda Taub. "Chile Woke Up: Dictatorship's Legacy of Inequality Triggers Mass Protests," *The New York Times*, Nov. 3, 2019, https://www.nytimes.com/2019/11/03/world/americas/chile-protests.html; Mark Johanson, "How a $0.04 Metro Fare Hike Sparked Massive Unrest in Chile," *Vox*, Oct. 29, 2019, https://www.vox.com/world/2019/10/29/20938402/santiago-chile-protests-2019-riots-metro-fare-pinera.
36. A referendum finally approved the project. Rose-Ackerman, Egidy, and Fowkes (2015), p. 214. Completion of the project has been delayed until 2025,

and costs are rising. Uschi Götz and Dieter Nürnberger, "Stuttgart 21: Entgleisung eines Bahnprojekts," *Deutschlandfunk*, Feb. 4, 2018, https://www.deutschlandfunk.de/stuttgart-21-entgleisung-eines-bahnprojekts.724.de.html?dram:article_id=409964 (accessed Nov. 23, 2020).

37. Barvosa (2018).
38. On Poland, see B. Ackerman (2019).
39. The Hungarian environmental groups, whose leaders I interviewed in 2002, had low budgets and few staff, and faced cutbacks in outside support from international donors. A similar situation existed in Poland. Rose-Ackerman (2005).
40. Constitutional texts can be ambiguous, and much of the debate in US constitutional law centers on interpretative disagreements. B. Ackerman (1993, 2000a, 2009).
41. For example, in 2001 the Constitutional Court held that, in spite of the language of the Law on Normative Acts, consultation was not constitutionally required unless the groups to be consulted were explicitly listed in the statute. Because the law mentions no specific groups, no one could claim a right to be heard. The decision is 10/2001 (IV.12).
42. Article 79, sect. 1 gives ". . . everyone whose constitutional freedoms or rights have been infringed . . . the right to appeal to the Constitutional Tribunal for its judgment on the conformity to the Constitution of a statute or another normative act upon which basis a court or organ of public administration has made a final decision on his freedoms or rights or on his obligations specified in the Constitution." Konst. Pol., art. 79, sect. 1.
43. European Commission, "The Environmental Implementation Review 2019: Country Report: Poland" (2019), https://ec.europa.eu/environment/eir/pdf/report_pl_en.pdf (accessed April 9, 2020).
44. Summarized in Walsh (2016).
45. Walsh (2016).
46. Stein, Tommasi, Echebarría, Lora, and Mark (2005), p. 81.
47. Hammergren (2002), p. 3. See also Oynadel (2019).
48. Kerche (2007).
49. For example, in Argentina the Supreme Court has been quite independent, although it has tended to defer on sensitive political issues. Tommasi and Spiller (2007); Dix (2004). See also Oynadel (2019).
50. Popkin (2005), p. 25; Costa Rica is mentioned positively in Dakolias (1996), p. 12. But see Dodson and Jackson (2003), pp. 236–37. They claim that the council in Costa Rica was dependent on the Supreme Court until 1999

reforms that excluded the judiciary from membership and did not actively police judicial corruption.

51. Popkin (2005).
52. See the discussion in Chapter 7 of "hard-look" review in the American context.
53. Perroud (2018). Leila Abboud, "Macron to close training school of French Elite," *Financial Times*, April 8, 2020.
54. See the critique of restrictive US standing doctrines in Chapter 7.
55. Rose-Ackerman (1996), pp.25–26. The statutes are the Clean Water Act, 33 U.S.C.A. § 1365, and the Clean Water Act § 304(g).
56. Lessig (2011).
57. Cain, Ferejohn, and Fiorina (1987).
58. On legislative corruption and conflicts of interest see Rose-Ackerman and Palifka (2016), pp. 341–73, and the sources cited therein.
59. Lambert-Mogiliansky (2011).
60. Rose-Ackerman and Palifka (2016).
61. J. M. Ackerman and Sandoval (2006).
62. R. J. Fisman (2001); Khwaja and Mian (2005).
63. D. Fisman et al. (2012).
64. For example, *Motor Vehicle Manufacturers' Assoc. v. State Farm Mutual Automobile Insurance Co.*, 463 U.S. 29 (1983). On bias in agency decision-making, see Kuehn (2015)
65. Several civil-society groups have tracked President Trump's conflicts of interest. See, for example, CREW, "Trump Passes 2,300 Conflicts-of-Interest," Aug. 15, 2019, https://www.citizensforethics.org/press-release/new-report-trump-conflict-of-interest/ (accessed April 9, 2020).
66. For background see Jack Ewing and Kevin Granville, "VW, BMW, and Daimler Hindered Clean-Air Technology, European Regulator Says," *The New York Times*, April 4, 2019.
67. Payoffs by BAE involving British contracts with the Saudis are discussed in Rose-Ackerman and Billa (2008).
68. Phase 1 of the official report on the fire was issued in October 2019; work on Phase 2 began in January 2020 and is ongoing. https://www.grenfelltower-inquiry.org.uk/phase-1-report (accessed April 21, 2021).
69. Jacob Frenkel, "Criminal Prosecution Exposure in Boeing Investigation May Come to Light with Expert Report," *Forbes*, Aug. 28, 2019, https://www.forbes.com/sites/jacobfrenkel/2019/08/28/criminal-prosecution-

exposure-in-boeing-investigation-may-come-to-light-with-expert-report/#4b630bfb49a1.

70. Elf paid bribes of at least €305 million around the world between 1989 to 1993 to secure contracts and made large political contributions in France (McPherson and MacSearraigh, 2007). On water see Julio Godoy, "Water and Power: The French Connections," May 19, 2014 (update of original article from Feb. 4, 2003): https://publicintegrity.org/environment/water-and-power-the-french-connection/ (accessed Nov. 23, 2020).
71. Heilbrunn (2005).
72. Anderson and Tverdova (2003).
73. Rauch and Evans found that merit recruitment and promotion were the keys to good performance in the 35 countries they studied. Salary levels played little role in performance. Rauch and Evans (2000). On Latin American public administration see Cortázar et al. (2014).
74. 26 USC § 501(c). Colinvaux (2014).
75. Olaf Scholz. "Gemeinnützigkeit für Vereine soll eingeschränkt werden," *Die Zeit Online*, Nov. 22, 2019, https://www.zeit.de/politik/deutschland/2019-11/olaf-scholz-steuerpolitik-gemeinnuetzigkeit-vereine.
76. "Tunnel vision . . . arises when an agency so organizes or subdivides its tasks that each employee's individual conscientious performance effectively carries single-minded pursuit of a single goal too far, to the point where it brings about more harm than good" (Breyer [1993], pp. 18–19).

Bibliography

Ackerman, Bruce. 2019. *Revolutionary Constitutions: Charismatic Leadership and the Rule of Law.* Cambridge MA: Harvard University Press, 2019.

———. *We the People: The Civil Rights Revolution.* Cambridge MA: Harvard University Press, 2009.

———. "The Living Constitution." *Harvard Law Review* 120 (2007): 1727–1812.

———. "The Emergency Constitution." *Yale Law Journal* 113 (2004): 1029–91.

———. *We the People: Transformations.* Cambridge MA: Harvard University Press, 2000a.

———. "The New Separation of Powers." *Harvard Law Review* 113 (2000b): 633–729.

———. *We the People: Foundations.* Cambridge MA: Harvard University Press, 1993.

Ackerman, Frank, and Lisa Heinzerling. *Priceless: On Knowing the Price of Everything and the Value of Nothing.* New York: The New Press, 2004.

Ackerman, John M. "Understanding Independent Accountability Agencies." In *Comparative Administrative Law*, edited by Susan Rose-Ackerman and Peter L. Lindseth, 265–76. Cheltenham UK: Edward Elgar, 2010.

Ackerman, John M., and Irma Sandoval. "The Global Explosion of Freedom of Information Laws." *Administrative Law Review* 58 (2006): 85–130.

Adler, Jonathan H. "Redefining 'Waters of the United States' Regulation." *Regulation* 42 (2019): 16–23.

Adler, Matthew D., and Eric A. Posner. *New Foundations of Cost-Benefit Analysis.* Cambridge MA: Harvard University Press, 2006.

Akerlof, George. "The Market for Lemons." *Quarterly Journal of Economics* 84 (1970): 488–500.

Anderson, Christopher J., and Yuliya V. Tverdova. "Corruption, Political Allegiances, and Attitudes toward Government in Contemporary Democracies." *American Journal of Political Science* 47 (2003): 91–109.

Arrow, Kenneth J., Maureen L. Cropper, George C. Eads, Robert W. Hahn, Lester B. Lave, Roger G. Noll, Paul R. Portney, et al. "Is There a Role for Benefit-Cost Analysis in Environmental Health and Safety Regulation?" *Science* 272 (1996): 221–22.

Arrow, Kenneth J., and A. C. Fisher. "Environmental Preservation, Uncertainty, and Irreversibility." *Quarterly Journal of Economics* 88 (1974): 312–19.

Arrow, Kenneth J., and R. C. Lind. "Uncertainty and the Evaluation of Public Investment Decisions." *American Economic Review, Papers and Proceedings* 60 (1970): 365–76.

Atkinson, Giles, Ben Gross, Nicholas Hanley, and Susana Mourato. "Environmental Valuation and Benefit-Cost Analysis in UK Policy." *Journal of Benefit-Cost Analysis* 9 (2018): 97–119.

Autin, Jean-Louis. "La Motivation des Actes Administratifs Unilatéraux, entre Tradition Nationale et Évolution des Droits Européens." *Revue Française d'Administration Publique*, n° 137–38 (2011/1): 85–99.

Avitzer, L., and Brian Wampler. "The Spread of Participatory Democracy in Brazil: From Radical Democracy to Good Government." *Journal of Latin American Urban Studies* 7 (2005): 37–52.

Balleisen, Edward J., and Melissa B. Jacoby. "Consumer Protection after the Global Financial Crisis." *Georgetown Law Journal* 107 (2019): 813–43.

Baranger, Denis. "Executive Power in France." In *The Executive and Public Law*, edited by Paul Craig and Adam Tomkins, 217–42. Oxford: Oxford University Press, 2006.

Barker, Alan, ed. *Quangos in Britain*. London: Macmillan, 1982.

Barnett, Kent. "How the Supreme Court Derailed Formal Rulemaking." *George Washington Law Review Arguendo* 85 (2017): 1–24.

Barvosa, Edwina. *Deliberative Democracy Now: LGBT Equality and the Emergence of Large-Scale Deliberative Systems*. Cambridge UK: Cambridge University Press, 2018.

Batie, S. S., and H. H. Shugart. "The Biological Consequences of Climate Change: An Ecological and Economic Assessment." In *Greenhouse Warming: Abatement and Adaptation*, edited by N. J. Rosenberg, W. E. Easterling III, P. R. Crosson, and J. Darmstadter, 121–31. Washington DC: Resources for the Future, 1989.

Beetham, David. "Evaluating New vs. Old Forms of Citizen Engagement and Participation." In *Evaluating Democratic Innovations: Curing the Democratic Malaise?*, edited by Brigitte Geissel and Kenneth Newton, 56–67. Abingdon UK: Routledge, 2012.

Beierle, Thomas C., and Jerry Cayford. *Democracy in Practice: Public Participation in Environmental Decisions.* Washington DC: Resources for the Future, 2002.

Bell, Joanna. "*ClientEarth (No 2)*: A Case of Three Legal Dimensions." *Journal of Environmental Law* 29 (2017): 343–53.

Bentham, Jeremy. *An Introduction to the Principles of Morals and Legislation.* Buffalo NY: Prometheus Press, 1988 (1789).

Bermann, George, and Etienne Picard, eds. *An Introduction to French Law.* Austin TX: Wolfers/Kluwer, 2008.

Bétaille, Julien. "La procédure de l'étude d'impact après la Loi portant engagement national pour l'environnement: Des insuffisances récurrentes." *Revue juridique de l'environnement* (Spécial) (2010): 241–51.

Biernat, Stanislaw. "Poland." In *Administrative Justice in New European Democracies*, edited by R. H. Langan II, D. J. Galligan, and C. S. Nicandrou, 501–13. Oxford UK: Centre for Socio-Legal Studies, University of Oxford, 1998.

Binmore, Ken. *Rational Decisions.* Princeton NJ: Princeton University Press, 2009.

Blatrix, Cécile. "La démocratie participative en représentation." *Sociétés contemporaines* 74 (2009): 97–119.

———. "Genèse et consolidation d'une institution: Le débat public en France." In *Le débat public: Une expérience française de démocratie participative*, edited by Cécile Blatrix et al., 43–56. Paris: Le Découverte, 2007.

Blatrix, Cécile, Laurent Mermet, and Judith Raoul-Duval. *Research on Public Participation in Environmental Decision-Making: Approaches, Context, Stakes and Perspectives across Borders.* Report Summing Up the Main Outcomes of an International Conference at Oxford University, April 12–13, 2011 (2011). http://concertation-environnement.fr/documents/seminaires/CDE_Oxford_2011_EN.pdf (accessed Nov. 6, 2020).

Boardman, Anthony, David H. Greenberg, Aidan R. Vining, and David L. Weimer. *Cost-Benefit Analysis: Concepts and Practice.* 5th ed. Cambridge UK: Cambridge University Press, 2018.

Böckenförde, Ernst-Wolfgang. *Staat, Verfassung, Demokratie.* Frankfurt-am-Main: Suhrkamp, 1992.

Boiteux, Marcel. "On the Management of Public Monopolies Subject to Budgetary Constraints." *Journal of Economic Theory* 3 (1971): 219–40.

Bourg, Dominique, and Kerry H. Whiteside. "France's Charter for the Environment: Of Presidents, Principles and Environmental Protection." *Modern and Contemporary France* 15 (2007): 117–33.

Bowen, Jeff, and Susan Rose-Ackerman. "Partisan Politics and Executive Accountability: Argentina in Comparative Perspective." *The Supreme Court Economic Review* 10 (2003): 157–210.

Boy, Daniel, et al. *Le Grenelle de l'environnement: Acteurs, discours, effets*. Paris: Armand Colin, 2012.

Bozóki, András, and Dániel Hegedüs. "An Externally Constrained Hybrid Regime: Hungary in the European Union." *Democratization* 25 (2018): 1173–89.

Brand, Donald R. "The President as Chief Administrator: James Landis and the Brownlow Report." *Political Science Quarterly* 123 (2008): 69–94.

Breger, Marshall J., and Gary J. Edles. *Independent Agencies in the United States: Law, Structure, and Politics*. Oxford: Oxford University Press, 2015.

Brennan, Geoffrey, and James Buchanan. *The Power to Tax: Analytical Foundations of a Political Constitution*. Cambridge UK: Cambridge University Press, 1980.

Brenner, Michael. "Das Innere Gesetzgebungsverfahren im Lichte der Hartz IV–Entscheidung des Bundesverfassungsgerichts." *Zeitschrift für Gesetzgebung* 26 (2011): 394–404.

Bressman, Lisa Schultz, and Michael P. Vandenbergh. "Inside the Administrative State: A Critical Look at the Practice of Presidential Control." *Michigan Law Review* 105 (2006): 47–99.

Breyer, Stephen. *Breaking the Vicious Cycle: Toward Effective Risk Regulation*. Cambridge MA: Harvard University Press, 1993.

Brissy, Stéphane. "L'autorégulation des professions." *Droit social* 2016/2: 137–41.

Brown, L. Neville, and John S. Bell. *French Administrative Law*. 5th ed. Oxford: Oxford University Press, 1998.

Bruggemeier, Gert, Josef Falke, Christian Joerges, and Hans-W. Micklietz. "Examples of Product Safety Legislation." *Hanse Law Review* 6 (2011): 135–236.

Buchanan, James M., and Gordon Tullock. *The Calculus of Consent*. Ann Arbor: University of Michigan Press, 1962.

Buge, Éric. "À la recherche du Diamant de Micromégas: Quelques réflexions à propos du grand débat national et de la Convention Citoyenne pour le Climat." *Archives de philosophie du droit* 62 (2020) 205-225.

Buge, Éric, and Camille Morio. "Le grand débat national: Apports et limites pour la participation citoyenne." *Revue du droit public* (2019): 1205–38.

Burgsmüller, K. "Die Errichtung selbständiger Bundesoberbehörden Gemäss Art. 87 Abs. 3 Satz 1 Gg—Ihre Stellung innerhalb der Bundesverwaltung und ihr Verhältnis zu den Behörden der Länder." Dissertation, Köln, 1967.

Burnett, Jason K., and Robert W. Hahn. "A Costly Benefit: Economic Analysis Does Not Support EPA's New Arsenic Rule." *Regulation* 24/3 (Fall 2001): 44–49.

Buzbee, William W. "Deregulatory Splintering." *Chicago-Kent Law Review* 94 (2019): 439–86.

Cafaggi, Fabrizio. "Transnational Private Regulation and the Production of Global Public Goods and Private 'Bads'." *European Journal of International Law* 23 (2012): 695-718.

Cai, Y., K. L. Judd, T. M. Lenton, T. S. Lontzek, and D. Narita. "Environmental Tipping Points Significantly Affect the Cost-Benefit Assessment of Climate Policies." *Proceedings of the National Academy of Sciences* 112 (2015): 4605–11.

Cain, Bruce, John Ferejohn, and Morris Fiorina. *The Personal Vote: Constituency Service and Electoral Independence.* Cambridge MA: Harvard University Press, 1987.

Calabresi, Stephen, and C. S. Yoo. *The Unitary Executive: Presidential Power from Washington to Bush.* New Haven CT: Yale University Press, 2008.

Caleb, Nelson. "Standing and Remedial Rights in Administrative Law." *Virginia Law Review* 105 (2019): 703–804.

Cane, Peter. "Standing Up for the Public." *Public Law* (1995): 276–87.

Carey, John M., and Matthew Soberg Shugart, eds. *Executive Decree Authority.* Cambridge UK: Cambridge University Press, 1998.

Carpenter, Daniel, and David A. Moss, eds. *Preventing Regulatory Capture.* Cambridge UK: Cambridge University Press, 2014.

Cent, Joanna, Malgorzata Grozinska-Jurczak, and Agata Pietrzyk-Kaszynska. "Emerging Multi-Level Environmental Governance: A Case of Public Participation in Poland." *Journal for Nature Conservation* 22 (2014): 93–102.

Chambers, S. "Rhetoric and the Public Sphere: Has Deliberative Democracy Abandoned Mass Democracy?" *Political Theory* 37 (2009): 323–50.

Cheibub Figueiredo, Argelina, and Fernando Limongi. "Presidential Power, Legislative Organization, and Party Behavior in Brazil." *Comparative Politics* 32 (2000): 151–70.

Chevallier, Jacques. "Le Défenseur des Droits: Une intégration réussie?" *Revue française d'administration publique* 147 (2013): 747–60.

———. "Défenseur des droits: Unité ou diversité?" *Revue française d'administration publique* 139 (2011a): 433–45.

———. "De la Administration démocratique à la démocratie administrative." *Revue française d'administration publique* 137–38 (2011b): 217–27.

———. "Le débat public en question." In *Pour un droit commun de l'environnement: Mélanges en l'honneur de Michel Prieur*, 489–508. Paris: Dalloz, 2007.

Clark, Alistair. "Public Administration and the Integrity of the Electoral Process in British Elections." *Public Administration* 93/1 (2015): 86–102.

Coglianese, Cary. "Citizen Participation in Rulemaking: Past, Present, and Future." *Duke Law Journal* 55 (2006): 943–68.

———. "Is Satisfaction Success? Evaluating Public Participation in Regulatory Policymaking." In *The Promise and Performance of Environmental Conflict Resolution*, edited by Rosemary O'Leary and Lisa B. Bingham, 69–86. Washington DC: RFF Press, 2003.

———. "Assessing Consensus: The Promise and Performance of Negotiated Rulemaking." *Duke Law Journal* 46 (1997): 1255–1349.

Cohen, Henry. *Awards of Attorneys' Fees by Federal Courts and Federal Agencies*. CRS94–970. Washington DC: Congressional Research Service, Office of Congressional Information and Publishing, 2008.

Cohen-Eliya, Moshe, and Iddo Porat. "American Balancing and German Proportionality: The Historical Origins." *I-CON* 8 (2010): 263–86.

Colinvaux, Roger. "Political Activity Limits and Tax Exemption: A Gordian's Knot." *Virginia Tax Review* 34 (2014): 1–62.

Collins, Craig E. "Selection of Administrative Intervenors: A Reappraisal of the Standing Dilemma." *George Washington Law Review* 42 (1974): 991–1029.

Commission Nationale du Débat Public. *2009–2010: Rapport d'activité*. Paris: CNDP, 2011.

———. *2017–2018: Rapport annuel*. Paris: CNDP, 2019.

Conseil d'État, *Rapport public: Consulter autrement, participer effectivement*. Paris: CE, 2011.

———. *Rapport public*. Paris: CE, 2010.

Cortázar, Juan Carlos, et al. *Serving Citizens: A Decade of Civil Service Reforms in Latin America*. Washington DC: Inter-American Development Bank, 2014.

Craig, Paul. *Administrative Law*. 8th ed. London: Sweet & Maxwell, 2016.

———. *EU Administrative Law*. 2nd ed., Oxford: Oxford University Press, 2012.

Crettez, Bertrand, Bruno Deffains, and Olivier Musy. "Convergence of Legal Rules: Comparing Cooperative and Non-Cooperative Processes." *Review of Law and Economics* 12 (2016): 13–35.

———. "On the Dynamics of Legal Convergence." *Public Choice* 156 (2013): 345–56.

Croley, Steven. "White House Review of Agency Rulemaking: An Empirical Investigation." *University of Chicago Law Review* 70 (2003): 821–85.

Cross, Frank B., and Emerson H. Tiller. "Judicial Partisanship and Obedience to Legal Doctrine: Whistleblowing on the Federal Courts of Appeal." *Yale Law Journal* 107 (1998): 2155–74.

Curato, N., and M. Böker. "Linking Mini-Publics to the Deliberative System: A Research Agenda." *Policy Sciences* 49 (2016): 173–90.

Curato, N., J. S. Dryzek, S. A. Ercan, C. M. Hendriks, and S. Niemeyer. "Twelve Key Findings in Deliberative Democracy Research." *Daedalus* 146 (2017): 28–38.

Curtin, Deidre. "Delegation to EU Non-Majoritarian Agencies and Emerging Practices of Public Accountability." In *Regulation through Agencies in the EU: A New Paradigm of European Governance*, edited by Rodolphe Muñoz Damien Geradin and Nicolas Petit, 88–119. Cheltenham UK: Edward Elgar, 2005.

Custos, Dominique. "The 2015 French Code of Administrative Procedure: An Assessment." In *Comparative Administrative Law*, edited by Susan Rose-Ackerman, Peter Lindseth, and Blake Emerson, 284–301. Cheltenham UK: Edward Elgar, 2017.

———. "Independent Administrative Authorities in France: Structural and Procedural Change at the Intersection of Americanization, Europeanization and Gallicization." In *Comparative Administrative Law*, edited by Susan Rose-Ackerman and Peter Lindseth, 277–92. Cheltenham UK: Edward Elgar, 2010a.

———. "Le statut du responsable public et la réception de la notion d' 'accountability.'" In *L'influence du droit européen sur les catégories juridiques du droit public français*, edited by Jean-Bernard Auby, 275–85. Paris: Dalloz, 2010b.

———. "The Rulemaking Power of Independent Agencies." *American Journal of Comparative Law* 54, Supplemental Issue (2006): 615–40.

Dakolias, Maria. *The Judicial Sector in Latin America and the Caribbean: Elements of Reform*. Technical Paper 319. Washington DC: The World Bank, 1996.

D'Alberti, Marco. *Diritto amministrativo comparato: Transformazioni dei sistemi amministrativi in Francia, Gran Bretagna, Stati Uniti, Italia*. Translated by Christine Marciasini. Bologna: Il Mulino, 1992 (trans. 1995).

Dann, Philipp. "Verfassungsgerichtliche Kontrolle gesetzgeberischer Rationalität." *Der Staat* 49 (2010): 630–46.

Davis, Kevn E., and Michael J. Trebilcock. "The Relationship between Law and Development: Optimists versus Skeptics." *American Journal of Comparative Law* 56 (2009): 895–946.

De Bellis, Maurizia. "Public Law and Private Regulators in the Global Legal Space." *International Journal of Constitutional Law* 9 (2011): 425–48.

Delaunay, Bénédicte. "De l'enquête publique au débat public, la consultation des personnes intéressées." *La semaine juridique—Administrations et collectivités territoriales* n° 8 (Feb. 21, 2011).

———. "Les limites aux recours contre les décisions de la Commission Nationale du Débat Public." *Actualité juridique, droit administratif* 60 (2004): 2100.

Della Cananea, Giacinto. *Due Process of Law beyond the State: Requirements of Administrative Procedure.* Oxford: Oxford University Press, 2016.

Dempsey, Paul Stephen. "The Rise and Fall of the Interstate Commerce Commission: The Tortuous Path from Regulation to Deregulation of America's Infrastructure." *Marquette Law Review* 95 (2011–2012): 1151–90.

———. "The Rise and Fall of the Civil Aeronautics Board—Opening Wide Floodgates of Entry." *Transportation Law Journal* 11 (1979): 91–186.

Denninger, Erhard. *Verfassungsrechtliche Anforderungen an die Normsetzung im Umwelt- und Technikrecht.* Baden-Baden: Nomos, 1990.

Derlien, Hans-Ulrich. "German Public Administration: Weberian Despite 'Modernization.'" In *Comparative Bureaucratic Systems*, edited by Krishna K. Tummala, 97-122. Lanham MD: Lexington Books, 2005.

DeShazo, J. R., and Jody Freeman. "The Congressional Competition to Control Delegated Power." *Texas Law Review* 81 (2003): 1443–1519.

Dewey, John. *The Public and Its Problems.* Athens GA: Ohio University Press, 1927 (1954).

Dix, Sarah. "Judicial Politics in Argentina." Ph. D. diss., Yale University, 2004.

Dodson, Michael, and Donald W. Jackson. "Horizontal Accountability and the Rule of Law in Central America." In *Democratic Accountability in Latin America*, edited by Scott Mainwaring and Christopher Welna, 228–65. Oxford: Oxford University Press, 2003.

Dohler, Marian. "Institutional Choice and Bureaucratic Autonomy in Germany." In *The Politics of Delegation*, edited by Alec Stone Sweet and Mark Thatcher, 101–24. London and Portland OR: Frank Cass, 2003.

Dooling, Bridget C. E. "HHS Entries in OIRA's Latest Regulatory Reform Report: Cutting Red Tape in the Medicare Program Delivers Cost Savings While Other Deregulatory Efforts Fall Short." Regulatory Studies Center ed. *Spotlight*, November 26, 2018.

Dross, Miriam. "Germany." In *Access to Justice in Environmental Matter and the Role of NGOs: Empirical Findings and Legal Appraisal*, edited by Nicolas de Sadeleer, Gerhard Roller, and Miriam Dross, 65–82. Gronigen: Europa Law Publishing, 2005.

Dryzek, John S. *Foundations and Frontiers of Deliberative Democracy*. Oxford: Oxford University Press, 2010.

Dryzek, John S., and Aviezer Tucker. "Deliberative Innovation to Different Effect: Consensus Conferences in Denmark, France, and the United States." *Public Administration Review* (September/October 2008): 864–76.

Dupré de Boulois, Xavier. "Les actes administratifs unilatéraux." In *Traité de droit administratif*, edited by Pascal Gonod, Fabrice Melleray, and Philippe Yoka, 160. Paris: Dalloz, 2011.

Durance, Philippe. "De la décision politique à la décision publique: Participation des citoyens et innovation sociale." In *Créativité et innovation dans les territoires*, edited by Michel Godel, Philippe Durance, and Marc Mousli, 107–17. Paris: Conseil d'Analyse Économique, 2010.

Durner, Wolfgang. "Öffentlichkeitsbeteiligung und demokratische Legitimation im Energie-Infrastrukturrecht." Kolloquium Anlässlich der Verabschiedung von Prof. Erbguth, Rostock, 2014.

Eifert, Martin. "Conceptualizing Administrative Law—Legal Protection versus Regulatory Approach." In *Debates in German Public Law*, edited by Hermann Pünder and Christian Waldhoff, 203–18. Oxford: Hart, 2014.

Elkins, Zachery, Thomas B. Ginsburg, and Beth Simmons. "Taking Rights Seriously: Treaty Ratification, Constitutional Convergence, and Human Rights." *Harvard International Law Journal* 61 (2013): 201–34.

Elliott, E. Donald. "Re-Inventing Rulemaking." *Duke Law Journal* 41 (1992): 1490–96.

Elliott, Mark C., and Stephen Tierney. "Political Pragmatism and Constitutional Principles: The European Union (Withdrawal) Act 2018." *Public Law* 1 (January 2019): 37–60.

Elstub, Stephen. "Mini-Publics: Issues and Cases." In *Deliberative Democracy: Issues and Cases*, edited by S. Elstub and P. McLaverty. Edinburgh: Edinburgh University Press, 2014.

Epstein, Richard A. *Takings: Private Property and the Power of Eminent Domain.* Cambridge MA: Harvard University Press, 1985.

Eskridge, William N., and John Ferejohn. *A Republic of Statutes: The New American Constitution.* New Haven CT: Yale University Press, 2010.

Evans, Paul. *Braking the Law: Is There, and Should There Be, an Executive Veto over Legislation in the UK Constitution?* The Constitution Unit, University College London, October 2020.

Everson, Michelle. "Good Governance and European Agencies: The Balance." In *Regulation through Agencies in the EU: A New Paradigm of European Governance,* edited by Damien Geradin, Rodolphe Muñoz, and Nicolas Petit. Cheltenham UK: Edward Elgar, 2005.

Farber, Daniel A. "Regulatory Review in Anti-Regulatory Times." *Chicago-Kent Law Review* 94 (2019): 383–438.

Farber, Daniel A., Lisa Heinzerling, and Peter M. Shane. "Reforming 'Regulatory Reform': A Progressive Framework for Agency Rulemaking in the Public Interest." *Issue Brief* 2018. https://www.acslaw.org/wp-content/uploads/2018/10/Oct-2018-APA-Farber-Heinzerling-Shane-issue-brief.pdf.

Farhang, Sean. *The Litigation State: Public Regulation and Private Litigation in the United States.* Princeton NJ: Princeton University Press, 2010.

Farina, Cynthia R., and Mary J. Newhart. *Rulemaking 2.0: Understanding and Getting Better Public Participation.* Ithaca NY: Cornell Law School, 2013. https://scholarship.law.cornell.edu/cgi/viewcontent.cgi?article=1014&context=ceri.

Feinstein, Brian. "Congress in the Administrative State." *Washington University Law Review* 95 (2018): 1187–1247.

———. "Designing Executive Agencies for Congressional Influence." *Administrative Law Review* 69 (2017): 259–90.

Fesler, James W. "The Brownlow Committee Fifty Years Later." *Public Administration Review* 47 (1987): 291–96.

Fiorina, Morris, and Roger G. Noll. "Voters, Legislators and Bureaucracy: Institutional Design in the Public Sector." *American Economic Review, Papers and Proceedings* 68 (1978): 256–60.

Fisahn, Andreas. *Demokratie und Öffentlichkeitbeteiligung.* Tübingen: Mohr Siebeck, 2002.

Fishkin, James S. *When the People Speak: Deliberative Democracy and Public Consultation.* Oxford: Oxford University Press, 2009.

Fisman, David, Raymond J. Fisman, Julia Galef, Rakesh Khurana, and Yongxiang Wang. "Estimating the Value of Political Connections to

Vice-President Cheney." *B. E. Journal of Economics Analysis and Policy, Advances* 13 (2012): Issue 3.

Fisman, Raymond J. "Estimating the Value of Political Connections." *American Economic Review* 91 (2001): 1095–1102.

Forsyth, Christopher, ed. *Judicial Review and the Constitution.* Oxford and Portland OR: Hart Publishing, 2000.

Fowkes, James. *Building the Constitution: The Practice of Constitutional Interpretation in Post-Apartheid South Africa.* Cambridge UK: Cambridge University Press, 2016.

Fox, Ruth, and Joel Blackwell. *The Devil in the Detail: Parliament and Delegated Legislation.* London: Hansard Society, 2014.

France, Pierre, and Antoine Vauchez. *Sphère Publique, Intérêts Privés: Enquête sur un Grand Brouillage.* Paris: Presses de Sciences Po, 2017. (Available in English as Antoine Vauchez and Pierre France, *The Neoliberal Republic: Corporate Lawyers, Statecraft, and the Making of Public-Private France.* Ithaca, NY: Cornell University Press, 2021.)

French, D., and M. Laver. "Participation Bias, Durable Opinion Shifts and Sabotage through Withdrawal in Citizens' Juries." *Political Studies* 57 (2009): 422–50.

Frier, Pierre-Laurent. "Vice de procédure." In *Répertoire de contentieux administratif*, edited by F. Gazier and R. Drago. Paris: Dalloz, 2012.

Fung, Archon. "Mini-Publics: Deliberative Designs and Their Consequences." In *Deliberation, Participation, and Democracy*, edited by S. Rosenberg, 159–83. New York: Palgrave Macmillan, 2007.

———. "Survey Article: Recipes for Public Spaces: Eight Institutional Design Choices and Their Consequences." *Journal of Political Philosophy* 11 (2003): 338–67.

Furlong, Scott, and Cornelius M. Kerwin. "Interest Group Participation in Rulemaking: A Decade of Change." *Journal of Public Administration and Theory* 15 (2005): 353–70.

Galligan, Denis J., and Daniel M. Smilov, eds. *Administrative Law in Central and Eastern Europe 1996–1998.* Budapest: Central European University Press, 1999.

Gärditz, Klaus Friedrich. "Temporale Legitimationsasymmetrien." In *Management von Unsicherheit und Nichtwissen*, edited by Hermann Hill and Utz Schliesky, 253–84. Baden-Baden: Nomos, 2016.

Geissel, Brigitte. "Impacts of Democratic Innovations in Europe: Findings and Desirata." In *Evaluating Democratic Innovations: Curing the Democratic*

Malaise?, edited by Brigitte Geissel and Kenneth Newton, 163–83. London: Routledge, 2012.

Gerson, Jacob E., and Anne Joseph O'Connell. "Deadlines in Administrative Law." *University of Pennsylvania Law Review* 156 (2008): 923–990.

Gilson, Ronald J., Henry Hansmann, and Mariana Pargendler. "Regulatory Dualism as a Development Strategy: Corporate Reform in Brazil, the United States, and the European Union." *Stanford Law Review* 63 (2011):475–537.

Gluck, Abbe, and Lisa Schultz Bressman. "Statutory Interpretation from the Inside—an Empirical Study of Congressional Drafting, Delegation, and Canons—Part I." *Stanford Law Review* 65 (2013): 901–1026.

———. "Statutory Interpretation from the Inside—an Empirical Study of Congressional Drafting, Delegation, and Canons—Part II." *Stanford Law Review* 66 (2014): 725–802.

Golden, Marissa Martino. "Interest Groups in the Rule-Making Processes: Who Participates? Whose Voices Get Heard?" *Journal of Public Administration and Theory* 8 (1998): 245–70.

Gollier, Christian. *Pricing the Planet's Future: The Economics of Discounting in an Uncertain World*. Princeton NJ: Princeton University Press, 2013.

Goodin, Robert E., and John S. Dryzek. "Deliberative Impact: The Macro-Political Uptake of Mini-Publics." *Politics & Society* 34 (2006): 219–44.

Grisinger, Joanna. "Law in Action: The Attorney General's Committee on Administrative Procedure." *Journal of Policy History* 20 (2012): 379–418.

Grönlund, K., M. Setälä, and K. Herne. "Deliberation and Civic Virtue: Lessons from a Citizen Deliberation Experiment." *European Political Science Review* 2 (2010): 95–117.

Grove, Tara Leigh. "Foreword: Some Puzzles of State Standing." *Notre Dame Law Review* 94 (2018): 1883–92.

Habermas, Jürgen. *The Theory of Communicative Action*. Vol. 1: *Reason and Rationalization of Society*. Translated by Thomas McCarthy. Boston: Beacon Press, 1981.

Haemer, Robert B. "Reform of the Toxic Substances Control Act: Achieving Balance in the Regulation of Toxic Chemicals." *Environmental Lawyer* 6 (1999): 99–134.

Hage, Maria, Pieter Leroy, and Artur C. Petersen. "Stakeholder Participation in Environmental Knowledge Production." *Futures* 42 (2019): 254–64.

Hahn, Robert W., and Patrick M. Dudley. "How Well Does the U.S. Government Do Benefit-Cost Analysis?" *Review of Environmental Economics & Policy* 1 (2007): 192–211.

Hahn, Robert W., and Robert E. Litan. "Counting Regulatory Benefits and Costs: Lessons for the U.S. and Europe." *Journal of International Economic Law* 8 (2005): 473–508.

Hahn, Robert W., and Andrea Renda. "Understanding Regulatory Innovation: The Political Economy of Removing Old Regulations before Adding New Ones." SSRN 2017 https://papers.ssrn.com/sol3/papers.cfm?abstract_id=3022552 (accessed Nov. 6, 2020).

Hall, Joseph. *Characters of Virtues and Vices*. Edited by Ben Ross Schneider, Jr. Renascence Editions, Eugene OR: University of Oregon, 1998 (1608). http://www.luminarium.org/renascence-editions/hallch.htm.

Hammergren, Linn. *Fifteen Years of Judicial Reform in Latin America: Where We Are and Why We Haven't Made Much Progress*. New York: United Nations Development Program, 2002.

Hammerschmid, Gerhard, Steven Van de Walle, Rhys Andrews, and Philippe Bezes, eds. *Public Administration Reforms in Europe: The View from the Top*. Cheltenham UK: Edward Elgar, 2016.

Hańderek, Piotr. "Current Situation of Regional Development in Poland." In *Public Participation in Regional Development in Central Europe*, edited by Petr Pelcl, 48–56. Szentendre, Hungary: Aarhus Convention and Regional Development Project, Regional Environmental Center, 2002.

Hansard Society, Commission on Parliamentary Scrutiny. *The Challenge for Parliament—Making Government Accountable*. London, 2001. https://www.hansardsociety.org.uk/publications/reports/the-challenge-for-parliament-making-government-accountable-the-report-of (accessed Nov. 6, 2020).

Harlow, Carol. *Accountability in the European Union*. Oxford: Oxford University Press, 2002.

Harlow, Carol, and Richard Rawlings. *Law and Administration*. 3rd ed. Cambridge UK: Cambridge University Press, 2009.

Harvey, Hosea H. "Constitutionalizing Consumer Financial Protection: The Case for the Consumer Financial Protection Bureau." *Minnesota Law Review* 103 (2019): 2429–76.

Haveman, Robert H., and Julius Margolis, eds. *Public Expenditures and Policy Analysis*. Chicago: Markham, 1970.

Heal, Geoffrey. "Discounting: A Review of the Basic Economics." *University of Chicago Law Review* 74 (2007): 59–77.

Heilbrunn, John R. "Oil and Water? Elite Politicians and Corruption in France." *Comparative Politics* 37 (2005): 277–96.

Heinzerling, Lisa. "Inside EPA: A Former Insider's Reflections on the Relationship between the Obama EPA and the Obama White House." *Pace Environmental Law Review* 31 (2014): [i]–369.

———. "Markets for Arsenic." *Georgetown Law Journal* 90 (2002): 2311–39.

Herz-Roiphe, D. "The Young, the Old, and the Economists: Rethinking How Agencies Account for Age in Cost-Benefit Analysis." *Yale Journal of Health Policy, Law & Ethics* 14 (2014): 350–75.

Hickey, Kevin J. *Agency Delay: Congressional and Judicial Means to Expedite Agency Rulemaking*. Washington DC: Library of Congress, 2018.

Hicks, John R. "The Four Consumers' Surpluses." *Review of Economic Studies* 11 (1943): 31–41.

———. "The Valuation of the Social Income." *Economica* 7 (1940): 105–24.

Hilliard, Nadia. *The Accountability State: US Federal Inspectors General and the Pursuit of Democratic Integrity*. Lawrence: University Press of Kansas, 2017.

Houk, Carole S., Mary P. Rowe, Deborah A. Katz, Neil H. Katz, Lauren Marx, and Timothy Heeden. *The Ombudsmen in Federal Agencies*. Washington DC: Administrative Conference of the United States, 2016.

House of Commons, Public Administration Select Committee. *Who's Accountable? Relationships between Government and Arm's-Length Bodies*. House of Commons First Report of Sessions 15 (2014). London: Stationary Office, 2015.

House of Lords. *The Regulatory State: Ensuring Its Accountability*. London: Stationary Office, 2004.

———. *Statistics on Business and Membership, Session 2016–17: 18 May 2016 to 27 April 2017*. London: Stationary Office, 2016–2017.

Huettner, David A. "Product Market Definition in Antitrust Cases When Products Are Close Substitutes or Close Complements." *Antitrust Bulletin* 47 (2002): 133–42.

Jackson, Vicki. "Constitutional Comparisons: Convergence, Resistance, Engagement." *Harvard Law Review* 119 (2005): 105–28.

Jauvert, Vincent. *Les intouchables d'état*. Paris: Robert Laffont, 2017.

Jégouzo, Yves. "Principe et idéologie de la participation." In *Pour un droit commun de l'environnement: Mélanges en l'honneur de Michel Prieur*, edited by Michel Prieur, 577–88. Paris: Dalloz, 2007.

Jordão, Edgardo. *Le juge et l'administration: Entre le contrôle et la déférence.* Brussels: Bruylant, 2016.

JUSTICE. *To Assist the Court: Third Party Interventions in the UK.* London: JUSTICE, 2016. https://justice.org.uk/assist-court-third-party-interventions-public-interest/.

Kagan, Elena. "Presidential Administration." *Harvard Law Review* 114 (2001): 2245–2319.

Kagan, Robert. "American and European Ways of Law: Six Entrenched Differences." In *European Ways of Law: Toward a European Sociology of Law*, edited by Volkmer Gessner and David Nelkin, 41–70. Portland OR: Hart Publishing, 2007.

Kaldor, Nicholas. "Welfare Propositions of Economics and Interpersonal Comparisons of Utility." *Economic Journal* 49 (1939): 549–52.

Kaliarnta, Sofia, Maria Hage, and Sabine Roeser. "Involving Stakeholders in Risk Governance: The Importance of Expertise, Trust, and Moral Emotions." In *Trade, Health and the Environment: The European Union Put to the Test*, edited by Marjolein van Asselt, Michelle Everson, and Ellen Vos, 235–53. New York: Routledge, 2014.

Kaplow, Louis. "Discounting Dollars, Discounting Lives: Intergenerational Distributive Justice and Efficiency." *University of Chicago Law Review* 74 (2007): 79–118.

Karpen, Ulrich. "Regulatory Impact Assessment: Current Situation and Prospects in the German Parliament." *Amicus Curiae* 101 (2015): 14–19.

Karpowitz, Christopher F., and Chad Raphael. *Deliberation, Democracy, and Civic Forums: Improving Equality and Publicity.* Cambridge UK: Cambridge University Press, 2014.

Katzen, Sally. "A Reality Check on an Empirical Study: Comments on 'Inside the Administrative State.'" *Michigan Law Review* 105 (2007): 1497–1510.

Kavanagh, Aileen. "Reasoning about Proportionality under the Human Rights Act 1998: Outcomes, Substance and Process." *Law Quarterly Review* 130 (2014): 235–58.

Kerche, Fábio. "Autonomia e discricionariedade do Ministério Público no Brasil." *Dados—Revista de ciências sociais* (2007): 259–79.

Kerwin, Cornelius M., ed. *Rulemaking: How Government Agencies Write Law and Make Policy.* Washington DC: CQ Press, 2003.

Kerwin, Cornelius M., and Scott R. Furlong. "Time and Rulemaking: An Empirical Test of Theory." *Journal of Public Administration Research and Theory* 2 (1992): 125–31.

Ketcham-Colwill, Peter. "Presidential Influence over Agency Rulemaking through Regulatory Review." *George Washington Law Review* 82 (2014): 1622–53.

Khwaja, Asim Ijaz, and Atif Mian. "Do Lenders Favor Politically Connected Firms? Rent Provision in an Emerging Financial Market." *Quarterly Journal of Economics* 120 (2005): 1371–1411.

Kies, Raphäel, and Patrizia Nanz. *Is Europe Listening to Us? Successes and Failures of EU Citizen Consultations.* Farnham UK: Ashgate, 2013.

Kilmnik, Kenneth S. "Germany Occupational Safety and Health Regulation from an American Perspective." *Dickinson Journal of International Law* 6 (1988): 143–235.

Koh, Harold. *The National Security Constitution: Sharing Power after the Iran-Contra Affair.* New Haven CT: Yale University Press, 1990.

Könen, Daniel. "Die Rolle des Bundeskartellamtes im Beschwerdeverfahren." *Nomos* 28 (2013): 36–38.

Kotulla, Michael, and Michael Rolfsen. "Zur Begründbarkeit von Zustimmungsvorbehalten zu Gunsten des Bundestages beim Erlass von Rechntvorordnungen." *Neue Zeitschrift für Verwaltungsrecht*2010: 943–49.

Krawiec, Kimberley D. "Don't 'Screw Joe the Plummer': The Sausage-Making of Finance Reform." *Arizona Law Review* 55 (2013): 53-103.

Kropp, Sabine. "Federalism, People's Legislation and Associative Democracy." In *Citizen Participation in Multi-Level Democracies*, edited by Cristina Fraenkel-Haeberle, Sabine Kropp, Francesco Palermo, and Karl-Peter Sommermann, 48–66. Leiden: Brill/Nijhoff, 2015.

Krotoszynski, Ronald J., Jr., Johnjerica Hodge, and Wesley W. Wintermyer. "Partisan Balance Requirements in the Age of New Formalism." *Notre Dame Law Review* 90 (2015): 941–1017.

Kuehn, Robert R. "Bias in Environmental Agency Decision Making." *Environmental Law* 45 (2015): 957–1020.

Kühne, Ulrich. *Amicus Curiae.* Tübingen: Mohr Siebeck, 2015.

Kunreuther, H., and P. Slovic. "Science, Values, and Risk." *Annals of the American Academy of Political and Social Science* 545 (1996): 116–25.

Kuztenov, Ivan. "The Legality of Golden Shares under E.U. Law." *Hanse Law Review* 1 (2015): 22–29.

Kysar, D. A. "Discounting . . . on Stilts." *University of Chicago Law Review* 74 (2007): 119–38.

Lafont, C. "Deliberation, Participation, and Democratic Legitimacy: Should Deliberative Mini-Publics Shape Public Policy?" *Journal of Political Philosophy* 23 (2015): 40–63.

Lambert-Mogiliansky, Ariane. "Corruption and Collusion: Strategic Complements in Procurement." In *International Handbook on the Economics of Corruption*, edited by Susan Rose-Ackerman and Tina Søreide, 108–40. Cheltenham UK: Edward Elgar, 2011.

Landes, William M., and Richard Posner. "The Independent Judiciary in an Interest Group Perspective." *Journal of Law and Economics* 18 (1975): 875–901.

La Porta, Rafael, Florencio Lopez de Silanes, and Andrei Shleifer. "The Economic Consequences of Legal Origins." *Journal of Economic Literature* 46 (2008): 285–352.

La Porta, Rafael, Florencio Lopez-de-Silanes, Andrei Shleifer, and Robert W. Vishny. "Law and Finance." *Journal of Political Economy* 106 (1998): 1113–55.

———. "Investor Protection and Corporate Valuation." *Journal of Finance* 57 (2002): 1147–70.

———. "Legal Determinants of External Finance." *Journal of Finance* 52 (1997): 1131–50.

———. "The Quality of Government." *Journal of Law, Economics, and Organization* 15 (1999): 1–33.

Lascoumes, Pierre. "Des acteurs aux prises avec le 'Grenelle Environnement': Ni innovation politique, ni simulation démocratique, une approche pragmatique des travaux du Groupe V." *Revue participations* 1 (2011): 277–310.

Lasser, Mitchel de S.-O.-l'E. "The Europeanization of French Law." *Cornell Law Review* 90 (2005): 995–1083.

———. *Judicial Transformations: The Rights Revolution in the Courts of Europe.* Oxford: Oxford University Press, 2009.

Lawson, Gary. "The Risk and Rise of the Administrative State." *Harvard Law Review* 107 (1994): 1231–54.

Lazarus, Richard. "The National Environmental Protection Act in the U.S. Supreme Court: A Reappraisal and a Peek behind the Curtain." *Georgetown Law Review* 100 (2012): 1507–86.

Lessig, Lawrence. *Republic Lost: How Money Corrupts Congress—and a Plan to Stop It*. New York: Twelve, 2011.

Levin, Ronald M. "The Regulatory Accountability Act and the Future of APA Revision." *Chicago-Kent Law Review* 94 (2019): 487–549.

Lewis, David E. "Deconstructing the Administrative State." *Journal of Politics* 81 (2019): 767–89.

Lewis, Kevin M. *The Federal Tort Claims Act (FTCA): A Legal Overview.* Washington DC: Congressional Research Service, 2019.

Liebenberg, Sandra. "The Democratic Turn in South Africa's Social Rights Jurisprudence." In *The Future of Social Rights*, edited by K. G. Young, 187–211. Cambridge UK: Cambridge University Press, 2017.

Light, Paul. *A Government Ill Executed: The Decline of the Federal Service and How to Reverse It*. Cambridge MA: Harvard University Press, 2008.

Lijphart, Arend. *Patterns of Democracy: Government Forms and Performance in Thirty-Six Countries*. 2nd ed. New Haven CT: Yale University Press, 2012.

———. *Democracy in Plural Societies: A Comparative Exploration*. New Haven CT: Yale University Press, 1977.

Lindgren, Karl-Oskar, and Thomas Persson. "Participatory Governance in the European Union." In *Handbook on Participatory Governance*, edited by Hubert Heinelt, 225–45. Cheltenham UK: Edward Elgar, 2018.

Little, I.M.D. *A Critique of Welfare Economics*. Oxford: Oxford University Press, 1958 (republished 2003).

Lodge, Martin, and Lindsay Stirton. "Accountability in the Regulatory State." In *The Oxford Handbook of Regulation*, edited by R. Baldwin, M. Cave, and M. Lodge, 348–70. Oxford: Oxford University Press, 2010.

Luskin, Robert C., James S. Fishkin, and R. Jowell. "Considered Opinions: Deliberative Polling in Britain." *British Journal of Political Science* 32 (2002): 455–87.

Magat, Wesley A., Alan J. Krupnick, and Winston Harrington. *Rules in the Making: A Statistical Analysis of Regulatory Agency Behavior*. Washington DC: Resources for the Future, 1986.

Maggetti, Martino, and Koen Verhoest. "Unexplored Aspects of Bureaucratic Autonomy: A State of the Field and Ways Forward." *International Review of Administrative Sciences* 80 (2014): 239–56.

Magill, M. Elizabeth. "Congressional Control over Agency Rulemaking: The Nutrition Labeling and Education Act's Hammer Provisions." *Food and Drug Law Journal* 50 (1995): 149–90.

Magnetter, P. "Between Parliamentary Control and the Rule of Law: The Political Role of the Ombudsman in the European Union." *Journal of European Public Policy* 10 (2003): 677–94.

Majone, Giandomenico. *Regulating Europe*. London: Routledge, 1996.

———. "Two Logics of Delegation: Agency and Fiduciary Relations in EU Governance." *European Union Politics* 2 (2001): 103–22.

Mansbridge, Jane. *Beyond Adversary Democracy*. Chicago IL: University of Chicago Press, 1983.

Mansbridge, Jane, James Bohman, Simone Chambers, Thomas Christiano, Archon Fung, John Parkinson, Dennis F. Thompson, and Mark E. Warren. "A Systemic Approach to Deliberative Democracy." In *Deliberative Democracy at the Large Scale*, edited by John Parkinson and Jane Mansbridge, 1–26. Cambridge UK: Cambridge University Press, 2012.

Mantel, Jessica. "Procedural Safeguards for Agency Guidance: A Source of Legitimacy for the Administrative State." *Administrative Law Review* 61 (2009): 343–406.

Marcou, Gérard, and Johannes Masing. *Le modèle des autorités de régulation indépendantes en France et en Allemagne.* Société de Législation Comparée Paris: Université de Paris/CNRS UMR 8103, 2011.

Markus, Ludwig. "Die Bundesnetzagentur auf dem Weg zur Independent Agency? Europarechtliche Anstöße und verfassungsrechtliche Grenzen." *Die Verwaltung* (2011): 46–55.

Marrani, David. "The Intersection between Constitution, Human Rights, and the Environment: The French Charter for the Environment and the New Ex Post Constitutional Control in France." *Environmental Law Review* 16 (2014): 107–21.

Mascott, Jennifer L. "Who Are 'Officers of the United States'?" *Stanford Law Review* 70 (2018): 443–564.

Mashaw, Jerry. *Creating the Administrative Constitution: The Lost One Hundred Years of American Administrative Law.* New Haven CT: Yale University Press, 2012.

———. "Improving the Environment of Agency Rulemaking: An Essay on Management, Games, and Accountability Law and Contemporary Problems." *Law and Contemporary Problems* 57 (1994): 185–257.

———. *Due Process in the Administrative State.* New Haven CT: Yale University Press, 1985.

Mashaw, Jerry, and David Berke. "Presidential Administration in a Regime of Separated Powers: An Analysis of Recent American Experience." *Yale Journal on Regulation* 35 (2018): 549–616.

Masing, Johannes, and Gérard Marcou, eds. *Unabhängige Regulierungsbehörden: Organisationsrechtliche Herausforderungen in Frankreich und Deutschland.* Tübingen: Mohr Siebeck, 2010.

Massot, Jean. "Legislative Drafting in France: The Role of the Conseil D'État." *Statute Law Review* 22 (2001): 96–107.

Mast, Reinhard. "Braucht es ein Verbandsklagerecht im Denkmalschutzrecht?" *ZRP, Beck-Online* (2019): 237.

Mathews, Jud. "Proportionality Review in Administrative Law." In *Comparative Administrative Law*, edited by Susan Rose-Ackerman, Peter Lindseth, and Blake Emerson, 405–19. Cheltenham UK: Edward Elgar, 2017.

Mayhew, David. *Congress: The Electoral Connection*. New Haven CT: Yale University Press, 1974.

McCubbins, Mathew D., Roger G. Noll, and Barry R. Weingast. "Structure and Process, Politics, and Policy: Administrative Arrangements and the Political Control of Agencies." *Virginia Law Review* 75 (1989) 431–489.

———. "Administrative Procedures as Instruments of Political Control." *Journal of Law, Economics, and Organization* 3 (1987): 243–77.

McGarity, Thomas. "Some Thoughts on Deossifying the Rulemaking Process." *Duke Law Journal* 41 (1992): 1385–1462.

———. "Administrative Law as a Blood Sport: Policy Erosion in a Highly Partisan Age." *Duke Law Journal* 61 (2012): 1671–1762.

McPherson, Charles, and Stephen MacSearraigh. "Corruption in the Petroleum Sector." In *The Many Faces of Corruption: Tracking Vulnerabilities at the Sectoral Level*, edited by J. Edgardo Campos and Sanjay Pradhan, 191–220. Washington DC: The World Bank, 2007.

Mehde, Veith. "Political Accountability in Germany." In *Political Accountability in Europe: Which Way Forward?*, edited by Hansko Broeksteeg, Luc Verhey, and Ilse Van den Driessche, 101–19. Groningen: Europa Law Publishing, 2008.

Meinel, Florian. "Confidence and Control in Parliamentary Government: Parliamentary Questioning, Executive Knowledge, and the Transformation of Democratic Accountability." *American Journal of Comparative Law* 66 (2018): 317–68.

Melnick, R. Shep. *Regulation and the Courts: The Case of the Clean Air Act*. Washington DC: The Brookings Institution, 1983.

Mendelson, Nina A. "Agency Burrowing: Entrenching Policies and Personnel before a New President Arrives." *New York University Law Review* 78 (2003): 557–666.

Merrill, Thomas W. "Article III, Agency Adjudication, and the Origins of the Appellate Review Model of Administrative Law." *Columbia Law Review* 111 (2011): 939–1003.

Merrill, Thomas W., and Katheryn Tongue Watts. "Agency Rules with the Force of Law: The Original Convention." *Harvard Law Review* 116 (2002): 467–592.

Metzger, Gillian. "1930s Redux: The Administrative State under Siege." *Harvard Law Review* 131 (1917): 1–95.

Michaels, Jon D. *Constitutional Coup: Privatization's Threat to the American Republic.* Cambridge MA: Harvard University Press, 2017.

Moe, Terry. "Control and Feedback in Economic Regulation: The Case of the NLRB." *American Political Science Review* 79 (1985): 1094–1116.

Morand-Deviller, Jacqueline. *Cours de droit administratif.* 11th ed. Paris: Montchrestien. 2009.

Mueller, Dennis C. *Public Choice III.* Cambridge UK: Cambridge University Press, 2003.

Nelson, David, and Susan Webb Yackee. "Lobbying Coalitions and Government Policy Change: An Analysis of Federal Agency Rulemaking." *Journal of Politics* 74 (2012): 339-353.

Nesti, Giorgia. "Strengthening the Accountability of Independent Regulatory Agencies: From Performance Back to Democracy." *Comparative European Politics* 16 (2016): 1–18.

Neudorf, Lone. "Intervention at the UK Supreme Court." *Cambridge Journal of International and Comparative Law* 1 (2013): 16–31.

Newell, R. G., and W. A. Pizer. "Discounting the Distant Future; How Much Do Uncertain Rates Increase Valuation?" *Journal of Environmental Economics and Management* 46 (2003): 52–71.

Nicholas, Barry. "*Loi, Règlement* and Judicial Review in the Fifth Republic." *Public Law* (August 1970): 251–76.

Nielson, Aaron L. "In Defense of Formal Rulemaking." *Ohio State Law Journal* 75 (2014): 237–92.

Niemeyer, Simon J. "The Emancipatory Effect of Deliberation: Empirical Lessons from Mini-Publics." *Politics & Society* 39 (2011): 103–40.

Noguellou, Rozen. "Le Conseil d'État et la régulation des télécommunications." *Revue du droit public et de la science politique en France et à l'étranger* n° 3 (2010): 825–53.

Nolte, Jakob. "Rationale Rechtsfindung im Sozialrecht." *Der Staat* 52 (2013): 245–65.

Nordhaus, William. *The Climate Casino: Risk, Uncertainty, and Economics for a Warming World.* New Haven CT: Yale University Press, 2013.

Nou, Jennifer. "Civil Service Disobedience." *Chicago-Kent Law Review* 94 (2019): 349–82.

———. "Agency Self-Insulation under Presidential Review." *Harvard Law Review* 126 (2013): 1755–1837.

Noveck, Beth Simone. *Smart Citizens, Smarter State: The Technologies of Expertise and the Future of Government.* Cambridge MA: Harvard University Press, 2015.

———. "The Electronic Revolution in Rulemaking." *Emory Law Journal* 53 (2004): 433–522.

O'Connell, Anne Joseph. "Bureaucracy at the Boundary." *University of Pennsylvania Law Review* 162 (2014): 841–927.

———. "Agency Rulemaking and Political Transitions." *Northwestern University Law Review* 105 (2011): 471–534.

———. "Auditing Politics or Political Auditing?" Public Law Research Paper. Berkeley CA, 2007. http://papers.ssrn.com/id=964656.

O'Donnell, Guillermo A. "Horizontal Accountability in New Democracies." *Journal of Democracy* 9 (1998): 112–26.

OECD, *Improving Governance with Policy Evaluation: Lessons from Country Experiences*, Paris: OECD, 2020 (https://doi.org/10.1787/89b1577d-en (accessed Nov. 14, 2020).

Owen, David, and Graham Smith. "Survey Article: Deliberation, Democracy, and the Systemic Turn." *Journal of Political Philosophy* 23 (2015): 213–34.

Oynadel, Juan Carlos. *Assessing Judicial Reforms in Developing Countries: Trust in Law and Criminal Procedure in Chile.* Cham, Switzerland: Springer, 2019.

Page, T. "On the Problem of Achieving Equity and Efficiency Intergenerationally." *Land Economics* 73 (1997): 580–96.

Pahis, Stratos. "Corruption in Our Courts: What It Looks Like and Where It Is Hidden." *Yale Law Journal* 118 (2009): 1900–1943.

Palermo, Francesco. "Participation, Federalism, and Pluralism: Challenges to Decision Making and Responsible Constitutionalism." In *Citizen Participation in Multi-Level Democracy*, edited by Cristina Fraenkel-Haeberle, Sabine Kropp, Francesco Palermo, and Karl-Peter Sommermann, 31–47. Leiden: Brill/Nijhoff, 2015.

Parrillo, Nicholas R. "Federal Agency Guidelines and the Power to Bind: An Empirical Study of Agencies and Industries." *Yale Journal on Regulation* 36 (2019a): 165–272.

———. "Should the Public Get to Participate before Federal Agencies Issue Guidance?: An Empirical Study." *Administrative Law Review* 71 (2019b): 57–126.

Pateman, Carole. "Participatory Democracy Revisited." *Perspectives on Politics* 10 (2012): 7–19.

Pech, Laurent, and Kim Lane Scheppele. "Illiberalism Within: Rule of Law Backsliding in the EU." *Cambridge Yearbook of European Legal Studies* 19 (2017): 3–47.

Perroud, Thomas. "Les études d'impact dans l'action publique en France: Perspective critique et propositions." *Politiques et management public* 35 (2018): 215–42. https://pmp.revuesonline.com/article.jsp?articleId=39935.

Petersen, Niels. "Gesetzgeberische Inkonsistenz als Beweiszeichen, eine Rechtsvergleichende Analyse der Funktin on Konsistenzargumenten in der Techtspreachung." *Archiv des Öffenlichen Rechts* 138 (2013): 108–34.

Phelps, Edmund. "The Golden Rule of Accumulation: A Fable for Growthmen." *American Economic Review* 51 (1961): 638–43.

Pildes, Richard H., and Cass R. Sunstein. "Reinventing the Regulatory State." *University of Chicago Law Review* 62 (1995): 1–129.

Pogrebinschi, Thamy. "The Squared Circle of Participatory Democracy: Scaling up Deliberation to the National Level." *Critical Policy Studies* 7 (2013): 219–41.

Popkin, Margaret. "Participación ciudadana en la reforma de la justicia." In *Sociedad civil y reforma judicial en América Latina*, edited by Centro Nacional para Tribunales Estatales: Fundación para el Debido Proceso Legal, 23–32. Washington DC: Due Process of Law Foundation, 2005.

Posner, Eric A., and Adrian Vermeule. *The Executive Unbound: After the Madisonian Republic*. Oxford: Oxford University Press, 2010.

Posner, Richard. "Theories of Economic Regulation." *Bell Journal of Economics and Management Science* 5 (1974): 335–58.

Potter, Trevor. "Money, Politics, and the Crippling of the FEC: A Symposium on the Federal Election Commission's Arguable Inability to Effectively Regulate Money in American Elections." *Administrative Law Review* 69 (2017): 447–66.

Pourtois, Hervé. "Mini-publics et démocratie délibérative." *Pouvoir, participation et capacité* 32 (2013): 21–41.

Prado, Mariana Mota. "Assessing the Theory of Presidential Dominance: Empirical Evidence of the Relationship between the Executive Branch and Regulatory Agencies in Brazil." In *Comparative Administrative Law*, edited by Susan Rose-Ackerman, Peter Lindseth, and Blake Emerson, 181–97. Cheltenham UK: Edward Elgar, 2017.

Prado, Mariana Mota, and Michael J. Trebilcock. *Institutional Bypasses: A Strategy to Promote Reforms for Development*. Cambridge UK: Cambridge University Press. 2019.

President's Commission on Administrative Management. *Report and Special Studies (Brownlow Report)*. Washington DC: Government Printing Office, 1937.

Prieur, Michel. *Droit de l'environnement*. 6th ed. Paris: Dalloz, 2011.

Prosser, Tony. *Law and the Regulators*. Oxford: Oxford University Press, 1997.

Psygkas, Athanasios. *From the "'Democratic Deficit" to a "Democratic Surplus": Constructing Administrative Democracy in Europe*. Oxford: Oxford University Press, 2017.

———. "Accountability." In *Oxford Handbook of Comparative Administrative Law*, edited by Peter Cane, Herwig Hofmann, Eric Ip, and Peter Lindseth, 443–466. Oxford: Oxford University Press, 2020.

Pünder, Hermann. "More Government with the People: The Crisis of Representative Democracy and Options for Reform in Germany." *German Law Journal* 16 (2015): 713–40.

———. "Administrative Procedure—Mere Facilitator of Material Law versus Cooperative Realization of Common Welfare." In *Debates in German Public Law*, edited by Hermann Pünder and Christian Waldhoff, 239–60. Oxford UK: Hart, 2014.

———. "Democratic Legitimation of Delegated Legislation—a Comparative View on the American, British and German Law." *International Comparative Law Quarterly* 58 (2009): 353–78.

Rabin, Robert L. "Federal Regulation in Historical Perspective." *Stanford Law Review* 38 (1986): 1189–1326.

Radin, Beryl A. *Beyond Machiavelli: Policy Analysis Reaches Midlife*. 2nd ed. Washington DC: Georgetown University Press, 2013.

Rae, Douglas W. "The Limits of Consensual Decision." *American Political Science Review* 69 (1975): 1270–94.

Rask, M., S. Maciukaite-Zviniene, and J. Petrauskiene. "Innovations in Public Engagement and Participatory Performance of the Nations." *Science and Public Policy* 39 (2012): 710–21.

Raso, Conner. "Agency Avoidance of Rulemaking Procedures." *Administrative Law Review* 67 (2015): 65–132.

Rauch, James, and Peter Evans. "Bureaucratic Structure and Bureaucratic Performance in Less Developed Countries." *Journal of Public Economics* 75 (2000): 49–71.

Ray, Brian. *Engaging with Social Rights: Procedure, Participation, and Democracy in South Africa's Second Wave*. Cambridge UK: Cambridge University Press, 2016.

Reed, Mark S. "Stakeholder Participation for Environmental Management: A Literature Review." *Biological Conservation* 141 (2008): 2417–31.

Reitz, John C. "Political Economy and Separation of Powers." *Transnational Law & Contemporary Problems* 15 (2006): 579–625.

Renn, Ortwin, Thomas Webler, and Peter Wiedemann, eds. *Fairness and Competence in Citizen Participation.* Cham, Switzerland: Springer, 1995a.

Renn, Ortwin, Thomas Webler, and Peter Wiedemann. "The Need for Discourse on Citizen Participation: Objectives and Structure of the Book." In *Fairness and Competence in Citizen Participation*, edited by Ortwin Renn, Thomas Webler, and Peter Wiedemann, 1–16. Cham, Switzerland: Springer, 1995b.

Reuchamps, Min, and Jane Suiter. *Constitutional Deliberative Democracy in Europe.* Washington DC: Rowman & Littlefield, 2016.

Revesz, Richard L., and Michael A. Livermore. *Retaking Rationality: How Cost-Benefit Analysis Can Better Protect the Environment and Our Health.* New York: Oxford University Press, 2008.

Richardson, Mark D. "Politicization and Expertise: Exit, Effort, and Investment." *Journal of Politics* 81 (2019): 878–91.

Roca, Elisabet, Gonzalo Gamboa, and J. David Tàbara. "Assessing the Multidimensionality of Coastal Erosion Risks: Public Participation and Multicriteria Analysis in a Mediterranean Coastal System." *Risk Analysis* 28 (2008): 399–412.

Roe, Mark J. "Legal Origins, Politics, and Modern Stock Markets." *Harvard Law Review* 120 (2006): 460–527.

Rose-Ackerman, Susan. "Executive Rulemaking and Democratic Legitimacy: 'Reform' in the United States and the United Kingdom's Route to Brexit." *Chicago-Kent Law Review* 94 (2019): 267–313.

———. "The Limits of Cost/Benefit Analysis When Disasters Loom." *Global Policy* 7(S1) (2016): 56–66.

———. "Putting Cost-Benefit Analysis in Its Place: Rethinking Regulatory Review." *University of Miami Law Review* 65 (2011): 335–56.

———. "Public Administration and Institutions in the LAC Region." In *Latin American Development Priorities: Costs and Benefits*, edited by Bjørn Lomborg, 515–90. Cambridge UK: Cambridge University Press, 2009.

———. "Judicial Independence and Corruption." In *Global Corruption Report 2007: Corruption in Judicial Systems*, edited by Transparency International, 15–24. Cambridge UK: Cambridge University Press, 2007.

———. *From Elections to Democracy: Building Accountable Government in Hungary and Poland.* Cambridge UK: Cambridge University Press, 2005.

———. "Establishing the Rule of Law." In *When States Fail: Causes and Consequences*, edited by Robert Rotberg, 182–221. Princeton NJ: Princeton University Press, 2004.

———. "Public Law versus Private Law in Environmental Regulation: European Union Proposals in the Light of United States and German Experience." In *Law and Economics of the Environment*, edited by Erling Eide and Roger van der Bergh, 13–39. Oslo: Juridish Forlag, 1996.

———. *Controlling Environmental Policy; The Limits of Public Law in Germany and the United States.* New Haven CT: Yale University Press, 1995.

———. "Consensus versus Incentives: A Skeptical Look at Regulatory Negotiation." *Duke Law Journal* 43 (1994): 1206–20.

———. *Rethinking the Progressive Agenda: The Reform of the American Regulatory State.* New York: The Free Press, 1992.

———. "A New Political Economy?" *Michigan Law Review* 80 (1982): 872–84.

Rose-Ackerman, Susan, and Benjamin Billa. "Treaties and National Security." *New York University Journal of Law and Politics* 40 (2008): 437–96.

Rose-Ackerman, Susan, and Raquel de Mattos Pimenta. "Corruption in Brazil: Beyond the Criminal Law." In *Corruption and the Lava Jato Scandal in Latin America*, edited by Paul F. Lagunes and Jan Svejnar, 199–212. Abingdon UK: Routledge, 2020.

Rose-Ackerman, Susan, Diane Desierto, and Natalia Volosin. "Hyper-Presidentialism: Separation of Powers without Checks and Balances in Argentina and the Philippines." *Berkeley Journal of International Law* 29 (2011): 101–88.

Rose-Ackerman, Susan, Stefanie Egidy, and James Fowkes. *Due Process of Lawmaking: The United States, South Africa, Germany, and the European Union.* Cambridge UK: Cambridge University Press, 2015.

Rose-Ackerman, Susan, and Bonnie Palifka. *Corruption and Government: Causes, Consequences, and Reform.* 2nd ed. Cambridge UK: Cambridge University Press, 2016.

Rose-Ackerman, Susan, and Thomas Perroud. "Policymaking and Public Law in France: Public Participation, Agency Independence, and Impact Assessment." *Columbia Journal of European Law* 19 (2013): 225–312.

Rose-Ackerman, Susan, and Lena Riemer. "Strengthening Democracy through Public Participation in Policy-Making: The EU, Germany, and the United States." *Yale Journal on Regulation: Notice and Comment* 36 (May 6, 2019). https://yalejreg.com/nc/strengthening-democracy-through-public-participation-in-policymaking-the-eu-germany-and-the-united-states-by-susan-rose-ackerman-lena-riemer/.

Ross, Richard J. "The Commoning of the Common Law: The Renaissance Debate over Printing English Law, 1520–1640." *University of Pennsylvania Law Review* 146 (1998): 323–461.

Rothstein, Bo. "Social Trust and Honesty in Government: A Causal Mechanism Approach." In *Creating Social Trust in Post-Socialist Societies*, edited by János Kornaii, Bo Rothstein, and Susan Rose-Ackerman, 13–30. New York: Palgrave, 2004.

Rousseau, Jean-Jacques. *The Social Contract*. Translated by Victor Gourevitch. Cambridge UK: Cambridge University Press, 1997 (1762).

Rubinfeld, Daniel L. "Market Definition with Differentiated Products." *Antitrust Law Journal* 68 (2000): 163–86.

Ruffert, Matthias. "The Transformation of Administrative Law as a Transnational Methodological Project." In *The Transformation of Administrative Law in Europe*, edited by Matthias Ruffert, 3–52. Munich: Sellier, 2007.

Russell, Meg. *The Contemporary House of Lords: Westminster Bicameralism Revived*. Oxford: Oxford University Press, 2013.

Russell, Meg, and Philip Cowley. "The Policy Power of the Westminster Parliament: The 'Parliamentary State' and the Empirical Evidence." *Governance* 29 (2016): 121–37.

Ruthig, Josef, and Stefan Storr. *Öffentliches Wirtschaftsrecht*. 4th ed. Heidelberg: C. F. Müller, 2015.

Ryan, Alan, ed. *Utilitarianism and Other Essays: J. S. Mill and Jeremy Bentham*. New York: Penguin Books, 1987.

Salop, Steven, and David T. Scheffman. "Raising Rivals' Costs." *American Economic Review—Papers and Proceedings* 73 (1983): 267–71.

Samidas, Dexter, and David A. Weisbach. "Paretian Intergenerational Discounting." *University of Chicago Law Review* 74 (2007): 145–70.

Samuelson, Paul. *Foundations of Economic Analysis*. Cambridge MA: Harvard University Press, 1947.

Saurer, Johannes. "Die Mitwirkung des Bundestages an der Verordnungsgebung nach § 48b Bimschg." *Neue Zeitschrift für Verwaltungsrecht* 2003: 1176–89.

Sayid, Amena H. "Air Pollution: We Already Spent the Money, Keep Air Toxics Rule: AEP, Duke to EPA." *Administrative Law Bulletin* 2018/7 (2018).

Scalia, Antonin. "The Doctrine of Standing as an Essential Element of Separation of Powers." *Suffolk University Law Review* 17 (1981): 881–900.

Schlacke, Sabine, Christian Schrader, and Thomas Bunge, *Informationsrechte, Beteiligung und Rechtsschutz im Umweltrecht: Das Aarhus-Handbuch*. 2nd ed. Berlin: Erich Schmidt, 2019.

Schlozman, Kay Lehman, and John T. Tierney. *Organized Interests and American Democracy.* New York: Harper & Row, 1986.

Schmidt-Aßmann, Eberhard. "Legitimacy and Accountability as a Basis for Administrative Organisation and Activity in Germany." In *Legitimacy in European Administrative Law: Return and Reconstruction*, edited by Matthias Ruffert, 49–57. Groningen: Europa Law Publishing, 2011.

Schmidt-Aßmann, Eberhard, and Wolfgang Hoffmann-Reim, eds. *Methoden der Verwaltungsrechtswissensschaft.* Baden-Baden: Nomos, 2004.

Schmidt-Aßmann, Eberhard, and Christoph Möllers. "The Scope and Accountability of Executive Power in Germany." In *The Executive and Public Law*, edited by Paul Craig and Adam Tomkins, 268–89. Oxford: Oxford University Press, 2006.

Schmitter, Chris. "Going Back in Time: The Search for Retroactive Rulemaking Power in Statutory Deadlines." *Minnesota Law Review* 97 (2012–2013): 1114–44.

Schneider, Jens-Peter. "German Tradition in Administrative Law: Obstacles to a Common Legal Framework?" In *Administrative Law in Europe: Between Common Principles and National Traditions*, edited by Matthias Ruffert, 51–65. Groningen: Europa Law Publishing, 2013.

———. "Regulation and Europeanisation as Key Patterns of Change in Administrative Law." In *The Transformation of Administrative Law in Europe*, edited by Matthias Ruffert, 309–23. Munich: Sellier, 2007.

Schuck, Peter. "Public Interest Groups and the Policy Process." *Public Administration Review* 37 (1977): 132–40.

Schulz-Nieswandt, Frank. *Berufsgenossenschaften und Europarecht.* Berlin: Duneker & Humblot, 2011.

Schwarze, Jürgen. *European Administrative Law.* 1st ed., rev. London: Sweet and Maxwell, 2006.

Scott, Colin. "Agencies for European Regulatory Governance: A Regimes Approach." In *Regulation through Agencies in the EU: A New Paradigm of European Governance*, edited by Damien Geradin, Rodolphe Muñoz, and Nicolas Petit, 67–87. Cheltenham UK: Edward Elgar, 2005.

Scott, Thomas, and Jeffrey H. Bowman. "Obstacles to Effective Enforcement of the Federal Election Campaign Act." *Administrative Law Review* 52 (2000): 575–608.

Seidenfeld, Mark. "Playing Games with the Timing of Judicial Review: An Evaluation of Proposals to Restrict Pre-Enforcement Review of Agency Rules." *Ohio State Law Journal* 58 (1997): 85–130.

Shane, Peter M. *Madison's Nightmare: How Executive Power Threatens American Democracy.* Chicago: University of Chicago Press, 2009.

Shapiro, Martin. "A Comparison of US and European Independent Agencies." In *Comparative Administrative Law*, edited by Susan Rose-Ackerman and Peter Lindseth. Research Handbooks in Comparative Law, 293–308. Cheltenham UK: Edward Elgar, 2010.

———. *Who Guards the Guardians? Judicial Control of Administration.* Athens, GA: University of Georgia Press, 1988.

Shapiro, Sidney A., and Robert L. Glickman. *Risk Regulation at Risk: Restoring a Pragmatic Approach.* Stanford CA: Stanford University Press, 2003.

Shapiro, Sidney A., and Richard W. Murphy. "Arbitrariness Review Made Reasonable: Structural and Conceptual Reform of the Hard Look." *Notre Dame Law Review* 92, no. 1 (2016): 331–80.

———. "Constraining White House Political Control of Agency Rulemaking through the Duty of Reasoned Explanation." *U.C. Davis Law Review* 48 (2015): 1457–1509.

Sharma, Lisa T., Stephen P. Teret, and Kelly D. Brownell. "The Food Industry and Self-Regulation: Standards to Promote Success and to Avoid Public Health Failure." *Farming Health Matters* 100 (2010): 240–46.

Shugerman, Jed Handelsman. "The Dependent Origins of Independent Agencies: The Interstate Commerce Commission, the Tenure of Office Act, and the Rise of Modern Campaign Finance." *Journal of Law & Politics* 31 (2016): 139–86.

Siems, Mathias. "Legal Origins: Reconciling Law & Finance and Comparative Law." *McGill Law Journal* 52 (2007): 55–82.

Silvia, Stephen J. *Holding the Shop Together: German Industrial Relations in the Postwar Era.* Ithaca NY: Cornell University Press, 2013.

Skahan, Kelly Ann. "Ineffective by Design: A Critique of Campaign Finance Law Enforcement in the U.S., Australia, and the U.K." *Washington International Law Journal* 27 (2018): 577–608.

Sólyom, László, and Georg Brunner, eds. *Constitutional Judiciary in a New Democracy: The Hungarian Constitutional Court.* Ann Arbor: University of Michigan Press, 2000.

Sossin, Lorne. "The Puzzle of Independence and Parliamentary Democracy in the Common Law World: A Canadian Perspective." In *Comparative Administrative Law*, edited by Susan Rose-Ackerman, Peter L. Lindseth, and Blake Emerson, 159–81. Cheltenham UK: Edward Elgar, 2017.

Spieker, Arne. "Stakeholder Dialogues and Virtual Reality for the German Energiewende," *Journal of Dispute Resolution* (2018): 75–86.

Stack, Kevin M. "Interpreting Regulations." *Michigan Law Review* 111 (2012): 355–421.

———. "Constitutional Foundations of Chenery." *Yale Law Journal* 116 (2007): 952–1021.

Stein, Ernesto, Mariano Tommasi, Koldo Echebarría, Eduardo Lora, and Mark Payne. *The Politics of Policies: Economic and Social Progress in Latin America*. Washington DC: Inter-American Development Bank and The David Rockefeller Center for Latin American Studies at Harvard University, 2005.

Steinbach, Armin. "Das Behörderliche Unabhangigkeitsparadigma im Wirtschaftsverwaltungsrecht." *Die Verwaltung* 50 (2017): 537–69.

Steinberg, Rudolf. "Untergesetzliche Regelwerke und Gremien." In *Reform des Atomrechts*, edited by Rudolf Steinberg, 82–100. Baden-Baden: Nomos, 1994.

Stephenson, Matthew C. "A Costly Signaling Theory of Hard Look Judicial Review." *Administrative Law Review* 58 (2006): 753–814.

Stewart, Richard B. "The Reformation of Administrative Law." *Harvard Law Review* 88 (1975): 1667–1813.

Stigler, George. "The Theory of Economic Regulation." *Bell Journal of Economics and Management Science* 2 (1971): 3–21.

Stolzenberg, Philipp, and Brian Wampler. "Participatory Budgeting." In *Handbook on Participatory Governance*, edited by Hubert Heinelt, 291–314. Cheltenham UK: Edward Elgar, 2018.

Stone Sweet, Alec, and Jud Mathews. "Proportionality, Balancing and Global Constitutionalism." *Columbia Journal of Transnational Law* 47 (2008): 72–165.

Strauss, Peter L. "Private Standards Organizations and Public Law." *William & Mary Bill of Rights Law Journal* 22 (2013–2014): 497–562.

———. "Overseer or 'the Decider'? The President in Administrative Law." *George Washington Law Review* 75 (2007): 696–760.

———. "Presidential Rulemaking." *Chicago-Kent Law Review* 72 (1997): 965–86.

———. "From Expertise to Politics: The Transformation of American Rulemaking." *Wake Forest Law Review* 31 (1996): 745–77.

———. "Rules, Adjudications, and Other Sources of Law in an Executive Department: Reflections on the Interior Department's Administration of the Mining Law." *Columbia Law Review* 74 (1974): 1231–75.

Sunstein, Cass R. "The Office of Information and Regulatory Affairs: Myths and Realities." *Harvard Law Review* 126 (2013): 1838–78.

———. "Precautions against What? Perceptions, Heuristics, and Culture." In *The Reality of Precaution*, edited by Jonathan Weiner et al., 492–515. Washington DC: RFF Press, 2011.

———. "The Arithmetic of Arsenic." *Georgetown Law Journal* 90 (2002a): 2255–2309.

———. *The Cost-Benefit State: The Future of Regulatory Protection*. Chicago: American Bar Association, 2002b.

———. "Health-Health Tradeoffs." In *Risk and Reason*, edited by Cass R. Sunstein, 133–52. Cambridge UK: Cambridge University Press, 2002c.

———. "Deliberative Trouble: Why Groups Go to Extremes." *Yale Law Journal* 110 (2000a): 71–119.

———. "Nondelegation Canons." *University of Chicago Law Review* 67 (2000b): 315–44.

———. "What's Standing after Lujan—of Citizen Suits, Injuries, and Article III." *Michigan Law Review* 91 (1992): 163–236.

Surowiecki, James. *The Wisdom of Crowds: Why the Many Are Smarter Than the Few and How Collective Wisdom Shapes Business, Economics, Societies, and Nations*. New York: Doubleday, 2004.

"Symposium on Legal Origins." *The American Journal of Comparative Law* 57 (2009): 768–876.

Szabados, Tamás. "Recent Golden Share Decisions in the Jurisprudence of the Court of Justice of the European Union." *German Law Journal* 16 (2015): 1099–1130.

Thatcher, Mark. "Independent Regulatory Agencies and Elected Politicians in Europe." In *Regulation through Agencies in the EU: A New Paradigm of European Governance*, edited by Damien Geradin, Rodolphe Muñoz, and Nicolas Petit, 47–66. Cheltenham UK: Edward Elgar, 2005.

———. "Delegation to Independent Regulatory Agencies: Pressures, Functions and Contextual Mediation." In *The Politics of Delegation*, edited by Mark Thatcher and Alec Stone Sweet, 125–47. Oxford: Frank Cass, 2003.

Thatcher, Mark, and Alec Stone Sweet, eds. *The Politics of Delegation*. London: Frank Cass, 2003.

Théophile, Didier, and Hugues Parmentier. "L'étendue du contrôle juridictionnel dans le contentieux du contrôle des concentrations en droit interne et communautaire." *Concurrences: Revue des droits de la concurrence* 1 (2006): 39–46.

Tiller, Emerson H., and Frank Cross. "A Modest Proposal for Improving American Justice." *Columbia Law Review* 99 (1999): 215–34.

Toby, James S. "Fixing Failures of U.K. Electoral Management." *Electoral Studies* 32/3 (2013): 597–608.

Tomkins, Adam. "Political Accountability in the United Kingdom." In *Political Accountability in Europe: Which Way Forward?* edited by Luc Verhey, Hansko Broeksteeg, and Ilse Van den Driessche, 243–69. Groningen: Europa Law Publishing, 2008.

———. "The Struggle to Delimit Executive Power in Britain." In *The Executive and Public Law*, edited by Paul Craig and Adam Tomkins, 16–51. Oxford: Oxford University Press, 2006.

Tommasi, Mariano, and Pablo T. Spiller. *The Institutional Foundations of Public Policy in Argentina: A Transactions Cost Approach*. Cambridge UK: Cambridge University Press, 2007.

Torres-Spelliscy, Clara, and Kathy Fogel. "Shareholder-Authorized Corporate Political Spending in the U.K." *University of San Francisco Law Review* 46 (2011): 525–80.

Tozzi, Jim. "OIRA's Formative Years: The Historical Record of Centralized Regulatory Review Preceding OIRA's Founding." *Administrative Law Review* 63 (2011): 37–70.

Traeger, C. P. "On Option Values in Environmental and Resource Economics." *Resource and Energy Economics* 37 (2014): 242–52.

Truchet, Didier. *Droit administratif*. 5th ed. Paris: Presses Universitaires de France—PUF edition, 2017.

Tsebelis, George. *Veto Players: How Political Institutions Work*. Princeton NJ: Princeton University Press, 2002.

Tucker, Adam. "Parliamentary Scrutiny of Delegated Legislation." In *Parliament and the Law*, edited by Alexander Horne and Gavin Drewry, 347–72. Hart: Oxford UK, 2018.

Tucker, Paul. *Unelected Power: The Quest for Legitimacy in Central Banking and the Regulatory State*. Princeton NJ: Princeton University Press, 2018.

Verhey, Luc, Hansko Broeksteeg, and Ilse Van den Driessche, eds. *Political Accountability in Europe: Which Way Forward?* Groningen: Europa Law Publishing, 2008.

Verhoest, Koen, Sandra Van Thiel, Geert Bouckaert, and Per Laegreid, eds. *Government Agencies: Practice and Lessons from 30 Countries*. Houndsmill, Basingstoke UK: Palgrave Macmillan, 2012.

Verkuil, Paul R. *Valuing Bureaucracy: The Case for Professional Government.* Cambridge UK: Cambridge University Press, 2017.

Vining, A. R., and David L. Weimer. "Welfare Economics as the Foundation for Public Policy Analysis: Incomplete and Flawed but Nevertheless Desirable." *Journal of Socio-Economics* 21 (1992): 25–37.

Vogel, Laurent. "Making Lies Sound Truthful: Applying the Standard Cost Model to European Health and Safety Law." In Laurent Vogel and Eric Van den Abeele, *Better Regulation: A Critical Assessment*, Report 113, 7–52. Brussels: European Trade Union Institute, 2010.

Von Neumann, John, and Oskar Morgenstern. *Theory of Games and Economic Behavior.* 3rd ed. Princeton NJ: Princeton University Press, 1953.

Voßkuhle, Andreas. "The Reform Approach in the German Science of Administrative Law: The 'Neue Verwaltungsrechtswissenschaft'." In *The Transformation of Administrative Law in Europe*, edited by Matthias Ruffert, 89–141. Munich: Sellier, 2007.

Voßkuhle, Andreas, and Thomas Wichmeyer. "Neue Verwaltungsrechtswissenschaft' against the Backdrop of Traditional Administrative Law." In *Comparative Administrative Law*, edited by Susan Rose-Ackerman, Peter Lindseth, and Blake Emerson, 85–101. Cheltenham UK: Edward Elgar, 2017.

Wagner, Wendy. "Participation in the US Administrative Process." In *Elgar Research Handbook on Comparative Law and Regulation*, edited by Francesca Bignami and David Zaring, 109–28. Cheltenham UK: Edward Elgar, 2016.

———. "Administrative Law, Filter Failure, and Information Capture." *Duke Law Journal* 59 (2010): 1321–1432.

Wagner, Wendy, Katherine Barnes, and Lisa Peters. "Rulemaking in the Shade: An Empirical Study of EPA's Air Toxic Emissions Standards." *Administrative Law Review* 63 (2011): 99–158.

Wald, Patricia M. "A Response to Tiller and Cross." *Columbia Law Review* 99 (1999): 235–61.

Walker, Christopher J. "Modernizing the Administrative Procedure Act." *Administrative Law Review* 69 (2017): 629–70.

Wallerath, Maximilian. "Berufsgenossenschaftliche Selbstverwaltung zwischen autonomer und heteronomer Steuerung—Zur Rechtsetzungsbefugnis der Berufsgenossenschaften nach § SGB VII § 15 SGB VII." *Neue Zeitschrift für Sozialrecht* (1997): 1–19.

Walsh, Jessica. *A Double-Edged Sword: Judicial Independence and Accountability in Latin America.* International Bar Association, Human Rights Institute,

London UK, 2016. https://www.academia.edu/28085583/A_Double-Edged_Sword_Judicial_Independence_and_Accountability_in_Latin_America?email_work_card=view-paper.

Walters, Daniel E. "Capturing the Regulatory Agenda: An Empirical Study of Agency Responsiveness to Rulemaking Petitions." *Harvard Environmental Law Review* 43 (2019): 175–223.

Wampler, Brian. *Participatory Budgeting in Brazil: Contestation, Cooperation, and Accountability*. State College PA: Penn State University Press, 2007.

Weber, Max. "Politics as a Vocation." In *Max Weber: Essays in Sociology*, edited by H. H. Girth and C. Wright Mills. New York: Oxford University Press, 1946 (1916).

Weingast, Barry R., and Mark J. Moran. "The Myth of the Runaway Bureaucracy: The Case of the FTC." *Regulation* 6/3 (1982): 33–38.

Wendel, Matthias. *Verwaltungsermessen als Mehrebenenproblem*. Tübingen: Mohr Siebeck, 2019.

West, William F. "Formal Procedures, Informal Processes, Accountability, and Responsiveness in Bureaucratic Policy Making: An Institutional Analysis." *Public Administration Review* 64 (2004): 66–80.

Whiteside, Kerry H., et al. "France's 'Grenelle de l'Environnement': Openings and Closures in Ecological Democracy." *Environmental Politics* 19 (2010): 449–67.

Wiener, Jonathan. "The Diffusion of Regulatory Oversight." In *The Globalization of Cost-Benefit Analysis in Environmental Policy*, edited by Michael A. Livermore and Richard L. Revesz, 123–41. Oxford: Oxford University Press, 2013.

———. "Better Regulation in Europe." In *Current Legal Problems 2006*, edited by J. Holder, C. O'Cinneide, and C. Campbell, 447–518. Oxford: Oxford University Press, 2006.

Wiener, Jonathan B., and Alberto Alemanno. "Comparing Regulatory Oversight Bodies: The US Office of Information and Regulatory Affairs and the EU Regulatory Scrutiny Board." In *Comparative Administrative Law*, 2nd edition, edited by Susan Rose-Ackerman, Peter L. Lindseth, and Blake Emerson, 333–51. Cheltenham UK: Edward Elgar, 2017.

Wiener, Jonathan B., Michael D. Rogers, James K. Hammitt, and Peter H. Sand, eds. *The Reality of Precaution: Comparing Risk Regulation in the United States and Europe*. Washington DC: RFF Press, 2011.

Wilke, Helmut. *Smart Governance—Governing the Global Knowledge Society*. Chicago: University of Chicago Press, 2007.

Wilson, Richard. "Underestimating Arsenic's Risk." *Regulation*, Fall 2001: 50–53.

Wu, Tim. "Network Neutrality, Broadband Discrimination." *Journal of Telecommunications & High Technology Law* 2 (2003): 141–75.

Yackee, Jason Webb, and Susan Webb Yackee. "From Legislation to Regulation: An Empirical Examination of Agency Responsiveness to Congressional Delegations of Regulatory Authority." *Administrative Law Review* 68 (2016): 395–444.

———. "Testing the Ossification Thesis: An Empirical Examination of Federal Regulatory Volume and Speed, 1950–1990." *George Washington Law Review* 80 (2012): 1414–85.

———. "Administrative Procedures and Bureaucratic Performance." *Journal of Public Administration Research and Theory* 20 (2009): 261–82.

———. "A Bias toward Business? Assessing Interest Group Influence on the U.S. Bureaucracy." *Journal of Politics* 68 (2006): 128–39.

Yackee, Susan Webb. "Participant Voice in the Bureaucratic Policymaking Process." *Journal of Public Administration Research and Theory* 25 (2015): 427–49.

Yeatman, William. "Deadline Citizen Suits." *Appalachian Natural Resources Law Journal* 8 (2013–2014): 51–90.

Zhang, Wentong. "The Revolving Door." *Notre Dame Law Review* 90 (2015): 1265–1308.

Ziller, Jacques. "Political Accountability in France." In *Political Accountability in Europe: Which Way Forward?* edited by Hansko Broeksteeg, Luc Verhey, and Ilse Van den Driessche, 81–98. Groningen: Europa Law Publishing, 2008.

General Index

Index of Selected Cases

Page numbers are in **boldface**.

England and Wales High Court

England and Wales Court of Appeal

Queen's Bench Division

United States

U.S. Supreme Court

U.S. Courts of Appeals